Literary Polemics

Bataille, Sartre, Valéry, Breton

Literary Polemics

Bataille, Sartre, Valéry, Breton

Suzanne Guerlac

STANFORD UNIVERSITY PRESS

STANFORD, CALIFORNIA

For my mother,
and in memory
of my father

Acknowledgments

An earlier version of Chapter 1 was published as "'Recognition' by a Woman!" in *YFS* 78 (1990). An earlier version of Chapter 2 appeared as "Transgression in Theory" in *Ethics, Politics, and Difference in Julia Kristeva's Writing*, ed. Kelly Oliver (New York: Routledge, 1993).

I would like to thank the following friends and colleagues for helpful discussion and suggestions concerning various parts of this study: Scott Bryson, Margaret Cohen, Jonathan Culler, Vincent Descombes, Marc Gotlieb, Josué Harari, James Meyer, Claire Nouvet, Clark Poling, Michael Randall, and Philip Wood. I would also like to thank graduate students both at Johns Hopkins and at Emory upon whom I tried out many of the ideas developed here, as well as my very helpful copy editor, Ann Klefstad, and editors, John Ziemer and Helen Tartar, at Stanford University Press. Last but not least, I am very grateful to Clifford Holland for his love and support throughout and to my daughter Catie—for being Catie.

S.G.

Contents

Literary Polemics

Bataille, Sartre, Valéry, Breton

Introduction

◡

This study began as an investigation of *Tel Quel* and gradually moved
back in time across generations—all the way back to Bergson. It became
an attempt to map the intellectual (and to a certain extent the cultural)
site of the emergence of theory, and to remap the modern. I could say I
became interested in *Tel Quel* in the course of my study of Lautréamont
and the sublime, for *Tel Quel* critics, like the Surrealists, were fascinated
by him.[1] In retrospect, however, I see that perhaps just the reverse was
true: I became interested in Lautréamont because of a myth of theory that
saw its reflection in the myth of Lautréamont—pure text without author,
wrenched from history.

During the 1960's and 1970's, the eruption of theory was presented as
an epistemic break. It was hailed as an intellectual breakthrough so radical as to be quite discontinuous with the past. To this extent the advent
of theory reorganized the field of questioning both prospectively and retrospectively. On the one hand, *Tel Quel* canonized a body of preferred
avant-garde texts (both literary and theoretical), designating them as worthy of further critical attention. At the same time, the milieu of *Tel Quel*
nullified prominent figures from the preceding generations. In so doing, it
effectively detached theory from the cultural polemics of the previous
decades, polemics associated with the phenomena of pure art, automatism, transgression, and engagement.

In an exceptional gesture, Philippe Sollers alludes to "la dimension his-
torique de ce qui arrive [the historical dimension of what is happening]"
in a short text commemorating the centenary of avant-garde activity from
Lautréamont (1868) to *Tel Quel* (1968). In this account, Sollers leaps over
the first half of the twentieth century to what he calls the "more radical
reserves inscribed at the end of the last century (Lautréamont, Mallarmé,
Marx, Freud)." He trivializes the cultural contributions of the 1950's (existential phenomenology and the new novel) and skirts surrealism, pure

art, and structuralism, dismissing them parenthetically as "cultural spin-offs" which he characterizes as an "après après coup."[2] Most significantly, however, the 1920's, 1930's, and 1940's receive no mention, although it was during this period that artists, critics, and intellectuals worked through the nineteenth-century inheritance *Tel Quel* wants to claim for itself—Lautréamont, Mallarmé, Hegel, and Freud. These were the generations that battled over the questions *Tel Quel* subsequently makes its own. "If the meaning of an ideology's answers is to be understood," Althusser has written, "it must first be asked the question of its questions."[3] The questions of *Tel Quel* go back to precisely the decades Sollers omits from the brief historical sketch he presents in *Théorie d'ensemble*. The powers subsequently claimed for theory are a displacement of powers attributed to literature, variously theorized in terms of modernist pure art, transgression, automatism, and engagement.

Discourses of the previous generation—those of Sartre, Valéry, and Breton—have been neutralized in part by myths of incompatibility between them. When I speak of myths of incompatibility, I do not mean to imply that differences between these figures are illusory; on the contrary, the polemics of these decades were substantial. But the best way to appreciate the substance of such differences is to reconstruct a sense of the common ground from which these voices could be said to emerge. The point is not to reduce dissonance, but to nuance apparent incompatibilities, to give them context. It is a question of rereading effaced texts in order to retrieve relations that problematize stereotypes of incompatibility.

The terms "pure art," "engagement," "automatism," and "transgression" have been pinned down so far apart from one another in the fabric of received ideas that the texts that present them have become almost indecipherable to us. We have lost track of the codes that animate them and of the dialogic aspect of their elaboration. These figures respond to one another. Bataille's voice emerges in knowing contestation first with Breton and then with Sartre. Sartre was consistently aware of Bataille, since his journal *Critique* was the principal rival to Sartre's *Les Temps Modernes*, and a number of authors published in both reviews. Sartre was a respectful reader of Valéry, who was Breton's close friend and mentor during the 1920's. These are all banal and familiar facts, yet we tend to ignore them. When we recognize the specific dynamics of these proximities, however, through an appeal to the complicated interactions of the philosophical subtexts (specifically the discourses of Hegel and Bergson) that contribute to their elaboration, we can let the facts of cultural proximity enter into our thinking. We can adjust the framework that positions these figures in sets of neutralizing oppositions. By exploring the proximities among transgression, engagement, automatism, and pure art, we can more

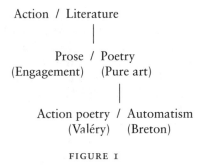

FIGURE I

easily recognize the issues at stake in the cultural polemics that informed the emergence of theory. To this extent we can enhance our critical understanding of the accomplishments and the limits of theory.

In the case of all the figures we investigate, the divisive issue concerns relations between poetry and action. In a moving letter to René Char, Bataille wrote of the "radical incompatibility" between poetry and action. "Although the debate concerning literature and engagement appears to have subsided," he declares in 1950, "its decisive nature has not yet been clearly perceived."[4] Indeed the difference poetry/action cuts through a number of overlapping debates of the 1920's, 1930's, and 1940's. In the first place, we could associate the fundamental opposition between action and poetry with ideological debates concerning the antinomy between art and revolution. But an implicit version of the split between poetry and action opens up within the literary, or "art," side of that fundamental opposition, for there is also a debate between realism and poetry. To the extent that engagement is a myth of transparent prose and is hence associated with realism, we have a confrontation between prose and poetry that conventionally pits Sartre against Valéry, Breton, and Bataille. Finally, the fundamental antinomy returns as an internal division among the voices that defend poetry against prose. A voluntarist poetics (Valéry's modernist poetics of perfection) is opposed first by surrealist automatism and subsequently by the more recent notion of textual productivity, which, theorized in terms of Bataille's notion of transgression, takes poetic language as a model. This synchronic analysis of the problem is represented schematically in Fig. 1.

The position of Valéry is pivotal in these debates. For some he represents poetry against the subordination of art to politics and against prose. For others he represents "literature," in the pejorative sense, against the avant-garde transvaluation of literature into poetry, understood in the very large sense that will be displaced by the terms "literarity" and "text" during the years of structuralism and poststructuralism. At the same time, Sartre's antimodernist image becomes more entrenched as the modernist conflict over the Sartrean question—that is, What is literature?—intensifies in relation to the challenge posed by the avant-garde activities of Dada and surrealism. This is the struggle that can be retraced through the writings of Bataille, Blanchot, Barthes, and others. Although one could say that Sartre's role in this literary polemic recedes, nevertheless the question of literature is still posed in relation to imperatives of action, an optic that sometimes reveals the grotesque misery of literature, its *impuissance*, and at other times its sublime or sacred powers.

If this were a historical study, I would have begun with Bergson and gone on to analyze his influence on Valéry, Breton, Bataille, and Sartre, in that order, before arriving at *Tel Quel*. But I am more interested in the schematic relations of ideological opposition outlined above. Instead of following a chronological orientation, therefore, I have begun with Bataille, the only figure who survives the "break" of theory. To this extent he is a liminal figure. He belongs both to the generation of *Tel Quel*, who reinvented transgression, and to the decades he shared first with Breton and then with Sartre. Because of this double historical inscription, Bataille opens a textual path back to these earlier figures and mediates broader links between *Tel Quel* and discourses it has suppressed or effaced.[5] Part I of this study analyzes the appropriation of Bataille by *Tel Quel* and the importance of trangression for poststructuralism. As a theoretical term, "transgression" enables Kristeva to reconcile (in theory) the antinomy of art and revolution (which is also to say the cultural positions associated with Breton the avant-gardist and Sartre the militant) in *La Révolution du langue poétique*.

In Part II I pursue the question of "incompatibilities" among Sartre, Valéry, and Breton. I propose readings of engagement, pure art, and automatism that attempt to demystify stereotypes concerning these discourses, and which emphasize differences rather than oppositions between the various positions.[6] I begin with Sartre because Bataille elaborated the notion of an incompatibility between poetry and action in relation to the pressures of engagement in the 1950's. I then consider Valéry because pure poetry is usually the term ideologically opposed to the theory of engagement as a myth of prose.[7] Next I move to Breton and pursue the question of the tension between poetry and action at work within the realm of poetry itself, a tension that introduces the issues of modernism and avant-gardism.

Whereas the conventional reading of engagement considers that it subordinates art to political or moral values, the reading I propose places a literary absolute at the heart of engagement, and considers *Qu'est-ce que la littérature?* in proximity to Valéry. The myth of prose, I suggest, is a gift from poetry. Valéry the pure poet has already elaborated a notion of poetry as action; he introduces the dynamic between text and reader that Sartre will call the paradoxical dialectic of reading and place at the heart of his analysis of the essence of literature as mutual recognition of freedoms. But the clichés concerning Valéry are no more valid than those pertaining to Sartre. As I argue in Chapter 4, Valéry's notion of poetry as action (his modernist poetics of effort and perfection) has been misread to the extent that it is viewed from the perspective of an ideological opposition between surrealist automatism and pure poetry. Reading Valéry in proximity to Breton, I show that Valéry anticipates the affirmation of surrealist automatism, and that *Monsieur Teste* presents an allegory of automatism. Lastly, I suggest that automatism is misread when it is interpreted on the basis of a linguistic paradigm (for example, according to Lacan's theory of the unconscious) or viewed in exclusively dialectical terms. I emphasize what I call the surrealist affirmation, and Breton's critique of incipient modernism.

What unites these rereadings is the gradual reintroduction of the effaced discourse of Bergson. In most cases this subtext coincides with, and is masked by, the more obvious philosophical subtext of Hegel, as well as related structures borrowed from the domain of French sociology. Both "transgression" and "engagement" emerge as corrections of the Hegelian scene of the struggle for recognition from a vantage point that appeals to Marcel Mauss's theory of the potlatch. Once the correction is recognized, however, we also perceive that in both cases, the notion of action that is at play in them is not always the one associated with Hegelian negativity of consciousness in the face of the givens of nature. For Bataille, the teachings of Kojève concerning the end of history posed the question of the end of action, in the Hegelian sense. In Sartre, a postrevolutionary end of history also inflects the operative concept of action, and the notion of history he explicitly invokes requires an appeal to a Bergsonian notion of action as free invention, one we can subsequently recognize in the elaboration of literary engagement in *Qu'est-ce que la littérature?*

The oppositions of Valéry to both Sartre and Breton diminish when we interpret Valéry's concept of action in relation to Bergson instead of Hegel. Likewise, surrealism appears in a fundamentally affirmative light when it is read in proximity to the energies of symbolism and from the point of view of Bergson's analyses of dream and mental action—or what Valéry called "le travail de l'esprit."[8] Indeed, here, as in the *Poésies* of Lautréamont-Ducasse which so impressed Breton, negation and contradiction are far less important than a conception of affirmation linked to Nietzsche and Bergson. The Hegelian scene of recognition plays no part in the dynamics of psychic automatism. Instead it is a question of the operations of *reconnaissance* as theorized by Bergson. What this illuminates is that memory and time, as well as the visual image and a notion of fiction, play a crucially important role in surrealist affirmation.

If this were a historical study whose principal aim was to elucidate the thinking of *Tel Quel*, I would have devoted a chapter to Nietzsche, who is only mentioned in passing in these chapters. As Gilles Deleuze has pointed out, there are certain similarities between the "anti-philosophies" of Nietzsche and Bergson.[9] Nietzsche has been much discussed in relation to French theory, whereas (before Deleuze) Bergson's name is not usually mentioned. I have chosen to emphasize Bergson instead of Nietzsche both for this reason and because the treatment of Nietzsche in the milieu of theory has largely absorbed his thinking into the linguistic or rhetorical model of analysis that predominates within poststructuralism, as an inheritance from structuralism. Bergson, on the other hand, provides another thinking of affirmation (as Deleuze argues, his thinking is not dialectical in the Hegelian sense), one that invites us to reconsider the visual register, taking into account the question of unconsciousness (*inconscience*). Since the figure of Bergson is so deeply (and broadly) embedded in the French cultural context, the effacement of this discourse poses interesting questions.

The readings presented in Part II depend upon retrieving the effaced subtext of Bergson, and in the last part of this study I explore Bergson's thinking in more detail. I analyze the ways in which his discourse organizes the issues that became central to the polemics of the next generation. I explore in more general terms the ways in which the intertext of Bergson illuminates proximities among transgression, engagement, automatism, and pure art, proximities suggesting a reconfiguration of our conception of the modern and hence of the distinction between modern and postmodern. The last chapter explores the ideological pressures associated both with the eclipse of Bergson's thinking and the depreciation of surrealism. It also returns to Bataille to recontextualize the figure I take primarily as a theorist in the opening chapter, and to situate him in relation to issues that pertain to Bergson. In my conclusion I return to *Tel Quel* and to the question of theory, which I consider as a displacement of the powers of literature at issue in the literary polemics of the previous generation.

This study emerged from a meditation upon the intellectual pressures of the present moment. Some striking intellectual reversals have occurred. For years it has been a question of the demise of the subject. Recently, we hear about a "politics of identity" that implies collective subjectivity. The social, which used to be considered the arena of the dissolution of the subject into various linguistic, symbolic, and semiotic structures, is now often constructed on the model of individual subjectivity. Referentiality returns to a foundational role, with the privilege given to biological facts of gender and race, in addition to social class and other features of what Sartre called "situation."

The question confronts us then, what do we do with theory? Do we discard it, either in favor of a committed but sometimes uncritical attitude, or simply in favor of more traditional esthetic or intellectual virtues? Do we try to appropriate it (and misappropriate it), applying its operations or concepts to incompatible domains defined in terms of empirical fact and the unified subject? Or do we continue to repeat the theoretical discourse of the past two-and-a-half decades, as if it were eternally valid? None of these solutions is appealing. I felt the need therefore to explore broad relations, and especially to cross the ideological boundaries of generations, in order to unblock channels of discussion.

It is impossible, however, to explore broad relations and to respect detail at every level—the analysis would be interminable. As a result, I have had to generalize at times, or to use short-hand formulations, which necessarily oversimplify. I speak of "theory," for example, fully aware that no such thing exists as a unified body. I speak of *Tel Quel* as if it were a single entity, when of course it names a constantly changing milieu associated with a review that reversed itself dramatically over the twenty years of its existence, and which published a wide range of authors.[10] I speak of poststructuralism, without going into the dissensions between figures associated with this label. I have tried to respect detail as a reader of texts. Precisely because of the emphasis on textual reading in recent decades, however, I felt it was important to explore some of the broad presuppositions that affect our thinking and that are not usually acknowledged. These involve cultural stereotypes that would continue to structure our field of thinking if left unchallenged. Although most people would be willing to acknowledge a few of these stereotypes as such, the task was to challenge a number of them simultaneously, in an effort to pose the question of the modern, and of the postmodern, differently.

Part I

Abstract

Part I of this study attempts to analyze the centrality of the term "transgression" to the theoretical enterprise of *Tel Quel*. In Chapter 1 I trace a series of readings of Bataille's *L'Erotisme* within the *Tel Quel* context (essays by Foucault, Hollier, Sollers, and Derrida) to show how "transgression" became a theoretical operation of crucial importance to poststructuralism. I then contrast these accounts with a reading which approaches Bataille more contextually, that is, taking into account both Caillois's treatment of the sacred and the influence of Kojève. I read eroticism as a strategic displacement of the Hegelian recognition scene (the master/slave dialectic) and explore what Bataille understood by an "erotic phenomenology."

Chapter 2 analyzes Kristeva's *La Révolution du langage poétique* in order to do two things: to demonstrate the essential role the theoretical term "transgression" played in the strategies of poststructuralist theory, and to illuminate the extent to which Kristeva's study reworks literary polemics inherited from the previous generation, specifically the antinomy between art and revolution that came to be associated with the names of Breton and Sartre. (This, as we shall see, is largely due to the force of Sartre's critique of surrealism in *Qu'est-ce que la littérature?*, and his refusal to take Breton's own engagement seriously.)

In order to make this link, I have chosen to analyze Kristeva's study as representative of larger issues and features of theory in the *Tel Quel* milieu. Whereas some American and French critics do not consider Kristeva's influence to be equal to that of Barthes, Foucault, Lacan, or Derrida, the *Tel Quel* milieu consistently put Kristeva forward as a figure of theoretical legitimation or validation. In their *Dictionnaire encyclopédique des sciences du langage*, for example, Ducrot and Todorov invoke the new "elaboration conceptuelle en France . . . autour de la revue *Tel Quel* (R. Barthes, Ph. Sollers *et surtout J. Kristeva*)" (my emphasis) to justify their appendix introducing the notions of text and writing (*écriture*) as well as *signifiance* and *sémanalyse*, all of which are presented in terms of a transgressive epistemic break. I would argue that it is perhaps precisely because Kristeva was not strictly speaking a philosopher (like Derrida) or a pyschoanalyst (like Lacan, although she subsequently became one), or a writer (like Barthes) that she became paradigmatic of "the theorist." She is a theorist precisely as an interdisciplinary thinker who tries to engage semiotics (displaced, via psychoanalysis, to *sémanalyse*) and linguistics with Marxism and revolution from the perspective of an avant-garde poetics. *Tel Quel*, as both a review and a publishing concern that brought out important works of Barthes, Foucault, and Derrida at a crucial moment in the emergence of theory, leveraged each of these figures by virtue of the ground it provided. Kristeva's *La Révolution du langage poétique*, which was so philosophically dense that large portions of it had to be omitted from the English translation, effectively wedded cultural avant-gardism to revolution once and for all. It is perhaps for this reason that she, along with Derrida, Lacan, Barthes, and Foucault, remains canonical within the field of theory even as the site of theory shifts from poststructuralism to "cultural studies."

CHAPTER I

Bataille

The Fiction of Transgression

"I write for whoever, upon entering my book, would fall into it as into
a hole, and would never come out."
    —Georges Bataille, in M. Surya, *Georges Bataille, la mort à l'œuvre*

If there is a single term poststructuralist theory could not do without, it
is "transgression," inherited from Georges Bataille. Bataille elaborated a
notion of transgression most explicitly in *L'Erotisme* (1957), an essay that
reworked material from a previously unpublished piece, "L'Histoire de
l'érotisme," and that harks back to a study of "erotic phenomenology"
projected as early as 1939. But eroticism is only one modality of transgression, which refers us to an experience of the sacred, the "motive force"
of Bataille's thinking.[1] Bataille distinguishes the sacred from the profane
in economic terms borrowed from the ethnographer Marcel Mauss, whose
work impressed Bataille in the late 1920's. In "La Notion de dépense"
(1933), Bataille distinguished between what he calls the restrained or utilitarian economy, and the general economy of sovereignty. Whereas the
former implies production, saving, and exchange, the latter implies consumption, expenditure, and reciprocity. This economic distinction remains
constant throughout Bataille's career, even as it operates in quite different
registers—those of revolutionary politics, of mystical experience, and of
literary community.

"La Notion de dépense" dates from the period following Bataille's
break from the surrealists, prompted by Breton's declaration of support
for the Communist revolutionary cause. These were the years of Bataille's
own form of engagement, his involvement with Le Cercle Démocratique,
a revolutionary group organized by the dissident communist Boris Sou-

varine, and of his intense involvement with the teachings of Alexander Kojève on Hegel. They will be followed, toward the end of the decade, with Bataille's investment in the group enterprises of Contre-Attaque, Acéphale, and the Collège de Sociologie, the last two devoted to an exploration of "sacred sociology." If Breton was the avant-gardist, Bataille was the ultra- (and perhaps anti-) avant-gardist. If Breton announced his adherence to communist revolution, Bataille placed himself at the extreme left, and was in a problematic relation even to this milieu. Bataille was not only at the cultural margins during the 1930's, he was at the edge of those margins. He was in a relation of contestation first to Breton, then to Le Cercle Démocratique, and subsequently to Sartre. Of all the figures of his generation, it was this most hypermarginal and erratic character that was privileged by the avant-garde theorists of *Tel Quel*. In this chapter I would like to explore why this was so, to analyze the appropriation of transgression by contemporary theory, and to measure certain displacements that took place in the course of theoretical rereadings of Bataille.

So powerful was the impact of Bataille upon the *Tel Quel* generation that the difference between structuralist and poststructuralist thinking itself was officially characterized in terms of Bataille's distinction between restrained and general economies. Structuralism was accused by poststructuralism of remaining Hegelian: that is, of operating binary oppositions (or contradictions) in relation to a framework of unified totality. To the extent that the movement of Hegelian dialectic puts every term to work in the service of a subsequent development of that totality, poststructuralist critics identified structuralism with the utilitarian or restricted economy and championed a nontotalizable or general one.

Derrida launches what we could call poststructuralist critique with his analysis of Husserl in *La Voix et le phénomène* (1967) and his elaboration of the force and dynamics of *différance*. Temporality, ontological difference, and the structure of the unconscious as analyzed by psychoanalysis are all invoked to put into question the presupposition of the horizon of presence crucial to the phenomenological undertaking. The post-phenomenological critique is then directed explicitly at structuralist thinking with the essays collected in *Marges de la philosophie* (1972). Here Derrida exposes the presuppositions of structural linguistics and semiotics, attacking the structure of the sign itself as a reinscription of metaphysical oppositions which, in Derrida's view, presuppose a horizon of presence. He specifically challenges the status of the transcendental signified, the term that had been brought into question in the reading of Husserl. The philosophical argument is elaborated within the literary domain in *De la grammatologie* (1967), where Derrida opposes writing to speech (as a necessary moment, on his analysis, of the phenomenological perspective) and launches a theory of writing elaborated in terms of *différance*. In an essay on Lautréamont published in *Tel Quel*, Philippe Sollers characterizes this theory of writing in terms of Bataille's operation of transgression. "God-meaning . . . is a figure of linguistic interdiction," he writes, "whereas writing—which is metaphoricity itself (Derrida) *transgresses* the hierarchic order of discourse and of the world associated with it, through the introduction of a specific difference [*écart*]."[2] Never mind Sollers's misprision (as Derrida will subsequently make clear in "Le retrait de la métaphore," *différance* does not operate through metaphor in grammatology); the important point is that he invoked Bataille's term "transgression" to characterize the break introduced by, or as, poststructuralism. This gesture will be repeated again and again, as we see, for example, in Ducrot and Todorov's *Encyclopedic Dictionary of the Sciences of Language* where the rhetoric of transgression is frequently invoked to characterize the epistemic break—the "Copernican revolution"—introduced by poststructuralism. Whereas Bataille elaborates transgression as a kind of supplement to philosophical discourse, Sollers borrows this language to characterize a philosophical shift, a move away from Hegel (associated with phenomenology and its appropriation by existentialism) toward late Heidegger. Sollers and Foucault both contribute essays that reconfigure "transgression" in terms of Heidegger's thinking of the question of the limit in relation to time and ontological difference. Transgression, they hope, will put to rest an exhausted Hegelian paradigm.[3]

By 1967, when Derrida published his now canonical essay on Bataille, "De l'économie restreinte à l'économie générale,"[4] transgression can be invoked as a quasi-philosophical term, or at least a term carrying the authority of philosophical discourse. More significantly, however, it emerges as a theoretical term that elaborates a "transgression of philosophy," one performed by literature as it communicates with theory (or by theory as it communicates with poetry). This is the program *Tel Quel* will put forth in the 1968 manifesto "La révolution ici maintenant."[5] In the writings of Kristeva, as we shall see, the transgression of philosophy will be reread as a revolutionary gesture; it becomes a Marxist revolutionary practice.[6] Bataille's thinking on transgression both sets the *Tel Quel* agenda and enables crucial moments of what Sollers will subsequently call "the dream of theory."[7]

If one had to isolate the single gesture of Bataille that had the greatest impact for avant-garde thinking of the 1960's and 1970's, it would be the insertion of the ethnological distinction sacred/profane into the discourse of philosophy (or of Hegel). Foucault meditates on this interlarding of philosophy and religion in his important essay "Préface à la transgression," which appeared in a special issue of *Critique* devoted to Bataille in commemoration of his death in 1963.[8] Foucault's essay is worth analyzing in some detail, for it anticipates in very precise terms (one could even say it generates) the role transgression will come to play within the theoretical enterprise of poststructuralism, particularly among those associated with *Tel Quel*. Foucault first tentatively proposes that transgression might be understood as an equivalent of profanation in a world that no longer gives any positive meaning to the sacred. He identifies transgression with eroticism. "Thus," he writes, "at the depths of sexuality, of its movement that nothing ever limits . . . an experience is formed [*se dessine*], that of transgression" (PT 754).

After the preliminary paragraphs linking transgression to sexuality, the avant-gardism of Sade, and the nihilism of Nietzsche, Foucault moves on to a philosophical elaboration of transgression. Whereas Bataille emphasized the dual operation of transgression/interdiction in *L'Erotisme*, Foucault defines transgression as a "gesture which concerns the limit." It is reduced to a simple gesture, one Foucault characterizes as a flash of lightning, and hence associates with the figure of the line.[9] The move into the philosophical register is marked by this representation of a line, one that gesturally depicts the Heideggerian ontology of limitation: the coming into being, or appearance, of beings on the horizon of Being. Foucault nuances his initial formulation further on in the essay when he speaks of a "play of limits and of transgression." Transgression, then, includes two gestures, which are ambiguously one: the inscription of a line and its crossing. "The limit and transgression owe to one another the density of their being," Foucault writes, "non-existence of a limit that could absolutely not be crossed; vanity of the return of a transgression that would only cross an illusory or shadowy limit" (PT 755). Thus transgression is not exterior to the limit that is transgressed. The two are inseparable, and yet not the same. They are different. In the next sentence, however, the event of transgression is once again hypostatized, as it was through the figure of the line. It is given an existential status as "this *existence* so pure and so entangled [*enchevêtrée*]" (my emphasis).

Once posited in these terms, however, transgression can be distinguished from other existences and immunized against other discourses. In the first place, Foucault insists, it must be distinguished from the language of ethics. What Bataille calls "evil" in *Literature and Evil*, Foucault explains, has nothing to do with moral discourse. Nothing is negative in transgression, which affirms both the limited and the unlimited. At the same time, however, Foucault holds that this affirmation affirms nothing because it does not posit anything. Positing entails the dialectical moments of concrete negation and synthesis, whereas transgression, Foucault writes (anticipating the publication of Derrida's analysis of *différance*) is the affirmation of difference. This formulation introduces the next big step in Foucault's argument: the notion of a philosophy of transgression, glossed in Heideggerian terms as a "philosophy of non-positive affirmation, that is, the *épreuve* [ordeal/trial] of the limit." This is the crucial step for the theoretical enterprise of *Tel Quel*.

Foucault wrote this sentence three years before Derrida's first essay on grammatology was published in 1966, also in *Critique*. He anticipated certain features of the Derridean analysis of différance when he alluded to Nietzschean affirmation and Blanchot's "principle of contestation." His major point emerges in the following rhetorical question, which brings us to the crux of the matter. Speaking of transgression, he writes:

No dialectical movement, no analysis of fundamental laws [*constitutions*] and of their transcendental foundation [*leur sol*] can be of help in thinking such an experience or even the access to this experience. Might not the instantaneous play of the limit and transgression be today the essential test of a thinking of "origin" which Nietzsche bequeathed to us . . . a thinking that would be absolutely, and in the same movement, a Critique and an Ontology, a thinking that would think finitude and being? (PT 757)

Thus we arrive tentatively at a "philosophy" of eroticism, where philosophy is neither cognitive nor rational, but involves "an experience of finitude and of being, of the limit and of transgression." It is a question of philosophy as experience, one that has not yet found its language. "Would it be an exaggeration," Foucault writes, "to say . . . that it would be necessary to find a language for the transgressive that would be what dialectic has been for contradiction?" (PT 759). Foucault has moved us to the ground of ontology, or to ontology as a question of grounding. With this move transgression has become a question of language—and of the language of philosophy.[10]

We are at a peculiar juncture here. Foucault brings to his reading of Nietzsche the discovery of structuralism, namely, that the subject is in language, and not the other way around. No explicit mention is made of the structuralist subtext, but it is implicit in the following account of the fracture of the subject of philosophy:

The philosopher knows that "we are not everything"; but he learns that the philosopher himself does not inhabit the totality of his language like a secret god . . . he discovers that next to him there is a language which speaks and of which he is not the master; a language that strives, and that fails. . . . And above all he discovers that at the very moment of speaking, he is not necessarily lodged inside his language . . . and that at the site of the speaking subject . . . a void has hollowed itself out. (PT 751)

Foucault's analysis introduces the following crucial reversal: if transgression constitutes a philosophy, what is transgressed is the position of the philosopher—and to this extent philosophy itself—through the limitlessness of language. Here we have a preview of the fundamental program of poststructuralism, or of theory in the context of *Tel Quel*. The philosopher, Foucault writes, finds "not outside language, but in it, at the center of its possibilities, the transgression of his philosophical being." This will be the starring role of transgression—the transgression of philosophy by language, that is, by the "nondialectical language of the limit that only unfolds in the transgression of the one who speaks it." This is what we will read a decade later in Ducrot and Todorov's *Dictionnaire encyclopédique des sciences du langage*, where it is a question of the "Copernican revolution" of theory. In Foucault's essay, then, transgression becomes a function of (even an experience of) a relation to the finitude of being. A thinking of transgression, Foucault concludes, marks an interrogation of the limit which replaces the totalizing gesture of Hegel: "The gesture of transgression replaces the movement of contradictions," Foucault writes, by "plunging the philosophical experience into language" (PT 767–68).

"Perhaps one day," Foucault speculates concerning the philosopheme "transgression," "it will appear as decisive for our culture as the experience of contradiction used to be for dialectical thinking." This is precisely the role transgression, as constituted in the essay by Foucault, will play for the thinking of poststructuralism and the avant-gardism of *Tel Quel*. Transgression is meant to take over from contradiction. Appropriations of Bataille's notion of transgression reveal a desire to get beyond dialectical thinking into a new field of language and of thinking, one in which it would be possible, as *Tel Quel* will put it, to "faire communiquer théorie et fiction [make theory and fiction communicate, or open out onto, one another]." Speaking of the language of transgression he adumbrates here, Foucault writes toward the end of his essay: "It is possible . . . to find the scorched roots, the promising ashes, of such a language in Bataille."[11] The shadow of the phoenix in this figure is already an indication that the operation of contradiction will be difficult to get beyond completely. Transgression, as we shall see, implies a greater proximity to Hegel than Foucault's essay suggests.

Four years later (and one year after the appearance of Derrida's *De la grammatologie*) Sollers publishes a reading of Bataille's *L'Erotisme* in an essay entitled "Le Toit, Essai de lecture systématique."[12] Transgression (now synonymous with eroticism) becomes identified with writing or text, that is, with what the director of *Tel Quel* will characterize as the "wrong side or inside out [*envers*]" of literature. "Le Toit" reaffirms Foucault's point of departure, namely, the distinction between transgression, understood as a "philosophy of eroticism," and the popular notion of sexual liberation. Sollers labels the latter "pseudo-transgression" and dismisses it. He then reminds his readers that Bataille had posed transgression as a "dual operation," an interplay between transgression and interdiction. He reaffirms that neither operation can take place, or have meaning, without the other, thereby reinscribing the term "interdiction," which played an ambiguous role in Foucault's analysis, as we have seen.

Sollers goes on to interpret interdiction in terms of the opposition between discourse and silence, a move that constitutes the major step in the transposition of Bataille's eroticism into the key of language, writing, and text. Interdiction is read as discursive constraint upon language and meaning: "the world of discourse is the mode of being of interdiction . . . interdiction is the signifier itself (in the world of discourse . . .)" (T 29). Sollers does not invent here, for Bataille has made this identification. What is exceptional, however, is the exclusive emphasis on this register. The important point is that Sollers retains the broader philosophical claims made for Bataille's thinking by Foucault, while restricting transgression to the textual level. Thus he pursues one branch of Bataille's thinking concerning the fundamental structural difference between the sacred and the profane, and extends to it the supreme philosophical authority Foucault granted Bataille in the name of a "philosophy of transgression" that would go beyond the limitations of the Hegelian dialectic and proceed to the transgression of philosophy! The net effect is an inflation of the claims made for transgression in the linguistic, textual, or poetic register. These claims are then articulated with an evolving poststructuralist theory of writing and text.[13]

It is ironic that Bataille's thinking should have become so wedded to language. For Bataille initially rejected language altogether for silence, the silence of a *non-savoir* (non-knowledge) which was not at all a philosophical concept nor primarily a poetic mood or language effect. It was an experience of emotional intensity. Sacrifice, performed within the context of sacred ritual, could bind the members of a community together more forcefully, Bataille believed, and more enduringly, than anything words could do because of its overwhelming affective shock. What was at stake was a shared experience of radical immediacy, and the ultimate event of such immediacy was the experience of another's death. When this intimate experience was shared, a powerful collective bond was established. Sacrifice provides something like what one could call the "regulative idea" of *non-savoir* for Bataille. His relation to poetry (or to nondiscursive textual practices) existed as a function of this idea, and to this extent was ambivalent and unstable.

In Sollers's essay, the identification of transgression and nondiscursive language enables a theoretical link with psychoanalysis, where interdiction as repression is marked by linguistic parapraxis, or slips of the tongue. With respect to language, Sollers suggests, there is a fundamental transgression—a "scandal"—namely, the fact that discourse simply does not work. "There is nothing in the thing of what we say of it," he writes, " . . . nothing in what we say that 'belongs' to the thing or which replaces it." This, we recognize, amounts to the "scandal" Saussure had announced as the arbitrariness of the sign. Although fundamental, Sollers wants to suggest, this transgression "would recognize the necessity of the interdiction to which it finds itself bound," that is, the "as if" of language's capacity to signify. On this account, then, interdiction is identified with the communicative function of language which serves as the basis for discursive exchange. Thus, a Saussurian structuralist moment is read back into Bataille, who was not at all concerned with this kind of problem (which worried Paul de Man)—the inefficacy of language truthfully to represent the world. Bataille was more inclined to feel that discursive language worked all too well, flattening out and homogenizing human experience in the process.

On Sollers's reading, transgression becomes a "space of organic effervescence of language." It is organic, Sollers implies, in relation to the fundamental transgression, the scandal of the arbitrariness of the sign. It occurs in an agonistic relation to the interdiction of language as discursive event. What is at stake here (and it is barely concealed) is a return to the old polemic against realism that Breton (among others) launched in the previous generation and which has continued to haunt esthetic avant-gardism and the theoretical enterprise associated with it to the present day. "Eroticism is the anti-matter of realism" (T 36), Sollers declares, in a formula that reveals clearly what is at stake in the *Tel Quel* appropriation of eroticism for theory.

Transgression becomes explicitly polemical when it is analyzed in linguistic terms. For Sollers, the dual operation transgression/interdiction becomes a "dialectic of war," where "interdiction or transgression provisionally gets the upper hand, depending on whether the field of objects and things (the domain of the discontinuous) wins out or whether the dimension of crossing beyond objects and things (the continuous) wins out" (T 30). Once the conflict is set up in such oppositional terms, the earlier proviso concerning the peculiar logic of reciprocity of interdiction/transgression (the logic of the dual operation) is neglected. It becomes a question of taking sides. Indeed, in spite of Sollers's explicit opening declaration that eroticism is not simply an apology of transgression, it becomes precisely that. For once interdiction is opposed to transgression, other binary oppositions enter the argument, culminating in the one between "literature" and "writing." Literature implies representational discourse and thus belongs on the side of interdiction; writing, which is transgressive, belongs with poetry, madness, and excess.[14]

"Le Toit" works out in rigorous detail various analogies which will subsequently be taken for granted in the milieu of *Tel Quel*. Thanks to suggestive allusions to historical and dialectical materialism, the agon between transgression and interdiction takes on epic proportions. In the process, the reach of eroticism as "philosophy of transgression" is vastly extended, as is the rhetoric of its violence:

Eroticism—the fact that its theory is only produced today in the wake of Sade— takes on all its meaning: not only is it what, in history, presents itself as the end of the theological, philosophical and pre-scientific era—as that which visibly *puts an end to* their logical presuppositions—but moreover the *rape/violation* [*le viol*] of the individual constituted during this period, the organic and economic unity that was its support: the whole erotic *mise en œuvre* [putting into a work] and, as its fundamental principle, the destruction of the closed being that is the *partenaire de jeu* in the moral state. . . . All in all eroticism, understood as the unveiled richness and the avowal [*aveu*] of language—as its power of expenditure and of gratuitousness—involves . . . a function of penetration and destruction of discourse. (original emphasis)[15]

This is then related to the materialist dialectic of Marx. But let us make the analogy explicit. Discourse is in the position of the woman violated in a gesture of transgressive eroticism that is performed by, or as, an "unveiled richness . . . of language." Discourse is not only penetrated and opened, but also destroyed, as is the unified (closed) subject of discourse— implicitly the bourgeois subject. The world-historical framework of dialectical progression (the allusion to revolution) makes it difficult to see in what sense *this* transgression—the transgression of writing and text— could be said to retain the force of interdiction. The problem will not go away. We shall see in the following chapter how it returns in Kristeva's *La Révolution du langage poétique*, and how it will entail her critique of the very Derridean discourse Sollers had credited with opening up the possibility of a philosophy of eroticism in the 1960's.

By the end of his essay, Sollers announces bluntly that transgression has become writing. First, he cites Bataille to the effect that "eroticism, considered gravely, tragically, represents a reversal." Then he adds the decisive commentary: "But we see right away how writing takes charge of this reversal from this point on, how it then has the same status and ultimately the same meaning as eroticism . . . writing . . . finally takes over from transgression" (T 41). Text becomes the object of eroticism. Once again, we have the citation and then the gloss. First Bataille: "Eroticism . . . is nevertheless expressed by an object," and then Sollers: "this object . . . has a name: the detour, the detour of the text" (T 36). Lastly, eroticism becomes the name of the subversive program formally announced by *Tel Quel* the following year: "faire communiquer théorie et fiction."[16]

Sollers has entitled his "systematic reading" of Bataille "Le Toit," a figure borrowed from Bataille's *L'Expérience intérieure*, where it evokes "the interrelationship between all the opposed possibilities [la relation entre elles de toutes les possibilités opposées]." In Sollers, it is meant to evoke the dual structure of eroticism as interdiction/transgression precisely in the role Foucault had anticipated it would play once it had found its language: that of displacing the Hegelian logic of contradiction. What it found with Sollers, of course, was not its language, but quite simply, language. The figure of "le toit"—the roof of the temple—is posed by Sollers as a nondialectical alternative to the ostensibly dialectical point of surrealism, the "point of the esprit where life and death . . . cease to be perceived as contradictory." Sollers writes: "The difference between these two formulations is essential (it would enable us, no doubt, to understand how Bataille and Breton are situated in irreconcilable positions with respect to Hegel)" (T 26).[17] Sollers fleshes out what Foucault had hypothetically proposed in his "Préface à la transgression." "Le Toit" moves Bataille's terms "eroticism" and "transgression" toward the field of language, writing, and text. "Text," or "signifier," has replaced the woman as object of desire. The metaphor of "le toit," which figured the two worlds of the sacred and the profane and the dual operation of interdiction and transgression for Bataille, becomes an emblem of writing in its difference from literature: "the emblem of the 'roof / home of writing' . . . the two hands, one that writes and one that dies." "Le toit" (the expression also signifies "home" and in this sense suggests an allusion to Heidegger's statement that language is "the house of Being") not only prepares the ground for the shift from structuralism to poststructuralism, it announces this shift as imperative through the figure of excess. "According to a 'dying' logic," Sollers writes, "it is necessary that an excess, which, no matter what the current logic, does not cease putting to death, correspond to a system of formal relations." As theoretical discourse gains currency, eroticism and transgression come to stand for the transgression of structuralism by poststructuralism on the one hand, and the transgression of philosophy by writing or theory, on the other.

"*L'Erotisme* is a clear book . . . its exposition conceals itself because . . . of its extreme simplicity," Sollers had written. His reading of Bataille's text, however, simplifies a little too much, for it overlooks the explicit statement by Bataille that the relation between the two "worlds" of transgression and interdiction is itself dialectical—a question of *aufhebung*. If transgression replaces *aufhebung*, as Hollier has stated, intensifying the force of Foucault's hypothetical claim, it does so through a specific reinscription of *aufhebung*, one which Derrida undertakes to analyze in his essay on Bataille.[18] Sollers cites Bataille: "Transgression is different from a return to nature, it removes the interdiction without doing away with it," and he asks rhetorically, by way of comment, "What can this operation, whose gesture is irreducible to classical rationality, mean?" (T 27). Derrida responds to this question when he cites Bataille's note concerning the dual operation of transgression/interdiction—"There is no need to stress the Hegelian nature of this operation which corresponds with the moment of dialectic expressed by the untranslatable term *aufheben* (to surpass while maintaining.)"[19] If transgression replaces *aufhebung*, it is, as we shall see, because eroticism reinscribes the *aufhebung* in another register, that of the sacred.

Derrida's essay reveals the dynamics of a double writing in Bataille's text, one that displaces the terms of Hegel's *Phenomenology* while retaining certain of its movements. And, not surprisingly, the displacements signaled by Derrida largely coincide with those performed by poststructuralist writers in relation to the totalizing thinking of structuralist linguistics and semiotics. As we shall see, this also implies that poststructuralism itself becomes imbued with the aura of the sacred—or, more specifically, of the sublime.[20] From here on in, for *Tel Quel* critics such as Kristeva, the subversion of philosophy by writing goes hand in hand with the theorizing of writing. The project to formalize the infinite play of *signifiance*, for example, announced by Ducrot and Todorov in the *Dictionnaire*, reveals the full extent of *Tel Quel*'s ambitions for what Sollers called, retrospectively, "the dream of theory."[21]

Henceforth, what Ducrot and Todorov call the poststructural "shift [*basculement*] to the side of the signifier" will be characterized in terms of a "materiality" of text. On Saussure's analysis, the signifier is one side of the sign that Saussure compares to a sheet of paper. On the front, as it were, is the signifier—an inscribed mark, or audible sound—and on the back, the signified or mental idea. When you cut out one side of the sign, the other side is delimited correspondingly. On this basis the sign divides into "materialist" and "idealist" components, associated with the signifier and the signified respectively. The notion of the "materiality" of the text rhetorically acknowledges Marxist dialectical materialism. At the same time, it alludes to the discourse of psychoanalysis and to the way in which the body is associated with unconscious drives and impulses in opposition to the conscious mind, construed as the field of signifieds. Rhetorically, at least, Marx and Freud can be reconciled through the extension of the term "materiality" to the linguistic domain. Furthermore, the materiality of text can be associated with the discourse of eroticism and the specific excess the body introduces in relation to the ostensible stability of the unified subject of consciousness. As Sollers writes, "What the flesh presents to the body . . . is an 'impersonal plethora' just as poetic language appears to scientific discourse as a fundamentally 'repugnant' putting into play of the subject of discourse" (T 34). Poetry, text, writing, *signifiance*, and so on, all enjoy the dilation of the "impersonal plethora."

In 1966, Denis Hollier reminded his readers that "the opposition of the sacred and the profane is the basis for all aspects of the thinking of Bataille."[22] In the poststructuralist appropriation of Bataille, however, the dimension of the sacred is evacuated. It is displaced by the psychoanalytic register and the difference conscious/unconscious, by the ontological difference elaborated by Heidegger, and by Derrida's theoretical elaboration of différance in its difference from the metaphysics of presence. Although the three paths of displacement are quite distinct, taken together they mark a reformulation of the religious question of the sacred (which, since Durkheim, is related to the implicitly political issue of social cohesion) in terms of a question of philosophy, and of its end. The ethnographic perspective that had deliberately introduced a dimension of cultural otherness is lost when the question of transgression is transposed back into the European intellectual tradition in this way. As demonstrated by his investment in the collective experiences of the Cercle Démocratique, of Contre-Attaque, Acéphale, and the Collège de Sociologie, however, Bataille's marginal status is deliberate and is precisely a function of his refusal of the exclusively philosophical register—that is, of philosophy unalloyed by an experiential impact where intensity of affect is the moving force. Throughout the 1930's in particular (the period that saw the emergence of "La Notion de dépense") Bataille was interested in questions of power and action. In the poststructuralist context, the discourse of psychoanalysis appropriates these issues. Interdiction and transgression are interpreted in relation to desire. With Lacan, the unconscious itself is analyzed in linguistic and rhetorical terms; it too becomes a field of language forces. The meaning of materiality is attenuated when materialism is restricted to the materiality of text.

Rereading

The canonization of Bataille within the avant-garde canon, the theoretical privilege accorded him (quite exceptionally among writers of his generation), contaminated the reception of his writings, which the poststructuralist glosses rendered both all too familiar, and unfamiliar at the same time. So much was made of Bataille's writing, writing that became emblematic of writing per se (in the new theoretical sense), that it became all but impossible to read him.

When we return to the text of *L'Erotisme*, conscious of the strategic shifts of emphasis that have occurred in the poststructuralist rereading of Bataille, we find a few surprises. Readers introduced to Bataille through *Tel Quel* (which is to say most contemporary readers of Bataille, and certainly most of his American readers) will have absorbed the poststructuralist identification of transgression with polysemia and the infinite play of *signifiance*, characterized as the literary equivalent of perversity. They will be familiar with Sollers's association of text with flesh and the erotics of an "impersonal plethora." For these readers it is surprising to hear Bataille explicitly reject, in his analysis of eroticism, the experience of the orgy in favor of the determinate dialectical relation to the woman as object of man's desire. If we pursue this puzzling detail, a different reading of Bataille opens up, one that places the question of the sacred, or the difference sacred/profane, back at the center of Bataille's thinking. Once this focus is reestablished we can recognize how the issue of the sacred impinges on the question of philosophy for Bataille. We can then reconsider how transgression informs the question of the essence of literature and of its powers for Bataille—a question imposed by Sartre and the imperative of engagement.

Bataille begins his discussion of eroticism with what he calls "a philosophical detour," a schematic opposition between continuity or fusion on the one hand, and discontinuity or separation on the other. In Hegelian terms, this would correspond to the difference between identity and difference, the latter introduced through the negativity of consciousness. It might be more fruitful, however, to take a philosophical detour through Bergson, who opposes the discontinuity of ordinary or intellectual experience and the continuity of duration.[23] For it was Bergson, not Hegel, who accompanied this distinction with a critique of language (in the name of discontinuity) which could only have appealed to Bataille. And it was Bergson who introduced the constellation of terms that return together in Bataille: the distinctions between homogeneity and heterogeneity as well as between utility and nonutility, and above all the notion of communication. "We perceive duration as a current that one cannot go back up," Bergson writes in *L'Evolution créatrice*, "it is the depth [*fond*] of our being, we feel it well enough, the very substance of things with which we are in communication." It is in roughly this sense that the term "communication" functions in Bataille, where it refers us to the experience of intimate immediacy that transgression is said to open up to us. Eroticism is characterized as just such a moment of communication, that is, as a movement from separation back to an experience of fusion.

Given this point of departure, we have all the more reason to expect the sacred orgy (extreme case of the loss of separateness through fusion) to become the privileged erotic experience. Bataille surprises us, then, when he declares the orgy to be "necessarily disappointing," and proceeds to focus exclusively on heterosexual eroticism *à deux*, a gendered scenario of man's relation to woman as erotic object.[24] The orgy, it seems, involves too radical a loss of separateness for Bataille. "Not only is individuality itself submerged in the tumult of orgy," he complains, "but each participant denies the individuality of the others. All limits are completely done away with." Although radical fusion may be the ultimate meaning of eroticism, as Bataille declares, this meaning only emerges when the erotic experience is structured in intersubjective terms and intersubjectivity is modeled on a relation of subject to object. In Bataille's theory of eroticism, the presence of an erotic object is required. It is a question of losing oneself knowingly, and not too completely after all.

Whereas the philosophical tradition poses man as the rational animal, Bataille poses him not only as the erotic animal but simultaneously as the religious animal. He must therefore delimit the human realm from the animal one, although, as Bataille points out, these are usually identified in discussions of sexuality. It is for this reason that eroticism is defined here as the *conscious* activity of the sexual animal and distinguished from merely sexual activity, which pertains to the animal world. It is for the sake of this lucidity, ultimately, that erotic experience is staged as a relation to an erotic object and that, as Bataille puts it, "a dialectic is necessary."[25]

The object of desire, Bataille writes in "L'Histoire de l'érotisme," is the "mirror in which we ourselves are reflected." The woman mirrors the man's transgression. "Ordinarily a man cannot have the feeling that a law is violated in his own person," Bataille writes:

which is why he awaits the confusion of a woman, even if it is feigned, without which he would not have the consciousness of a violation. . . . It is a question of marking, through shame, that the interdiction has not been forgotten, that the *dépassement* has taken place in spite of the interdiction, in consciousness of the interdiction. (H 134)

The man's transgression is reflected in the woman's shame which, real or play-acted (*jouée*), signifies eroticism. The problem with the orgy is that it produces a negation of limits but does not give this negation to consciousness. To this extent it does not give the experience to us as meaning. The erotic object, on the other hand, does precisely that. It is a paradoxical object, Bataille writes, "an object which signifies the negation of the limits of any object" (*E* 143). In the possession of the erotic object man comes into consciousness—of loss, of death, and of himself as erotic subject. Lucidity lies at the heart of what Bataille thinks through the word "fiction."

The erotic object must not only be a woman, but a woman as object, which for Bataille means a prostitute. In "L'Histoire de l'érotisme," Bataille contrasts his theoretical erotic object with actual experience. In real life, he acknowledges, autonomous women are at least as desirable as prostitutes—usually more so. It is customary, he writes, to wish for "the movements of more real beings, existing for themselves and wanting to respond to their own desire," instead of the "frozen figures [*figures figées*]" of prostitutes, "beings destroyed as ends in themselves" (H 124). If the passivity of the prostitute is less desirable erotically, however, it turns out to be of crucial importance philosophically. For in relation to autonomous, desiring women—women as subjects—one "cannot avoid struggle which would lead to destruction" (H 124). It is in order to avoid such struggle, Bataille concludes, that "we [men] must . . . place this object equal to ourselves, *in the frame of the dead object*, of the infinitely available object" (H 124, my emphasis)—hence the figure of the prostitute portrayed here as a work of art, indeed, a kind of still life.

It is just here that we find the note already mentioned concerning the *necessity* of dialectic. And it is here that we can begin to see the paradoxical proximity of Bataille to Hegel, and of sovereignty to mastery. From what has been said so far it should be clear that a version of Hegelian recognition is at play in Bataille's theory of eroticism. A determinate object of desire is required because a dialectic is necessary. A dialectic is necessary for the sake of recognition, that is, in order to achieve the self-consciousness of man as erotic animal. This dialectic yields a kind of meaning even in its nondiscursiveness, even in its silence, or *non-savoir*. It is precisely to avoid the kind of struggle to the death that occurs in Hegel's master/slave dialectic that the woman must not be a desiring subject, and must be placed in the frame of the dead object. And even when this precaution is taken, even with this correction of the recognition scene, we are not entirely free of the subordination associated with mastery. For the sovereign moment of erotic possession does subordinate object to subject. Does this mean that Bataille's thinking is still dialectical after all?

It is more exact to say that Bataille's thinking is dialectical again, in a repetition that renders the pertinence of the dialectical movement difficult to decide. The repetition operates in a rigorous way. The discrepancy between Bataille and Hegel, between sovereignty (as it operates in eroticism) and mastery, is less a formal or conceptual difference than a temporal or rhythmic one. Bataille takes a step back from Hegel, or, to be more precise, Kojève.[26] But it is a choreographed step in a paradoxical dance. In the Hegelian struggle for recognition, the positions of master and slave

are designated when one subject concedes victory to another, thereby sacrificing his or her autonomy in order to survive.[27] Instead of being killed by
his opponent he undergoes "dialectical suppression." His life is spared but
his status as subject is annulled. To be a slave is to be considered no better than a thing. It is to be reduced, in Kojève's words, to the status of "living cadaver"—like the prostitute, in other words, in Bataille's theory. The
master, on the other hand, succeeds in finding satisfaction. In Kojève's
words, "he succeeds in getting to the heart of things [*au bout de la chose*]
and satisfying himself in pleasure [*jouissance*]." With Kojève's version of
the Hegelian scenario in mind, we recognize that in Bataille's theory of
eroticism, the woman is cast in the role of the already *aufgeheben* slave.
She is given the status of thing, while the man enjoys the role of the master who can take the things of this world for his pleasure. In other words,
and this is the important point, Bataille begins the dialectical relation to
the erotic object just where the Hegelian master/slave dialectic concludes.
What we have in Bataille, then, is something like a second-order scene of
recognition.

Now in Kojève's version of the Hegelian story (and this is where he dif-
fers from Hegel and engages with a revolutionary myth) the slave will
eventually regain his autonomy through work. He can do so because in
the intense experience of fear of death that prompts his capitulation to the
master, he has crossed the threshold from a merely animal "sentiment de
soi" to a distinctly human self-consciousness. For Kojève, in other words,
the fear of death serves the same function as the actual risk of death in
Hegel's account. The intensity of this anxiety yields self-consciousness.
For Bataille, erotic desire is an equivalent of the fear of death elaborated
by Kojève. But since Bataille does not grant the erotic object this desire,
she does not undergo this anxiety, and therefore cannot enter into the historical, dialectical progression toward autonomy. Thus what Kojève found
tragic about the Hegelian recognition scene—the fact, as he put it, that
the master is not "recognized by another man," but merely by a slave—
is not simply comic for Bataille. It becomes the opportunity, and the specific virtue, of eroticism: "recognition" by a woman!

Eroticism, then, or what will come to be known as transgression, involves a peaceful correction of Hegel's scene of recognition—a recognition essential to the specifically human, that is, lucid, experience of eroticism as distinct from mere brute sexuality. To appreciate this point, we
must look more closely at the mechanism (*ressort*) of eroticism. Bataille
presents it as a dynamic equilibrium (*jeu de balance*) between interdiction
(*l'interdit*) and transgression. If, for a moment, we interpret Bataille's opening opposition between fusion and discontinuity in Hegelian terms, that
is, in terms of identity and difference (or negativity), we see that it lines

up with a number of other oppositions that enter into Bataille's elaboration as he leads up to the presentation of the "dual operation" of transgression/interdiction—oppositions between violence and reason, nature and culture, as well as between the sacred and the profane. According to one line of development here, the imposition of interdiction upon a violence of nature inaugurates a human world of work, consciousness of death, and restricted sexual activity. It thus marks a passage from the animal world to the human order. Just where Hegel would place his anthropogenic scene of the struggle for recognition, however, Bataille's theoretical elaboration splits in two.

In the first place, Bataille substitutes the unconscious negativity of interdiction for the negativity of consciousness Hegel opposes to continuity or identity, thereby injecting an ethnological term into the discourse of philosophy. This shift introduces a new dimension into the Hegelian dialectic of human history: the structural difference (or difference of level) between the sacred and the profane. Bataille refers the reader to Roger Caillois's analysis of the sacred in *L'Homme et le sacré*. He credits Caillois with the discovery of the dual operation of interdiction and transgression that Bataille considers to be the very mechanism (*le ressort*) of eroticism. The reference to Caillois, however, renders Bataille's use of the word "sacred" ambiguous, since Caillois not only analyzes an ambivalence in what he terms the primitive sacred, he also opposes this primitive sacred to a modern, monovalent sacred. Whereas Caillois emphasizes the distinction between ancient and modern versions of religious experience, Bataille mixes the two together. In *L'Erotisme* the opposition sacred/profane sometimes coincides with the opposition between transgression and interdiction, while at other times both transgression and interdiction are said to belong to the world of the sacred in its primitive ambivalence. In the course of his exposition of eroticism, Bataille switches blithely from one of these frameworks to the other.

Following the Hegelian, teleological line of development, Bataille suggests that the imposition of interdiction upon the violence of nature both sacralizes that violence and opens the domain of reason, thereby inaugurating the realm of history or culture. On this line of development transgression is said periodically to introduce the force and violence of the sacred into the profane world of reason in order to rejuvenate the system. This formulation implies a correspondence between the oppositions sacred/profane and transgression/interdiction. Bataille conflates Hegel's and Kojève's anthropogenic story of the dialectical passage from animal to man (or from desire to self-consciousness) with an anthropological narrative of the emergence of culture from nature. At other times, however, Bataille presents interdiction as a refusal of violence that he characterizes as a step back—a *recul*—prompted by a feeling of horror. Transgression, then, occurs as a *rebondissement*, a rebounding of violence produced by positive emotions of attraction or fascination (*E* 75). Here Bataille emphasizes the emotional nature of interdiction itself. This implies an irrational foundation of the domain of reason, for reason is set up by interdiction on the authority of feeling. We see how far we are from the more schematic treatment of interdiction in much of early poststructuralist theory.

It is in the context of this affective elaboration that Bataille transposes transgression and interdiction into the economic terms first introduced in "La Notion de dépense." He identifies transgression and interdiction with the operations of expenditure and accumulation, respectively. The important point is that the economic formulation is not introduced for the sake of abstraction or theoretical articulation. Bataille insists upon the fact that it depends upon an emotional logic of attraction and repulsion. I say emotional *logic* because it is a question here of an equivalent, on the order of feeling, of the abstract moments of affirmation and negation in Hegel's logic. In the dual operation of transgression/interdiction, Bataille writes, the emotional ambivalence is so intense that the only clear distinction between the two moments of the mechanism of the sacred is the economic one. "Getting and spending are the two phases of this activity," Bataille writes, " . . . seen in this light, religion is like a dance in which a step back [*recul*] is followed by a spring forwards [*rebondissement*]" (*E* 68–69). The *ressort* of eroticism involves just this dance, for the word *ressort*, as the *Robert* dictionary indicates, itself includes the meanings of both a *recul* and a *rebondissement*. And the dance is Bataille's playful and intimate version of the Hegelian dialectic. Only here, instead of a sober dialectical synthesis, the vertigo of the dance yields "a deeper harmony [*un accord plus profond*]" (*E* 69), an allusion to what Bataille elsewhere elaborates in the name of communication. By substituting interdiction for the Hegelian negativity associated with action or work, and by placing the woman, as "living cadaver," in the position of the slave, Bataille appears to have elided the scene of recognition altogether. But he has only postponed it. His version of the scene of recognition—eroticism as relation to the erotic object—occurs in a second moment, a *reprise* of the dialectical turn that yields the experience of the sacred.

Bataille places interdiction, the negative moment in the development from animal to human in Kojève's diachronic story, in a dialectical relationship with its counterpoint (*contrecoup*), transgression. "There is no need to stress the Hegelian nature of this operation," Bataille writes, as we recall, in a note to his text, "which corresponds with the moment of dialectic expressed by the untranslatable German verb *aufheben* (to surpass while maintaining)."[28] Bataille thus superimposes this dialectical mechanism, this *ressort*, onto the Hegelian development of the negativity of consciousness and the passage from the condition of animal to human being. At the same time, he suspends this story before the scene of the struggle for pure prestige, thereby interrupting one Hegelian development with another. To be even more precise we might say that he interrupts the development of one Hegelian movement with the same movement at another moment of its development. Bataille syncopates Hegel.

Throughout *L'Erotisme* Bataille calls attention to the ruses of his text, to what he calls "changes of emphasis," which reveal the posturing of various theoretical gestures and tones. He even explicitly signals the superimposition of what Caillois had distinguished as primitive and modern versions of the sacred. This conflation operates through a strategic alignment of the philosophically grounded oppositions continuity/discontinuity (invoked by Bataille in the opening line of his essay) and nature/reason (linked to the opposition of animal to human) with the philosophically problematic ethnological oppositions sacred/profane and interdiction/transgression borrowed from Caillois. This alignment joins two theoretical stories together precisely through the ambiguity introduced by the recourse to two different versions of the sacred—primitive and modern—which yield two different accounts of the relation between the sacred and the profane. Transgression, Bataille writes,

is complementary to the profane world, exceeding its limits but not destroying it. Human society is not only a world of work. Simultaneously—or successively—it is made up of the profane and the sacred, its two complementary forms. The profane world is the world of interdictions. The sacred world depends on limited acts of transgression. (*E* 67–68)

The modern, monovalent sacred is here opposed to the profane, which is identified with interdiction. Bataille then shifts to the other track, though not without first signaling the move. "This way of seeing is a difficult one," he acknowledges,

in that *sacred* has two contradictory meanings simultaneously. Basically whatever is subject to prohibition is *sacred*. Interdiction [*l'interdit*] designating negatively the sacred thing, has not only the power to give us . . . a feeling of fear. . . . This feeling can change to one of devotion. . . . Man is at the same time subject to two movements: one of terror, which rejects, and one of attraction, which commands fascinated respect. Interdiction and transgression correspond to these two contradictory movements. (*E* 68)

Here it is a question of the ambivalence of the primitive sacred, which depends upon the emotional ambivalence of horror and fascination, or repulsion and attraction, which affects both interdiction and transgression.

To operate this slippage from the monovalent sacred, which is identified with transgression, to the ambivalent sacred, which requires the dual operation transgression/interdiction, Bataille can rely upon the ambiguity of the word "interdiction" (*l'interdit*), which, in French, refers both to the rule (or the act) of exclusion and to the object rendered taboo.

In *L'Erotisme*, Bataille finesses the double inscription of the word "sacred" (and the double movement of his argument) so elegantly that we hardly notice it despite the signal he provides. In "L'Histoire de l'érotisme," however, the dance with Hegel is much more explicit. The steps are traced out more boldly. Whereas in *L'Erotisme*, as we see in the passage cited above, Bataille characterizes the complementarity between profane and sacred worlds as simultaneous *or* successive, here he depicts the double movement of interdiction and transgression as "almost simultaneous" (H 66). In this elaboration Bataille takes Kojève's definition (derived from Hegel) as his point of departure: the dialectical progression of the self-creation of man as negation of the givens (*les données*) of nature. In a second moment, he proposes that the cultural world—as negation of the natural one through the imposition of interdiction (Bataille's ethnological correction of Hegel's philosophical story)—itself becomes the horizon of the given, which impinges on the freedom of the subject. This leads to the moment of transgression, where what was previously negated returns as desirable, for it no longer exists in relation to the constraints of the *donnée* (H 69). It is in this context that Bataille describes the two movements of interdiction and transgression as "almost simultaneous"— a negation and its *contrecoup*. "This double movement," he explains, "does not even imply distinct phases. I can, for the sake of exposition, speak of it as two moments [*en parler en deux temps*]. But it is a question of a totality [or organic unity, *ensemble solidaire*]" (H 66). It is impossible to speak of one without the other, just as it is impossible to separate the ebb from the flow of the ocean tides. "The duplicity of eroticism," Bataille writes, "is unintelligible as long as the totality of this double movement of negation and return is not grasped" (H 66).

The dual operation interdiction/transgression does not just involve two moments, one of negation and one of return. It involves two (double) moments of negation *and* return. First there is the moment of interdiction, presented as a negation of the state of nature which yields the passage to culture. Then comes transgression as a negation of this horizon of culture which has itself taken on the quality of the given (the *donnée*). This negation (or transgression) of the cultural given yields the passage to the sacred and to man as religious animal. This, we remember, was Bataille's ethnological correction of the philosophical topos that defines man as rational animal.

The dizzying character of this movement—this dance—has to do with its temporality. The two points of view concerning the "duplicity of erot-icism," the successive and the simultaneous versions of relations between interdiction and transgression, correspond to two positions with respect to history. The successive implies a situation within history, whereas the simultaneous refers us to a position at the end of history. Thus the rhythm of point and counterpoint, of ebb and flow, involves not just two mo-ments, but two times or temporalities: the profane temporality of history and of work, and the sacred one in which time stops. The double move-ment itself is sequential. To say yes, Bataille writes, one must have been able to say no. Logically, then, transgression cannot precede interdiction. But it is also simultaneous with interdiction because, in the instant, there is no such thing as before or after. Transgression, *la fête*, opens a mythic time that is not linear. Finally, the two movements are both simultaneous and sequential to the extent that they collapse the two moments of He-gel's scene of recognition: the anthropogenic moment, which corresponds to the self-consciousness of the master, and the end of history, which cor-responds to the self-consciousness of the sage as subject of absolute knowl-edge.

In "L'Histoire de l'érotisme," Bataille is explicit about the relation be-tween his thinking of eroticism and a Hegelian notion of the end of his-tory, which Kojève insisted upon in his lectures and interpreted in revo-lutionary terms.[29] "History, to my mind, will have finished," Bataille writes, "when the disparity of rights and of level of subsistence are re-duced: such would be the conditions for *an ahistorical mode of existence of which erotic activity is the expression*" (H 163; my emphasis). Eroti-cism, then, would be a postrevolutionary mode of experience. At the end of history, Kojève wrote, the sage is content to retrace the path already traveled. This is precisely what Bataille does in this study of eroticism that he calls an "erotic phenomenology" (H 524), alluding back to the project he had identified for himself as early as 1939. Eroticism involves not the mastery of the lord, but the sovereignty of the sage. Bataille's version of the scene of recognition—man's relation to the erotic object, the beauti-ful woman prostitute—refers us to this moment of sovereignty. "By what right," Kojève had asked, "can we affirm that the State will not engender in man a new desire, other than that of Recognition, and that it will not consequently be negated one day by a negative or creative action other than that of struggle or work?" (K 468). Eroticism is Bataille's answer to Kojève's rhetorical question. "Questioning has meaning only as elaborated by philosophy," Bataille writes in his conclusion to *L'Erotisme*, "the su-preme questioning is that to which the answer is the supreme moment of eroticism—that of eroticism's silence" (E 275).

Eroticism requires a scene of recognition in order to provide a conscious experience of transgression, and thereby to engender, for man, the status Bataille refers to as "religious animal." In this corrected, second-order version of the master/slave dialectic, it is not a question of real struggle to the death, as in Hegel's scenario, but of a fiction of death—a philosophical equivalent of *la petite mort* of erotic *jouissance*. Recognition operates through a fiction of death. But it is not a question of a fictive death, as in the case of the dialectically suppressed slave according to Hegel. It is rather a matter of a fiction, or illusion of death as absolute recognition, or recognition of the absolute. The fiction does not occur by default, for want of the real thing. It is the positive result—the meaning—of this dialectic. The *figure figée* of the prostitute, the beautiful erotic object, is essential to the staging of this fiction.

"The dialectic has a positive result," Hegel wrote, "because it has a specifically determined content, because the result is not . . . empty and abstract nothingness, but the negation of certain specific determination."[30] The problem with the orgy, for Bataille, is that it involves abstract negation in Hegel's sense. Whereas in *L'Erotisme* it is the specific beauty of the erotic object that lends concreteness to the desire for possession; beauty presents the erotic object to desire. For Bataille, beauty is the meaning of the erotic object, a meaning (*sens*) that gives this object—this woman— its value (*E* 131). In a woman's nudity, Bataille writes, "the potential beauty of this nakedness and its individual charm are what reveal themselves . . . the objective difference in fact, between the value of one object and that of another" (*E* 131). Beauty provides the specific determinations negated in the act of erotic possession.

"The decisive element in the distinct constitution of erotic objects is a bit disconcerting," Bataille concedes; "it presupposes that a human being can be considered as a thing" (H 119). He goes on to discuss various modes of subordination or alienation, passing in review man's domestication of animals and the master's domination over the slave before arriving at the question of relations between women and men. Of the slavery of Hegel's master/slave dialectic Bataille writes, "the fiction thanks to which our ancestors regarded their fellow men as things is full of meaning" (H 120). Slavery aside, Bataille writes, in a charmingly ambiguous turn of phrase, men have generally tended to "voir les choses dans les femmes [to see things in women / consider women as things]" (H 120). Before marriage, girls are considered the property of their fathers or brothers. It is for this reason that women, unlike the maenads, are granted a reified status. It is because they have the form and determinateness of an object, as object of exchange, that they can function as objects of erotic desire. Whereas the maenads fled in disorder, Bataille writes, "the object of desire . . . ornaments herself with the greatest care and offers an immobile figure/face [*figure*] to the temptation of he who would possess her" (H 121). The problem with the orgy, then, is that its participants, like the maenads, cannot be captured in order to be exchanged. They cannot be stabilized in order to function as the support of a figure or a fiction.

Bataille's study is a history of eroticism in the sense that it explores the dialectical development of the contradiction (or dual operation) of gift-exchange as it is associated with the problem of incest. The duplicity of eroticism, the dual operation of transgression/interdiction, corresponds to this economic contradiction. Bataille opens "L'Histoire de l'érotisme" with a rambling discussion of Lévi-Strauss's theory concerning the prohibition of incest. On the one hand, he says, the theory emphasized the expenditure associated with sexual interdiction because of the exchange of women. He calls the prohibition of incest "the law of the gift" because it sets in motion the movement of "generosity" associated with the circulation of women in exchange (H 29). It is in this sense that he describes potlatch as "at once beyond calculation and the epitome of calculation" (H 39). Bataille regrets that Lévi-Strauss did not emphasize the relation between the exchange of women (or the potlatch) and the structure of eroticism. Testily, he states that the anthropologist "would no doubt not go so far as to say what I say: that it is a question of a dialectical process of *development*" (H 36, original emphasis).

Bataille's dialectical development of the insight he shared with Lévi-Strauss involved a superimposition of various stories concerning a struggle for pure prestige. He combines elements from Hegel's analysis of the struggle for recognition (which requires the fiction of the servile man as object) with anthropological stories of potlatch as struggle for pure prestige, and of women as objects of exchange. In other words, he combines elements of the formal structure of the master/slave dialectic with one anthropological story of interdiction (the prohibition of incest) and one story of transgression (potlatch) which includes the gift and sacrifice. If the Hegelian fiction of slavery is "full of meaning" for Bataille, it is because it provides the point of articulation for these overlapping stories.

Paradoxically, for Bataille the erotic object operates in the registers of both the restricted and the general economies. To the extent that the relation to the erotic object includes elements of the Hegelian scene of recognition, there is subordination in the sovereignty of eroticism. There is possession in a nonreciprocal relation. On the other hand, the woman gives herself to the man. Erotic possession belongs not to the restricted economy of utility, but to the general economy of expenditure. Interdiction, as law of the gift, thus repeats the "double movement" Bataille attributes to the dual operation of interdiction/transgression. Interdiction (the interdiction of incest) precedes eroticism as relation to the erotic object because it is necessary to the constitution of that object. This movement corresponds to the first line of development of Bataille's theory, the story of history along the lines of Hegel-Kojève. At the same time, the woman as erotic object is necessary for transgression since she provides the "recognition" of erotic sovereignty; she is necessary for the transgressiveness of erotic possession per se.

In other words, there is no pure origin of transgression, no origin of the economy of expenditure. The dance of interdiction/transgression goes all the way back—or circles round. There is no transgression that is not mediated by interdiction, no *rebondissement* without a moment of *recul*. But neither is interdiction primary. The historical narrative refers us back to a (violent) animal sexuality from which we step back in horror. "To the extent that the tumultuous movement of the senses occurs," Bataille writes, "it requires a step back, a renunciation, the step back without which no one would be able to leap ahead so far. But this step back requires the rule, which organizes the dance and assures that it will spring forth again indefinitely" (H 36). If woman is at the center of eroticism, as Bataille claims, it is as the paradoxical object that marks the limit between law and transgression, or their interpenetration.

In *L'Erotisme* Bataille figures the dual operation of interdiction/transgression through the image of the chrysalis. The emotions of desire and anxiety associated with interdiction and transgression, Bataille writes,

are . . . in the life of man, what the chrysalis is to the final perfect creature, the *perfect animal*. The inner experience [*L'expérience intérieure*] of man is given at the instant when, bursting out of the chrysalis, he feels that he is tearing himself, not something outside that resists him. He goes beyond the objective awareness bounded by the walls of the chrysalis and this process, too, is linked with this reversal [*renversement*]. (E 39)

As an intermediate form between the larva and the image, the chrysalis figures the transitional stage between animal existence and the emergence of the "perfect animal"—man as religious animal—from the limits of historical time. The image thus figures both the story of interdiction as entry into history (passage from larva to chrysalis, or from man to animal) and transgression as a leap out of history at the moment of the imago or image. Elsewhere in Bataille the appearance of the image on the walls of the Lascaux caves marked the emergence of civilized man from the "larval" state of animal existence. There, what Bataille called the "sacred moment of figuration" signals the beginning of history and of art. The figure of the chrysalis, therefore, accommodates Bataille's *syncope*, both moments of his *ronde* with Hegel. It does so through the insistence of the image (or figuration) per se. It both duplicates and delays the image through the hesitation of the moment implied in the metamorphosis of the chrysalis: the imago.

I have suggested that the dialectic of the erotic object is necessary to Bataille's theory of eroticism as the support of figuration or fiction—the fiction of death in particular. We can perhaps learn something more about what fiction means in Bataille, or how it operates, by examining the figure of the chrysalis. If the chrysalis figures a movement toward sovereignty, and sovereignty, as Bataille writes in the text on Lascaux, pertains to "the one who is an end in himself," then the chrysalis is an image of man as erotic animal.[31] If, however, woman is always at the center of eroticism, she is also at the center of this image, although in a manner that bypasses what the image gives us to see and operates through the language of the figure. For another word for *chrysalide* is *nymphe*, which, in a first meaning, refers to a mythological goddess, or rather, as the *Robert* specifies, "her image in the form of a naked young girl." In addition to the zoological meaning, however (which is synonymous with chrysalis), the dictionary also gives an anatomical meaning: "the small lips of the vulva." The synonym of the chrysalis, then—the nymph—signifies the woman's sex. It clothes or figures it with the image of nakedness.

In its form, Bataille writes, eroticism is fictive. The fiction is what ensures the lucidity, or consciousness, necessary to distinguish eroticism from mere animal sexuality. It is necessary to erect man as erotic animal, and religious animal as well. The woman (the erotic object) is essential to eroticism in order to render it perceptible (*saisissable*), in order to figure eroticism, to present it to consciousness through the mediation that distinguishes it from animal sexuality. Yet what is figured through the dialectic of the erotic object, what is seized by consciousness, is loss or expenditure. With eroticism, we are left with a fiction that does not represent anything, but must nevertheless be staged or performed—a fiction of death. Its appearance requires the presence of the "paradoxical object" (the beautiful woman prostitute), an object that signifies the absence of any object.

With the metaphor of the chrysalis we have the sex of the woman hidden within the figure of metamorphosis. The chrysalis names one moment of the process which it also "figures," though only as an accumulation or juxtaposition of latent figures—the larva and the imago—which serve both to veil and to reveal one another. The metamorphosis, as image, passes not into another image of something, but into the word "image" per se, the imago. The linguistic level introduces a latent figuration that gives us the image, to the extent that it names it—imago. But it does not give us anything to see. Likewise the image of the woman's sex (or of the naked girl) is veiled by the linguistic alibi of the synonym, *nymphe*. This corresponds to the way beauty operates in Bataille's account of eroticism, where it is associated with nakedness. Nakedness is a revelation of beauty which reveals the "individual charm" of a woman—"the objective difference, in fact, between the value of one object and that of another" (*E* 131). At the same time, the beauty of the nude woman serves as a veil. It exerts a charm that seduces the man into desiring the woman's nonbeautiful parts—the *nymphe* in the anatomical sense. "The beauty of the desirable woman suggests her private parts, the hairy ones, to be precise, the animal ones. . . . Beauty that is a negation of animality and awakens desire ends up by exasperating desire and exalting the animal parts" (*E* 143–44). In the figure of the chrysalis, the nymph as image—the figuration of the mythological goddess through the image of the naked girl—clothes the naked fact of the woman's sex with an image of nakedness, a kind of seductive artifice or prestige.

The positive result of the dialectic of erotic sovereignty is a fiction, one "invented expressly." "We approach the void," Bataille writes, "but not to fall into it. We want to become intoxicated with dizziness and *the image of the fall is enough*" (*E* 94, my emphasis). But this is an image, like the word "imago," which is not, in itself, an image *of* anything. The positive result of the dialectical movement of interdiction/transgression is neither discursive meaning, nor radical loss of meaning such as we find in the textual practice of *signifiance* with its indefinite deferral of meaning. Rather it is a fiction—a desired or intentional fiction (*fiction voulue*)—a seductive illusion or *praestigium* of death.

As I have already indicated, the transgression of eroticism has been appropriated as a model (or antimodel) for text and *signifiance*, and hence for the "communication," or mutual contamination, between theory and literature (or writing) evoked in *Tel Quel*. The version of transgression that has been appropriated for *signifiance*, however, is one which would imply an orgiastic eroticism. This is elaborated by Barthes in *Le Plaisir du texte* in relation to the notion of *jouissance*. We have seen that a close reading of *L'Erotisme* is at odds with Sollers's reading of transgression, specifically his reading of the woman as figure for the *interdit* and the signifier. Transgression is not a function of what Sollers called "the flesh [*la chair*]" or "the impersonal plethora" in opposition to "the body [*le corps*]." It is rather a function of bodies, determinate bodies that can enter into a dialectical relation, if only a merely formal or fictive one. This reading has shown the extent to which the question of the limits of philosophy was posed by Bataille specifically in relation to Hegel. I have stressed the centrality of the structure of recognition in the elaboration of eroticism and emphasized the importance of the notion of fiction in Bataille, a term that dropped out of the language of *Tel Quel* in the early 1960's. Increasingly, the issues of avant-gardism have come to be articulated in opposition to realism and to phenomenology. It was therefore convenient to equate discourse, in Hegel's sense, with the esthetic project of realism. Clearly the sense of "fiction," as it pertains to Bataille, has nothing to do with realism. But it does have something to do with meanings (although not discursive ones) and with lucidity—that *se saisir* (bringing to consciousness) which is essential to transgression for Bataille.

In Bataille's theory of transgression, fiction (or figuration) is necessary to enable consciousness of the erotic moment. Likewise the theory of sacrifice requires a fictive negation. For the moment of "se saisir"—the *se saisir* (bringing to consciousness) of a *désaisissement* (loss of consciousness)—is the experience common to eroticism, laughter, sacrifice, and poetry. It is what Bataille calls the "being in the instant."[32] It is in this sense that poetry, for Bataille, is event.[33] Lucidity, which we have considered in relation to the question of eroticism, is evoked as a "giving to visibility [*donner à voir*]" in Bataille's discussion of poetry. Poetry, Bataille writes, "is a cry that gives to visibility [*un cri qui donne à voir*]." In the same context he writes that sacrifice "gives to visibility that in the object which has the power to excite desire or horror"—that is, the sacred.[34] And he adds a temporal characterization of the encounter with "what is" when he defines sacrifice as "the burning moment of the passage where what already is no longer is, or what no longer is is for sensibility, more than what was." In this essay he defines the sacred, which he identifies with the poetic, as an intensity one experiences on the level of sensibility, independently of the operations of intelligence. Poetry and sacrifice, he writes, have the same impact: "[They] render sensible, and as intensely as possible, the content of the present instant."[35] We see from this early essay that the notion of fiction in Bataille has an important temporal dimension. Fiction gives us to see what linear time denies to us. When we neglect or efface the notion of fiction in Bataille (as theoretical rereadings of him tend to do) we lose this temporal dynamic. When the instant (or the "event") is interpreted in terms of transgression it becomes reduced to a point or line. This facilitates its association with the Heideggerian question of limitation. What is lost, however, is the affective dimension, as well as the force of time.

Kristeva

Reconciliations—In Theory

By the 1940's, both Breton and Sartre had undertaken (in their quite different ways) to resolve the conflict between art and revolution. For Sartre it was a question of the antinomy between speech and action; for Breton it was a question of the dual task of interpreting the world and transforming it. Both attempts failed. Indeed, they failed in such a way that each figure came to represent one horn, as it were, of the dilemma Breton had diagnosed: the impossible choice between esthetic avant-gardism (or formal innovation) and revolutionary commitment.[1] The surrealist came to stand for esthetic avant-gardism and the existentialist for social responsibility or revolution. This was the inheritance of the *Tel Quel* generation.

If, as Foucault wrote in 1963, "The attentive gaze that *Tel Quel* directs at Breton is not a retrospective one," *Tel Quel* was also far from oblivious to Sartre—appearances notwithstanding.[2] Although the review opens in 1960 with an appeal to Valéry's conception of pure art in implicit opposition to Sartrean engagement, as the review matures it undertakes to replace surrealism's rhetorical call for a synthesis of the two great theorists of freedom, Marx and Freud, with a more systematic, a more explicitly theoretical articulation of these two discourses, which had come to stand for revolution on the one hand and (avant-garde) art on the other. With *Tel Quel*, art and revolution do become reconciled—in theory—and theory itself is rendered *engagé*, thanks to the theoretical operator inherited from Bataille: transgression. We have seen how Bataille's thinking of transgression was appropriated for theory and noted specific displacements that occurred in the process of this rereading of Bataille. We can now explore what this appropriation accomplished for theory in an analysis of Kristeva's *Révolution du langage poétique*. Kristeva's study represents the most systematic effort to perform the reconciliation of art and revolution in the *Tel Quel* context.[3] This work is not merely a study of the "revolutionary" poetics of figures such as Lautréamont and Mallarmé, it also presents a theory of poetic language that affirms avant-garde poetic practices to be revolutionary in and of themselves in a concrete sociopolitical sense. Avant-garde poetic language, Kristeva claims, generates a new instance of the subject—a revolutionary subject—through the operations of its signifying process, *signifiance*. This revolutionary subject is posed not just as a new modality of subjectivity, but also as an agent of revolution. "The signifying process," Kristeva writes of this mode of textual productivity, "gives itself as agent, an 'ego' [*un moi*], that of the revolutionary" (206).[4]

Art, for Kristeva, transvalued as avant-garde poetics, is a vehicle for the manifestation of a radical negativity. This is not the usual Hegelian negativity of consciousness, but a "nonsymbolized"—that is, materialist—negativity. Kristeva is reading Hegel through Freud and Bataille. With the negativity of what Kristeva calls the *rejet* (rejection), it is a question of repressed material that neither passes into symbolic representation (or distortion) as in dream work nor receives a merely intellectual acknowledgment, as in denial (*dénégation*).[5] Instead, it produces something new, a "marking [*marquage*] in the signifying material" (163). Kristeva identifies the negativity of the *rejet* with Freud's death instinct and with Bataille's term "expenditure." She characterizes it as a "movement of the material contradictions that generate the semiotic function" (119), a movement that coincides with the infinite processes of signifiance. At the same time, Hegel and Freud are read together with Marx, as we see in this summary of what is at stake in Kristeva's enterprise:

> The aim of ancient philosophy was to explain the world. Dialectical materialism, on the other hand, wants to transform it. It speaks to a new subject, the only one capable of understanding it. This is not simply a subject of explanation, of cognition and knowledge but an elusive subject [*sujet insaisissable*] because one that *transforms* the real. This subject, which includes the movements of the subject of knowledge, emphasizes *process* [*le procès*, that is, process and trial] more than identification, *le rejet* more than desire, *heterogeneity* over the signifier, *struggle* more than structure. (178–79, original emphasis)

It is the question of the status of the subject within the theoretical articulation of art and revolution, the status of "to give oneself an 'ego,'" that I would like to examine more closely in the text and argument of *La Révolution du langage poétique*.

Kristeva takes the phenomenological given of the subjective position of speech as her point of departure. She then undermines the stability of this position, displacing the structure of signification to the operations of signifiance. She presents signifiance as a transgression of the symbolic by the semiotic, oedipal, and pre-oedipal moments, respectively, in a genetic psychoanalytic account of the emergence of the subject. Poetic language is offered as an exemplary instance of this process occurring as text. Here, however, the notion of text is expanded to stand for a general signifying practice, one that opens out directly onto the social-historical world. Poetic language is thus transplanted from the bourgeois realm of esthetics to the revolutionary field of text, that is, to the field of text that Kristeva constitutes here as revolutionary. The notion of text is dislodged from the printed page and displaced to the social-historical world.

The term "transgression," borrowed from Bataille, operates on three levels in Kristeva's analysis. First, it occurs in relation to an account of the constitution of the subject as "subject in process/subject on trial [*sujet en procès*]." This involves a displacement of the traditional psychoanalytic account of a passage from pre-oedipal to oedipal stages, for here the pre-oedipal (the semiotic) returns to transgress the law of the symbolic. Transgression also occurs in the register of art. Avant-garde poetic language is considered paradigmatic of the transgression of the symbolic by the semiotic which occurs through the process of signifiance. It transgresses discursive operations of language and the associated notion of truth. Last, through the notion of text that generalizes the art process of signifiance, transgression is transposed into the sociopolitical domain as revolution. Earlier, we argued that transgression was the one term poststructuralism could not live without. Here we see that transgression is the very mechanism of signifiance, of which both art and revolution are considered merely specific modalities.[6] Thanks to the insistence of the operation of transgression, and to the revolutionary flavor of its rhetoric, Kristeva's analysis appears to present a seamless progression from art to revolution.

And yet, as Sartre had reminded his readers of the previous generation, (avant-garde) art and revolution have different requirements when it comes to the question of the subject. This remains true in Kristeva's argument. It is the transgression of the phenomenological subject, the subject of the symbolic, which constitutes the revolutionary force of poetic language for Kristeva. The "art" subject, in other words, is a pulverized or exploded one, not unlike the subject of surrealist automatism.[7] This association is hardly surprising, of course, given that Kristeva's study emphasizes the poetics of Lautréamont-Ducasse, whom Breton considered one of the principal precursors of surrealist automatism. In recognition of this affinity, Kristeva writes: "It is in the so-called 'art' practices that the semiotic, condition of the symbolic, also reveals itself to be its destroyer" (47). Taken to the limit, then, as the author acknowledges, esthetic avant-gardism would mark a foreclosure of the symbolic, or of the thetic moment that positions the subject. This, of course, is the position of Artaud, exemplary figure of avant-garde madness.

Political revolution, on the other hand, requires a unified subject of action, as Sartre had argued in *Qu'est-ce que la littérature?* in response to this passage from the *Surrealist Manifesto*:

Everything leads us to believe that there exists a certain point in the mind . . . where life and death, the real and the imaginary, past and future . . . the high and the low, are no longer perceived as contradictory. . . . One seeks in vain for any other motivation for Surrealism than the hope of determining this point.

Sartre comments contemptuously:

Is this not to proclaim his [Breton's] divorce from the working-class public? For the proletariat engaged in struggle needs to distinguish the real from the imaginary, life from death at every moment in order to succeed. . . . It is not by chance that Breton cites these oppositions: they all involve categories of action; revolutionary action, in particular, needs them. (189)

We are in the 1940's here, but the problem has not fundamentally changed by the 1970's. The conflicting demands placed on the subject by avant-garde art and revolution produce symptoms in Kristeva's argument—symptoms of what Breton had called the artist's dilemma. The most notable one is Kristeva's ambivalence toward Derridean grammatology. She implicitly acknowledges that her theoretical project belongs within the field of grammatology when she pauses over the Greek etymology of her term "semiotic"—trace, gramme, engraved or written sign, and so on. She also explicitly recognizes her debt to Derrida's critiques of phenomenology and structuralism: "The functioning of writing [*écriture*], the trace and the *grammé*, introduced by J. Derrida in his critique of phenomenology and subsequent versions of it in linguistics points to an essential aspect of the semiotic" (40). At the same time, however, she charges that "the grammatological deluge of meaning [*la crue grammatologique*] abdicates the subject and is obliged to ignore its functioning as social practice" (142). To our surprise we find that Kristeva repeats the thrust of Sartre's attack against Breton in her criticism of Derrida, thereby inscribing the register of engagement within her argument. She insists that the term "semiotic," as she uses it, is to be distinguished from Derridean différance. For, "being part of a signifying practice which includes the symbolic instance . . . it *must* be situated in relation to the subject" (142, my emphasis). The register of obligation (or responsibility) can be heard as overtone to an ambiguous mode of logical necessity which attaches, as we shall see, to one version of the structure of transgression as it pertains to signifiance.

In order to reconcile the demands of both art and revolution, Kristeva must accommodate the (grammatological) term "semiotic" to the (Sartrean) imperatives of revolution. The author's ingenious strategy is to revolutionize différance. What she calls "the revolution of différance" (144) is characterized in terms of expenditure, ecstasy, and eroticism—terms borrowed from Bataille's notion of the general economy and associated with transgression. In textual terms, however, to revolutionize différance means to attach its operations to a subject. But clearly this cannot be the unified subject of the symbolic, or what is called in the language of phenomenology the thetic subject. Instead, Kristeva poses the very mechanism of transgression—*le rejet* —as agent of the "practice" of signifiance. This radical negativity of expenditure becomes "the maintained and reinforced agent of the signifying process" (162). In other words, the *rejet* itself is posed as subject![8] This is quite astounding. The *rejet* stands for the negativity specific to the transgression of the symbolic (as instance of the unified subject) by the semiotic. Kristeva has claimed that this negativity is so radical that it threatens to destroy the thetic position and "cannot be located in any ego [*moi*]" (164). Nevertheless, it functions as an ego here: "In the social configuration of capitalism . . . [*le rejet*] emerges with all its clear-cut force . . . acts through a negativity" (177), and so on. The *rejet* is a subject of action. As activating force of the process of signifiance, it enables signifiance to become a practice—and to become revolutionary.

The status of the *rejet* as agent, even as "'ego'—that of the revolutionary," is maintained and reinforced textually when the *rejet* is written as *actant* in a number of mini-fables or small narrative sequences.[9] Kristeva writes, for example, that "decentering the subject, the *rejet* sets its pulverization [*pulvérization subjectale*] against the structures of the natural world, collides with them, rejects them and has them at its disposal [*en est dis-posé*]" (203). Or again: "Out of the heterogeneity of its practice *and its experience* [*le rejet*] produces new symbolizations. This is *the mechanism of innovation* which . . . characterizes social practice" (179, my emphasis). As not merely "motor" but "mechanism of innovation," the *rejet* becomes, in effect, the subject of action and invention—the subject of experience!—necessary to the revolutionary project. If grammatology abdicates the subject, to revolutionize grammatology apparently means to write it in relation to an agency of the *rejet* itself. "The return of the heterogeneous element in the movement of différance," Kristeva writes, " . . . provokes the revolution of différance" (144). The heterogeneous *is* the *rejet*, and the *rejet* is heterogeneous because, as *pulsion* (usually translated as "drive"), it must be situated at the limit of body and psyche. Différance, then, is revolutionized by being written in relation to the theoretical fiction of a revolutionary subject, which is itself produced by writing the very mechanism of transgression—the *rejet*—into narrative sequence.

If the *rejet* functions as *actant*, the fable being told here is precisely the story of the engendering of this "different subject." It is the story of "the signifying process / trial of signifiance [*procès de la signifiance*] . . . transforming the opaque and impenetrable subject . . . into the subject in process / on trial [*le sujet en procès*]" (105). It is the story of a "transformation of the thetic position: the destruction of the old one and the formation of another" (59). The fable involves the possibility of "a subject who speaks its being put in process / on trial through action [*un sujet parlant sa mise en procès dans l'action*]" (210, original emphasis) and of "situating oneself beyond 'art' through 'art'" (211). In other words, the underlying fiction is the reconciliation of the positions of Breton and Sartre, or of art and revolution. Ironically, Kristeva's formulation is so abstract that it could be said to characterize both of the "antagonistic" positions, at least as we have read them here. As we shall see, however, this fable also suggests a story concerning the constitution of theory. To this extent we could say that theory emerges through the reconciliation—in theory—of the incompatible positions of Sartre and Breton.

In *Qu'est-ce que la littérature?* Sartre accuses Breton of skepticism. He understands this in the Hegelian sense of adherence to an irreducibly negative moment, one associated with the nondialectical negativity of the *néant*. Here is the thrust of Sartre's attack:

> I perceive a very serious contradiction at the origin of Surrealism . . . to speak in Hegelian terms I would say that this movement had the concept of totality . . . and that in its concrete manifestations it realized something completely different. The totality of man is necessarily a synthesis, that is to say the organic unity of all its secondary structures. . . . Hegel writes of skepticism: "Thought becomes perfect thought annihilating the being of the world in the multiple variety of its determinations and real negativity." . . . Thus surrealist man is an addition, a mixture, but never a synthesis.[10]

Sartre opposes engaged prose to poetry in a gesture of opposition to this esthetics of skepticism. Kristeva addresses the issue of skepticism in fundamentally the same terms. In *La Révolution du langage poétique*, a chapter entitled "Scepticisme et nihilisme selon Hegel et dans le texte" marks the transition between a section entitled "Heterogeneity" and one entitled "Practice." In her discussion of skepticism Kristeva defends her notion of text against precisely the kind of charge Sartre had made against Breton. In so doing, she explicitly acknowledges the limits of avant-gardism. In the passage already cited, which links radical negativity to madness, she implicitly associates the perspective of radical avant-gardism with formalism—one horn of Breton's dilemma of the modern artist. "To try to coincide with the logic of the mobile and heterogeneous chora," she writes, " . . . is ultimately to foreclose the thetic. . . . The foreclosure of the subjective and representative thetic phase marks the limit of avant-garde experience: it leads to madness" (182).[11]

But we are about to leap from one horn of the dilemma to the other, as it were, for suddenly it is no longer a question of Hegel being corrected by the materialism of Freud; instead he is corrected by Marx's materialism. It is precisely here that Kristeva introduces her discussion of practice with an appeal to Marxism as philosophy of the subject. "At this point," she writes, "*it is necessary* . . . to reintroduce the way . . . in which Marxism thinks the subject," and she adds, still in a hybrid register of obligation mixed with necessity, "one *must* . . . take up again the subject who says 'I' and struggles in a social community. *It is necessary* to hear the discourse of this subject as well as the heterogeneous contradiction he has deferred and which poets have made it their task to explore" (190, my emphasis).

The turning point in Kristeva's analysis, the turn toward praxis that introduced the need for a subject of spontaneity or innovation, is accompanied by an appeal to prose, or at least to narrative. "The signifying process," Kristeva writes here, "whose heterogeneous contradiction is the moment of fierce struggle, *ought* to be inscribed according to a historical logic in this representational narrative [materialist history] which itself attests to the historical process underway in revolutionary class struggles" (191, my emphasis). The step to praxis thus reintroduces the question of meaning that was dismissed earlier.[12] It suddenly emerges as a question of "capital importance." The survival of the social function of art is at stake, Kristeva adds, in an unmistakable, though somewhat reluctant, allusion to Sartre.[13]

We seem to have a contradiction here, or at least a certain ambiguity. It is a version of the same ambiguity Kristeva explicitly places at the heart of signifiance as "heterogeneous" relation between the symbolic and the semiotic, associated with the transgression of the former by the latter. And it is for just this reason that an appeal to narrative makes sense, both on the macro-level of the fable of materialist history, and on the micro-level of the textual constitution of the *rejet* as revolutionary hero in small narrative sequences. For, as Kristeva tells us in an earlier chapter entitled "Four Signifying Practices," the logic of narrative is to remove contradiction.[14] A narrative moment (a moment of non-disjunction) is altogether appropriate to Kristeva's theoretical project, which, as she acknowledges, concerns the process of signifiance in its very ambiguity. The practice of text, she explains, involves not simply the negativity of the *rejet*, but also a renewal (*relance*) of the *rejet* which provisionally positions a new thetic moment. "Our conception of the *rejet* will oscillate between these two poles [negativity and renewal] and this ambiguity will present the ambiguity of the process itself, divided and unitary," she writes (148).

An appeal to narrative serves the interests of Kristeva's theoretical project, which involves a reconciliation of art and revolution—which is also to say, of the positions of Breton and Sartre. Whereas the transgressive force of poetic language entails the pulverization of the unified subject through the material (or libidinal) force of the *rejet*, the process of signifiance "gives itself an agent, an 'ego'—that of the revolutionary," by posing the rejet itself as narrative subject, and in this specific sense, making a subject of it. This grammatical subject of action becomes the heroic revolutionary subject that engenders new social and cultural forms. If, as Kristeva suggests, text has a social function, if it produces "a different subject, able to establish new social relations and thus inscribe itself in the process of the subversion of capitalism," Kristeva generates that subject textually. Art and revolution, apparently incompatible when it comes to the question of the subject, are theoretically reconciled here through the narrative or textual engendering of this "different" subject.

These textual moments of slippage from theoretical discourse to narrative (or fiction) are crucial to the success of Kristeva's theoretical enterprise. But they cannot do the job alone. They cannot resolve the tension between the conflicting demands placed on the subject by avant-garde art and revolution. They receive support from the philosopheme "transgression," which includes within itself both terms of the ambiguity of this theoretical project: the unified subject and the exploded subject. Transgression involves precisely "the simultaneity of the limit (which is the One) and the . . . crossing [*franchissement*] of that boundary" (159). Indeed, if Kristeva could be said to succeed where surrealism was said to fail (by Sartre and then again by *Tel Quel*), it is largely because of the mechanism of transgression. More precisely, it is thanks to the way Bataille elaborated this term. Bataille's philosopheme absorbs the tension between the subject of art and the subject of revolution.

Transgression, as we have already indicated, emerges as a critical term through Caillois, Mauss, and Durkheim—that is, at the unlikely intersection of an incipient structuralism and a reflection on the sacred.[15] We have already seen in the last chapter how Bataille's thinking of transgression was appropriated for theory; how specific displacements occurred in the process of identifying transgression with writing and text. We are now in a position to explore what this appropriation accomplished for theory. What Kristeva receives from Bataille is not only Bataille as read by Foucault, Sollers, and Hollier, but also the fact emphasized in the reading of *L'Erotism* proposed in the preceding chapter: namely, Bataille's textual interweaving of two distinct versions of the sacred (and hence of transgression) into his theoretical discourse. For these two versions of the sacred, we remember, Bataille refers us to Caillois's *L'Homme et le sacré*, which contrasted a primitive sacred and a modern one. The first, as we have seen, operates dialectically; the second does not. The important point is that these two distinct structures of the sacred accommodate the requirements of the double practice of signifiance in Kristeva's theory: art and revolution. "Pseudo-transgression" (to borrow Sollers's formula for the modern sacred) suits the (avant-garde) art subject. On the other hand, insistence on the moment of interdiction in the dual operation interdiction/transgression associated with the primitive (dialectical) version of the sacred retains the relation to the subject necessary for the revolutionary moment in the sociopolitical field. It is thanks to this structure of transgression that Kristeva can claim that, unlike grammatology which "abdicates" the subject, the semiotic "ought to be situated in relation to the subject." This is because it is "part of the signifying practice which includes the symbolic."

Bataille combines two versions of transgression such that, coming after him, Kristeva can profit from the hesitation produced by the difference between them, at the same time that she appears to embrace a stable philosopheme. Since, in her argument, transgression is the mechanism of signifiance, and signifiance, as we have seen, requires two different instances of the subject—the "pulverized" one in the case of avant-garde art, and the productive subject in the case of text, as this belongs to the social-historical domain—her argument can capitalize on the fact that two different structures are quietly held within the single operator "transgression." Without the special valences of this term (and they are not intrinsic to the concept but are rather due to the way in which Bataille has elaborated it), the tension between the two structures of the subject would threaten to undermine Kristeva's studiously rigorous and relentlessly theoretical articulation of art and revolution. Transgression, for Kristeva, functions like a theoretical equivalent of *mana*, whose role, as Lévi-Strauss puts it, is "to enable symbolic thinking to operate despite the contradiction inherent in it."[16] Here it enables her to reconcile theoretically the conflicting claims of art and revolution, and to do so in the precise terms of the effaced positions of Breton and Sartre. It enables her to generate theoretically a subject who is revolutionary in the double sense of "formally innovative"—the exploded subject of avant-garde art—and "politically active"—the engaged subject Sartre opposes to the passive subject position of surrealist art.

If I proposed earlier that the theoretical reconciliation of the positions of Breton and Sartre was not only an accomplishment of theory, but could be said to be constitutive of theory as such, it is because in *La Révolution du langage poétique* the structure of transgression also helps Kristeva generate a subject of theory that overlaps with the theoretical fiction of the revolutionary subject. In her chapter "Skepticism and Nihilism in Hegel and in the Text," Kristeva distinguishes between the modern text and its nineteenth-century avant-garde precursors. In an implicit allusion to Adorno, she claims that the modern text includes a self-reflexive moment. Unlike "art," she maintains, text is not simply a marking of the negativity of the *rejet*, that nondialectical negativity associated with Freud's death instinct, that is, of the material or the heterogeneous. It includes a second moment. It "unfolds the contradiction *and* represents its formation" (184, original emphasis). Text, Kristeva continues, "introduces into the *rejet* a reversal [*retournement*] of the *rejet* itself which constitutes the signifying relation [*la liaison signifiante*] . . . [it] introduces *discourse* into the *rejet*" (187, my emphasis). Here we have a theoretical elaboration of the moment of meaning (*sens*) alluded to earlier. More precisely, we have an elaboration of meaning in relation to the event of theory per se—as well as its subject. With an implicit allusion to Adorno's analysis of modernity, Kristeva inflects the moment of Hegelian self-consciousness in the direction of a psychoanalytic encounter in which the reader occupies the position of analysand and text plays the role of analyst.

Kristeva defines text as "a practice of the *rejet* which includes the heterogeneous contradiction as its key moment [*moment fort*] and the signifying thesis [*la thèse signifiante*] as a necessary pre-condition." Thanks to the latter, she adds, "the text is already on its way to scientific knowledge of the process that animates it [*l'agite*] and exceeds it" (187). This is to say that the "heterogeneous condition" of the subject (the heterogeneity semiotic/symbolic) is doubled by two moments of text: its practice, on the one hand, and the knowledge (*connaissance*) of this practice—critique or theory—on the other. Thus we arrive at "the subject of science or of theory" (188).

This development parallels the one we have already analyzed. A gap between art and the social (or revolutionary) imperative is still at issue. Only now "art" and "theory" substitute for the dyad "art" and "revolution." The operation of these terms still corresponds with what Kristeva calls the dialectical conditions of the subject, and with the processes of significance and transgression. "Combining heterogeneous contradiction whose mechanism is possessed by the text, with revolutionary critique of the established social order . . . is a most difficult thing to do" (191), Kristeva acknowledges in an understated tone. And she adds: "The moment of the semantic and ideological binding [*liaison*] of drive rejection [*rejet pulsionnel*] . . . *ought* to be a binding [*devrait être une liaison*] in and through an analytic and revolutionary discourse" (191, my emphasis). The register of obligation returns (all the more awkward in the weaker tense of the conditional), leading us to this crucial conclusion: "Articulated in this way, heterogeneous contradiction approaches [*côtoie*] critical discourse." Critical discourse is defined as the "representative [*représentant*] of a social revolutionary practice." Knowledge (*connaissance*)—or theory—has become a necessary moment in the articulation of art and revolution operated through transgression. It constitutes the moment of practice, activating the relation to the subject by performing the moment of meaning (*sens*). The revolutionary subject, constructed, as we have seen, through the philosopheme "transgression," overlaps with the critical subject—the subject of theory. This is not altogether unlike the parallels we shall find between Sartre's figure of the reader and the subject of praxis in the *Critique of Dialectical Reason*. In the case of Kristeva, however, not only is a moment of theory a necessary condition for the articulation (or reconciliation) of art and revolution, but this reconciliation is the raison d'être of theory.

"I maintain that Surrealism is still in a preliminary phase," Breton wrote in the *Second Manifesto*, and he continued: "The fact is that generally speaking these preliminaries are 'artistic' in nature. However, I foresee that they will come to an end and that at that point the earthshaking [*boulversantes*] ideas that Surrealism holds in reserve will erupt resoundingly . . . and give themselves free rein."[17] *Tel Quel*'s step into theory advances the surrealist project beyond its preparatory phase, while at the same time it displaces it in the direction of Sartre. Theory itself is *engagé*; it is a revolutionary practice. Theory—specifically Kristevan *sémanalyse*—will in turn be characterized as a transgression of philosophy, or, if this honor is to be reserved for Bataille, at least as a transgression of structuralism or structuralist semiotics.

Transgression in Theory

The theoretical magic of transgression plays a crucial role in the constitution of the notion of the theoretical subject, and endows theory itself with transgressive, sacred, or magical force. To appreciate the continuities between the transgressive and revolutionary force associated with theory itself and the theory of transgression or revolution in *La Révolution du langage poétique* we need only look back at the portrayal of the theoretical breakthrough of Kristevan *sémanalyse* in the appendix to Ducrot and Todorov's *Dictionnaire encyclopédique des sciences du langage*, published some months before Kristeva's book appeared in print.[18] *Sémanalyse*, the authors write, "gives us to understand the production of meaning as by definition *incompatible with representation* [*hétérogène à tout représentable*]" (451, original emphasis). Text, we are told here, "has always functioned as a field of transgression in relation to the system which organizes our perception, our grammar, our metaphysics and even our science" (443–44). Indeed, this transgressive field is so radical that the shift from structuralist semiotics to poststructuralist *sémanalyse* is characterized as a "Copernican revolution," an epithet conventionally attributed to the revolutionary force of Kantian critical philosophy. To reinforce the implicit allusion to Kant, everything prior to the poststructuralist thinking of *sémanalyse* is characterized as "pre-critical" (449).

What does it mean if we take the metaphor "pre-critical" seriously? It means that from the point of view of the grammatological critique, the structure of the sign implies an equivalent of metaphysical illusion. The critical project of Kant is initiated as an analysis of representation, an investigation of the link between representations in our minds and the external world. The *Critique of Pure Reason* establishes that these mental representations do not give us truth about anything outside the mind. They only give us the outside world as it appears to us, that is, as representation. This occurs through the operations of the schematism, the coordination of the receptive operations of the (reproductive) imagination, which takes in data from the outside, and the spontaneous operations of the understanding, which attaches concepts to that material. We recognize an analogy between the intuition of clear and distinct ideas (criticized by Kant) and the ideology of communication, the belief in the use of signs to truthfully represent the world through the operations of reference.

The grammatological critique, which uses the structure of the Saussurian sign itself as a model for the relation of writing to speech, charges that the structure of the sign implies the presupposition of a "transcendental signified": a mental idea that would transparently correspond to something in the world without mediation by anything external to it acting as a signifier. If the structure of the sign implies a "transcendental signified," then this signified enjoys a privilege and a priority. Construed in terms of the activity of communication, this implies a temporal priority as well. It presupposes that the subject first has an idea to be expressed and then attaches a material signifier to it. From the point of view of deconstruction, of course, this is (phono)logocentrism. Todorov and Ducrot characterize the "Copernican revolution" of poststructuralism as a "shift [*basculement*] to the side of the signifier, now considered primary [*dont on souligne alors la primauté*]." A movement along a chain of signifiers is posed as a condition of possibility of signification: "the signified is always already in the position of signifier" (439). The science of semiotics thus passes from the analysis of the structure of the sign (analyzed by Saussure in terms of the system of *langue*), to the actual use (*mise en acte*) of the sign in the process of signification or communication on the level of speech (*parole*). Meaning is not a given that we express or exchange at will. It operates as "effects of meaning," said to emerge from the dynamic operation of signifiance as movement along a signifying chain or text.

In the *Dictionnaire*'s portrayal of the transgressive force of Kristevan *sémanalyse*, we recognize something like the violence to purpose associated with the Kantian sublime. The sublime is transgressive of the positions of phenomenality (of subject and object). It tears us out of the *as if* of the principle of reflective judgment (the purposiveness of nature), which grounds the judgment of taste a priori. Imposing an abrupt return to the critical attitude, it reinscribes the transcendental horizon, reminding us that nature consists only of appearances constructed through representation. It is in relation to this structure that we can appreciate the more far-reaching epistemological (or anti-epistemological) claim that transgression—or a philosophy of eroticism—implies a transgression of philosophy. In Kant the sublime is "transgressive" with respect to the field of empirical knowledge. It is in relation to this structure, or this difference, that we can understand the sense in which the signifying infinity (*infinité signifiante*) associated with the productivity of text (according to *sémanalyse*, on Ducrot and Todorov's account) is "transgressive" to the field of structuralist semiotics and everything that rests upon it—"transgressive with respect to the system according to which our perception, our grammar, our metaphysics and even our science are organized."

The esthetics of the sublime has always operated at the limit of esthetic (in the narrow sense) and ethical or political domains, just as it has been situated at the limit of philosophy or metaphysics. It carries a critical force that has both enhanced and challenged the space of the narrowly esthetic. In Kant the experience of the esthetic sublime serves as a reminder of the subject's moral destination. It reinscribes, albeit negatively and painfully, the autonomous moral subject in its difference from the cognitive subject. One could say that it is precisely in the marking of this difference that the domain of freedom, as Kant writes in the introduction to the *Critique of Judgment*, is "meant to make itself felt in the realm of nature." I would argue that the structure of the sublime plays an analogous role for the theorists of *Tel Quel* except that the place of the moral subject is taken by a political one—the revolutionary subject. In the Kantian esthetic sublime there is a negation of the cognitive or phenomenological subject at the same time that a relation to the moral subject is imposed. This is the kind of dissonance that constitutes the revolutionary (and the theoretical) subject in Kristeva; Bataille's term transgression performs this dissonance for her. For in parallel with the event of the Kantian sublime, the transgressive field of text pulverizes the phenomenological (thetic) subject at the same time that it obliges a relation to the revolutionary subject.

The transgressive force that is authoritatively attached to theory in the *Dictionnaire* has repercussions for the reception of theory. Readers are asked to accept its radical discontinuity with respect to intellectual activity of the past. We are asked to consider it as radically originary, indeed a form of *Ursprung* (radical origin, literally an "originary springing forth"). In 1972, Ducrot and Todorov find themselves constrained to relegate their discussion of a then still emerging poststructuralism—the recent "conceptual elaboration in France . . . around the review *Tel Quel* (R. Barthes, Ph. Sollers and above all J. Kristeva)"—to an appendix to their encyclopedic dictionary of the sciences of language. It is here that we find a discussion of such terms as *texte*, *signifiance*, *écriture*, and *sémanalyse*. The *Dictionnaire encyclopédique* undertakes to consolidate and organize knowledge concerning the sciences of language. It attempts to provide a general overview, one intended to serve the interests of the incipient science of semiotics. The authors find themselves caught in a kind of historical syncope, however, undertaking to shore up the field of structuralist semiotics at the very moment that poststructuralism breaks onto the scene and renders the structuralist optic obsolete. The *Dictionnaire* gives 1969 as the date of the emergence of the science of semiotics, the year of the inauguration of the review *Semiotikà*. By 1972, the authors acknowledge, semiotics has not yet succeeded in legitimizing itself as a science. It is haunted by "a certain uncertainty as to fundamental principles and concepts; in particular that of the sign itself" (210). Hence, we are left to infer, the project of the *Dictionnaire*, whose mission is to clarify these fundamental concepts. The "new research" underway, however, throws a wrench into this project. For, as the authors explain, even though these new critics "situate themselves in relation to a semiotic perspective," they call into question the most fundamental terms of structuralist linguistics, the terms upon which the enterprise of semiotics was founded. They call into question the sign itself! This is why this new research cannot simply be incorporated into the *Dictionnaire encyclopédique*. Nor, however, can these new writings be ignored—"it would have been unthinkable not to give them their due [*de ne pas leur faire leur place*]." Not wanting to risk the incoherence that would result from including this material "in the same time framework [*dans le même temps*] as the body of concepts upon which today's sciences of language are based, and which, precisely, it puts into question," the authors decide on an appendix. This gesture, of course, completely detaches poststructuralist thinking from any historical context and marks the radical heterogeneity of the poststructuralist departure—its status as epistemic break. It implies that the whole history of the sciences of language, from Aristotle and Saint Augustine up to the review *Semiotikà*, can be comprehended within the same encyclopedia, but that what "arrives" during the late 1960's cannot. This is radically heterogeneous with respect to the past. To the extent that recourse to this appendix parallels Kant's treatment of the relation between the sublime and the beautiful in the third *Critique* (where the analytic of the sublime is an appendix to the theory of taste), it reinforces the claim that poststructuralism amounts to a Copernican revolution for Western thought. During the 1960's and 1970's, then, the eruption of theory was presented as an epistemic break. It was hailed as an intellectual breakthrough so radical as to be quite discontinuous with the past.

In 1983, after the demise of *Tel Quel*, the new review *Infini* opens with a retrospective glance by Kristeva in an essay entitled "Mémoires." It gives us this account of Kristeva's first encounter with *Tel Quel*:

Around the end of 1961, I think it was, the Communist student review *Clarté* published a large photo of Philippe Sollers and a text in which he explained, basically, that only socialist revolution could provide a fertile social ground [*terrain social*] for avant-garde writing. This was my first encounter with *Tel Quel*. And the first seduction.[19]

With Sollers (who identifies revolution with avant-garde art production) in the role of Breton, the image poses the terms of theory and of its seductiveness: avant-garde art and revolution. Another memory surfaces a few lines down, an evocation of the milieu of Kristeva's student days in Paris which provides a further clue to this seductiveness:

The Ecole des Hautes Etudes providing a counterbalance to the Sorbonne, *Tel Quel* developing in spite of the *NRF* or *Les Temps Modernes . . . the dilemma of engagement* was reconfigured [*remodelé*] for us, displaced. It was transformed into an implication, a complete inclusion within the intellectual adventure that we lived as practice. (my emphasis)

Kristeva's formula, "the dilemma of engagement," condenses the language of Breton (the "dilemma" of the modern artist) and that of Sartre ("engagement"). It also suggests the direction, if not the meaning, of the remodeling of engagement by *Tel Quel*. What this remodeling involved was a displacement of the question of engagement toward the questions of language and of signifying practices, one that resulted in a diffusion of the issue of engagement. To the extent that avant-garde poetics became a model for signifying practices in general, this remodeling of the problem of commitment brings it closer to surrealist engagement in which revolution was considered a subcategory of the more comprehensive problem that Breton (from his "pre-critical" horizon) called "expression." We could even say that *Tel Quel*'s displacement of the problem of engagement goes in the direction of Breton's position, as it was critically portrayed by Sartre: avant-gardism and radical negativity.

This is precisely the way the question of engagement is reconfigured in *La Révolution du langage poétique*. Approximately forty years after *Qu'est-ce que la littérature?* Kristeva turns engagement inside out. She succeeds in substituting the taboo term "poetry" (precisely the avant-garde poetry at the origin of surrealist automatic writing, which, as we have seen, was the real target of Sartre's attack) for the Sartrean term "prose" as the instrument of engagement. In other words, she renders revolutionary that which Sartre attacked in the name of revolution: esthetic (or anti-esthetic) avant-gardism. What is more, she does this by reworking basically the same argument Sartre had used against Breton: that of a radical negativity. Transvalued as a force of innovation, this negativity itself becomes the subject of action—engaged and revolutionary. Engagement is displaced from prose to poetry and the strategies of that displacement serve the esthetic avant-gardism Sartre so violently rejected in *Qu'est-ce que la littérature?* The immediate success of *La Révolution du langage poétique* was not only a result of its theoretical merits, or of the marvelous *disponibilité* of the new philosophical operator, transgression. It was also a function of the persistence of concerns inherited from the previous generation. The revival of questions concerning relations between art and revolution, in the context both of May 1968 and of the Chinese Cultural Revolution, prepared the receptiveness of a specifically "theoretical" resolution of the two cultural positions associated with the names Breton and Sartre—avant-gardism and engagement. The reconciliation of these positions occurs in the domain of theory; it is also one of the crucial gestures deciding the enterprise of theory. To the extent that this reconciliation engenders a subject of theory, as we have seen in our analysis of Kristeva, it constitutes theory as a practice.

Part II

Abstract

The first part of this study attempted to demystify the notion of the absolute rupture of theory. I linked the activities of *Tel Quel* to the polemics of the preceding generation and resituated transgression in this context. Part II will explore these polemics further through close analysis of the notions of engagement, pure art, and automatism. This analysis calls into question a number of stereotypes.

Although Bataille himself had been politically committed during the 1930's, and had opposed a concept of action to the "mere art" of the orthodox surrealists, by the 1940's Sartre had become Bataille's principal interlocutor and rival. Specifically in response to Sartre's attack on Baudelaire, Bataille opposed poetry to action and declared a radical incompatibility between the two. As we shall see, the antinomy between poetry and action (which rephrases the opposition between art and revolution) runs through each of the various polemical positions—engagement, pure art, and automatism—and structures the field of struggle between them.

In Chapters 3, 4, and 5, I analyze Sartre, Valéry, and Breton in terms of this tension between poetry and action. By inflecting the term "action" in the direction of Bergson, instead of Hegel (where it is an operation of negation), we find that the antinomy softens and proximities emerge between figures usually posed in opposition to one another. We have already seen that Bataille's analysis of the transgression of eroticism involved a displacement of the Hegelian scene of recognition, or the master/slave dialectic. Eroticism involves a playful reenactment of this struggle, which turns risk into erotic fiction and evacuates the dimension of violence.

As we shall see in Chapter 3, Sartre's paradoxical dialectic of reading, which is central to his theory of engagement, also involves a reworking of the recognition scene and a correction of it. In Chapter 4 we see that Valéry's poetics of perfection does not depend upon a Hegelian negativity of work but rather upon a *"travail de l'esprit* [mental activity]" that approaches what Bergson understood by invention. My analysis shows that the account of reading that Sartre invokes to displace the master/slave dialectic is anticipated by Valéry, and before him by Bergson. The negativity of the recognition scene is also absent in Breton's theory of automatism, which I trace through a number of critical essays as well as through an analysis of *Nadja*. In its place, Breton elaborates a complex interaction between perception and representation that Bergson had theorized in terms of a quite different notion of "recognition."

CHAPTER 3

Sartre

Reading Engagement

"If literature is not everything, it is not worth one minute of our
time. That is what I wanted to say by 'engagement.'"
—Jean-Paul Sartre, *Situations 9*

The "incompatibility of literature and 'engagement,'" Bataille declares in
1950, " . . . is precisely one of opposites."[1] Bataille identifies engagement
with project, or action, and action with prose. In other words, he takes
Sartre at his word. Speech is action, Sartre affirms in *Qu'est-ce que la littérature?*; the prose writer uses language like a tool. For Bataille, the utilitarian economy associated with such instrumentality is incompatible with
his conception of literature as poetry. What Bataille calls "poetry of the
instant" (specifically in opposition to the temporality of project he associates with engagement) is transgressive; it enjoys a general, as opposed
to a restricted, economy.

The ideological opposition affirmed by Bataille—literature (poetry) versus action (prose)—has for the most part been accepted uncritically. But
what if the theory of engagement were itself a symptom of the "neurosis"
Sartre diagnosed in himself in *Les Mots*: the tendency to consider literature as an absolute? What if, at the heart of engagement, there were a general economy of sovereignty instead of a utilitarian one? What if an equation of literature and the absolute was the very mechanism of engagement,
and engagement was a myth of literature?

Simone de Beauvoir tells us that the ambition of the founding group of
Les Temps Modernes, where the essays that now make up *Qu'est-ce que
la littérature?* were first published, was to produce a new ideology for the
postwar era.[2] Sartre affirms that the myth of literature a society holds is

central to its broader ideology. Indeed, his theory of engagement provides a new myth of literature—the myth of prose—which serves as the ideological core of an existentialist humanism and of a democratic socialism. Prose is the myth of language restored to an originary innocence—a pure signifying force—through the healing powers of a literary practice.

To appreciate the mythic character of Sartre's theory of writing, we need only read *Qu'est-ce que la littérature?* backwards. If the last chapter, "The Situation of the Writer in 1947," portrays language in a state of crisis, the preceding one, "For Whom Does One Write?", diagnoses the fundamental problem of an antinomy between speech and action. It also asserts that this antinomy can only be overcome in a classless society, that is, after the revolution that would end history as class struggle.[3] As we move back to "Why Write?", we recognize that the essence of literature presented abstractly there corresponds to this ideal that still awaits concrete realization in a postrevolutionary utopia. When we return to the opening chapter, however, we realize that "What Is Called Writing?" presents the resolution of the fundamental antinomy between speech and action as a fait accompli. The faultless efficacious force of prose is summarized there by the formula "speech is action [*parler, c'est agir*]." This implies that the dialectical resolution of contradiction has already occurred. Sartre's essay presents a myth of literature that corresponds to the ideological dream of democratic socialism: the utopia of a classless society.

Sartre opens *Qu'est-ce que littérature?*, then, with a myth of prose in which transparency stands for an unimpeded instrumental force of signification. The transparency of prose is flatly contrasted to the opacity of the nonsignifying forms of poetry and painting. Speech is action. Writing is figured by speech operating in the mode of discrete acts of nomination or performative speech acts: "The writer is a speaker, s/he designates, demonstrates, gives orders, refuses, calls out / questions [*interpelle*], implores, insults, persuades, insinuates" (25). Words are instruments of designation and the prose writer (*prosateur*) is defined as a person who uses words like tools. But words are unusual instruments, for they belong to our subjectivity. They provide us with a sixth sense; they are a kind of extension of the body, an antenna, which can be used for self-protection. "When one is in danger . . . one grabs any old tool," Sartre writes in a celebrated passage, and " . . . once this danger is passed, one no longer remembers whether it was a hammer or a log. And anyway, one never knew, one just needed an extension of one's body . . . it was a sixth finger, a third leg, in short a pure function that we assimilated for ourselves."

Just when the rhetoric of action intensifies, even dramatizing a scene of danger, Sartre qualifies his initial formula, "speech is action." Prose is now defined as "a certain secondary moment [of action] that one might call action by unveiling":

> Thus, when I speak I unveil the situation by my very project of changing it; I strike its very heart [*je l'atteins en plein coeur*], I pierce it and fix it beneath my gaze; now I have it at my disposal [*j'en dispose*], with each word I utter I engage myself a little further with the world, and at the same time, I emerge from it a little more, for I go beyond it into the future. (28)

We are still at the scene of danger, the danger described as "an enterprise either between me and others or between the other and me." The French word *entreprise* suggests "project," and to this extent evokes engagement. But it also means a conflict or struggle between two individuals.[4] What is at stake here, in other words, is a scene of intersubjective encounter. The danger that erupts into Sartre's text is the struggle to the death of the Hegelian recognition scene or master/slave dialectic. Words are weapons in a verbal sublimation (or secondary moment) of this violent encounter.

In *Being and Nothingness* the intersubjective encounter passes through the objectifying gaze. Here speech is "action by unveiling" because "to look at something is to change it [*voir c'est changer*]." The identity of speech and action is mediated by a linguistic gesture of unveiling that passes figuratively through the gaze. It is speech as gaze that is figured as a transpiercing in the passage cited above, and as a pistol shot. But the target of such gestures is not a referential object in an act of signification. It is another subject. The game is one of seeing oneself be seen [*se voir vu*], a kind of ironic (because disempowering) version of the moment of self-consciousness in Hegel's scene of recognition. In Hegel, recognition occurs as a fight to the death. When the slave prefers defeat to death s/he validates the master's powers, powers of negative consciousness that entail potential mastery not only over the slave, but over nature in general as well.[5] The master achieves self-consciousness through recognition by the slave. In *Qu'est-ce que la littérature?* Sartre's paradigm is at once Hegelian and Husserlian. Sartre models the directionality of the sign upon an intentional structure of consciousness borrowed from Husserl. He superimposes this intentional consciousness onto the Hegelian narrative of the emergence of self-consciousness in the scene of recognition. In other words, instead of following Husserl toward the ideality of meaning associated with the expressive sign, Sartre invokes the Hegelian master/slave dialectic in his elaboration of an intentionality (deictic force, or the capacity to indicate or refer) of the indicative sign. In Sartre's analysis of prose, a myth of semiological transparency serves a myth of instrumental force: speech as action.

The Charm of Prose

Conventionally, the transparency and instrumental force of prose are identified with a representational or expressive use of language, and considered in relation to the issue of literary realism. Engagement is construed
as a theory of realism, a special pleading in its favor in opposition to the
kind of avant-garde literary experimentation we associate with Breton,
who explicitly abandoned the term "literature" in favor of a new notion
of "poetry" on the basis of Verlaine's quip—"and all the rest will be
merely literature"—subsequently taken up, and "corrected," by *Tel Quel*.

From this perspective, one would expect Sartre to launch into the question of the engaged writer's subject matter once the signifying force of
prose had been firmly established. One would expect the transparency of
prose to operate in the service of something the writer wanted to express,
that is, in the service of values ostensibly superior to "merely esthetic"
ones. To the reader's surprise, however, Sartre does not take up the question of the writer's subject. Instead, in the manner of Proust, whose narrator in *Swann's Way* chides the young Marcel for his naive ideas concerning what it takes to be a great writer, Sartre mocks the whole question of the author's message:

Are we not in the habit of asking all aspiring young writers this fundamental question: "Do you have something to say?" By which we are meant to understand
something worth writing about. But how are we to know what is worthwhile,
without recourse to a system of transcendental values? (27)

Message, for Sartre, implies inauthenticity, for it either starts from cliché
or, if successfully received, ends up as one. It becomes "a completely dis-
embodied discourse . . . where human feelings, because they no longer
touch us, take on the status of exemplary feelings, and, to be more precise, of *values*" (original emphasis). "Message" implies a system of
preestablished values that Sartre, as existentialist philosopher, rejects. We
need only remember the scene depicted in *Existentialism Is a Humanism*
where a young man comes to ask Sartre what he should do. It is wartime.
His mother is very ill and alone. Should he join the troops on the front?
Should he stay with his ailing mother? Sartre responds that there are no
transcendental values to guide him in his choice; he must decide freely for
himself. Authorial message threatens to carry the kind of hidden ideological force that Sartre (before Barthes) detects in that which presents itself
as eternal verity.

In *Qu'est-ce que la littérature?* Sartre criticizes message in the same
terms he used in his opening pages to deprecate poetry and painting in opposition to signifying prose. Poetry is like painting, he argues, which "is

not at all readable." Speaking of the yellow streak in a painting by Tin-toretto, Sartre writes: "It is like an immense and vain effort, always ar-rested halfway between the sky and the earth, to express what, in [its] na-ture, it is impossible for it to express" (16). The yellow mark, he adds, does not signify anxiety; it is anxiety become thing (15). In very similar terms he criticizes the prose writer's message for being "a spirit turned into an object [*une âme faite objet*]" (38); it is opaque, reified. Oddly, then, when it is a question of what the powerful language of prose might actu-ally signify, the notion of message is depicted in terms of the same impo-tence and materiality that was invoked to establish the inferiority of non-signifying forms, painting and poetry, with respect to the signifying force of prose.

Unexpectedly, the transparency of prose is most explicitly elaborated in relation to the question of style, not substance. Defending himself against the charge of being insensitive to style, Sartre writes: "One is not a writer for having chosen to say certain things but for having chosen to say them in a particular way. And style, of course, determines the value of prose. But it must go unnoticed" (30). It is in this context that he in-vokes the traditional figure for transparency: the windowpane. "Since words are transparent and the gaze traverses them," he writes, "it would be absurd to slip in amongst them unpolished panes of glass" (30). The transparency of prose, it appears, is not an inherent property of language; it exists as a function of style.

Sartre's evasion of content in favor of a consideration of style suggests that although he champions a transparency of prose in the name of speech, and models the instrumentality of language on a Husserlian intentional-ity of consciousness, his conception of signification does not coincide with Husserl's notion of the expressive sign. Indeed, Sartre invokes not the ex-pressive sign but the indicative one, which (as Derrida's analysis of Husserl affirms) the phenomenologist suppressed in order to protect an ideality of meaning. For Sartre ideality of meaning implies the domain of those eter-nal verities—*valeurs*—that he derides in his dismissal of the notion of au-thorial message. To privilege it would not enhance the existentialist's ar-gument concerning the identity of speech and action.

From this point of view one would have to question any reading of en-gagement that identifies prose with representation or expression—with an ideology of realism. For if Sartre's myth of prose reduces the play of the signifier, as advanced critics have always maintained, it could be said to reduce the play of the signified as well. In Husserl the signified is specific to expressive signification. It is associated with the possibility of hearing oneself speak through an inner voice, even in the absence of any exteri-orization. "Expressions," Husserl wrote, "function meaningfully . . . even in solitary mental life, where they no longer seem to indicate anything." Citing this passage, Derrida comments: "By a strange paradox meaning would isolate the concentrated purity of its *ex-pressiveness* just at that moment when the relation to a certain *outside* is suspended . . . [this is] the phenomenological project in its essence."[6] Clearly, if Sartre were working from the Husserlian notion of the expressive sign, the message would be valued in relation to an ideality of meaning, or a *vouloir dire* [meaning / desire to express]. This is precisely not the case.

For Sartre the relation to the outside cannot be suspended, for not only is consciousness always consciousness *of* something, but it is the role of language to throw us into the world outside of ourselves. Words are depicted as "indicators [*indicateurs*] that cast the writer outside of himself, into the midst of things" (20), on the model of the operation of intentional consciousness. There is no semantic dimension here, and the epistemological one proposes a notion of truth as correct indication. It is a question of knowing whether words "correctly indicate a certain thing in the world or a certain notion" (25). Once again, we see that it is not so much transparency per se that is privileged here but a form of instrumentality. Transparency suggests unimpeded expression, whereas here it is a question of an instrumentality of indication. This is the role played by the sign construed as an "extension of our body . . . of our senses" (19).

A rhetoric of transparency becomes attached to this instrumentality, however, through the insertion of a linguistic variant of the intentional movement—a "to refer to" (*renvoyer à*), or a "to designate"—within the broader structure of intentional consciousness. Sartre construes consciousness as something that is "nothing but the outside of itself," a consciousness, therefore, without the interiority necessary for the gestation of a *vouloir dire*. To put this another way, we could say that the word's indication of a thing is in the service of (or structurally redundant to) consciousness itself, occurring as consciousness *of* something. The word is "transparent" to the vector of intentional consciousness, then, because it overlaps with its movement (hence the pertinence of the figure of the gaze already mentioned). But this transparency has little to do with the ideality of meaning we usually associate with an expressive or representational use of language.

We have gone into so much detail concerning transparency because Sartre defines prose in terms of this notion. "There is prose," he writes, "when, to speak like Valéry, the word passes through our glance [*le mot passe à travers notre regard*] as glass through the sun [*comme le verre au travers du soleil*]." The recourse to intertextual allusion introduces a textual opacity into Sartre's depiction of transparency. More significantly still, however, Sartre has borrowed from poetry to give to the very essence of prose, for the allusion is to a poem from *Charmes*: "Intérieur." What Sartre takes from Valéry is a poetic reversal of the conventional figure of transparency he himself invoked in his discussion of style—language as window onto the world. "Since words are transparent," he had written, "and the gaze traverses them, it would be absurd to slip in amongst them unpolished panes of glass" (30). One polishes the windowpane so that light might shine through it. In the conventional figure, then, meaning passes through the word as light (or our gaze) passes through the glass. Here, however, we move in the opposite direction: "the word passes through our gaze," and "the glass passes through the sun."

Valéry's poem reads as follows:

INTÉRIEUR

Une esclave aux longs yeux chargés de molles chaînes
Change l'eau de mes fleurs, plonge aux glaces prochaines,
Au lit mystérieux prodigue ses doigts purs;
Elle met une femme au milieu de ces murs
Qui, dans ma rêverie errant avec décence,
Passe entre mes regards sans briser leur absence,
Comme passe le verre au travers du soleil,
Et de la raison pure épargne l'appareil. (my emphasis)

INTERIOR

A slave with long eyes weighed down by limp chains
Changes the water in my vases, plunges into the nearest mirrors,
lavishes her pure fingers on the mysterious bed;
She places a woman within these walls
Who, wandering in my reverie with a sense of decency
Passes through my glance without disrupting its absence
As glass passes right through the sunlight
And spares the instrument of reason.[7]

The poem characterizes the difference between the inner life of revery and the outer world of perception and pure reason. In the manner of Mallarmé, it uses language to evoke presence in absence. The figure of the woman escapes the lucidity of reason, which registers mere absence. The gaze is a figure for the apparatus of reason, and the figure of the woman "passe entre mes regards," which we might render "passes through my gaze/glance," but which more literally suggests "slips through my glances"—an ingenious darting between glances so as not to be seen. The woman eludes the objectifying gaze because as inner vision or even memory image she is present as absence. In the poem, then, the woman "passe entre mes regards . . . / Comme passe le verre au travers du soleil" (she passes through my glance . . . / As the glass passes right through the sunlight). She is transparent in the sense of not being seen—transparent to the point of invisibility—at least as far as the eye of analytic reason is concerned. To this extent the woman stands for all the poetic features of language that give us so much difficulty in the translation of this poem, and which are indiscernible to (and hence impenetrable by) rational, or prosaic, intelligence. She is a figure for that interiority given in the title of the poem, and, if we want to consider the phonic equivalent of *verre* (glass) and *vers* (verse), a figure for poetry itself.

In Sartre's adaptation of Valéry's poetic language, the prose word occupies the place the woman holds in the poem. Sartre has changed Valéry's "passe entre mes regards" to "passe à travers notre regard," which corresponds more to our loose translation of "passes through our gaze" than to the literal meaning of slipping through and escaping from our glances ("regards" shifts from plural to singular). But he has retained Valéry's "comme le verre passe au travers du soleil." The expression "passer au travers," which signifies to "slip right through" something that offers no resistance, has a supplementary meaning of "to escape from danger." In Valéry's poem this meaning reinforces the theme of the vulnerability of interior vision in the face of the bright light of analytic reason, which knows only the alternative between objective presence and absence. The sun is the figure for pure reason; the inner vision of the woman escapes the danger of the objectifying glance. The presence-in-absence of the dream vision is figured by the transparency of the glass, that is, by the instrument of outer vision in its pure objectivity: the glass or the lens in its transparency. Inner vision subsists by becoming entirely transparent (transparent to the point of absence) to the transparency of outer vision. Here transparency operates not in the service of revealing something present, but of sustaining (and implicitly concealing) a presence in absence. The focus is on the transparency of the glass itself, not the clear appearance of an object that would be revealed (or unveiled) on the other side of the glass.

In his definition of prose, then, Sartre retains one half of Valéry's reversal of the topos of transparency while adjusting the other half. In his adaptation, the word passes though the glance instead of getting past it, as the glass passes through the sun. Sartre retains a principal feature of Valéry's poetic reversal of the topos of transparency even as he elaborates it in the context of an argument that depends upon the conventional topos in its unadulterated form. The displacement changes the direction of the movement. Significantly, it shifts it away from any object that would be revealed by the transparency of the glass and turns it back upon the source of light—the sun. It is turned back toward the sunlight, as a figure of the eye of consciousness: the word passes through the gaze in the sense that it is carried by means of it. This is consistent with the fact we emphasized earlier: namely, that transparency does not serve expression in Sartre's analysis. The gaze is the weapon in Sartre's version of the intersubjective encounter, and the word is a weapon in the verbal sublimation of that struggle that figurally passes through the gaze. The word passes through the gaze in a "secondary moment," or on a figural level. It is in this sense that prose is "action by unveiling," where unveiling is figured as a tran-spiercing.

At first glance, the secondary meaning of *au travers de*—to escape from danger—does not appear to be pertinent to the Sartre text. But it is not entirely irrelevant. It leads right into the apparent non sequitur that im-mediately follows the definition of prose: "When one is in danger . . . one grabs any old tool. . . . So it is with language." It leads, in other words, to the danger of another objectifying glance, the glance of the other in the intersubjective encounter. This is where transparency and instrumentality come together in Sartre's analysis. Language attaches to the operations of consciousness. To this extent, for Sartre, the word does pass through the glance, and not the other way around. The transparency associated with the instrumental operation of signification is figurally displaced here into the opacity of the instrument, the tool of self-defense or aggression, in the violent struggle between self and other. Transparency, in other words, is not a matter of what the eye might see; it does not operate in relation to an object and its representation. It attaches to the eye of the subject as a function of the intentional glance. As such it becomes instrumental. For, as Sartre writes, "to see something is to change it [*voir c'est changer*]." Transparency is activated as a piercing gesture once it is attached to the eye of consciousness. In Sartre's analysis in *Being and Nothingness* the in-tersubjective encounter operates through the gaze. In his analysis of prose as an instrument of intersubjective violence, the word is redundant to the operation of the glance—it passes through our glance (*le mot passe à tra-vers notre regard*). We can now better appreciate why the question of the author's message was trivialized. What is at stake in language as action (even sublimated into a secondary moment) is a version of struggle to the death.

I have given particular attention to the master/slave dialectic as it ap-pears in Sartre's text not only because it relates to Bataille's displacement of this same scene in his theory of the transgression of eroticism, but also because it returns, transposed into a peaceful and harmonious mode, in the second chapter of Sartre's study, "Why Write?" It returns in Sartre's discussion of the "dialectical paradox of reading," where it determines the very essence of the literary event. In this second chapter, Sartre shifts focus from the act of writing (figured by speech) to the written text itself. In the first chapter of *Qu'est-ce que la littérature?*, what Sartre calls "ac-

tion by unveiling" means that words unveil situation in a piercing gesture
that is modeled on the glance; in the second chapter the act of unveiling
becomes self-reflexive instead of transitive. The written work must be unveiled (*dévoilé*) in the phenomenological sense. For the work to be a work
and not merely black smudges on white paper, it requires an interpretive
act of reading. As unveiling, reading is the "dialectical correlative" of writing. The written work is construed as an appeal or address (*un appel*)
which, when freely responded to, dialectically resolves the oppositions between subject and object and inaugurates an intersubjective or reciprocal
recognition. In this way Sartre portrays the collaboration between writing and reading as a mutual recognition of freedoms. This is Sartre's peaceful and egalitarian substitute for Hegel's violent scene that fixes positions
of dominance. "The writer recognizes, by the very act of writing . . . the
freedom of the readers," Sartre writes. The reader reciprocates with recognition of the freedom of the writer. "To write is a certain form of willing
freedom [*vouloir la liberté*]" Sartre declares. It is in this quite specific sense
that writing is a question of the absolute and will always lie at the heart
of engagement.

In its very essence, writing is value for Sartre. It is value inasmuch as it
is an appeal to the freedom of the reader and therefore to a free invention
of value.[8] The event of reciprocal recognition, which occurs through the
collaboration of writing and reading, constitutes value per se as free act
of valuation. The experience of freedom, mediated through the work in
this way, is felt as esthetic joy. "We are in the presence of an essential structure of esthetic joy" (65), Sartre writes, " . . . esthetic joy accompanies the
positional consciousness that the world is value, that is, a task proposed to
human freedom" (66). Sartre calls this structure of esthetic joy an "esthetic modification of the human project" (66). Project itself depends upon
the experience of the world as value. This occurs as a function of esthetic
experience, or of the esthetic modification of experience. To this extent
the esthetic moment lies at the heart of engagement. The esthetic moment
(the essence of literature as mutual recognition of freedom) is central to
the structure and coherence of literary engagement and, as we shall see,
to the theoretical elaboration of engagement more generally. *Qu'est-ce
que la littérature?* is not a tract proposing a burden of social or political
commitment upon literature—literature in the service of theory. It is a serious interrogation of the essence of literature and a defense of its powers
and autonomy.[9] At the heart of engagement—that is, at the heart of the
essence of literature as "engagement . . . with freedom"—there is a space
of free invention. The embrace of freedoms in the dialectical paradox of
reading is not altogether unrelated to the embrace of eroticism. At the
heart of project, there is an economy of excess.

The Magic of Reading

To fully appreciate this point of view, we must analyze the dialectic of free-doms in more detail. In Sartre's version of the Hegelian master/slave dia-lectic, an existential question of essentiality replaces the issue of mastery. If human consciousness gives us the world (the "there is [of] being," *il y a de l'être*) it cannot be said to create that world through its representa-tions.[10] Artists, Sartre suggests, attempt to achieve essentiality through the act of creating. In order to feel fully essential, however, one would have to both produce something and unveil it, or bring it to appearance. Not being divine, we can only unveil what already exists for us as object. Thus when the artist wants to confirm his or her essentiality, recognition must occur in two stages. First, the objective status of the work must be con-firmed. Once this is established, the work can mediate the recognition of the writer's essentiality by the reader. Thus we have two overlapping dia-lectics condensed within this single *paradoxical* dialectic of reading. One is between subject and object, and pertains to the relation between the artist and his or her work. The other is the intersubjective dialectic be-tween writer and reader that is mediated by the first dialectic as it con-cerns the work. As with Bataille's eroticism, it is a question of a certain self-consciousness (a *se saisir*): "It is only through the consciousness of the reader that the writer can become conscious of his essentiality with re-spect to his work" (52). Revising the provisional definition of writing he gave in the first chapter, Sartre now proposes that to write is to "have re-course to the consciousness of others in order to become recognized as es-sential to the totality of being" (65).

The objective status of the work is problematic (and therefore requires recognition) only because it is a question of an esthetic object, an original creation or work of genius. If the artist were merely an artisan, if she or he made objects "according to the traditional norms with tools whose us-age is codified," the instrumental object thus produced would already have objective status. The craftsperson would not be essential to it, however, for in this case producing becomes just another mode of unveiling—a kind of technological unveiling. On the other hand, when "we ourselves pro-duce the rules of production" in the creation of an original work, we are essential with respect to our work, but the work lacks objective being; "We only find ourselves in our work" (47). It is impossible to stop the process of creation so that the perception required for recognition might take place: "When we try to perceive our work, we are still creating it . . . [we] mentally repeat the operations that have produced it." Only the reader's intervention interrupts this process. Thus writing implies reading as its dialectical correlative: "It is the combined effect of the author and the reader that will bring forth the concrete and imaginary object which is the work [*l'ouvrage de l'esprit*]" (49).

The tasks of producing and unveiling are thus distributed across the two interlocutory instances of subjectivity: the writer and the reader. But the work, like the woman in eroticism, is what Bataille would call a "paradoxical object." It receives its objective status by virtue of existing as something quite different from an object: as an extension of the subjectivity of the writer on the one hand and of the reader on the other. Faced with the book, the reader waits expectantly as the text unfolds before his or her eyes in time.[11] Reading mimes the operations of writing; the reader has to repeat the creative process of the writer in order to perceive the work. To this extent, he or she "synthesizes the operations of perception and creation" (51). Thus the reader not only contributes the moment of perception to the collaborative undertaking of creation/perception, he or she also repeats the moment of creation by reinventing what s/he reads: "the reader invents everything by perpetually going beyond the written word" (52). Reading is what Sartre calls "directed creation"; it operates "through the pure freedom of the reader" (53).[12]

Reading as directed creation, or reinvention, implies a notion of literary language quite different from the myth of prose Sartre presented in the first chapter of his book. Earlier, we read that the prose writer uses words like tools. Here the esthetic work is explicitly contrasted with the instrumentality of the tool. The dialectic of freedoms requires a rejection of instrumentality not just on the part of the writer who seeks essentiality, but also by the reader, who would retain his or her freedom. As we have seen, the writers invent their own rules of production, instead of fabricating a work "according to traditional norms with tools whose usage has been codified." The writer of the literary text does not use words in a codified manner, that is, s/he does not use them as tools—the artist's words do not "transpierce." We could almost say that like the painting and the fallen state of ordinary language, they "stop halfway along to their meaning." And necessarily so. For if the words of the literary text were piercing, if they carried an impaled meaning that imposed itself on the reader, the reader would no longer be free. And without the freedom of the reader, the writer's essentiality cannot be affirmed. "I can use a hammer to nail a crate [*clouer une caisse*] or to clobber my neighbor [*assommer mon voisin*]" (53), Sartre writes, in language that recalls the more violent scene of recognition evoked in the earlier chapter. But a book "is not like a tool, a means to a specific end." Literature is an end in itself. It cannot be placed in the service of anything else—not even a political goal. The literary work "proposes itself as end to the freedom of the reader" (54). The autonomy of literature is affirmed in ethical terms, that is, in relation to a Kantian notion of autonomy. The work "is not an instrument whose existence is manifest and whose end is indeterminate: it presents itself as a task to be carried out [*une tâche à remplir*], it places itself at the level of the categorical imperative" (55).

Sartre's theory of engagement is usually read as a theory of literature in the service of some higher value. Yet there is no higher value evoked in *Qu'est-ce que la littérature?* than freedom. What the writer requires from the reader is not subservience to any goal or value, but his or her freedom. And it is this requirement that entails a specific appeal to the structure of recognition and its correction. "To address oneself to a freedom as such it is necessary to recognize it . . . there is only one way to reach it [*l'atteindre*]: to recognize it." It is the mutual recognition of freedoms that establishes value as such. The work of art is value as call to freedom: "This absolute end, this transcendental imperative which is nevertheless consented to . . . by freedom itself [*repris à son compte par la liberté même*] is what we call value" (55). The experience of the value of the work implies an experience of the absolute.

The freedom of the reader, however, has further consequences for the act of reading and the operation of language. Not only do words not signify in the piercing or instrumental manner depicted in the discussion of prose in the first chapter, they no longer function as units of signification at all.[13] Here it is not a question of denotative meaning but of esthetic or "organic" meaning, what Sartre calls the "meaning of the work." He makes the distinction explicit in the following terms:

The literary object, even though it be realized through language, is never given in language; on the contrary it is silence and contestation of speech. Also, the hundred thousand words lined up in a book can be read one by one without the meaning of the work [*le sens de l'oeuvre*] springing forth; the meaning is not the sum of all the words, it is their organic totality. (51)

We hear echoes of Bataille (as well as of Blanchot and Valéry) in these allusions to silence and the contestation of language by literature—allusions that will be forcefully echoed in Sartre's late essay, *Plaidoyer pour les intellectuels*. But we must look more closely at Sartre's account of reading to appreciate what silence and the contestation of language might mean in *Qu'est-ce que la littérature?*

If the objectivity of the work is problematic because it remains too close to the subjectivity of the author—at its very limit—the work also attaches to the subjectivity of the reader.[14] It is for just this reason that the text can mediate the mutual recognition of freedom between the two instances of subjectivity. The reader's subjectivity comes into play because of the relationship between language and emotion. Words act as traps (*pièges*) for the reader's feelings. These emotions nevertheless remain free because they occur only as a function of what Sartre (echoing Proust) calls our "imaginary belief [*croyance imaginaire*]," which is freely given. It is on this basis that the reader lends emotion to the language of the text in a gesture that enables a self-recognition of freedom by itself. "All the feelings that occur on the basis of this imaginary belief are like specific modulations of my freedom; far from absorbing it or masking it, they are so many ways it has chosen to become aware of itself [*se révéler à elle-même*]" (57). Speaking of the experience of reading the novel *Crime and Punishment*, Sartre writes:

> But, by a reversal *that is particular to the imaginary object*, it is not the [character's] conduct that provokes my indignation or my esteem, but my indignation, my esteem, that give consistency and objectivity to his or her conduct. Thus the feelings of the reader are never dominated by the object and, as no external reality can condition them, they have their permanent source in freedom, that is, they are completely *generous*. (57, my emphasis)

The reader reads a novel. What Sartre calls the "generosity" of the reader depends on the fictional status of the work. For generosity depends on freedom and in the case of fiction, there is no real conditioning of the reader's emotions. These are free in the Kantian sense, for "no external reality can condition them" (57).

The word is read through emotions.[15] But the reader does not experience emotion as the by-product of reading, that is, in emotional response to the work once its meaning has been grasped. The gift of the reader's emotions is necessary for reading to occur at all. Without that gift, the words on the page are unable to carry out their signifying function. Speaking of the literary work, Sartre writes, "meaning is no longer contained in the words"; it is what links words together. Meaning would only be contained in the words if it were a question of an instrumental use of language, one in which, as Sartre put it, usage was codified by tradition. In the literary work the writer (like the genius in Kant) invents his or her own rules. Here it is the meaning of the work as a whole—what Sartre calls "organic" meaning—which enables the comprehension of individual words of the text. It is not enough for readers to let words signify, Sartre argues, they must fill the words with meaning through the force of their emotions. To read is to provisionally suspend one's critical faculties, to render oneself credulous, and to make a gift of one's feelings. The reader gives "the gift of his whole person . . . passions, opinions or prejudices, sexual temperament and scale of values. Only when this person gives himself with generosity, will freedom run completely through him or her and transform the most obscure depths of the person's sensibility."[16] The generosity of the reader is conditioned by, and conditions, his or her freedom. When I read, my emotions play themselves out as "particular modulations of my freedom." As such, they enable a self-recognition of freedom. Through these concrete modulations of our feelings, Sartre writes, we can become conscious of (*saisir*) our freedom. Thus for the reader the text plays a role analogous to the role the erotic object plays for the transgressive subject in Bataille. It functions as a mirror, enabling a coming to consciousness. It also serves as the ground for the determinate presentation (or figuration) necessary for this lucidity.

Sartre introduces the theme of generosity in connection with his phenomenology of reading. Once the link has been made between generosity and freedom in relation to the reader, Sartre goes on to label writing in general terms a "gift ceremony." The reader gives a gift of his or her whole person, the artist gives his or her writing—"a recuperation of the totality of being" which is "presented to the freedom of the reader" (64). The writer's gift, the recuperation of the objective world for the world of consciousness, is "consecrated" by the ceremony—indeed the "Passion"—of reading. Esthetic joy accompanies the recognition of "a transcendental and absolute end . . . a call . . . a value." The joy of this recognition, Sartre insists, is accompanied by a suspension of "the utilitarian chain of ends-means and means-ends relations." Esthetic joy is the sign of value, and value involves the self-recognition of freedom. Sartre explicitly distinguishes literature from the restricted or utilitarian economy of means-ends relations. Far from being a means to an end, something in the service of higher values, literature is absolute for Sartre. As such, it exceeds the economy of utility or project that Bataille identifies with Sartrean engagement. In Sartre's correction of the Hegelian master/slave dialectic, recognition involves not only a reciprocity of freedom (a mutual recognition of freedom on the part of writer and reader), but a certain generosity as well. This theme marks another point of intersection with our analysis of Bataille. For the theme of generosity is attached to the anthropological structure of the gift, and it was just this structure that prompted Bataille's elaboration of the general economy in his early essay "La Notion de dépense."[17] Sartre describes the dialectical dynamics of the literary gift ceremony in the following terms: "When I read, I place demands [*j'exige*]; what I read in this way, if my demands are met, incites me to demand more from the author, which means: I demand from the author that he or she demand more from me. And vice versa, the author demands that I carry my own demands to the highest degree. Thus when my freedom manifests itself it unveils the freedom of the other."[18] The recognition of the other's freedom involves an even greater demand of the same in reverse. This introduces an excessive economy without limit.[19] It is precisely the paradoxical economy of this reciprocal recognition by writer and reader—its excess—that encourages us to take the metaphor of the gift seriously and to read the theme of generosity in relation to the anthropological structure of reciprocal gift exchange so important to Bataille's theory of transgression.

The potlatch, Lévi-Strauss writes, involves a gesture of "surpass[ing] a rival in generosity."[20] The "essential characteristic" of the potlatch, according to the structural anthropologist, was the emphasis placed on the "positive aspect of reciprocity" (LS 61). Lévi-Strauss depicts the reciprocity of gift exchange as a kind of antidote to, or resolution of, the intersubjective violence of the Hegelian recognition scene. "The uninterrupted process of reciprocal gift exchange," he writes in 1947, "effects the transition from hostility to alliance, from anxiety to confidence and from fear to friendship. . . . The action of reciprocity [is] regarded as the most immediate form of integrating the opposition between self and other" (LS 68). This is precisely the role the "gift ceremony" of writing plays in *Qu'est-ce que la littérature?*[21]

The anthropological dimension of Sartre's thinking (and its evocation of the sacred) is not theorized in *Qu'est-ce que la littérature?* It surfaces only through disparate metaphors that initially strike the reader as idiosyncratic and out of keeping with the subject of engagement. One tends to neglect them. To appreciate the resonance of the anthropological code we must refer back to Sartre's study of the emotions. Emotions, Sartre writes, "are all tantamount to setting up a magical world." By "magical" Sartre understands "a consciousness rendered passive."[22] Here, as in the analysis of reading in *Qu'est-ce que la littérature?*, emotion occurs as a function of belief (75). When the generous reader makes a gift of his or her imaginary belief [*croyance imaginaire*], the body follows this leap of faith, and the emotions it carries are freely given. If, as Sartre writes, "the literary object is . . . by nature silence and a contestation of speech," (51) we might interpret this silence in relation to the body as it pertains to the activity of the feelings in reading. "In emotions," Sartre writes, "it is the body which . . . changes its relation with the world in order that the world may change its qualities" (E 60–61). It is in this sense that the words of a literary text act as traps; they trap our emotions and reflect them for us. The emotions of the reader become the flesh of the text.[23] Reading as "directed creation" yields an "absolute production of qualities, which freeze under our eyes into impermeable objectivities."[24] As Sartre explains in this study, feeling produces quality and "every quality [is] conferred upon an object only by a passage to infinity. . . . Emotion is . . . intuition of the absolute" (E 81). If prose is a myth, reading is magic—a magic of the absolute.

The Gift Ceremony

Readers of *Qu'est-ce que la littérature?* have found the depiction of the instrumentality of prose so compelling that they tend to overlook the shift away from instrumentality when it comes to the literary text. Sartre does not make an explicit distinction between discursive writing (or the writing of the intellectual) and literary writing here. Implicitly, however, the distinction cuts between the first and second chapters of Sartre's essay. The instrumental model of prose gives an account of the language of the intellectual, whereas the rest of the work addresses the question of literary writing.

In *Plaidoyer pour les intellectuels* (1965), Sartre makes the distinction between the instrumental writing of the intellectual and the noninstrumental writing of the literary artist explicit. The task of the intellectual is knowledge, which pretends to universality and hence requires an instrumental language such as the one depicted in the opening chapter of *Qu'est-ce que la littérature?*. In the second section of the *Plaidoyer* Sartre contrasts the discourse of knowledge, as modeled after the formal languages of mathematics and the sciences, to what he calls the "ordinary" language of the literary writer, which, he affirms, contains "a maximum of disinformation."[25] In *Qu'est-ce que la littérature?*, we remember, Sartre remarks in passing that "one isn't a writer because one has chosen to say certain things but because one has chosen to say them in a certain way . . . style, of course, determines the value of prose" (30). It is not until *Plaidoyer pour les intellectuels* that Sartre elaborates this point, one so at odds with the polemical connotations of engagement that it easily slips from our awareness. In this late essay, Sartre considers style not as an expression of subjective temperament, but in terms of the materiality of language. Style, in this specific sense, is central to Sartre's analysis of the superiority of the artist as writer over the intellectual. The artist values the material weight of the word; it is "as material reality" that the word "contains a significant share of *non-savoir*" (*P* 446)—a devil's share (*une part maudite*) we might say, with Bataille. Style, which communicates no knowledge, incarnates the universal singular.

The goal of the literary writer, Sartre affirms in the *Plaidoyer*, is to exploit the paradoxical situation of language—the fact that, as union of signifier and signified, the linguistic sign "has two faces [*est à double face*] as does being in the world [*comme l'être dans le monde*]." We recognize that something like the dialectical paradox of reading, as elaborated in the 1940's, returns in this account of the literary writer's special relation to language. For in *Qu'est-ce que la littérature?*, both in the case of the abstract reader theorized in the second chapter and in the case of the con-

crete historical public, the position of the reader contributes the singularization of the universalizing gesture of writing as unveiling. In *Plaidoyer
pour les intellectuels*, the paradox between the universal and the singular
is located within language itself, that is, in the relationship between the
two faces of the sign. It is the literary writer who puts the nonsignifying
face of the word—its materiality—to work in the name of style. When it
comes to the totalization of the universal singular, Sartre writes (in words
suggesting Bataille), "It must be accomplished in unknowingness [*dans le
non-savoir*]" (P 454).

The intellectual must strive to assume singularity (the concrete partic-
ulars of his or her position) against an ideology that claims a false universality. For this reason he or she must assume a vehemently critical
stance. Intellectuals must become revolutionaries and, unlike what Sartre
considers the false intellectual position of Camus, they must identify themselves as such. In other words, intellectuals must become Communists.
They must subject themselves to the Party, thereby making an uneasy alliance with the working class, which wants nothing to do with them. In
contrast, the literary writer "by his or her very craft [*métier*] confronts the
contradiction of the particular and the universal" (P 454), simply by using
language in a way that does not attempt to suppress the materiality of the
sign but exploits it to the maximum. As prefigured by Sartre's adaptation
of Valéry's poem "Intérieur," the word has become something like the
paradoxical object, which was the erotic object for Bataille. Here we are
not far from the position *Tel Quel* will assume in its theorizing of transgression.

It is because of these formal (and ontological) properties of language
that the literary writer, who engages with language in its paradoxical totality, can dispense with other displays of engagement.[26] The very existential structure of language as well as of the writer's craft (*métier*) provides the model for engagement that Sartre reformulates here in the following terms: "The engagement of the writer aims to communicate the
incommunicable and to maintain the tension between the whole and the
part, the totality and totalization, the world and being in the world as the
meaning of its work [*le sens de son oeuvre*]" (P 454). The communication
of the uncommunicable involves the universal singular status of "the being in the world of lived experience [*le vécu*]."[27] It is in these specific terms
that the engaged literary writer (now clearly a redundancy) communicates
a meaning. For the only meaning that matters is the "being in the world
of the universal singular"—the ontological condition of both human beings and language.

If we had not already passed through a reading of *Qu'est-ce que la littérature?* that insisted upon a number of implicit anticipations of Sartre's

discussion here, it would be tempting to say that Sartre had reversed himself by 1965, perhaps even become a reader of *Tel Quel*.[28] But it is not enough just to suspect Sartre of stepping back from the imperative of engagement, whose historical moment had passed by the time of the later essay. For *Plaidoyer pour les intellectuels* repeats the thrust of *Qu'est-ce que la littérature?*, or at least the thrust of the reading we have presented here.

Consider the following passage, in which Sartre writes that, if the work of art has all the characteristics of a universal singular,

> it is as if the author had taken the paradox of his or her *human condition* as means and the objectification in the world of this same condition in an object as end. Thus beauty, today, is nothing but the *human condition presented not as facticity* but as produced by a creative freedom (that of the author). And, to the extent that this creative freedom aims at communication, it addresses itself to the creative freedom of the reader and incites it to recompose the work through reading (which is also creation) . . . to freely seize [*saisir*] its own being-in-the-world as if it were the product of its freedom; in other words, as if s/he were the author responsible for his or her being in the world even while undergoing it [*tout en le subissant*] or, if you like, as if s/he were the world freely incarnated [*librement incarné*]. (P 445, my emphasis)[29]

We recognize a reelaboration of the paradoxical dialectic of reading in this passage. When we consider it closely, we see that it provides an important gloss of specific features of *Qu'est-ce que la littérature?* Here the "human condition," to which Sartre also refers in the earlier study where it is conventionally interpreted in more or less Marxist terms, signifies in an ontological/existential register. It is a question of "being in the lived world [*être dans le monde vécu*]," which implies the condition of the universal singular. But this condition is not to be presented in its facticity, that is, through techniques of literary realism or naturalism. Sartre criticizes realism in the strongest terms for portraying a world without freedom. He makes explicit here what we could only read between the lines in *Qu'est-ce que la littérature?*, namely, that "there is no privileged form [*forme prioritaire*]" when it comes to literary engagement. All writers present the human condition in freedom because the human condition—being in the world—corresponds to being in language. The goal of the writer, Sartre affirms, "is in no way to do away with the paradoxical situation of language but to exploit it to the maximum and to make one's being in language the expression of one's being in the world." In this context, to be responsible for the human condition (as ontological condition) comes much closer to Nietzsche, or even to Camus, than to Marx. This kind of responsibility is a form of affirmation.

But how does one make one's being in language the expression of one's being in the world? Through style, as it exploits the materiality of language. The writer, Sartre explains,

uses phrases as agents of ambiguity, as presentification of the structured totality which is the language [*la langue*], [the writer] plays on the plurality of meanings, uses the history of aberrant sounds [*l'histoire des vocables aberrantes*]; far from desiring to combat the limits of its language, he takes advantage of them [*il en use*] . . . style, in fact, communicates no knowledge; *it produces the universal singular* by showing, at the same time, language to be a generality producing the writer and completely conditioning him in his facticity, and the writer as adventure [*l'écrivain comme aventure*], turning back on his language [*se retournant sur son langage*], or assuming its idiotisms and its ambiguities in order to bear witness to its practical singularity and to imprison his relation to the world, as living world [*en tant que vécu*] in the material presence of words. (*P* 448–49, my emphasis)[30]

Here it becomes clear that the literary prose writer's use of language is preeminently poetic. Sartre approaches Valéry's definition of poetry when he explains, concerning a citation from Pascal, that "the meaning of this phrase is universal but the reader learns it through this abrupt nonsignifying singularity, style, which henceforth will attach itself so well to the meaning that one will only be able to think the idea through this singularization" (*P* 449). Valéry defines poetry in very similar terms, as that which refuses paraphrase and demands to be repeated in its material specificity. But is this so surprising? In *Qu'est-ce que la littérature?* Sartre identifies style with a hidden charm, and borrows, as we have seen, from Valéry's *Charmes* when he defines what he calls the "state of mind [*état d'esprit*]" of prose. We have seen the essence of literature, or literary prose, borrowed from poetry, and from a specifically poetic deformation of the conventional topos for the transparency of language usually associated with discursive prose. In *Plaidoyer pour les intellectuels*, Sartre characterizes the contemporary writer as a "poet who declares himself to be a prose writer [*poète qui se déclare prosateur*]" Perhaps it is Sartre who has been hiding poetry beneath a veil of prose.

The Question of History

How, then, are we to think Sartrean engagement? We are familiar with the story of a conversion, or a cure—a cure of Sartre's literary neurosis. "The war had provoked a veritable conversion in him," Simone de Beauvoir writes, " . . . it had revealed to him his own historicity."[31] According to the historian Anna Boschetti, this sort of conversion was the rule, rather than the exception, in the early years following the liberation. "The prewar social and political world was turned upside down," Boschetti writes,

" . . . intellectuals with no particular tendency towards extremism shared
the impression of living through a truly revolutionary situation. . . . In this
context, the attitude of the existentialists reveals itself to be simply a tendency of the period entirely consistent with the mood of the cultural world
as a whole [*conforme à l'humeur de toute l'intelligence légitime*]." It is in
this context, then, that Sartre commits himself to direct political involvement with the Rassemblement Démocratique Révolutionnaire (RDR).
What does this mean for literature, and for his relation to it? Does Sartre
turn his back on literature, or place it in the service of higher values? On
the contrary, says Anna Boschetti. *Qu'est-ce que la littérature?*, and the
theory of engagement more broadly,

[have] nothing to do with the subordination of literature to politics, as Gide and
other partisans of "pure" literature perceived it. *On the contrary, it is a passionate defense of literature against politics.* If Sartre repudiates irresponsibility and
gratuity with such vehemence, it is less to attack the partisans of form . . . than to
cleanse literature of a suspicion, to claim its absolute self-sufficiency [*son auto-
suffisance absolue*]. To proclaim that literature is already intrinsically political is
the best way to dispense with politics in the strict sense to which people would
like to enchain it. (my emphasis)[32]

Who or what wanted to enchain literature? The Communist Party,
Boschetti answers, which enjoyed an unprecedented cultural authority in
the post-Resistance years, and used it to promote "the dogma of action."
Thanks to the cultural authority Sartre had already achieved as both novelist and philosopher, Boschetti argues, he is able to "carry out a brilliant
reversal: he can hold that thinking, literature, not only are action in themselves, but that they are the highest form of action."[33]

Simone de Beauvoir speaks of Sartre's postwar conversion in very similar terms. She describes it as a shift from the register of being—the domain of literature as absolute and of literary glory—to doing.[34] Her analysis confirms that of Boschetti:

When he renounced being and decided to act [*faire*], he required that the work
[*l'œuvre*] always be a call [*appel*] and an engagement. *This did not at all imply
that he scorned literature, but [implied], on the contrary, a desire to restore its dignity;* if it [literature] were by essence divine, one could, by playing distractedly
with the pen, produce a sacred object. . . . So that it would not be degraded to the
status of mere diversion *it was necessary for man to identify it with his very existence, without dividing up his life. Engagement, in sum, is nothing but the total
presence of the writer to his or her writing.*[35]

But de Beauvoir also reveals that there was another reason for Sartre to
want to restore dignity to literature, a more personal reason. In the passage just cited, Simone de Beauvoir has just been discussing the relation-

ship between the "Présentation" of *Les Temps Modernes* (the initial call to engagement, which launched Sartre's new review), and the ambivalence Sartre experienced personally in the face of his overwhelming popular success as the author of *La Nausée*. De Beauvoir tells us that Sartre's favorite fantasy as a child was of himself as *poète maudit*, artist "unknown to all, and whom glory would strike after death or rather, on his deathbed, so that he might enjoy at least some measure of it." What overwhelmed Sartre in his early forties, his companion tells us, was an "idiotic glory":

Compared to the obscurity of Baudelaire, the idiotic glory that had struck Sartre was upsetting. . . . It had a high price. He saw an unexpected audience throughout the world: he saw himself denied that of centuries to come. Eternity had caved in . . . for him this was really the death of God who had survived, up to this point, beneath the mask of words. Sartre owed it to his pride to take on such a total catastrophe. He did so in the "Presentation."

In other words, in addition to the fall into history precipitated by wartime experiences, and the cultural pressure of the electorally legitimized left, there was the question of a paradoxical loss: "Fulfilled beyond measure [*démesurément comblé*] in winning everything, he had lost everything; consenting to lose everything, he nourished the secret hope that everything might be recuperated [*tout lui serait rendu*]" writes Simone de Beauvoir. It is at this point that we read: "He renounced being and decided to act." Being as eternal glory is renounced in favor of action because Sartre has received the indelible sign of its loss: the "idiotic glory" of popular success in the present. Sartre assumes this loss with a theory of attachment to the present: engagement.[36] Ironically, *Qu'est-ce que la littérature?* portrays a historical deterioration of the relations between writer and public at the very moment that Sartre himself "obtained an unexpectedly vast audience throughout the world."[37]

When we look closely at the story of Sartre's conversion, we see that it was overdetermined. This being so, we might wonder about the other conventional story concerning Sartre's career, that of his evolution from literary theorist during the 1940's to political theorist during the 1950's. According to this narrative (one adhered to by Boschetti and Aronson, among others) Sartre began to distance himself from literary engagement and to assume a firmer position vis à vis the Communist Party during the 1950's.[38] Literary engagement, theorized in the "Présentation" and in *Qu'est-ce que la littérature?*, is considered merely a transitional phase between Sartre the literary intellectual and Sartre the militant activist or Marxist theorist. But let us listen again to Simone de Beauvoir's remarks concerning the conversion of the 1940's. In light of the path we have been following here, she suggests a way to understand the place of literary or poetic action—of *poïein*, as Valéry would have it—within the project of a more militant engagement, that is, engagement after the accommodation with Marxism.

Literature, Simone de Beauvoir writes of the postwar period, was no longer something sacred for Sartre; it became a human concern: "Sartre respected literature," she writes, "to the point of confusing its destiny with that of humanity."[39] In the passage from being to doing, she tells us, practice replaced contemplation. We assume de Beauvoir has in mind what Sartre calls the fall into history in *Qu'est-ce que la littérature?* But in *La Force des choses* she reminds us that Sartre was intellectually very uneasy with the concept of history during this period, especially the Marxist concept of materialist history.[40] What Sartre objected to, she explains, was the idea of a dialectic of nature: "he analyzed . . . materialism as a revolutionary myth. At this point his thinking stopped short, for he was vague on the relation between freedom and situation, and even more so on the question of history."[41]

This will change with the *Question of Method* and the *Critique of Dialectical Reason*. The opening pages of the *Critique* review the charges against the dialectic of nature alluded to by Simone de Beauvoir. "The dialectic of nature," Sartre writes, "is nature without men. . . . Concrete man is removed—an absolute object is put in its place."[42] To avoid determinism, Sartre declares, Marxism "must become historical materialism, that is to say a materialism *from within*"—we hear echoes of the interiority Sartre inscribed ambivalently in the essence of prose through his adaptation of the lines taken from Valéry's poem. "This materialism," Sartre continues, "if it exists, can be true only within the limits of our social universe" (CR 33). History will be Marxist, and material, Sartre writes, but it must also always be human. Marxist dialectical materialism, therefore, must be corrected by anthropology, and anthropology by history. Likewise, I would argue, in order to be reconfigured as a "materialism from within," that is, in order to be human, history must in turn be corrected by art. The model for Sartre's theory of praxis is the act of reading as portrayed in the second chapter of *Qu'est-ce que la littérature?*. The dialectical paradox of reading evolves into the movement of dialectical reason. The free praxis of unification rewrites the myth of prose (and the magic of reading) in a Marxist idiom. Literature as action—"to speak is to act"—becomes praxis, the living logic of freedom, in the *Critique*.

Dialectical rationality, the "living logic of action," involves a "complex play" of praxis and totalization. We have already seen this complex play elaborated as reciprocal recognition in the paradoxical dialectic of reading, for reading exemplifies totalization. In the *Critique*, Sartre develops his concept of totalization, a concept that will become identified with history as truth, in opposition to totalities—things such as tools or machines that lend themselves to technological procedures and to analytical reason. We recognize the same fundamental opposition between instrumental and noninstrumental relations that Bataille theorizes in terms of the opposition between restricted and general economies.

Even in *Qu'est-ce que la littérature?*, the structure of the literary event functions as a model for the social domain: that is, for the utopian order of concrete mutual recognition of freedoms, and for the concrete overcoming of the hierarchical master/slave dialectic as the truth of social life in a class society. In the third chapter of this text, "For Whom Does One Write?", which presents a historical analysis of literary institutions, the discussion of the public concretizes and expands the abstract meditation on the position of the reader given in the previous chapter. The discussion of social or political freedom concretizes the theme of moral or metaphysical freedom—the freedom of the invention of writing and of the reinvention of reading. The essence of literature ("formal literature") provides a regulative idea both for "concrete literature" and for engagement in the social or political register. After the presentation of his schematic social history of literature, Sartre comments, "these considerations remain arbitrary if one does not place [them] back in the perspective of a work of art, that is, of a free and unconditioned call to freedom" (154). Sartre adds: "Our descriptions have enabled us to perceive a kind of dialectic of the idea of literature," such that, without trying to write a literary history (a *histoire des belles lettres*), we can "restore the movement of this dialectic throughout the last few centuries in order to discover, at the end, even if only as ideal, *the pure essence of the work of art*, and, conjointly, the type of public—*that is, of society*—that it requires" (155–56, my emphasis).

The very essence of literature, then, requires a certain sociopolitical reality. It requires it structurally in order to fulfill its essence concretely.[43] But, as we have already seen, "concrete literature [*la littérature en acte*] can only be equal to its full essence in a classless society" (160). Only after the revolution (only at the end of history) would the abstract figure of the reader become actualized as a universal public.[44] The essence of literature, then, yields the utopian social model precisely as correction to the violent and oppressive structure of the master/slave dialectic, which, in Kojève's reading of Hegel, corresponds with the history of class struggle. The ontology of the literary event itself, as founding moment of value (the absolute value of freedom as condition of possibility for the invention of any value, "the recognition of freedom by itself"), provides the model for the utopian goal in social relations. As such, it calls for its own concrete realization through revolution.

Revolution requires what Sartre calls "invention." "Historical action," he writes in this third chapter of *Qu'est-ce que la littérature?*, "never comes down to a choice between two raw givens, it is always characterized by the invention of new solutions . . . when an object is hidden from view [*caché à tous les yeux*] it has to be invented from scratch in order to be discovered/uncovered [*pour pouvoir le découvrir*]" (292). Invention itself is a form of unveiling, a bringing to appearance (or into being) of something hidden. Through the figure of invention, then, history is identified with the literary or creative process. What is more, to the extent that it can engender its own readership, Sartre suggests that literature can potentially resolve the antinomies of class contradiction. "In a word," he concludes, "literature is, by essence, the subjectivity of a society in perpetual revolution. In such a society, *it would resolve the antinomy between speech and action*" (163, my emphasis).[45]

"It is necessary to historicize the good will [*bonne volonté*] of the reader," Sartre writes in *Qu'est-ce que la littérature?* But it is not until the *Critique of Dialectical Reason* and the analysis of praxis as "logic of freedom" that Sartre effectively inserts the essence of literature into history as process. History is now considered a movement of totalization, like reading, instead of an accumulation of past events or relations. Sartre's theory of the collective agent of praxis, the group in fusion, develops his treatment of the three-term relation writer-text-reader introduced in his postwar essay. The structure of mediated and reciprocal recognition, which lay at the core of his conception of the essence of literature as "gift ceremony," returns in the dynamic multiplicity of the group in fusion in the *Critique of Dialectical Reason*.

Sartre emphasizes here that the difference between the series of the practico-inert and the group in fusion—the free subject of praxis that operates in a mode of totalization—involves the shift from a binary structure to a ternary one.[46] The fused group is defined as a three-term relation that includes self, other, and the third party. The position of the third party is mobile and relative. Each one can occupy that position with respect to another. The function of this term is to mediate reciprocity and thereby to neutralize the self-alienating, or oppositional, feature of the intersubjective encounter. To this extent, we could say that revolutionary praxis, the collective action of a group subject, activates the ternary structure of the literary event (the relation writer-text-reader) in relation to the invention— or co-creation—of history. It does so through revolutionary action.[47]

In the *Critique*, Sartre cites Marx from the *Eighteenth Brumaire* to the effect that "men make their own history . . . but under circumstances given and transmitted from the past." A little further on he rephrases Marx's declaration in the following terms: "The crucial discovery of dialectical investigation is that man is 'mediated' by things to the same extent as things are mediated by man" (CD 80). This was precisely the lesson of chapter 2 of *Qu'est-ce que la littérature?* in which recognition was mediated by text, thereby defusing the violence of the intersubjective encounter. The literary work, as both "thing" mediated by man and "thing" that mediated man (this was the thrust of the paradoxical dialectic of reading as recognition scene) enabled the mediated reciprocity of freedoms. This event becomes paradigmatic for the group in fusion in which the third party is modeled after the work.[48]

If we have considered Sartre's rethinking of the question of history in relation to his analysis of the essence of literature in sympathetic terms, Lévi-Strauss reaches a similar conclusion, though he formulates it as an attack. Sartre's conception of history in the *Critique*, he claims, "plays exactly the role of myth"; it "corresponds to no reality."[49] Lévi-Strauss returns to Sartre the charge Sartre had made against Bataille in his review of *l'Expérience intérieure*: that of being a "new mystic." The structuralist anthropologist charges Sartre with a "mystical conception of history" (SM 256). To the extent that history is presented in the *Critique* as a developing totalization, and that the model for this totalization, as I am arguing, is the literary event—specifically, in *Qu'est-ce que la littérature?* the reading of a novelistic fiction—I would suggest that if history corresponds to no reality it is precisely because it is, like eroticism, essentially fictive in its structure. We must read history (*histoire*) in terms of the double meaning it enjoys in French, where it signifies both history and fiction. Through this double meaning we can discern a certain pattern. In *La Nausée* it is a question of giving up the role of the historian (historian of fact) for the possibilities of the novel. In *Qu'est-ce que la littérature?*, an essence of art provides the kernel for the theory of engagement. Finally, in the *Critique of Dialectical Reason*, Sartre writes the dialectic of praxis, or historical action, in terms of the structure of the essence of literary art. Obviously, to the extent that Sartre's theory of action relies upon a dynamic literary structure, we must rethink Bataille's declaration concerning the incompatibility of literature and action.

And Valéry

There is one more question we must take up before we return to the issue of the ideological incompatibilities—and intellectual proximities—between Bataille and Sartre. If writing (or the literary event) enjoys a special privilege in Sartre's thinking, and if, as *Plaidoyer* reveals, Sartre's attitude to literary language is at times a poetic one, why does he continue to nominally subordinate poetry to prose? I would suggest that the insistence on prose does not reflect an esthetic preference or a political imperative but a theoretical pressure. The privilege of prose is a function of the importance of the practice of reading (and subsequently of praxis) as totalization.

In *Qu'est-ce que la littérature?* Sartre analyzes the paradoxical dialectic of reading in relation to the novel form. This is because the novel presents a totality realized only through a process of totalization. The meaning of the text must emerge as a function of this process. "The hundred thousand words lined up in a book can be read one by one without the meaning of the work springing forth [*sans que le sens de l'œuvre jaillise*] . . . meaning is not the sum of the words but their organic totality" (51)—that is, a totalization. Sartre requires that the temporality of reading correspond with the temporality of the form: narrative. The issue here is not realism but time.[50] The meaning of the text must unfold in time. To the extent that it does, the event of reading can return in the elaboration of Sartre's theory of praxis. Indeed, even the distinction between totalities (or series) and totalization (or the group in fusion) Sartre theorizes in the *Critique* is anticipated in the account of reading in *Qu'est-ce que la littérature?*. If reading involves both the "restoration of independent causal series . . . and . . . the expression of a deeper finality," it is the "causality which is the appearance . . . and it is the finality which is the deeper reality" (61). Finality implies totalization and requires the totalizing act of reading, as opposed to the totality engendered through series.[51]

From Sartre's point of view, there must be a parallel between the ongoing time of reading and the unfolding time of the story told. The theater provides Sartre with the maximum temporal correspondence between these frameworks.[52] It removes not only the omniscient narrator (to which Sartre strenuously objects) but any narrative presence at all. In this respect the theater might signify for Sartre an ideal actualization of the novel in its reading in the sense of a perfect correspondence between these two durations. Sartre claims that poetry is unreadable, not only because it turns words into things (we see both in *Plaidoyer* and in Sartre's response to Genet that Sartre can appreciate the materiality of the signifier) but also because it lacks a temporal thrust or *élan*. The modern poem, in particular, exists on the page like a painting; its unity, to the extent that it proposes one, is purely formal. It composes itself, through rereading, as a kind of static entity—a totality—instead of emerging through a synthetic process of totalization.[53]

It is ironic to consider that precisely this aspect of the myth of prose—the magic of reading—might be a gift of poetry. In the introduction to the course on poetics, the series of lectures Valéry presented at the Collège de France in 1937, we find an analysis of writing and reading as two consti-

tutive moments in the production of the work of art, an analysis that anticipates, in striking fashion, what Sartre will call the "paradoxical dialectic" of reading. In the opening remarks of his lecture, Valéry makes it
clear that he is not talking about poetics in the narrow sense. Nor is he
only interested in fine art. He is concerned more broadly with *poïein*,
which he glosses as "an action which culminates in works of the
mind/spirit (*l'esprit*)." Valéry analyzes this poïein in terms of two complementary systems: production and consumption (reading). Here, as in
Sartre, both moments are necessary for the work to be a work. And here,
as in Sartre, the interaction of the two systems involves a dialectic of freedoms and an excessive economy—the economy of charm.

The agency of poïetic production is "l'esprit," which is not a metaphysical entity, for Valéry, but a "force of transformation" which operates in a combinatory manner. "L'esprit" means concrete freedom ("la liberté en acte").[54] If writing involves such a poïein (action or production, or
faire), reading is a re-action, or repetition, of the processes of production.
The moment of reading, Valéry affirms, reconstitutes a state of mind analogous to the one involved in the production of the work: freedom in action. In the case of poetry, in particular, the economy of this poïein, this
production/consumption, is paradoxical, as it will be in Sartre. "The more
we give," Valéry writes of the experience of the reader of poetry, "the more
we want to give even as we believe we are receiving. . . . We feel that we
are possessors, even as we are magnificently possessed."[55] This is precisely
the poetic economy of what Valéry calls "charm." It appears to be this
economy that Sartre takes up again in the name of generosity when he
writes in *Qu'est-ce que la littérature?*, ten years after Valéry's course at
the Collège de France, "The more we experience our freedom, the more
we recognize that of the other, the more [the author] requires of us, the
more we require of him or her" (58).

It is precisely this "mutual possession" that constitutes the essence of
the work of art in Valéry's poetics. This is what brings the work into being. "The work of the *esprit* only exists in action [*en acte*]. Outside of this
action, what remains is nothing but an object that offers no particular relation to the spirit/mind [*esprit*]" (1349), Valéry writes. Reading endows
the word on the page with meaning and value; it gives it, in Valéry's
words, the "force and form of action." This is the crucial word for Sartre. Indeed, Valéry anticipates Sartre's resolution of the antinomy between
speech and action through a dialectic of reading. "Remove the voice and
the requisite voice [*Otez la voix et la voix qu'il faut*]," he continues, speaking of the reading voice that animates and performs the text, and "everything becomes arbitrary. The poem changes into a series of signs that are
related to one another only by being physically traced one after the other"

(1349)—mere black smudges on white paper, Sartre will write a few years later. Reading is magic—a charm—and prose a myth of poetry.[56] Ironically we recognize that the antinomy Sartre set out to resolve through the myth of prose—the antinomy between speech and action—has already been addressed, and to a certain extent resolved, by Valéry in the register of pure poetry. "It is truly strange that no one has thought to consider language as action," Valéry wrote in his notebook of 1942, " . . . to speak is to act [*parler, c'est faire*]." His course of poetics, begun in 1937, is premised upon just this affirmation: poïein is defined as "an activity [*un faire*] which ends up as a work of the spirit [*qui s'achève . . . en œuvres de l'esprit*]" (1342).

Valéry's analysis of reading as reinvention—what Sartre will call reading as "directed creation"—echoes an analysis Bergson had proposed in *Matière et mémoire*. Bergson cites the work of two experimental psychologists who, he claims, have refuted the doctrine that we read by deciphering one letter at a time. These researchers, he declares, have established that the process of reading is "a veritable labor of divination, our mind/spirit picking up certain characteristic traits here and there and filling in everything in between with memory images which, projected onto the paper, substitute themselves for the printed characters and give the illusion of them." Sartre's version of this analysis substitutes emotion for what Bergson called memories-images (*souvenirs-images*), but we recognize in Bergson the emphasis on "the living reality of the word embedded in the sentence [*qui s'organise avec la phrase*]" which anticipates what Sartre will call "organic reading."[57] We also find an anticipation of reading as reinvention, a concept that we find in both Valéry's poetics and Sartre's analysis: "Thus, we create or reconstruct incessantly," Bergson concludes, " . . . our distinct perception is truly comparable to a closed circle in which the perceptual image, directed to the mind [*esprit*] and the memory image thrown out into space run after one another" (*HB* 249). Finally, we recognize in Bergson's analysis of language acquisition an anticipation of Sartre's statement in chapter 2 of *Qu'est-ce que la littérature?* that we do not read word by word. "We do not learn to pronounce words first, but phrases," Bergson argues, " . . . a word always takes on its structure [*s'anatomose*] according to those which accompany it and according to the gait [*allure*] and the movement of the phrase of which it is a part, it takes on different features: just as each note of a melody vaguely reflects the entire theme" (HB 262, *Matière et mémoire*). Here Bergson compares the process of reading as reinvention to the unfolding of a musical phrase, which for Bergson is a figure for the experience of duration.[58] As we can see, the vitalist philosopher Bergson anticipates the distinction between series and totalization that will play such an important role for Sartre in the *Critique*. To the extent that Sartre's account of reading (and of praxis) echoes that of Bergson as well as Valéry, it is the vitality of prose that holds interest for Sartre, not its capacity to engender referential truth through representation. Sartre's notion of "action" in the theory of engagement is closer to a vitalist notion of action as activity in process—as freedom in action, or as the *vécu* (lived experience)—than to a Hegelian model of instrumental action. Paradoxically, this is revealed most clearly in the apparently least Bergsonian and most Marxist of texts—the *Critique of Dialectical Reason*.

And Bergson

Conventional accounts of precursors of Sartre's thought emphasize the German philosophers: Kant, Husserl, Hegel, and Heidegger. It was the French philosopher Bergson, however, who determined Sartre's choice to become a philosopher.[59] In light of the questions we have been investigating here, specifically the question of the incompatibility between Bataille and Sartre, it is helpful to remember that Bergson's philosophy of life, which opposed the mechanistic sciences and philosophies of knowledge, opened the existential question. *L'Evolution créatrice*, which dates from 1907 but was republished in 1941, asks in its opening line: "What . . . is the meaning of the word 'to exist'?" The question of existence, Bergson asserts, requires an inner knowledge, something quite different from our external judgments concerning inert objects. It is just this kind of "inner knowledge" that Sartre wants to inject into the concept of materialist history, as we have seen in our discussion of the *Critique of Dialectical Reason*.

Existence, Bergson insists, is synonymous with duration and vitality. Duration is defined as "the continual progress of the past that eats away at the future and fills it up [*gonfle*] as it moves forward," a definition that returns in Sartre's elaboration of the metaphysical structure of project in *Being and Nothingness*. The question of existence, and of its temporal dynamism, leads Bergson to the problem of the constitution of the self and its identity in *L'Evolution créatrice*: "What is our character," Bergson asks, "if not the condensation of the history we have lived?"[60] This is precisely the dimension of interiority that Sartre wants to reintroduce into the Marxist theory of history in the *Critique of Dialectical Reason*. Bergson argues that identity is a gradual condensation that always remains open in an indeterminate relation to the present, or to the future becoming present. "Our personality," he argues, " . . . constructs itself at every instant out of accumulated experience" (HB 499). He invokes the painted portrait as a figure for subjective identity:

The finished portrait is explicable . . . but even with the knowledge that explains it, no one, not even the artist, could have foreseen exactly what the portrait would be like, for to predict it would mean to have produced it before it was produced. So it is for the moments of our life, of which we are the artisans. Each one of them is a kind of creation . . . thus each one of our states, while it is part of us, changes our person, being the new form that we have just given ourselves.

Here is a notion of form as autoproduction that links form to action. For it is a question of action (*faire*) in this passage where existence is conceived in terms of duration and freedom means contingency. "It is thus correct to say," Bergson continues in a preview of Sartre, "that what we do depends upon who we are . . . but we must add *that we are, to a certain extent, what we do, and that we are continually creating ourselves*" (HB 500, my emphasis). This is what Bergson calls invention, and it is such a concept of invention that returns in Sartre's discussion of history both in *Qu'est-ce que la littérature?* and in the *Critique of Dialectical Reason.*[61]

Speaking of the emotional dimension of experience in his *Essai*, Bergson describes how ordinary social life flattens out our feelings and vitiates our experience of them as qualities. This is the world of the "conventional self," the world that is structured and contained by the pressures of social interaction and language. "But if now," Bergson adds,

some bold novelist, tearing off the carefully woven veil of our conventional self, were to show us a fundamental absurdity beneath this apparent logic, [to show us] beneath this juxtaposition of simple states an infinite interpenetration of a thousand diverse impressions which have already ceased to exist the moment one names them, we would praise such a novelist for having known us better than we know ourselves.[62]

Such a novelist, Bergson continues, would be able to convey the extraordinary and illogical experience of duration. He would give us a vision of the material world (*la matière*) "perhaps tiring for your imagination, but pure, and free of what the requirements of life [*les exigences de la vie*] make you add in external perception"—a vision, in other words, of the "moving continuity of the real" that corresponds to the experience of contingency in, or as, duration.

We could say that Sartre responded to Bergson's challenge with his novel *La Nausée*, for such is the revelation experienced by Antoine Roquentin.[63] Roquentin is disengaged from life, ready to have the veil torn away. The first symptom of his malaise is a breakdown of the instrumental relation to objects that produces a feeling of "disgust [*écoeurment*]." But this nausea is not without a certain pleasure at times, especially when Antoine is able to listen to his favorite ragtime tune in the cafe. The pleasure is quite explicitly a function of an unusual experience of time. It comes from a "tight duration of the music, that runs through and through our time and refuses it and tears it away from its dry little points; there is another time." When Antoine hears the song, "the duration of the music expanded, became swollen like a torrent. It filled the room . . . crushing our impoverished time against the walls. I am *in* the music."[64] In *Matière et mémoire* Bergson describes the qualitative synthesis of the experience of concrete duration in terms of the unity of a musical phrase (HB 74). In *La Nausée* it is through the experience of just such a musical phrase that Roquentin achieves something like an immediate experience of duration.[65]

The crucial revelation of duration as heterogeneous fusion occurs in the garden with the revelation of the absolute: the absurd as radical contingency. It begins, we remember, in the tramway on the way to the garden when language breaks down. It is no longer able to separate distinct things, to delimit subject from object: "Things were delivered of their names. . . . I am in the middle of things, unnameable . . . they are there before me" (N 179). Roquentin leaps off the tramway. He finds himself in the Public Garden—"I am suffocating, existence is penetrating me all over, through the eyes, the nose, the mouth . . . And all of a sudden, *the veil is torn [se déchire]*, I understood, I saw" (N 180, my emphasis).[66] In this vision, "existence was suddenly *unveiled* . . . it was the very stuff things are made of [*c'était la pâte même des choses*]." Individuated objects—the garden gate, the bench, the lawn—become mere appearance, "a varnish. This varnish had melted, there remained monstrous soft masses in disorder" (N 182). All that is left is an experience of qualities. Sartre concludes that the world of reason is not the world of existence (N 184) and that existence involves contingency.[67] This experience of contingency is a revelation of the absolute. It is "the key to existence, the key to my nauseas, to my very life." After the revelation, after the experience of the disorder that underlies any attempt at rational explanation, Antoine is free to abandon the historian's craft, free to leave Bouville—and free, perhaps, to write a novel.

"In reality," Bergson writes in *L'Evolution créatrice*, "a human being is a center of action. S/he represents a certain amount of contingency introducing itself into the world, that is, a certain quantity of possible action" (HB 717). Although Sartre will frequently inflect the term "action" in the direction of instrumentality, specifically in his adaptation of Husserl's theory of intentional consciousness, there is another inscription of action that refers us to Bergson's conception of free spontaneity and invention. For Bergson, the faculty of knowledge, which is an instrumental relation, is "annexed to the capacity for action" (HB 489). "The universe endures [*dure*]. . . . Duration signifies invention" (HB 503). Action is thought in relation to duration and spontaneity or invention. Invention, the term that returns in Sartre both in *Qu'est-ce que la littérature?* and in the *Critique of Dialectical Reason*, occurs as a function of the freedom of *l'esprit*, *l'esprit* that "gives more than it has" in what we could call a gesture of radical expenditure. For both Bergson and Sartre, action is a corollary of the dynamism of time, the lived time that implies vital interiority.

And Bataille

In the 1940's, Bataille elaborated his notion of a poetry of the event (*poésie de l'événement*) or of the instant in response to the ideological pressures of Sartrean engagement. The instant is posed in response to the thinking of project. It refers us to the moment of fusion Bataille evokes in the opening paragraph of his essay *L'Erotisme*. The instant involves an experience of immediacy, or "continuity," that Bataille also calls "communication." But it no more implies an experience of presence than it implies communication in the more recent sense of a representational use of language, that is, "communication" in the sense of Jürgen Habermas. The "instant," for Bataille, implies precisely a loss of presence in an awareness of temporal force or dynamism. In his essay "De l'âge de pierre à Jacques Prévert" Bataille, sounding much like Valéry, enjoins the poet to "cry out what is [*crier alors ce qui est*]." But he goes on to warn that the "misery of poetry" is a desire for permanence. "Between the man who cries out and the event that is," he writes, "language usually interposes itself, whose generality and immaterial nature inevitably yield duration, the immutable, and the Academy" (207). On first impression it might seem that Bataille is opposing the instant precisely to something like Bergson's notion of duration. Upon closer inspection, however, we recognize that Bataille is reiterating an earlier Bergsonian critique of language, which argues that language "crushes [*écrase*] immediate consciousness," that intuitive consciousness that yields an experience of duration. Duration, as Bergson presents it in the *Essai sur les données immédiates de la conscience* (as we shall see in more detail further on) is a dynamic, temporal, heterogeneous experience of qualitative intensities. It is the imposition of language upon this immediate experience that immobilizes the fluid dynamics of lived time and interrupts the experience of what both Bergson and Bataille call "continuity." As Sasso suggests, the notion of the Instant, in Bataille, is linked etymologically to "moment" or "moviementum (mouvement)."[68] The sacred and poetry, Bataille writes, are "par essence changement."[69] The "moral of the instant" involves "free mental activity" (209).[70] Sensibility, Bataille writes, is the domain of the instant.[71] Indeed, the instant as event of the sacred leads us not away from Bergsonian duration but to it.[72]

As Anna Boschetti among others has argued, the discourse of Bergson, which was immensely powerful through the 1920's, was subsequently displaced by that of Hegel (and Freud) during the 1930's as philosophers and thinkers grappled with the question of Marxism, the fact of communism in Russia, and the influence of the Communist Party in France. The importance of Hegel was reinforced, in this context, by the magnetism of Kojève. The discourse of Bergson is buried, at least on the level of explicit discussion. Indeed, for ideological and political reasons I shall take up further on, Bergson is not merely forgotten but systematically effaced. By the 1930's it is fashionable to be anti-Bergsonian.

If one cannot engage with Bergson's thinking philosophically in any explicit way, one can perhaps reengage with a version of it through the emerging field of sociology. I would propose that what Bataille rediscovers in the discourse of the sacred that he receives through the channels of ethnography and anthropology is a version of the vitalist thinking that had been popularized by the philosophy of Bergson (and a proliferation of Bergsonisms) during the teens and 1920's. Georges Sorel, for example, who represents a Bergsonism of the extreme left, participated in the Collège de Sociologie. The sacred provides a kind of collective equivalent of what Bergson analyzed in philosophical terms as an individual experience of intuition that could yield an experience of the absolute as real duration.[73] Bataille's use of the opposition between the sacred and the profane recapitulates Bergson's opposition between the vital and the automatic, that is, between pure duration as radical heterogeneity and the homogeneous "spatial" time of conventional experience. The collective experience of the sacred, lived as heterogeneous fusion and continuity that explodes the apparent coherence of the world faced by the discontinuous subject, recapitulates a Bergsonian thinking of duration on the collective level. The sacred yields the collective equivalent of what Bergson called "the deep self [*le moi profond*]" or the "fundamental self."

Bataille's formulation of the operation of poetry in his essay on Baudelaire anticipates the structure of transgression as it is theorized in *L'Erotisme*—as an injunction to *saisir le désaisissement*, to "bring the loss of self (or of consciousness) to consciousness." Reconsidering this formulation, we can now say that the *désaisissement* suggests the sacred moment of heterogeneity, which refers us back to the heterogeneous fusion of Bergson's analysis of real duration. The lucidity of this moment, the *saisir* of this *désaisissement*, marks a Hegelian (or Kojèvian) moment of self-consciousness, or a formally homologous moment—recognition by a woman. It is this structure of lucidity that requires the moment of figuration, or fiction, through which the transgression is lived.

Bataille's involvement with the sacred implied a commitment to a certain notion of action that he thematized in opposition to what he perceived as Breton's estheticism, or overestimation of poetry, in the 1930's. In the 1940's, however, it was turned against Sartre in the name of a refusal of action, which Bataille associated with poetry. By this time Bataille's view of political revolution had changed. It no longer exemplified for him irrational passion and energy, analogous to religious or sacred experience. In the post-Stalin, post-Hitler years, it had come to stand for the collective dimension of rational, utilitarian calculation. To the extent that action for Bataille had been pertinent in relation to the question of revolution, the political disaffection implies a shift in his discourse of action. Henceforth he understands action in relation to the polemic with Sartre. He construes the Sartrean imperative for action in terms of the existentialist notion of project, which he understands to mean a subordination of the present in view of an intentional, and utilitarian, action projected into the future. This, almost by definition, corresponds to the dynamics of the utilitarian economy in Bataille's terms.

The question of action, and of its economy and temporality, lies at the heart of the ideological disagreement between Bataille and Sartre. For Bataille, there is a fundamental incompatibility between poetry and action, when action is construed in the sense of project, that is, as useful action. For him, poetry itself *is* action, but it is action as event, the experience of being Bataille thematizes in terms of the instant in specific opposition to Sartre's intentional notion of project. "I go on about this at length," Bataille writes in 1946, "because today the problem is obfuscated by the polemic. . . . Is the writer responsible? Is s/he engaged?"[74] From Bataille's point of view, existentialism represents an evacuation of the sacred, a "flattening to the level of known things."[75] Engagement implies useful action, which inevitably forfeits the experience of the present moment in the name of a future goal.

As we have seen in some detail, however, the notion of action at stake at the deepest level of Sartre's thinking of engagement is not utilitarian. It does not subordinate literature to utilitarian ends or impose values to be upheld or represented in art. Indeed, it has more in common with the pure poet Valéry than with any ideology of socialist realism. Sartrean engagement requires a notion of action as free invention. Bataille and Sartre share an inheritance from Bergson that brings them closer together than the polemical rhetoric of the exchanges between them would suggest. For quite different ideological reasons, this inheritance had to be cut off. It thus became more difficult to retrieve the proximities that nuanced the "incompatibilities" between their respective positions.

We have read Bataille's *L'Erotisme* as a strategic writing-together of philosophy (Hegel as interpreted by Kojève) and anthropology (the universal rule of the prohibition of incest, and correlatively the economy of gift expenditure associated with the moment of transgression). Although not an explicitly political gesture, Bataille's insertion of the ethnographic distinction into the discourse of philosophy can be seen as a response to political pressures. Not least of these was the surrealist declaration of support for the Communist Party, which prompted the defection of those who came to be known as dissident surrealists—a group that included Antonin Artaud and Michel Leiris as well as Bataille.

Bataille's break from Breton was followed by Bataille's own problematic version of engagement during the 1930's. He passes from the dissident surrealist milieu to the dissident communist group of Boris Souvarine, Le Cercle Démocratique. We remember that it was in the review associated with this group, *La Critique sociale*, that Bataille published "La Notion de dépense." Bataille appeals to the economy of the potlatch to characterize the experience of social and political revolution. Like the early Sartre, Bataille does not accept the orthodox Marxist conception of history. From his point of view dialectical materialism is a version of economic determinism where the "utilitarian economy dictates." To the extent that ethnographic data concerning the potlatch had revealed to anthropologists a structure of symbolic exchange that does not conform to the rule of productive utilitarian exchange that lies at the heart of the Marxist conception of history, "La Notion de dépense" can be considered a critique of totalitarianism from a perspective that privileges superstructural cultural features over utilitarian economic ones.

Bataille's period of engagement roughly corresponds with the years of Alexandre Kojève's lectures on Hegel's *Phenomenology*, ongoing between the years of 1936 and 1939.[76] Bataille claims to leave these lectures completely overwhelmed—"broken, crushed, ten times killed [*rompu, broyé, tué dix fois*]"—because their impact on him was so strong.[77] Here is where philosophy and revolution converge. Whereas Souvarine was a dissident communist, Kojève was a faithful one. His interpretation of Hegel emphasizes a dialectical development of history toward a revolutionary end of history. The Russian philosopher orients his reading of Hegel around the master/slave dialectic, which Kojève reads as an account of class struggle. Kojève interprets Hegel to say that the slave, through his or her work, can achieve a position of mastery. From his revolutionary perspective, Kojève emphasizes Hegel's philosophical account of the end of history defined in terms of human action, that is, in terms of the negativity of consciousness with respect to the givens of nature. Whereas Hegel discerned the end of history in the figure of Napoleon, founder of the modern state, Kojève identified the end of history with Stalin. He therefore preached that the end of history was imminent.

This argument made a deep and lasting impression on Bataille, one that would affect his relationship to the political field and nourish his fascination with the question of the sacred. When one accepts the view that history as action is drawing to a close, the question becomes: What happens next? How can one think a "negativity without any use" when action would be displaced by desire? For Bataille the compelling scenario of the end of historical action became an added incentive to appeal to prehistorical experiences in order to work out ways of coping with a posthistorical moment. During the 1930's, then, Bataille is involved with an interrogation of the notions of action, knowledge, and desire in intimate dialogue with the philosophy of Hegel; an ambivalent relation to the practical ethos of extreme left politics; and an increasing fascination with the sacred.

In *Qu'est-ce que la littérature?* Sartre has also combined elements from Kojève's Hegel (the recognition scene as a passage to objectivity, and the question of positions of essentiality and inessentiality) with anthropological structures (gift exchange, as analyzed by Mauss and Lévy-Bruhl's conception of the "primitive" mentality and of magic). Though they do so in quite different ways, both Sartre and Bataille appeal to anthropological structures to correct the Hegelian scene of recognition and to resolve (and politically displace) the question of its violence. Whereas Bataille posed erotic transgression as answer to the question of philosophy (Hegel), Sartre writes the structure of reciprocity—or its economy—back into philosophy, specifically into the ethics of Kant. Sartre reads the freedom associated with the anthropological structure of reciprocal giving—the freedom of generosity or *dépense*—in terms of the Kantian realm of practical freedom, that other unconditioned realm of desire, desire in the mode of *volonté*, or will.[78]

There are proximities between the "paradoxical object" of Bataille's analysis of transgression in eroticism—the figure of the woman who enables the dialectic necessary to eroticism—and the dialectical paradox of reading that lies at the heart of Sartre's conception of both the literary event and engagement. Eroticism "corrects" the violent scene of the struggle for recognition in Hegel—the master/slave dialectic—and rewrites it in the nonviolent register of the amorous embrace. As we have seen, eroticism corresponds to an ahistorical mode of experience, one that would pertain to the notion of the end of history as this had been promulgated by the teachings of Kojève. It is the phenomenology of this spirit that Bataille gives us in his study of eroticism. Similarly, the essence of literature that Sartre presents through the dialectical paradox of reading in his theory of engagement corresponds to a fiction of the end of history—the classless society in which the essence of literature could become concretely realized. Like transgression, this essence of literature involves a correction of the Hegelian scene of recognition. Here the master/slave dialectic, which establishes positions of social dominance, is replaced by a mutual recognition of freedoms. This event grounds a conception of value; Sartre characterizes it as a specifically esthetic experience—an "esthetic modification of experience"—enabled by the literary work of art. Freedom determines the conception of value as act of free valuation. To this extent, it determines the notion of task, or project, that we associate with engagement. It is to freedom, and to freedom alone, Sartre affirms, that the writer is committed.[79] Engagement is not opposed to belief in an absolute value of art. On the contrary, an equation of literature and the absolute is itself the very mechanism of engagement, and not just of literary commitment. As we have seen, this equation is crucial to Sartre's elaboration of the notion of historical or political action in the *Critique of Dialectical Reason*.

CHAPTER 4

Valéry

The Work of Perfecting and the Chemistry of the Mind

Here is a man who presents himself as rational, cold, methodical, etc.

    We shall assume that he is just the opposite, and that what he appears to be is a function of his reaction against what he is.

           —Valéry, "Instants"

In the opening declaration of the review *Tel Quel*, Valéry is held up against Sartre in the following terms:

What needs to be said today is that writing is no longer conceivable without a clear anticipation [*prévision*] of its powers . . . a determination to give poetry the very highest value [*le plus haute place de l'esprit*]. All the rest will not be literature [*Tout le reste ne sera pas littérature*]. In this way the written work [*l'œuvre*] can truly become, in the words of Valéry, an "enchanted edifice."[1]

We are within the formula of the conventional opposition between poetry and action upon which, as we have seen, Bataille insisted in his letter to René Char, and which we have problematized in the preceding chapter. But if Valéry can be opposed to Sartre in a spirit of modernist avant-gardism in 1960, he soon becomes a figure of reaction in relation to writers such as Breton, Bataille, and Artaud. "The French avant-garde," Adorno writes, "has customarily placed Valéry among the reactionaries . . . to the right of Baudelaire . . . because of his authoritarian and classical cult of form."[2] This is the stereotype we would like to challenge.

    As Adorno's remark suggests, a version of the "incompatibility" between literature and action that Bataille identified in the context of engagement also resides within the literary term of that opposition, where we find a conflict between "action" poets (or pure poets) and non-action poets—artists of automatism or transgression.[3] It is as if *Tel Quel* catches up with this debate when a notion of significance (or textual productivity) displaces the initial high-modernist esthetic orientation of the review.

In this context, Valéry comes to stand for a hyper-intellectual poetics of effort and work that is now refuted by avant-garde theorists of textual productivity, itself modeled after a version of automatism. However, just as Sartre has been misunderstood because of a misperception concerning the status of action within the framework of literary engagement, so Valéry has been misinterpreted because of a comparable misreading of the term "action" and the associated ideas of effort, work, and will (*volonté*) as they pertain to his poetics. These are the notions I would like to explore in this chapter.

A poetics of work emerges historically with Baudelaire's rejection of a romantic notion of genius (one that appealed to an experience of inspiration associated with beautiful nature) in favor of a modern appreciation of the artificial. A modernist poetics of calculation reaches its high point with Valéry's presentation of the genius of Mallarmé, who, in Valéry's words, "carried the problem of the will [*volonté*] in art to the ultimate degree of perfection."[4] Valéry's essays on Mallarmé, published between 1920 and 1944, forged the myth of Mallarmé as genius of a pure modernist poetics of perfection. What Valéry especially admired in this poetry, he tells us, was its "essentially voluntarist [*volontaire*] character . . . demonstrated by the extreme perfection of the work that went into it" (V 641, "Lettre sur Mallarmé").

We begin our investigation of Valéry's conception of poetic effort with Mallarmé for two reasons. In the first place, it is here that Valéry's rhetoric of effort and of action is most intense. In the second place, Mallarmé is a crucial figure for theorists of text. The writing of Mallarmé survives the "Copernican revolution" of theory in the 1960's and 1970's, whereas that of Valéry does not. Indeed, it is one of the puzzles of literary criticism that we made the leap from work to play (and in this precise sense from the "modern" to the "postmodern") without ever leaving the universe of Mallarmé.[5] If Mallarmé exemplified "obstinacy in choice" and a "rigor of exclusion" (V 635) for Valéry, the language of Mallarmé also metaphorically authorized the ludic characterization of text for poststructuralist critics. Mallarmé supplied "the blank/whiteness" (*le blanc*), the spacing, the "weave" (*tissu*) and "fold" (*pli*) of text. He also provided a poetic elaboration of the dynamics of textuality itself with his "elocutionary disappearance of the poet," and of course the mime's "perpetual allusion, without breaking the glass." Mallarmé, whose role as modernist hero had been fashioned by Valéry, was subsequently recast as avant-garde hero, even as prophet of a poststructuralist antipoetics, in the milieu of theory.[6]

But how was it possible to get around the notorious difficulty of Mallarmé? How was it possible to pose this dense, crystalline writing as an instance—even an inaugural model—of textual productivity in its quasi-automatic operation? I would suggest that it was the very way Valéry wrote the myth of the modernist Mallarmé that enabled the subsequent effacement of a poetics of effort and intention, and the recasting of Mallarmé as an emblem of postmodernity. If the question of the difficulty of Mallarmé could be negotiated by poststructuralist critics, it was not only because of the theoretical possibilities that psychoanalysis made available, but also because of the dynamic tension between the voluntary and the automatic already at play in the poetics of Valéry. The high modernist poet-critic gave us an analysis of the mind at work (*l'esprit à l'oeuvre*) which precipitates into what will be called textual productivity.

Mallarmé: Defenses Against Automatism

Whereas lesser critics had dismissed Mallarmé because he was too hard to understand, Valéry turns this difficulty into a sign of the poet's genius. He found the poems to be such perfect jewels, he tells us, that he could only presuppose some hidden work involved in their production. Valéry imputes to Mallarmé, author of *Les Mots Anglais*, a "science of *his words*" (V 655, original emphasis).[7] For all his obscurity, Mallarmé is declared to be the poet of "pure and distinct ideas." Algebrist of language, poet of exact science, he is the Descartes of modern poetry.[8] Valéry opposes the art of the poet, characterized by "patience . . . obstinacy . . . and . . . industry" (V 648, "Je disais quelquefois") to mere natural poetic fact—"exceptional encounter in the disorder of images and sounds that come to mind" (V 648). For Valéry, Mallarmé personifies the art of the poet. "[He] created for himself a language that was almost entirely his own by his sophisticated [*raffiné*] choice of words," Valéry writes, " . . . refusing the easy solution advanced by common opinion [*la solution immédiate que lui souffle l'esprit de tous*] at every turn." This involved nothing less, Valéry concludes emphatically, than Mallarmé's "defending himself *against automatism*" (V 658, "Je disais quelquefois," original emphasis).

Automatism, in this context, is to be understood in the sense of Bergson, who opposed the vital and the voluntary as forces of spontaneity to the automatic as register of matter and necessity, and hence of repetition and reaction. "This entire study," Bergson writes in *L'Evolution créatrice*, "attempts to establish that the vital is in the direction of the voluntary . . .

the order of willed activity [*l'ordre du voulu*] as opposed to . . . that of
the inert and the automatic."[9] For Bergson, the world of interiority—the
world of the dynamic lived time of duration—is the locus of freedom in
relation to a mechanistic world of quantifiable matter. On Bergson's view,
because language is a function of convention and depends upon iteration,
it constrains our experience of duration and orients us toward the realm
of the automatic. Valéry shares Bergson's critique of language. It is in this
sense that he considers the refusal of conventional language to mark an
affirmation of the will (*volonté*) in relation to what he calls "the conflict
between the natural and effort." Effort is opposed to the natural, considered as domain of the automatic in the sense of repetition and reaction.
Although the contemporary ear tends to hear "effort" and "work"
through the filter of the discourse of Bataille, in which effort and work
imply a utilitarian economy and relations of instrumentality, for Valéry
these terms are on the side of the vital in opposition to the mechanism of
reification. This is the core of the misunderstanding that has resulted from
an oversimplification of Valéry's complex elaboration of *le travail de l'e-
sprit*, or "mental work," which should be analyzed in terms of what Bergson called "le travail élémentaire de l'esprit" in *Matière et mémoire* (HB
223).

The art of the poet, Valéry writes in "Lettre sur Mallarmé," involves a
"hidden work" (V 640) which is difficult to analyze because it is indiscernible. When Mallarmé brings out a copy of *Un coup de dés*, however,
Valéry finds evidence of its energies in the arrangement of black type and
white space on the pages of the book. "Having read me his *Coup de
dés* . . . Mallarmé finally had me look at the book itself [*me fit enfin con-
sidérer le dispositif*]," writes Valéry:

It was as if I saw a figure of thought [*une figure de la pensée*] placed in our space
for the first time . . . here, truly, extension spoke, dreamed, gave birth to temporal forms; anticipation [*l'attente*], doubt, concentration, were *visible things*. My
sight was directed at silences that had become embodied [*qui auraient pris corps*].
(V 624, "*Le Coup de dés*, Lettre au directeur de Marges," original emphasis)

It is not the existence of the literary masterpiece that displays Mallarmé's
genius. Valéry had already appreciated the work itself upon hearing the
text read. What reveals the art of the poet, the work that went into the
perfection of his poetry, is the "figure of thought" Valéry sees before his
eyes and which provides an imprint of the creative process that engendered the work. The book's typography registers this trace.

With *Un coup de dés*, Valéry writes, Mallarmé has attempted to "*finally elevate a page to the power of the starry sky!*" (V 626, "*Le Coup de
dés* . . . ," original emphasis). The allusion is to Kant's figure for the moral

law: the starry sky at night. Valéry sees stars on the pages of *Un coup de dés*, stars and constellations that he reads as signs of "the ideal spectacle of the creation of language" (V 624). After an evening spent with Mallarmé poring over the pages of this book, the text not only comes to figure the sky but the sky itself appears to Valéry as text. The sublime spectacle of the pages of *Un coup de dés*—text as sky—returned in the spectacle of the summer sky—sky as text—moves the high-modernist critic to anticipate a postmodern hallucination of text:

The innumerable heavens of July were enclosing everything in a sparkling group of other worlds . . . it felt to me that I was caught in the very text of the silent universe, a text made up of splendours and enigmas . . . an interweaving [*tissu*] of multiple meanings; which gathers together order and disorder. (V 626)

It also prompts this amusing reflection:

We were walking. . . . I was thinking of the marvelous endeavor [of *Un coup de dés*]: what a model, what a lesson, up above! Where Kant, quite naively, perhaps, thought he saw the Moral Law, Mallarmé no doubt perceived the Imperative of poetry: a Poetics. (V 626)

The comparison between Kant's ethics and Mallarmé's poetics presupposes an identification of pure poetry with the universe of language as pure form. This is what Valéry sees on the pages of *Un coup de dés*. He associates this universe of language with the Kantian ethical realm, the domain of freedom. The comparison links the purity of pure poetry to this freedom from what Kant called the "pathological" determinations of the world of nature as representation, the sensory forms of time and space. In this context, then, the automatic is to be understood on analogy with the world of nature as representation, from which the Kantian practical domain enjoys autonomy. The automatic is thus to be thought in relation to what Mallarmé called *la parole brute* or "common speech"—the ordinary language of comprehension and exchange, from which poetic language is meant to distinguish itself.[10] The defense against automatism, then, gives access to the universe of language in and of itself. This is the object, or material, of the poet's work. What the typography of *Un coup de dés* makes visible, then, is the universe of language—letters and words—worked over by the spirit—*l'esprit*—of the poet.

When it comes to giving a more concrete account of the calculation or science of Mallarmé, however, Valéry can only characterize it negatively. The poet's rigor is one of exclusion and refusal: "In literature, the *austere work* of the writer manifests itself, and operates, by refusals" (V 641, "Lettre sur Mallarmé," original emphasis). It is the rigor of this refusal, the number of possible solutions rejected along the way, that attests to the

poet's virtue.[11] The defense against automatism is rephrased here as a conflict between effort and the natural. Poetic virtue, on analogy with moral
virtue, involves a "resistance to the facile," a "desire to reject whatever
does not conform to the law one has given to oneself" (V 641). As in
Kantian ethics, however, the law one gives to oneself cannot be prescribed
or even specified. Valéry does no more here than suggest the symbolist
ideal of a "mystical union" between sound and sense. To hope to realize
this goal, he adds, is to expect a miracle, for "there is no case where the
relation of our ideas to the groups of sounds that name them one by one
is not completely arbitrary or by pure chance" (V 648, "Je disais quelquefois"). The natural and the automatic, it seems, will not be easy to resist,
given the arbitrariness of the sign.

Valéry presents the rigorous poetics of Mallarmé negatively, that is, by
revealing what the poet specifically rejects. These "negative characteristics" are to be taken as signs of the poet's hidden work. "Everything that
appeals to the majority was expunged from this work," he writes of Mallarmé:

There is no eloquence, no narration, no maxim, no direct appeal to ordinary passions; no giving in to familiar formulas. . . . [There is] a way of speaking which is
always unexpected; speech that never tends to repetition or to the vain delirium
of natural lyricism . . . always subject to the condition of music and to the conventional laws whose object is to *regularly* check any collapse [*chute*] into prose—
these are a few negative characteristics by which such works gradually make us
all too aware of the usual expediencies, weaknesses, idiocies, and inflations that
abound, *helas*, in all the poets. (V 647, original emphasis)

The specific refusals enumerated here indicate the kind of facile solutions
the poet must resist, the automatic literary reflexes against which the poet
must defend him- or herself. But this defense against one form of automatism—the clichéd literary reflexes that come to mind most readily, or
most naturally—approaches another automatism, the "psychic automatism" of Breton. Indeed, it is striking to what extent Valéry's account of
the "negative characteristics" of Mallarmé's pure poetry overlap with the
antipoetics of Breton.[12] Even the difficulty of Mallarmé is not alien to the
horizon of Breton's automatism, if we consider the operations in and of
themselves, independent of esthetic (or antiesthetic) intent. "The difficulty
one first experiences in comprehending," Valéry writes of Mallarmé's
poetry,

is due to the extreme contraction of the figures, the fusion of the metaphors, the
rapid transmutation of tightly knit images, which undergo a kind of discipline of
density . . . and which are consistent with the intention to keep the language of
poetry always radically, even absolutely, distinct from the language of prose. (V
668, "Stéphane Mallarmé")

The operations Valéry describes here are not so different from those sur-realist automatism is said to share with dream work—"condensation, dis-placement, substitution, touch-ups [*retouches*]," as Breton puts it in *Les Vases communicants*. And for surrealism, of course, both dream work and automatic writing succeed (in their own ways, and for their own reasons) in "keep[ing] language . . . distinct from the langage of prose."[13] There is thus some common ground here between (surrealist) automatism and the "defense against automatism" Valéry attributes to Mallarmé. Perhaps the extreme of the voluntary is not so far removed from the extreme of au-tomatism, at least as this is understood by Breton.

The Course on Poetics: Figures of Thought

Although Valéry makes some of his strongest claims for a rigorous poet-ics of calculation in his writings on Mallarmé, these essays do not go very far in analyzing the poet's art or labor of precision (*travail de précision*) (V 709, "Mallarmé"). One turns, then, to the "Première leçon du cours de poétique" for a theory of the poet's work. As we have already seen in the previous chapter, Valéry identifies poetry and action in this essay, in which he presents an analysis of writing and reading as two constitutive moments in the production of the work of art, an analysis that strikingly anticipates what Sartre will call the "paradoxical dialectic of reading" a decade later. We have seen how crucial this moment is to Sartre's argu-ment concerning the essence of literature as well as to his elaborations of praxis in the *Critique of Dialectical Reason*. Although I have already dis-cussed certain parallels between Valéry's poetics and Sartre's account of reading, I would like to look more closely at the notion of action Valéry elaborates here, specifically in relation to the work of the poet.

If we approach the "Première leçon" in the hope of finding a more de-tailed analysis of the poet's work—the poet's art of calculating poetic per-fection as it is invoked in relation to Mallarmé—we come away disap-pointed. For here we find only the irrepressible *travail de l'esprit* itself, which seems to run quite automatically. As "liberté en acte," or freedom in action, *l'esprit* is a spontaneous source of productivity. Radically inde-terminate, it operates as a "combinatory force" ad infinitum, like a per-petual motion machine.[14] "Reduced to its own substance," Valéry an-nounces here, "*l'esprit* does not have the finite at its command . . . it ab-solutely cannot bind itself [*se lier lui-même*]" (V 1353). A question arises, then, concerning the articulation between the terms *volonté*, or will, and *esprit* in the discourse of Valéry.

This question is all the more pressing since Valéry informs us here that the will cannot effectively intervene in the operations of the creative spirit (*esprit créateur*). "When it tries to turn towards the mind itself and to impose itself [*se faire obéir*] our will [*volonté*] is always reduced to a simple halt, to a maintenance, or else a renewal, of certain conditions" (V 1353). All one can do is to slow, or shut down, the operation of the system as a whole. The will is quite helpless when it comes to the mechanism of *l'esprit*: "we can only act directly on the freedom of the system of our *esprit* . . . we simply wait for the desired effect to present itself . . . we can do nothing but wait. *We have no means to achieve in ourselves exactly what we want to obtain*" (V 1353, original emphasis). To our surprise, then, in place of an analysis of the poet's concentrated effort, of his or her art or industry, we find an involuntary moment of waiting or anticipation (*attente*). Patience has overtaken obstinacy and there is little trace of industry in this art of the poet. "There is a lot of chance in all this," we could say with Proust, who spoke, of course, of the workings of involuntary memory. The central problem of Valéry's poetics, it soon becomes clear, is not the will, or even the means, to perfection. It is how *l'esprit*—a dispersive machine of infinite variation—can yield a finite work at all. The fundamental problem is poïein itself, the activity, the *faire*, of *l'esprit* as passage from indeterminacy to act.[15]

"Vaporization and centralization of the Self. That is everything," Baudelaire wrote.[16] Valéry's poetics dramatizes this formula.[17] For the indefinite machinations of mental activity to yield a finite work, the naturally dispersive character of *l'esprit* must counter itself by a gesture of concentration that requires effort. L'esprit "struggles against its own nature and its accidental and momentary activity" (V 1351), Valéry writes of the *l'esprit en acte*, "It seems to escape into the work from the instability, incoherence, and inconsistency that it recognizes in itself and which constitute its usual mode of operation" (V 1351). This is the moment of effort, and without it there would be no passage to act, or to *oeuvre*, at all. There would be only the perpetual slippage of infinite spontaneous variation. In the course on poetics conflict between the natural and effort is engaged within *l'esprit* itself. Here, more and more, the "natural" comes to mean the automatic in the register of the accidental; that is, in something like the surrealist sense. This movement plays itself out simply to enable the production of a work.

Effort, then, is not a voluntary cognitive action in the utilitarian sense. It involves a tension of concentration, one moment in an energetics. It marks a rebellion against the indeterminacy of mental action and an escape from it into the facticity of a work. But it is as if this moment of concentration were so foreign to the operation of the creative spirit that it required an intervention from the outside. The work, Valéry affirms, "is the end result of a series of inner modifications, as disorderly as you please, but which must necessarily resolve itself at the moment the hand acts . . . this hand, this external action, necessarily resolves the state of indeterminacy, for better or for worse" (V 1351). Is the work of the poet, then, a matter of handwork? Does the hand itself work automatically? Whereas the text needs the reader's voice to become animated as a work, to overcome the inertness of "a series of signs linked only by the fact that they are physically traced one after the other" (V 1349), the moment of material tracing appears to be essential for the work to come into being at all. Valéry summarizes his poetics in the following very abstract formula: "in the production of the work, action comes into contact with the indefinable" (V 1357). Action comes into contact with the indefinable, or the indeterminate, in the mystery of writing—"miraculous escape [*échappée*] out of the closed world of the possible into the world of fact" (V 1357).

If we compare the "Première leçon" to the essays on Mallarmé, we see that the gesture of concentration in *l'esprit*'s struggle with its own nature corresponds to the effort of the modernist poet. The pure poet's austere work amounted to a rigor of exclusion, a refusal of the ordinary. Likewise, the creative spirit's concentration involves a series of refusals of given possibilities in favor of others yet to come—"the missing image or word." Only here the negative moment appears less heroic, less virtuous, and more passive. The negative poetics earlier ascribed to the artistic will of Mallarmé the perfectionist now appear as a function of the perpetual motion, the infinite variation, of the psyche itself. *L'esprit* does not make corrections on the basis of any esthetic principle or precise formal requirement; it does not make them under the direction of a creative will at all.

Desire, only alluded to in passing in the essays on Mallarmé as "the principle . . . that engenders the poetic act" (V 653), becomes central to Valéry's poetics here, where the artist's work consists almost exclusively of desiring and waiting. "We present our desire to ourselves," Valéry writes, "the way one opposes a magnet to a confused mass of shavings, from which one tiny piece suddenly separates itself off from the rest" (V 1353). The *attente*—a moment of passive waiting identified with an indefinite desire—is paramount. The image suggests Proust, on the one hand—the vague pressure toward the missing image from the past sought in vain by the voluntary memory, but retrieved involuntarily—and Breton's *Les Champs magnétiques* on the other. This is a far cry from the rhetoric of calculation that characterized Mallarmé the algebrist and the "extreme perfection" of his labor.[18]

When the concentration that resists the dispersive instability of *l'esprit* is presented in slightly more active terms—"The mind which produces . . . resorbs the infinite variety of the incidents . . . rejects the indifferent substitutions of images, sensations, impulses and ideas that run through the other ideas" (V 1351)—we realize that the moment of effort theorized in the treatment of Mallarmé only mirrors the dispersive, or affirmative, operations of *l'esprit* itself. For in its very instability, in the ongoing self-substitution of its unremitting variation, the psyche already performs a work of perpetual self-correction. "As soon as *l'esprit* is in question," Valéry writes in the concluding paragraph of this essay, "everything is in question; everything is disorder and any reaction to disorder is disorder too" (V 1358).

For this reason, even the tension of refusal that aims at closure is indeterminate, mirroring the fundamental indeterminacy of the mind at work (*l'esprit à l'oeuvre*) as freedom in action. The poet waits until the desired word emerges, or until the hand that writes intervenes. But even this outside intervention is not definitive, for, as Valéry warns, "nothing is irrevocable. Here the next instant has absolute power over the product of the preceding instant" (V 1353). The process of self-correction remains indefinitely open, thanks to the "treasure of possibilities" provided by the activity of *l'esprit* as a spontaneous force of combination.

The surprising thing, Valéry remarks, is that the very instability of *l'esprit* is its most precious asset in the creative act:

The mind at work, which struggles against its mobility, against its constitutional uneasiness . . . and its own diversity . . . finds . . . incomparable resources in this very condition. . . . The instability, the incoherence . . . are also treasures of possibilities. . . . They provide reserves from which *l'esprit* can expect anything [*peut tout attendre*], reasons to hope that . . . the missing image or word is closer than it realizes [*l'image, le mot qui manque sont plus proches de lui qu'il ne le voit*]. (V 1352)

Valéry tells us nothing specific about this desire for the missing word or image, but more and more the work of the poet becomes identified with it.

"It seems that in this order of mental phenomena," Valéry concludes, "there are some very mysterious relations *between desire and the event* . . . the spiritual event that puts an end to our waiting" (V 1353, original emphasis). The allusion, of course, is to "Mimique" by Mallarmé:

The scene illustrates only the idea, not the actual action, in a hymen (from which the dream proceeds) . . . between desire and accomplishment, the perpetuation and its memory, now anticipating, now remembering [*remémorant*] in the future, in the past, through a false appearance of the present. Thus operates the mime, whose performance [*jeu*] is limited to a perpetual allusion without breaking the glass; he installs a pure atmosphere of fiction.

Mime is appropriate here, for Valéry's course on poetics is itself a mime of theory—"perpetual allusion without breaking the glass." Substantively, the analysis does not yield explanation or clarification but only the revelation of a mystery.[19] Formally it is tautological: poetics is poïein, poïein is *faire*, and *faire* is passage to act. Production, in other words, is production. The poïein of *l'esprit* is precisely a "mute soliloquy of the phantom, white like an unwritten page." It is a soliloquy of *l'esprit*, the spontaneity of "freedom in action" in its indeterminate productivity. It is a *hymen* (both union and barrier) between desire and accomplishment. Were there no union, there would be no work; were there no barrier, we would have an economy of utility, not of "charm" or fiction.

The work of art, Valéry explains, exemplifies the highest type of human action precisely because it involves "an action prompted not by something situated in the outside world, where we find the goals of ordinary action . . . [it is] therefore unable to give us the kind of formulas for action that would ensure being able to obtain what one set out to accomplish" (V 1358). Valéry anticipates Sartre in *Qu'est-ce que la littérature?* here, for it is a question of the idiosyncrasy of genius—creation without rule. The "Première leçon" seemed to promise an analysis that would support the rhetoric of rigor and calculation of the essays on Mallarmé with a theoretical elaboration. We can now appreciate why this analysis was necessarily impossible, or at least beside the point. The phenomenon of genius—pure invention—is not subject to analysis because it resists imitation or repetition. It is precisely because of the noninstrumental nature of the work of art that the artist's "perfectionist work" must always remain, as Valéry put it in the case of Mallarmé, a hidden work. It is for this reason that the economy of work or exchange is displaced within a framework of desire to the paradoxical economy of charm, where possession yields only desire for more. "We feel we are possessors, whereas we are magnificently possessed" (V 1355), Valéry says of the reader's charmed experience of the work of art. The same applies, in a more subtle way, to the activity of the poets themselves.

Toward the end of his lecture on poetics, Valéry reiterates the theme of a defense against automatism—the superiority of art or industry to natural poetic fact—introduced earlier in relation to Mallarmé. "Art consists of defending oneself against the unevenness [*inégalité*] of the moment" (V 1357), he declares. The defense against automatism is a defense against chance. And yet this essay has made it quite clear that the chance encounter, the *trouvaille*, is just what the creative spirit yearns for: "We implore our spirit for a manifestation of unevenness" (V 1352), Valéry writes a few pages earlier in the same essay. At the limit between desire and accomplishment, then, we find Valéry's ambivalence toward the accidental or the automatic. The conflict between the natural and effort haunts Valéry's own poetics at every turn.[20]

The figure for the mysterious relations between desire and event in the operation of poïein is Minerva—or, more precisely, "mysterious relations" between Minerva and Jupiter. Valéry compares "the miraculous escape out of the closed world of the possible . . . into the world of fact" to an "armed Minerva, produced by the spirit of Jupiter, an old image, still full of meaning!" (V 1357). Minerva, goddess of wisdom or spirit, coming fully formed into being from the spirit of Jupiter, figures poïein itself as passage to act. Once this figure has been made explicit, we recognize its shadow in Valéry's description of his first impression of *Un coup de dés*:

> Here, truly, extension spoke, dreamed, gave birth to temporal forms; anticipation [*l'attente*], doubt, concentration, were *visible things*. . . . There were murmurs, insinuations; it was like thunder for the eyes, a whole spiritual tempest blew from page to page to the extreme point of thought, to the ineffable point of rupture: there the marvel [*prestige*] occurred. (V 625, "Le coup de dés, lettre . . . ," original emphasis)

Rereading this passage with the lecture on poetics in mind, we can discern Minerva emerging from the spirit of Jupiter in the thunder of this spiritual tempest. The *figure de la pensée* that Valéry perceived in the layout of *Un coup de dés* gives a visible trace of the processes of mental activity portrayed in the "Première leçon." We now recognize "anticipation, doubt and concentration" as familiar features of mental action [*le faire de l'esprit*]. This *figure de la pensée*, then, is thunder for the eyes as "extension engendered temporal forms [*l'étendue enfantait des formes temporelles*]."

If the image of Minerva is full of meaning here, however, it is because the French word "minerve" also signifies "printing machine," the very mechanism of the typography that first revealed to Valéry the visible signs of the mental work of Mallarmé. The hidden figure, then, for the *figure de la pensée* is the printing machine. "The writer's mind sees itself in the mirror provided by the printing press," Valéry writes in "Pièces sur l'art."[21] Minerva, goddess of the spirit, figures intellectual invention in the explicit mode of effort or concentration, whereas "minerve" as "small printing machine" figures the operation of *l'esprit* itself as dispersive machine, as "reserve," or "treasure of possibilities" (V 1352). It figures the "automatism" of *l'esprit* as a combinatory force (V 646, "Je disais") of infinite potential. The ambivalence of Valéry toward the automatic is carried by the hidden work of this double figure.

At the Heart of the Mind: "Descartes"

Valéry's critical essays form a sustained reflection on "the whole system of the mind [*l'esprit*]," an ongoing meditation on the problem of genius. A series of essays on Descartes spanning 1925 to 1943 largely overlaps with the texts on Mallarmé. The question of genius is thus meditated concurrently in the registers of poetry and philosophy.

Valéry turns to Descartes for clues to a poetics in the large sense he sets out in his course—*poïein* as mental action. He looks to Descartes as the inventor of method, a "system of exteriorizable operations that does the work of *l'esprit* better than *l'esprit* itself" (V 800, "Descartes"). But just as what fascinated Valéry in his lecture on poetics was the artistic process more than the esthetic product, so also in the case of Descartes what interests him is not the content of the philosopher's thought, but the processes of his thinking.[22] Or, more precisely still, the process of his writing. Valéry looks to Descartes as the author of *A Discourse on Method*. It is less the Cartesian method per se that interests him than the text of the *Discourse*, which Valéry considers a "living monument" to the philosopher's genius.

Descartes, Valéry writes:

built himself a tomb with his own hands, one of those enviable tombs. He put the statue of his *esprit* in it, so distinct, so true to behold, that one could swear it was still living, speaking to us in person, that there were not three hundred years between us, but that exchange [*commerce*] were possible with it, as if there were only the interval between one *esprit* and another, or even between one soul and itself. His monument is this Discourse. (V 789, "Fragment d'un Descartes")

Once again, it is a question of something like a mime. This mute soliloquy concerns genius. It occurs at that junction where what is most intimate meets what is universal and hence most impersonal—method. When we read the *Discourse* of Descartes, Valéry claims, we hear our own thoughts: "[Descartes] has assumed this voice which first of all teaches us all our own thoughts and silently detaches itself from our directed expectation [*attente dirigée*]" (V 789).[23] It was Descartes's goal, he affirms, "to make us hear himself/oneself [*nous faire entendre soi-même*], that is, to inspire in us his necessary monologue and to make us pronounce his own wishes [*de nous faire prononcer ses propres vœux*]. *It was a matter of our finding in us what he found in himself* [*en soi*]" (V 790, original emphasis).[24]

We must appreciate the oddness of this *nous faire entendre soi-même*. It is something quite different, for example, from the *hypsos* of the Longinian sublime, where the listeners feel as if they have uttered the words themselves. For there one mistakes one's own voice for that of the other, the real speaker. Likewise, something like identification of self and other is implied by Valéry's definition of poetry as that which we feel compelled to repeat word for word, and, to a certain extent, by his account of reading as reinvention. With the "nous faire entendre soi-même," on the other hand, the very terms of identification are disrupted. The indefinite *soi-même* puts the identity of the subject into question. It blurs the difference between monologue and dialogue, amalgamating the interlocutory positions. We are left with an indefinite subject which must be read as both singular and universal at the same time.

What fascinates Valéry, then, is not the universality of method but the singularity of tone and voice. Paradoxically, the universality of Descartes's discourse is a function of its intimacy—"an intimate speech where there are no effects or stratagems; as our most intimate and most sure possession [*propriété*] . . . [it] can only be universal" (V 789–90, "Fragment d'un Descartes"). Indeed, so intimate is this voice that it speaks *our* thoughts before we have even thought them ourselves: "It assumes this voice which first of all teaches us all our own thoughts" (V 789). And this is no accident. For it was, we remember, Descartes's goal to "have us understand himself/ourselves [*nous faire entendre soi-même*]." For Valéry, this proximity of the personal to the impersonal (the *nous* to the *soi*) is at once the paradox, and the special charm, of Cartesian method, where "genius applies itself to reducing the need for genius" (V 800).

It is not the intellectual content that is of lasting value in the philosopher's work.[25] Valéry is interested in "the very workings of thought itself [*le travail propre de la pensée*]": "It is the substitutions and the transmutations that I imagine operating there, the vicissitudes of lucidity and will, the interventions and interferences that occur, that enchant the amateur of the life of the mind." For the poet, the vicissitudes of mental action are poetic in and of themselves, as we see in the strangely poignant *Monsieur Teste*. Valéry finds traces of the "vast Comedy" of psychic operations in the writing of Descartes. Just as he was able to detect a "figure de la pensée" in the typography of *Un coup de dés*, so he can discern traces of "the very workings of thought" in the writing of the philosophical text.

The content of a philosophical work, according to Valéry, becomes outdated, exhausted by virtue of being repeatedly challenged and refuted. What retains its full force, however, is the text and its "artistic vigor [*fermeté d'œuvre d'art*]." It is the writing of the *Discourse* that constitutes the monument to the genius of Descartes; the *Discourse* is a "living" monument to the extent that it holds traces of the vital energies that came together in the creation of the work—"the lively act of creators . . . and . . . the form of this act . . . their vital necessity of time past" (V 799). The philosopher's art—his poetry—presents an equivalent to the *figure de la pensée* Valéry perceived in *Un coup de dés*—an external manifestation of the processes of creative interiority. It is the art of the *Discourse* that provides the living statue of Descartes's *esprit*.

To the eye of the poet, Descartes's style is no less philosophical than the substance of Cartesian thought. Valéry defines philosophy here as an "exercise of thought upon itself" (V 798). To the extent that the poetic features of the philosopher's writing transmit the vital energies of the work of intellectual invention—"the force [*vertu*] that let it produce itself" (V 799)—and give us the spectacle of the transformations of mental action (V 799) involved in the work's production, they too qualify as a self-re-flexive exercise of thought. In this specific sense they are philosophical.

The vitality of the "artistic rigor" of the work is thus a function of the inexhaustible resources of mental activity familiar to us from the lecture on poetics. Valéry reiterates the indeterminacy of *l'esprit* here.[26] But in this essay, where it is ostensibly a question of a philosopher, not a poet, Valéry offers a less equivocal appreciation of the aleatory, the accidental, and the automatic. Here, it seems, no defense is necessary: "the essential disorder engenders . . . a momentary order, a necessity emerges from some arbitrary arrangement, the incidental occurrence engenders the law" (V 796). Valéry even goes so far as to identify genius with this fecund disorder: "the accidental, the superficial and its lively variations excite, illuminate, what is most profound and most constant in a person truly made for the highest spiritual destiny [*les hautes destinées spirituelles*]" (V 790). If the intimate voice of Descartes's *Discourse* opened onto the universal or the impersonal—the indefinite pronoun of the "nous faire entendre *soi*-même"— it seems that the reverse is also true. The lively variations of the accidental, the most superficial, involuntary, or automatic mechanisms of mental action, illuminate what is most profound and constant. They yield what is most personal—at least for someone "truly made for the highest spiritual destiny" (V 790). The arbitrariness of the impersonal and the automatism of variation characterize a notion of genius reserved for the special few.

Or, we should say, for the "Happy Few." For "borrowing a term from Stendhal," Valéry continues, "I will say that the true method of Descartes should be called egotism" (V 806). The Cogito, Valéry insists, is not a cognitive act. In fact, it is meaningless (V 825, "Une vue de Descartes"), but it has the power of a magic formula or mantra whose force resides in its enunciation. More poetry than prose, it is not meant to be understood but felt. Valéry compares the power of the Cartesian Cogito to exclamations, interjections, curses, and war cries, all utterances of phatic force "that thought cannot add anything to [*sur laquelle la pensée ne peut pas revenir*] except to declare that they do not mean anything in themselves, but have played a momentary role in a sudden, intimate modification of a living system" (V 825–26). Writing on Mallarmé, Valéry characterized the magical power of poetry as "what sings out or expresses itself at the most solemn, or most critical moments of life" (V 649, "Je disais"). He gave the magic formula as an example of such involuntary cries, which operate on the level of feeling and carry poetic force. It is in this sense that the mantra of the Cogito is "a reflex act of man" (V 826) for Valéry. At the core of method, we find reflex and poetry, and at the center of poetry, a prereflexive cry.[27]

At the heart of the mind (*au coeur de son esprit*) then, we find not intellect, but desire and feeling—"the feeling of the Self" (V 839). The key to the Cartesian position, Valéry writes, is Descartes's desire to "exploit *his treasure of desire* and of intellectual vigor"—"he couldn't desire [*vouloir*] anything else" (V 808, "Descartes," original emphasis). Once again, then, we find a problematic relation between will (*volonté*) and the free *esprit*. Or at least this is the case if we read *volonté* in terms of intentional consciousness, that is, as the *volonté* of a *vouloir dire* (to mean or to want to say). But that we must not do so is precisely the lesson of the essays on Descartes. They teach us to read will (*volonté*) as will to power. "For me," the poet-critic writes, "The Cogito is like a call sounded by Descartes to his egotistical powers. . . . At the sound of these words . . . the will to power invades the man, shores up the hero" (V 807).[28]

If the voluntary character of Mallarmé's poetics was enhanced by the portrayal of him in Cartesian terms—as algebrist and as poet of clear and distinct ideas—one wonders where, exactly, to locate the effort, the "hidden work" of Descartes, the Mallarmé of modern philosophy?[29] It is not intrinsic to the operations of method. For the essence of method, Valéry asserts, is to reduce effort, to substitute "a uniform treatment (*sometimes even a sort of automatism*) for the obligation to invent a special solution to each new problem" (V 800, my emphasis). In the case of Descartes, effort coincides with the philosopher's "treasure of desire." It occurs as a radical commitment to the self and to self-consciousness as the ground of certainty—"self consciousness, the consciousness of his whole being held together in his attention; a consciousness so voluntary and so precise that he makes an infallible instrument of his Self [*Moi*]. . . . His self is a geometer . . . one could say he took his Self, so strongly felt, as a point of origin of the axes of his thought" (V 805). *Volonté*, then, is a mode of freedom as spontaneity.

The Cartesian equivalent of Mallarmé's negative poetics is methodical doubt. It is Descartes's wholesale rejection of metaphysical dogma, his "implacable cleansing of the laboratory table of the mind [*l'esprit*]" (V 813, "Une vue de Descartes"). For Valéry, the Cogito is the clarion call to Descartes's pride and to his energies of self-assertion, self-reliance, and autonomy.[30] The Cogito animates the *Moi*. Once again the most impersonal, the reflex gesture, opens onto what is most interior—"the most pure, the least personal, Self, which must be the same in all people and . . . universal in each" (V 826). The voluntarism of Descartes, therefore, is one with his Egotism or will to power. This is what Valéry understands by "the madness of clarity [*la folie de la clarté*]" (V 797, "Descartes").

Descartes, Valéry suggests, lived his own version of the conflict between the natural and effort.[31] As we have seen, however, Valéry's Descartes also performs a certain reconciliation of the voluntary and the natural (or the automatic) precisely because of the mysterious relations set up between what is most personal—*le Moi*—and most impersonal—*le Soi*. "The I and the Me having to introduce us into modes of thinking that are entirely general, that is my Descartes" (V 806, "Descartes"; 839, "Une vue de Descartes"), Valéry insists. Descartes both personalizes *l'esprit* through the intimate voice of the *Discourse* and depersonalizes it through method. He introduces communication between the intimacy of the *Moi* (myself) and the impersonality of the *Soi* (oneself) which opens the virtue of work, or the voluntarism of effort, onto the *vertú* of an impersonal vital energy— a will to power and the autoproduction of a *se produire*.[32]

"Without knowing it," Valéry acknowledges of Mallarmé, "he played such a big role in my personal history [*histoire intime*] . . . [that] . . . I cannot speak of him in any depth without saying too much about myself" (V 634, "Lettre sur Mallarmé"). Valéry repeats the gesture of identification in enthusiasm that Baudelaire made with respect to both Poe and Wagner. Does Valéry's modernist myth of Mallarmé reveal something about Valéry?[33] Is there a "defense against automatism" (in the psychoanalytic sense, now) on the part of Valéry? The author of *Charmes* appears to defend specifically against an automatism of *l'esprit* itself as freedom in action. He appears to will his voluntarist poetics in spite of a desire for the accidental, a fascination with the overwhelming inventive powers of the mind in action as event of freedom (*liberté en acte*), and an enthusiasm for vitality.

The ambivalence of Valéry—the defense against automatism and the fascination with its force—might be understood as a function of the attraction of two conflicting notions of genius. Valéry wants to step away from an overpersonalized and romantic conception of genius as inspiration. He admires in Mallarmé "the most audacious and the most sustained attempt that has ever been made to overcome what I will call *naive intuition* in literature" (V 620, "Stéphane Mallarmé," original emphasis). In this spirit, Valéry moves in the direction of impersonality. M. Teste—"the being absorbed in his variation . . . who gives himself over entirely to the terrifying discipline of the free mind [*l'esprit libre*]" (V 18)—personifies the impersonality of *l'esprit*.[34] "What had he done with his personality?" (V 19), Valéry asks. But the desire to "conserve art, even while exterminating the illusions of the artist and the author," as he puts it in *Monsieur Teste*, brings Valéry uncomfortably close to the impersonality of Lautréamont-Ducasse and, to this extent, to the very formula of surrealist automatism—"Poetry must be made by all, not by one." To go too far in the direction of impersonality would be to sever connection with the modernist tradition of Baudelaire and Poe. Valéry compromises. He espouses a voluntarist poetics, but his complex elaboration of it is haunted by the energies of the impersonal, the radically spontaneous, and the automatic.[35]

Valéry's voluntarist poetics opposes perfectionist labor to a naive poetics of inspiration, on the one hand, and to natural poetic fact on the other. This reflects the situation of symbolist modernism, which marks a transition between a lingering romanticism and an emerging avant-gardism. Effort stands against both these tendencies. It stands for spontaneity, or freedom directed from within, against the presumed exteriority of the *daimon*, on the one hand, and of chance on the other. Effort is an index of autonomy. To this extent the poetics of a "defense against automatism," or of resistance to the facile, implies a resistance to all outside determinations. This is the thrust of Valéry's conceit: where Kant saw the moral law, Mallarmé saw poetry—a Poetics! The poetics of effort, and the rigor of refusal, coincide with the law of genius, that is, with a refusal of any rule other than the law one gives oneself.

As Valéry's analysis of Descartes suggests, however, the law one gives to oneself is the law of the self, the self of genius—"the purest and most impersonal self." When it comes to intellectual invention, the law one gives to oneself coincides with the autonomy, and the energy, of the will to power as law of self-affirmation—the *vertú* of a *se produire* (self-production). Valéry's poetics of effort tends toward a poetics—or poïetics—of poïein itself, a poetics of autoproduction and, to this extent, of the automatic in the surrealist sense. At moments—perhaps just long enough to mark the young Breton—Valéry approaches a notion of the automatic as register of the radical spontaneity of autoproduction. This is revealed most clearly in the problematic *Monsieur Teste*.

M. Teste: The Madness of Clarity

"There is no more rich poetic material in the world," Valéry writes of the inner workings of the mind in his essay on Descartes:

The life of the mind is an incomparable lyric universe, a complete drama lacking neither adventure, passion, suffering . . . nor comedy. . . . This world of thought, where one can discern the thought of thought and which extends from the mysterious center of consciousness to the luminous expanse where the madness of clarity is awakened, is as varied, as moving, as surprising . . . as admirable in itself as the world of affective experience dominated only by instinct. What could be more specifically human . . . than intellectual effort detached from any application? (V 796–97, "Descartes")

This drama of interiority provides the poetic material of Valéry's fiction of modern lyricism, *Monsieur Teste*. Teste is a figure of pure psychic will (*volonté*), of mental effort "detached from any application." "Will he find life or death at the extreme point of his attentive acts of will [*volontés attentives*]?", his wife asks, " . . . a little more of this absorption and I am certain he will make himself invisible!" (V 30). Absorption implies concentration, tension, and attention. Teste is a figure, then, for the willpower at the core of Valéry's poetics of effort. But to the extent that he embodies mental effort "detached from any application" we can already see that he will challenge the conventional formalist view of Valéry. He will call into question his identification with an intentional, or instrumental, poetics, and problematize the conventional portrait of the pure poet/critic as "rationalist, cold and methodical."

"The delicate art of duration," Valéry writes in *La Soirée avec Monsieur Teste*, "time, its distribution and its regimen . . . was one of the great areas of investigation of M. Teste . . . [who,] absorbed in his variation . . . gives himself over entirely to the terrifying discipline of *l'esprit libre*" (V 18). We recognize the dynamics of the *travail de l'esprit* as presented in the lecture on poetics. On the basis of our reading of that text, we can gloss *l'esprit libre* as another expression for *esprit* as "freedom in action." Teste dramatizes what the lecture at the Collège de France analyzes in abstract terms: the workings of the mind. Through its explicit appeal to the notions of duration and time, however, the Teste cycle also reveals a Bergsonian subtext which runs through Valéry and specifically informs the notion of will or *volonté*.

"In addition to consciousness and knowledge [*science*]," Bergson wrote, "there is life." Bergson rejects the Kantian focus on epistemology and objectivity and in its place affirms a philosophy of life. It is because philosophy posed the question of the relation between nature and consciousness in epistemological terms, he affirms in *Matière et mémoire*, that the relation of mind and matter has been analyzed on a spatial model. It became a question of representation, of mental images as duplicates of material entities in extension. What needs to be thought, Bergson insists, is a philosophy of life that considers experience from the perspective of action, not knowledge. Action, in this context, is to be understood in relation to a dynamic concept of life. "Beneath the speculative principles, so carefully analyzed by philosophers, there are tendencies that have not been studied and which are explained simply by the fact that it is necessary to live, in reality to act."[36] This change in perspective places emphasis not on space or spatial relations, in the Cartesian tradition of extension and mathesis, but on dynamic time, an active flow [*se découler*] of the lived time of becoming—time as rhythms of duration. Because of the requirements of practical action, however, this source of free action—duration—becomes blocked to our experience. Philosophical intuition (which for Bergson involves both action and effort) is required to retrieve contact with it. Teste's "terrifying discipline of the free mind" suggests the Bergsonian discipline of philosophical intuition, where what is sought is an immediate experience of duration, one in which, as Bergson puts it, "life . . . absorbs . . . intellectuality by going beyond it" (HB 665).

In *L'Evolution créatrice*, Bergson proposes the following investigation into the experience of intensity and time as duration: "We are going to ask consciousness to isolate itself from the outside world, and, by a vigorous effort of abstraction, to become itself again." It is a question of effort, but of the kind of effort we make to "go beyond pure reason [*le pur entendement*]" (HB 664). It is something like what Valéry called an "effort detached from any application," for, according to Bergson, intelligence is usually directed toward useful action in the outside world. "Let us concentrate on what . . . is simultaneously most detached from the outside world and the least penetrated by intellectuality," Bergson writes of philosophical intuition, and he continues:

Let us seek, in the deepest part of ourselves, the point where we feel innermost to our own life. We dive back into pure duration . . . the moments when we can take possession of ourselves again to this point are rare indeed: they coincide with our truly free actions. . . . Our feeling of duration, I mean the coincidence of our self with itself, admits of various degrees. But the more the feeling is deep and the coincidence is complete, the more the experience [*la vie*] into which it [pure duration] places us *absorbs intellectuality by going beyond it* . . . this state contains a *virtual intellectuality*, so to speak. Yet it goes beyond this, it remains incommensurable with it, being indivisible and new. (HB 664–65, *L'Evolution créatrice*, my emphasis)

Intuition could be said to involve what Valéry calls, in the case of Teste, a "terrifying discipline," because the act of philosophical intuition is extremely strenuous. "Intuition is laborious [*pénible*]," Bergson writes, "and cannot last . . . it is attached to a duration which is growth, perceives an uninterrupted continuity there and an unforeseeable newness; it sees, it knows that *l'esprit* draws out of itself more than it has" (HB 1275, *La Pensée et le mouvant*).

According to Bergson, the intuition of duration involves "the violent contraction of the personality upon itself." The *volonté* concentrates itself and gives us access to the experience of freedom that attaches to pure duration. Intuition involves an immediate form of self-reflection. In this sense no operation of recognition (in the Hegelian sense) is necessary or even possible. Intuition does not involve a mirroring; it is a temporal process instead of a spatial phenomenon. It is open. *Volonté*, in this context, is a force of invention, and hence of freedom. Indeed, *l'esprit* is *la liberté en acte* only as *volonté*. For Bergson, duration is the mechanism (*ressort*) of our will, our *volonté*. The voluntary overlaps with action as a modality of the vital—of *la vie*. "The vital is in the direction of the voluntary," Bergson writes, "in opposition to . . . the inert or the automatic" (HB 685, *L'Evolution créatrice*). In this sense *volonté* means indeterminacy in opposition to the determined state, the given necessity, of matter. *Volonté* is an instance of vital activity as "freedom in action [*liberté en acte*]." It signifies a force of becoming, a spontaneity that manifests itself as an expenditure of energy (HB 709, *L'Evolution créatrice*), that is, in relation to what Bataille would call a general economy.[37] The discourse of Bergson, then, proposes a conception of willful activity that has nothing to do with the intentional subject of a *vouloir dire*, or with any instrumental relation to meaning. *Volonté* is a category of life, not of knowledge or discourse. In this sense it is closer to Schopenhauer's conception of the will as force of becoming, and to the affirmative force of Nietzsche's will to power (both of which, as we have seen, were invoked in Valéry's essays on Descartes), than to a more restricted notion of subjective intention.

"One must become accustomed to thinking being directly," Bergson writes in *L'Evolution créatrice*, "one must try . . . to see for the sake of seeing [*voir pour voir*] and not for the sake of action. Then the Absolute reveals itself, very near to us, and, to a certain degree, in us. . . . It lives with us. It is like us, but, in certain respects, it is infinitely more concentrated and dense, it endures [*il dur*]" (HB 747).[38] Teste is the (anti-) hero of interiority precisely in this sense. He is the hero of a *voir pour voir*, witness to the dynamics of interiority as virtual processes of creation. His eye is poised at the limit between action and dream, between inside and out, at the maximum of the virtual on the point of actualization. He bears witness to the virtuality of genius within himself. Teste's question (which was also Nietzsche's), "What is humanly possible [*que peut un homme*]?" rephrases the question of genius in terms of the impersonality we saw thematized in the Descartes essay. Teste "wanted to conserve art—Ars—while exterminating the illusions of the artist and the author. He couldn't stand the stupid pretentions of the poets—or the crude pretentions of the novelists" (V 67). Art, transvalued as Ars, is to be understood as a kind of knowhow (in the sense of the French phrase *savoir faire*) a *se faire* of *l'esprit*, just as Valéry shifts the term "poetics" to "poïesis" or "poïétique" in his lecture. We could say that Valéry/Teste would substitute for the romantic, personalized conception of genius the process of a certain ingeniousness, an *ingénier*, which the dictionary describes as a "putting into play [of] all the resources of *l'esprit*." Thus, we read that Teste "carried dissociations, substitutions, similarities to an extreme point, but with an inevitable return, an infallible inverse operation" (V 65). Once again we recognize the terms of the "Première leçon."

Real genius, for Valéry, involves a knowledge of the power of mental operations and transformations, an ability to analyze "all the phases of the mind [*toutes les phases intellectuelles*]" (V 1161), as he puts it of Leonardo.[39] The name Teste has often been glossed in relation to the French word for head, *tête*, with the implication that Teste is all intellect, all cold calculation. But it is more a question of Teste as witness—"*Teste— témoin*." He is witness, precisely to the "mental action [*travail de l'esprit*]" depicted abstractly in the "Première leçon," and to the impersonal dynamics of genius as un-genius/ingeniousness (*in-génier*).[40] As witness, Teste must be always poised in a state of readiness. He exists in precisely the state of suspension or waiting (*attente*) that Valéry invoked in his lectures. Whereas for Bergson (who also emphasizes this moment) it is a question of a level of tension that accompanies an attentive readiness for action, in *Monsieur Teste* it is not a matter of action in the outside world, but of a mental action, a *faire de l'esprit*, which implies an inversion. Madame Teste compares her husband to a plant "whose roots would grow up to the light, instead of the foliage!", literalizing Bergson's remark to the effect that the philosophy of intuition consists in inverting the usual direction of the work of the mind (HB 1442, "La Pensée et le mouvant"). It is a question of action as invention in the sense of *poïein*. In *Monsieur Teste* Valéry is interested in virtual action. As if to better seize the instant of *poïein*, the passage from indeterminacy to act is suspended just at the moment of actualization, and thereby detached from any application—even from the actualization of *poïein* itself in the creation of a work.

As witness to the processes of inner life, Teste is a "man of attention."[41] "Imagine the eye," Valéry writes, "the act of looking rather than what is seen . . . and this only occurring by a consumption of the possible and a recharge. . . . Suppose someone who is the allegory and the hero of this seeing" (V 64).[42] Teste is the allegorical hero of a visionary vision—what Bergson calls a *voir pour voir*. It is not a question of a measured contemplative glance, however, but of a dynamic and vital seeing. Teste as witness, as seer, operates in a mode of radical expenditure.[43] His inner vision involves a "consumption of the possible and a recharge" (V 64); he is "the most complete *psychic transformer* that ever existed" (V 65).

With Teste we have something like a subjective interiority detached from any particular subject. We are reminded of the relation between the *moi* and the *soi* Valéry elaborated in the essay on Descartes. In the case of

Teste, however, as Valéry writes in one of the later fragments, "the psyche is at the peak of the separation between internal exchanges and values. . . . Thought (when it is Him [Teste]) is equally separated from its similarities and confusions with the World and . . . from affective values. He contemplates it in its *pure chance*" (V 65, my emphasis). Teste contemplates his own mental processes in their aleatory operation; he attests to mental functioning as pure chance. M. Teste is not only the hero of an allegory of seeing, as Valéry suggested, he is also the hero of an allegory of automatism—the kind of "psychic automatism" which will be elaborated by Breton.[44]

Through the figure of Teste we can better understand the puzzling role of anticipation (*attente*) in the lecture on poetics. Teste is a "man of anticipation [*homme d'attente*]" precisely as a "man of attention [*homme d'attention*]." The two go together. "To be alert [*Veiller*] is to foresee [*c'est prévoir*]—in the most general way," Valéry writes in his *Cahiers*.[45] He continues: "I am alert—means: If something happens, it will be responded to in the appropriate manner. This thing, in particular, will awaken the organizations and the acts necessary to divert or utilize what it announces. It is a way of gaining time . . . alertness, then, contains . . . a quantity of transformable energy—or tensions." Here we see that the notion of anticipation corresponds with a state of tension, and hence with effort. It involves a mode of virtuality poised on the edge of actualization. "The great interest of the moment of anticipation for Valéry," writes Judith Robinson, "is that it shows the implicit or virtual future that is already potential in the present moment" (R 147).[46] But for Valéry the past also inhabits the present, as we see in this citation from the *Cahiers*: "The return, the repetition, is an essential fact. Property of the present. Coincidence of a memory-perception with a perception-sensation which, by their union or rapprochement and complex composition yields the system Me-Present [*Moi-Présent*]" (V 136). This is a remarkably direct allusion to Bergson's theory of recognition (to be radically distinguished from Hegel's dialectic of recognition) which we shall explore in much greater length in connection with Breton in our next chapter. But we have already encountered a version of it in our discussion of Bergson's analysis of reading (and of language acquisition and comprehension) in *Matière et mémoire*, which, as we suggested, anticipates the theory of reading as reinvention that Valéry presents in his lecture on poetics. As we have shown, this returns as the "paradoxical dialectic of reading" in *Qu'est-ce que la littérature?* and in a different mode, in Sartre's theory of praxis in the *Critique of Dialectical Reason*. In Bergson, the theory of reading as "directed creation" parallels the analysis of perception according to which the subject needs to appeal to a spontaneously offered memory image in order to match it with the sensory material of an incoming perception. This mechanism which articulates memory (as relation to an absent object) and perception in a manner not unlike the way the Kantian schematism links perception with the understanding, is what Bergson calls recognition. Here memory replaces the understanding as the locus of spontaneous production. And here it is a question of conditions of possibility of experience in general, not (as in Kant) of cognitive knowledge.

What is the end of Teste? Precisely a breakdown of the operation of recognition in Bergson's sense. Together with the seeing that implies being, there is a "seeing which is called memory." In the "Fin de Monsieur Teste," the eye of the witness no longer contemplates the "boundaries of *l'esprit*." It becomes "the gaze that does not recognize . . . eye at the border between being and non-being." This is what Valéry calls the eye of the thinker. It involves the "agonizing gaze of a man who is losing recognition." The loss of consciousness is one with the loss of the function of recognition (not in the sense of Hegel, but of Bergson) which links together an "actual seeing [*voir actuel*]" and a "memory seeing [*voir souvenir*]." The dying Teste sounds like Bataille when he proclaims: "The syllogisms altered by the agony, the pain bathing a thousand joyous images, the fear joined to a beautiful past. . . . What a temptation death is . . . something unimaginable and which enters the mind sometimes in the form of desire, sometimes in the form of horror." We remember that in Bataille's *L'Erotisme* it was just such an affective ambivalence between fascination and horror that characterized the sacred. As we have already shown, the economic formulations of expenditure and accumulation that become associated with the sacred and with eroticism in Bataille depend upon this kind of emotional logic of attraction and repulsion. It is in this spirit, we could say, that Mme. Teste's Confessor writes to her that her husband is a "mystic without a god." Sartre, of course, will describe Bataille in precisely these terms, in his review of *L'Expérience Intérieure*.

The Lesson of Leonardo

La Soirée avec M. Teste, the first installment of what subsequently becomes the Teste Cycle, is published only two years after another essay that treats the drama of psychic operations: "L'Introduction à la méthode de Léonard de Vinci." Here it is a question of exploring the dynamics of genius by imagining the workings of Leonardo's mind. Valéry is concerned quite specifically with the duration of mental operations, what he calls (in the words used by Bergson, on the one hand, and Bataille on the other) the "*continuity* of this ensemble *l'esprit*" (my emphasis).[47]

Valéry imagines Leonardo's mind as the scene of a "personal comedy" in which mental images are the actors. He is not interested in analyzing these images; he wants to grasp their dynamism, to recapture a sense of their duration. He considers the "system" of these images in terms of their "frequency, their periodicity, the ease with which they enter into various forms of associations" (V 1159), operations we recognize from the lecture on poetics. In this essay Valéry identifies analogy as the principle of these various operations, and he defines analogy as "the faculty of varying images, of combining them, of making the part of one coexist with the part of another" (V 1159).[48] If analogy in general is the structural principle of this activity, however, Valéry warns against trying to understand these psychic operations through particular analogies to the material world. For, when it comes to these dynamics of *l'esprit*, he explains, "words lose their virtues [*vertus*]." Valéry insists on the indeterminacy of psychic processes in the continuity, or duration, of mental activity. It is precisely that indeterminacy he refers to in the lectures on poetics when he invokes the formula for poïein: passage from indeterminacy to act.[49] But in the early essay on Leonardo we are much closer to the Bergsonian subtext hidden in the "Première leçon." Valéry's refusal of external, scientific analogies for inner processes, and his general rejection of verbal descriptions of psychic operations coincide with two cardinal points of Bergson's early philosophy. First, outer experience is represented to us in spatial terms, and inner experience, which involves a temporal dynamic, is incompatible with spatial representation. Thus there can be no analogy between the world of extension and the world of interiority. Second, language functions in a spatializing mode, cutting up the qualitative material of experience into quantifiable pieces that cohere with respect to representations of objective reality. Hence, Bergson insists, duration is unrepresentable.

In this essay, Valéry's impossible task is to analyze a state of dynamic indeterminacy. He attempts this through imagination and identification. He undertakes to "imagine [*se figurer*] the operations and the paths of [Leonardo's] mind [*esprit*]." In a gesture of what Bergson would call "imaginative sympathy," he tries to imagine both Leonardo's works and the thinking that went into them from the point of view of their emergence—"The operations of the mind will be of interest to us when they are fluid, vacillating, still at the mercy of the moment" (V 1158). The poet/critic mimes the energies of Leonardo's mental activity—his personal comedy—just as the mind of Leonardo is said to "mime the strange situation of his own diversity."

The essays on Leonardo (like the fragments of the Teste cycle and the essays on Mallarmé and Descartes) evolve over time, in concatenation. In a later contribution to the Leonardo meditation, Valéry reveals to us that he had used himself as a model for his depiction of Leonardo in the earlier texts. The "*esprit* imagining an *esprit*" actually involved the projection of his own imagined mental operations onto Leonardo. From Valéry's point of view, this fact is insignificant, since at the level of mental operation he is concerned with here (at the level of genius), the psychic dynamics have general validity; they are impersonal. It is a question of the *soi*, not of the *moi*, as Valéry put it in the Descartes essay. From our point of view, however, when Valéry writes that his analysis of Leonardo's genius was a "portrait of my mental state" (V 1231) it is important. For it entitles us to apply the dynamics explored in the Leonardo meditations back to Valéry's other essays and extend them to his poetics as a whole.

In the essay "Léonard et les philosophes," Valéry meditates on the relations between the mental operations of philosophers and those of artists. He affirms that the artist goes beyond (*dépasse*) the philosopher (the reverse of Hegel's teleology) on the grounds that the artist's thinking more closely resembles that of a scientist. "Intellectual effort," he writes, "can no longer be regarded as converging toward a spiritual limit, the true. One has only to look inward [*s'interroger*] to find this modern conviction: all knowledge that does not include an effective power has only a conventional or arbitrary importance" (V 1240). Valéry anticipates Foucault here, although in doing so he invokes the very impetus of Bergson's thinking: the rejection of a philosophy of truth and knowledge in favor of a philosophy of life and vital force. "The value of all knowledge depends upon its being the description, or the recipe, of a verifiable power" (V 1240), Valéry insists.

What does he understand by "power" (*pouvoir*) here? Invention, or the power to create: "It is the power that matters to him," Valéry writes of Leonardo. "He does not separate comprehending from creating" (V 1253). It is in these terms that we must understand the superiority of the artist over the philosopher. As a philosopher, concerned with epistemological questions, "the limit one seeks to get back to [*rejoindre*] is simply what is." The artist, on the other hand, "spills out into the possible and makes himself the *agent of what will be*" (V 1243, original emphasis). Power, as "power to create," stands for dynamic agency, for an actualization of the possible. This is the kernel of Valéry's theory of poetry as action. "Axioms of a true knowledge," he summarizes, "can only be formulas of action. Do this, do that, that is, a sure external transformation suspended at the point of a conscious inner modification." This definition not only resonates with Sartre's myth of prose, it also corresponds with Bergson's account of the nature of free action as spontaneity. If we read Valéry's reflections on genius through the intertext of Bergson, we can understand action not in the instrumental mode of extension—the action of one billiard ball upon another—but as invention. This involves a kind of virtual action—action "suspended at the point of a conscious inner modification." Invention, Bergson insists, is freedom in action, it "brings into being what did not exist and might never have come into being" (HB 1293, "La Pensée et le mouvant").

"Léonard et les philosophes" provides the best refutation of the conventional portrait of Valéry as an intellectual poet. For here Valéry severely criticizes ideas as instruments of truth—ideas as idols. He presents a critique of language that is consistent with his well-known devaluation of prose and of prosaic reading. Leonardo, "whose philosophy was painting," proposes a new "figure of thought"—one that does not involve words. "Just as our thinking begins to deepen, that is, to approach its object . . . and not the arbitrary signs [*signes quelconques*] that excite the superficial ideas of things," Valéry writes, "just as we begin to live this thinking we feel it separate from all conventional language."

Once again, Valéry insists on the Bergsonian distinction between epistemology and experience. To think profoundly (that is, in relation to what Bergson called the "deep self [*moi profond*]" or the self as genius) is not to display rational prowess but to live one's thinking. This is what takes effort, as we see when Valéry continues. However much we may be used to construing thinking or knowing in terms of objectivity, and however quick these operations are to intervene, he writes:

With effort, by a sort of power of *enlargement* [*grossissement*] or by a sort of *pressure of duration*, we can separate it from our mental life at that instant. We feel that words are failing us, and we know that there is no reason that there should be words that correspond to us [*qui nous répondent*], that is . . . *that replace us*, for the power of words (and this is where their usefulness lies) is to bring us back to what we have already experienced, to regularize, or to institute repetition, whereas here we are ready to experience this mental life *which never repeats itself*. This is perhaps just what is meant by thinking profoundly, which does not mean: to think more usefully, more exactly, more completely than usual, but rather *to think far, to think as far as possible from verbal automatism*. (V 1263, original emphasis)[50]

The effort is one of inverting the path of rational thought, of expanding the temporal horizon at the expense of the spatial one. This effort corresponds to the "terrifying discipline" of Teste, and, in a different way, to the "hidden work" of Mallarmé.

We have come full circle to the central question of our reading of the essays on Mallarmé: the defense against automatism Valéry attributed to the pure art of Mallarmé and associated with the "extreme perfection of his work." The essay on Leonardo reveals that Valéry did not invoke this "defense" for purely literary reasons. He was not simply concerned with anxiety of influence, with questions of belatedness or the problem of cliché which haunts the literary sublime. The essays on Leonardo clearly reveal the importance of the Bergsonian subtext in Valéry's thinking. "Automatism" does not imply only what Mallarmé called "common speech [*la parole brute*]" as opposed to the "pure speech [*la parole pure*]" of poetry. The defense against automatism implies a challenge to the power of language in general. It implies an appeal to the related experiences of duration and invention, and strives for a living thought, a "mental life that never repeats itself."

For reasons I will discuss in greater detail further on, it is not surprising that the Bergsonian subtext comes through most clearly in the very early essays of Valéry—those on Leonardo and Teste—and is only implicit in later ones such as the "Première leçon de poétique." Having worked through these various texts, however, we might now consider Teste as a rewriting of the Leonardo essay in the mode of a defense against automatism, as this notion was expressed in patently Bergsonian terms in the Leonardo essay. The rhetoric of effort and will surrounding Teste is in the service of this defense. The lecture on poetics rewrites Teste—"fiction of modern lyricism"—in a more dispassionate and abstract register.

If we are attentive to the vitalist intertext in Valéry's writings, we recognize that the work of the poet has little to do with the instrumental effort of an intentional subject. We see that the concept of action to which Valéry appeals overlaps with the vital in its opposition to the inert. In this sense action pertains to freedom—a *liberté en acte*—which returns in Sartre's definition of literature and provides the basis for a figure of genius as *l'esprit libre*, or what Bergson has called the "deep self."

When action is understood as invention, and poetry is presented as action, the incompatibility Bataille affirmed between poetry and action dissolves. From this perspective, we can appreciate the ideological nature of Bataille's declaration, that is, the extent to which it depends for its force upon its opposition to a popular misconception of engagement. As we suggested in the beginning of this chapter, however, the "incompatibility" between poetry and action takes on a different meaning in relation to the earlier polemic which opposed Breton's surrealist automatism to Valéry's ostensible poetics of perfection—his "authoritarian cult of form." This polemic can be formulated in terms of an opposition between the "voluntary" (Valéry) and the automatic (Breton), one that repeats the thrust of the opposition Bataille declared between action and literature.

Once we become aware of the Bergsonian subtext in Valéry's poetics, however, this formulation becomes both ironic and potentially confusing. For surrealist automatism involves precisely an inversion, or reversal, of Bergson's category. At the same time, when we consider the vitalist subtext in Valéry, we see that the "voluntary" does not actually oppose psychic automatism. It does not imply the *volonté* of a *vouloir dire* or an intentional poetics. On the contrary, it signifies a force of freedom and spontaneity, one Bergson associates with duration. This conception of the voluntary not only resembles certain features of surrealist psychic automatism, it may have inspired Breton to effect the reversal of Bergson's term, that is, to rephrase duration and spontaneity in terms of Bergson's antithetical term: "automatism."

In view of Breton's close association with Valéry during his own formative years, it is plausible that Valéry's meditations on the *travail de l'esprit* played a role in the emergence of Breton's thinking of psychic automatism, which reverses the valence of the term "automatism" as it was initially elaborated by Bergson. For although Valéry consistently insists on the notion of authorial effort—"the will . . . and the calculations of the agent" (V 641)—his actual elaborations of this process, as we have seen, include an energetic tension between the voluntary and the "automatic" in the proto-surrealist sense of a pure spontaneity of *l'esprit*. Thus, although Breton turns against the explicit message of Valéry's high modernist poetics, the ethics of a "work of perfecting" inherited from the tradition of Poe and Baudelaire, perhaps he was nourished by the tensions that present themselves in the course of Valéry's attempts to elaborate this hidden work. Perhaps we can diagnose here what Valéry called a "special case of influence," one the pure poet defines in the following terms:

When a specific work or a man's whole *oeuvre* has an effect on someone, not because of all of its qualities, but because of a certain quality or qualities, influence takes on its most remarkable value. The separate development of a quality of one person by the whole power of the other person almost never fails to produce effects of *extreme originality*. (V 635, "Dernière visite à Mallarmé," original emphasis)

Valéry's poetic reflections turn around the notion of *l'esprit*, the insistent focus, as we have tried to show, of his critical essays. When *esprit* is read and translated as "mind," Valéry emerges as a cerebral poet, "rationalist, cold and methodical"—master, as Adorno put it, of an "authoritarian and classic cult of form." But Valéry gives us another definition of *l'esprit* in his collection of fragments, "Instants":

L'esprit is the collective pseudonym of a whole host of quite diverse characters—which find a way to express themselves through it . . . such as the stomach/womb [*ventre*], the heart, the sex and the brain itself. . . . If we knew how to determine this probably chemical plurality, whose emissaries come to excite [and] irritate the centers of images and of signs, to dominate each one according to the circumstances. . . . Sometimes the one answers, sometimes the other demands . . . they only have one apparatus of emission-reception. (V 380)

This more complex, and more vital, version of *l'esprit*—one that renders it all but untranslatable into English—is the one we need to keep in mind when we consider Valéry's poetics. "Chemist of *l'esprit*," chemist of what he calls, in the essay on Leonardo, "matter made up of time [*la matière faite de temps*]," Valéry presents an elaboration of the *travail de l'esprit* that provides an introduction to Breton's transvaluation of automatism from Bergson's pejorative automatism of material determinacy to Breton's *psychic* automatism of vital energies, one that gives free access to the full range of psychic forces and to the deep self.

Valéry might be considered a transitional figure between the positions of Sartre and Breton to the extent that his discourse combines a rhetoric of effort or work (and a language of action) with an economy of excess and expenditure; one, as he put it in *Monsieur Teste*, of "consumption and recharge [*consommation et recharge*]." An economy of work gives way to a paradoxical economy of desire. Artworks, Valéry writes, "force us to desire them all the more, the more we possess them, or they possess us" (V 1350). As he writes in the "Première leçon": "Satisfaction rekindles desire, the *response* revives the *demand, possession* engenders a growing *appetite* for the thing possessed: in a word, the *sensation* exalts its *anticipation* [*attente*] and reproduces it, without any fixed end . . . any act of resolution being able to directly abolish this effect of mutual excitation" (V 1407, original emphasis). Paradoxically, then, in his refusal of one sort of automatism, automatism in the sense of Bergson with which he identified the operations of conventional language (Mallarmé's "common speech"), Valéry approaches the elaboration of another kind of automatism, the psychic automatism that Breton will subsequently affirm in opposition to the ostensibly "voluntarist" poetics that Valéry has come to represent within the tradition of modernism.

CHAPTER 5

Breton: Angelic Truth

"Contemporary criticism is very unfair to symbolism," Breton wrote, " . . . you say that it was not surrealism's task to valorize it; historically, it was inevitably opposed to it, but criticism didn't have to follow in these footsteps [*lui emboîter le pas*]. It was up to criticism to retrieve, to install the drive belt [*courroie de transmission*]."[1] It is well known that Breton was a protégé of Valéry in his early years and that surrealism subsequently affirmed itself against his modernist poetics of "perfectionist work [*travail de perfection*]."[2] We need only look at Breton and Eluard's "correction" of Valéry's text "Littérature" (which they retitled "Notes sur la Poésie") to measure the distance Breton has put between himself and his early mentor. "A poem should be a festival of the intellect," Valéry writes. "It can be nothing else. . . . Festival: is a game, but solemn, orderly, meaningful; the image of what one is not ordinarily, of the state in which effort is rhythmical, redeemed [*racheté*]."[3] Breton and Eluard correct: "A poem should be a debacle of the intellect. It can be nothing else. Debacle: it is a run for your life [*un sauve-qui-peut*] but solemn, convincing: image of what one should be, of the state where effort no longer counts" (B 1015).[4] Attacking the romantic myth of inspiration, Valéry wrote: "What a disgrace to write, without knowing what language is, the word [*le verbe*], metaphors, changes of ideas and tone; without conceiving the structure or the duration of the piece, or the conditions of its end; hardly knowing the why of it, and not knowing the how at all! To blush / turn red [*rougir*] at being the Pythie" (V 550). Breton and Eluard correct this to read: "What pride to write, without knowing what language is, the word, comparisons, changes of ideas and of tone; without conceiving the structure of the duration of the work, or the conditions of its end; without having any idea of the why, any idea of the how! To turn green, to turn blue, to turn white at being the parrot" (B 1017). In simplest terms, we have a confrontation between effort and automatism.

The correction of "Littérature," undertaken in the manner of the "plagiarism" of Lautréamont-Ducasse, performs the "historically inevitable" opposition of surrealism to symbolism in its annulment of the modernist poetics of Valéry.[5] But then there is also the question of the *courroie de transmission.* We recall that in Valéry's celebrated essay on symbolism, he denies that there ever was such a thing as a symbolist literary movement, although he affirms a symbolist ethos: a shared commitment to "absolute adventure in the domain of artistic creation at the risk and peril of those who undertake it" (V 692, "Existence du Symbolisme")—"never have the powers of art . . . the virtue of poetry, been so close to becoming, in a certain number of spirits [*esprits*], the substance of an inner life that we could call 'mystical' . . . I say this from personal experience [*en connaissance de cause*]."[6] We have seen how Valéry's own explorations might be considered in this light. Staunch rejection of intellectualism, radical affirmation of interiority in the mode of invention, these are the broad lines of the symbolist inheritance that coincide with the surrealist commitment.[7] On the surface, the poetics of Valéry stands in starkest contrast to the position of his protégé, Breton. As the preceding chapter has shown, however, Valéry's conception of poetic effort was much more complex than the formalist notion he has come to represent. His exploration of the "intimate mechanics" of psychic operations may well have nourished Breton's appreciation of the various exploitations of psychic automatism he was introduced to by artists within the Dada milieu. We can only speculate how Valéry's meditations on the *travail de l'esprit* might have prepared the young Breton to accept the Dada formula of poetry as "dictatorship of *l'esprit*."[8]

Surrealism has mostly been read retrospectively in recent years—that is, from the point of view of poststructuralist theory and its concerns, specifically the interrelation between psychoanalysis and Marxism. From this perspective, surrealist automatism is often reductively analyzed in terms of the Lacanian unconscious. Breton is identified as a Hegelian, which disqualifies him from serious theoretical consideration. Bataille's ostensibly more advanced "philosophy" of transgression, as we have seen, is taken to represent a *dépassement* of the thinking of contradiction and held up against the alleged bourgeois idealism of Breton. If we are interested in the *courroie de transmission* that might link surrealism and symbolism, however, it is helpful to approach Breton's thinking from the point of view of its emergence (to borrow the phrase Valéry applies to the thought of Leonardo).[9] From this perspective, the early essays of Breton take on special importance. Initially published in small reviews, they date from the period of Breton's most serious reflection concerning the question of modernism.[10] They were republished in 1924 (the same year as the First Manifesto) in the collection *Les Pas perdus*—a title which means both "lost steps" (with a play on the opposite, "not lost") and "waiting room."

Les Pas Perdus: "The Taste for Innocence"

The essay that opens this collection is entitled "La Confession Dé-daigneuse" (The haughty confession; 1919). It is written for insiders and strikes today's readers as enigmatic and somewhat thin. This is perhaps because it was developed from a letter the very young Breton wrote to his prospective employer, Jacques Doucet, a wealthy man who wanted to play a role in the arts. Breton writes to Doucet to situate himself in relation to the cultural scene. Doucet will subsequently engage Breton—a poet in his early twenties much appreciated within established literary circles (that is, by Valéry, Proust, and Gide) and also familiar with the Dada milieu—as an art consultant; Breton will set up a private library for him and guide him in the acquisition of an art collection.

This letter was subsequently revised to form the essay that opens *Les Pas perdus*, an essay that reveals both a meaningful continuity with the symbolism of Mallarmé and a crucial break from it. Breton's first "confession" is an undying faith in poetry—"after all the disappointments it has already inflicted on me," writes the very young poet, "I still hold poetry to be the terrain where the terrible difficulties consciousness has with confidence have the best chance of being resolved." Indeed, Breton's faith in poetry will be unwavering throughout his career, even as his concept of it broadens and becomes more complex. The demoralization Breton alludes to in the passage cited above is of course linked to the First World War and to the general impact of modernization. In "La crise de l'esprit" (written in 1919, the same year as Breton's essay and as *Les Champs magnétiques*) Valéry announced a state of cultural crisis. "The military crisis is perhaps over," he wrote. "The economic crisis is visible in all its force"; and the intellectual crisis is "more subtle . . . [more] difficult to grasp" (V 990). It is fundamentally a moral crisis. "So many horrors would not have been possible," he wrote, "without so many virtues. No doubt a great deal of knowledge [*science*] was required to kill so many men, to dissipate so many goods, to annihilate so many cities in so little time; but moral qualities were no less necessary. Knowledge and Duty [*Savoir et Devoir*], have you thus become suspect?" (V 989). This is what Valéry will call a "crisis of confidence" (V 1056) in a later essay, "La Politique de l'esprit" (1933).[11] Breton's definition of surrealism in the Second Manifesto—"a total recuperation of our psychic forces" (B 791)—suggests a response to this crisis of confidence that appeals to certain features of the symbolist ethos,

including the unshakeable faith in poetry Breton admits to in "La Confession Dédaigneuse."

The special interest of this essay, however, is that in it we find both the
courroie de transmission between symbolism and surrealism and the crux
of surrealism's historical rejection of it. For if "La Confession Dédaigneuse" remains faithful to the symbolist ethos, it radically challenges
its modernist poetics. "People tend to think," Breton writes, "that the
meaning of what we write . . . no longer interests us, whereas . . . we are
attempting *to restore [restituer] content to form*" (B 198, my emphasis).
This is Breton's most telling confession, the one that most clearly announces the specific affirmation of Breton's surrealism as it emerges in opposition to Dada on the one hand and to the dominant current of modernism on the other—that of Mallarmé and Valéry in poetry and Cubism
in the visual arts.

This emphasis on content directly challenges the Mallarméan inheritance of poetic effacement. It anticipates the more explicit critique of Mallarmé in "Position surréaliste de l'objet," where Breton refers to "certain
nineteenth-century poets" who perceived the inferiority of poetry to music and who "thought it was possible to subordinate meaning to sounds,
and thus often ran the risk of simply gathering the empty shells of words."
Mallarmé is explicitly named a few lines further on when Breton charges
that the pure poet underestimated "the primordial virtue of poetic language," its universality. But if the criticism of Mallarmé becomes more explicit in the later essay, the "Confession" frankly reveals the affirmation
tied to that rejection: the restitution of meaning. Surrealism will break
from a symbolist poetics specifically in relation to this issue. As we shall
see, this restitution of meaning implies a broader rejection of the modernist tradition that emerges through the legacy of Mallarmé (handed
down by Valéry). In theoretical terms it implies a critique of the subsequent developments of this legacy: abstraction (in the context of the visual arts) and signifiance in the textual arts.

The question remains, however, what kind of meaning Breton has in
mind. Surely it is not a matter of a return to a broad thematic meaning in
the early romantic mode, one that operates through symbolic or mythic
content. The kind of meaning that interests Breton is lyrical meaning, but
in the mode of a *modern* lyricism. We know that Breton and Pierre
Reverdy engaged in prolonged discussions concerning what the nature of
a modern lyricism might be, and that it is in the context of these discussions that Reverdy comes up with the definition of the poetic image that
Breton will appeal to, and modify, in the First Manifesto—the image as a
coming together of two distant realities, which carries "emotive force and
poetic reality." Lyricism, and its ironic complication, is a legacy of ro-

manticism. In the spirit of Baudelaire, Valéry scorns what he called the "vain delirium of lyricism." Yet Mallarmé's solution to the problem of lyricism, the ascesis of pure poetry (sometimes considered a textual equivalent of abstraction) no longer satisfies Breton, whose concern with meaning is tied to a broad critique of esthetic modernism.

To pursue this question we must turn to Breton's short essay on Max Ernst, written in 1921 as preface to an exhibition catalogue and subsequently republished in *Les Pas perdus*. The exhibit was a show of Ernst collages at the Librairie Sans Pareil. The first exhibition of Ernst's work in Paris, it was staged as a Dada event. To show a German artist in Paris in 1921, so close to the end of the bloody war, was a radical gesture in itself, but the work that was shown struck even its most sophisticated viewers as revolutionary. Aragon writes that it was "the first event that led one to suspect the resources and possibilities of an absolutely new art."[12] Breton responded in the same spirit and immediately began to weave his own concerns into his reflections upon Ernst's work. He writes that "surrealism immediately found what it was looking for [*trouva son compte*] in the collages of 1920, which displayed a new precept of visual organization absolutely virgin, but corresponding to that which had been sought in poetry by Lautréamont and Rimbaud."[13] Breton's catalogue essay is not only framed by ruminations on automatism, it precisely anticipates the substance of the definition of the surrealist image that will be presented in the Manifesto three years later. In relation to Ernst's collages Breton refers to "this marvelous faculty of obtaining . . . two distant realities, without leaving the field of our experience, and of generating a spark from their encounter. By thus excluding all frame of reference," he adds, "we can estrange [*dépayser*] ourselves within our own memory."

The collages Ernst exhibited in Paris in 1921 were something quite different from the Cubist form of collage that had been practiced since the prewar years, conventionally known as *papier collé*.[14] Whereas these deal primarily with abstract relations in a given framework of representation, Ernst used photographs and other figurative materials as raw material. His collages developed out of Berlin Dada experimentation with photocollage and photomontage and involved the manipulation of mechanically reproduced figurative images. In *Beyond Painting* Ernst describes the discovery of this form of collage:

One rainy day in 1919, finding myself in a village on the Rhine, I was struck by the obsession which held under my gaze the pages of an illustrated catalogue showing objects designed for anthropologic, microscopic, psychologic, minerologic and paleologic demonstration. There I found brought together *elements of figuration so remote* that the sheer absurdity of that collection provoked a sudden intensification of the visionary faculties in me . . . it was enough at that time to embellish these catalogue pages, in painting or drawing, and thereby in gently reproducing *only that which saw itself in me*. I obtained a faithful *image of my hallucination* and transformed into revealing dramas my most secret desires—from what before had been only some banal pages of advertising. (my emphasis)[15]

Although Ernst used various figurative materials in his collages, including nineteenth-century engravings and woodcuts, some of the work Breton admired at the Librairie Sans Pareil involved photography. Ernst used photography in a variety of ways, sometimes fusing fragments of photographic images, or photographs of printed material. He also usually photographed his own collages, in order to erase the traces of his manipulations (and hence all indications of physical space as frame of reference) and signed this photographic reproduction of the actual collage, thereby conferring on it the value of the original work.[16]

It is clear that Ernst's use of photography interested Breton, for his catalogue essay opens with this remark: "The invention of photography dealt a fatal blow to old modes of expression, in painting and in poetry where automatic writing, which emerged at the end of the nineteenth century [Breton has in mind Lautréamont and Rimbaud] is a veritable photography of thought."[17] Here photography becomes a metaphor for automatism, but it is a question of a metaphorical, inner photography, which would give traces of inner processes—something like what Valéry called, in the case of Mallarmé, a *figure d'une pensée*—as a solution to the problem posed by photography in a literal sense and its mimetic scription of the external world. Consistent with his vehement repudiations of realism, Breton affirms that imitation is more effectively performed by the camera, the technical instrument designed for just this purpose.[18]

He poses the following dilemma: mimesis can no longer be the function of the artist or poet, but there are limits to the imagination that prevent us from coming up with anything radically new, that is, anything completely different from what a camera might record. "Unfortunately," Breton writes, "human effort, which tends to endlessly vary the disposition of existing elements, cannot be applied to the production of a single new element." Appealing to the Bergsonian subtext we have invoked concerning Valéry, we might say that this is because the imagination operates in relation to memory images; it is tied to the empirical world to the extent that it is a function of lived experience. "A landscape containing nothing earthly [*terrestre*]," Breton affirms, "is not within reach of our imagination." Even if we could conjure up such a thing, it would be meaningless to us, for we would have no emotional reaction to it—once again, lyricism is a central concern. With an eye on Ernst's specific solution to such difficulties, Breton summarizes the problem of modern art in the following terms: "It is just as sterile to rework a given image of an object . . . and the meaning of a word, as if it were up to us to rejuvenate it. We must pass through these acceptations, even if it means going on to distribute them, to group or order them in any way we please." Then comes the critical summation: "It is for not having recognized this essential freedom that symbolism and cubism have failed."

Here, then, we have another attack on the poetics of effacement. With the expression "it is equally sterile," Breton intimates the conventional charge made by opponents of Mallarmé—sterility—without mentioning the pure poet by name. Valéry's essays on Mallarmé, and his myth of the poet's rigorous will (*volonté*) attempt to respond to precisely this charge. But we can now better appreciate the relation of Breton's criticism of symbolist poetics to the question of meaning. We can appreciate the broader thrust of his argument, which implies a rejection of the entire agenda of what went on to become the hegemonic form of modernism. It is in this specific context that Breton proceeds to give a description of collage that will return as the definition of the surrealist image in the First Manifesto: "This marvelous faculty of attaining two distant realities, without leaving the field of our experience, and of drawing out a spark from their contact, and by denying us a system of reference, of estranging ourselves [*dépayser*, which can also mean "to take a holiday"] in our own memory."

The essay on Ernst confirms our sense that the content Breton proposed to restore to form is quite different from the content, say, of photographic realism. The sort of content that interests Breton involves the use of some anterior idiom—in Ernst's case figurative images that are redeployed or refigured. What is more, this restitution of content is tied to an explicit critique of dominant currents of modern art: symbolism and Cubism. The essay on Ernst enables us to perceive clearly the relation between the question of meaning and the surrealist challenge to what we might call, looking back, the modernist agenda. The fact that symbolism and Cubism are mentioned together indicates the reach of the young critic's theoretical thinking during this period when Breton is seeking the surrealist affirmation in the context of emerging modernisms.

We are in 1921; Breton is a 25-year-old poet. By this time he has already won the allegiance of the French literary establishment and sacrificed this support by turning toward automatism and Dada experimentation. At 25, he is not only on the verge of breaking definitively with his mentor Valéry, he is about to break with the French Dada group as well. This violent rupture will be precipitated by Tzara's refusal to participate in Breton's projected Congress of Paris, an event intended to promote a widespread reconsideration of the status of esthetic modernity in relation to both verbal and visual arts and within Europe as a whole.[19]

Why should such an event be deemed necessary? Because esthetic modernism, or avantgardism, is perceived to be at risk. We are in the postwar era, at a time of political conservatism and cultural retrenchment. Picasso is in his neoclassical period. Breton considers the French Dada movement to have declined into triviality, a farcical repetition of the early days of invention and resistance that characterized the exiled artists in wartime Zurich. He is concerned to shore up genuine experimentation in art. What is at stake is a form of spiritual renewal after the killing fields of the war and the disillusionment that followed. In other words, Breton is seeking the specificity of what will become the surrealist affirmation. It is in this context that he first launches his theory of the surrealist image, only here it goes by the name "collage."

The essay on Max Ernst makes clear that for Breton, writing and the visual arts must be thought in tandem for the question of automatism to emerge in its full force. Lyrical meaning, for Breton, is tied to a certain seeing. It includes a visual register, even when it is a question of texts. But just what does Breton see in the work of Ernst that might suggest an alternative to the modernist currents of symbolism on the one hand and Cubism on the other? A reconfiguring, whether in images or words, of meanings given by some anterior *parole* (speech).[20] We might interpret Breton's terse remarks to suggest that excessive interest in the play of the signifier leads to one form of sterility—the indefinite deferral of meaning in pursuit of "purer meaning," as Mallarmé put it—just as the insistence on the referent leads to the banality of realism. The choice between the signifier and the referent is a familiar one to us, since the alternative between avantgarde signifying practices (Artaud was for years the most common example) and realistic representation (Sartre's myth of prose as it is usually read) is conventionally presented to us in just these terms. In the two essays we have been considering, however, Breton suggests another line of development, an interest in the fictive and emotive potential of the signified as mental idea or image.

Saussure's notion of the linguistic sign can help us explore in more detail the kind of meaning at stake in what Breton calls the "restitution of content to form," as well as the parallelism Breton consistently maintains between verbal and visual art. We remember that in his course on linguistics, Saussure breaks the sign down into two elements, a signifier—the material mark or sound that is codified to carry a certain meaning—and a signified—a "thought," or mental idea. These two elements go together like two sides of a sheet of paper; when we cut through one (by distinguishing the signifier differentially from other signifiers) we necessarily cut the other as well. In the *Course in General Linguistics* the signified is presented by means of a visual icon. If we take the word "tree," for example, the signifier is given by the Latin signifier "arbor" and the signified is given by a small drawing of a tree. Within the semiotic structure of the sign, then, we have both verbal and visual components. These are yoked together such that the linguistic sign can be used to refer to an object in the world—a referent.

In the essay on Ernst, the question of meaning is posed in relation to the position of the signified, not the referent, and the visual register is an important feature of it. When Breton writes that the imagination cannot conjure up anything radically new, that we must "pass through the acceptations" of an anterior parole in order to be able to distribute them, to group them "according to whatever order we please"—he is speaking of both poetry and the visual arts. In relation to the collages, the "acceptations" he has in mind are mental ideas in the sense of the semiotic signified. The photos Ernst borrowed from eclectic catalogues function as so many signifieds that the artist freely redistributes and reconfigures.

What the essay on Ernst suggests, in other words, is that the "already given image of an object" offered by the catalogue images can itself be considered part of the work of language—the other half of the sign that Saussure annotated through the drawing of a visual image. The "given image" and the "meaning of the word" overlap. For this image already implies an associated name, and the name, as a term with semantic value, carries a mental idea or image. Hence "a landscape that contains nothing earthly [*terrestre*] is not within reach of our imagination." Our imagination (in the literal sense of an imaging faculty) includes a semantic dimension; the word "landscape" already implies the word "land" which implies earth. A landscape with nothing earthly is not within reach of our imagination because of the intimate relation of imagination to language, and of language to image. Dialectical negation cannot engender something of this order. For negation could only yield an absence of landscape; it could not generate one to which nothing earthly contributes. If we cannot invent something radically new, Breton proposes, then it is a question of borrowing given signs—that is, given meanings—and of combining them in new ways.

We have seen that for Breton the verbal and the visual modes of automatism are parallel and that Breton's thoughts turned to Rimbaud and Lautréamont at the sight of Ernst's collages. When people speak of Lautréamont in relation to surrealism, they usually refer to the *Chants de Maldoror* and its metaphoric power, invoking the celebrated formula of the chance encounter of the sewing machine and the umbrella on the dissecting table. In Ernst's collages, however, Breton would have found a visual equivalent of the writing Lautréamont practiced in his other work, *Poésies* (which was not signed with the pseudonym Lautréamont but with his given name, Isidore Ducasse). This was a mode of rewriting (or "correcting") that Lautréamont-Ducasse called "plagiarism," boldly announcing, "Plagiarism is necessary." What Lautréamont did was to take classic passages from French literature—fragments from Pascal, for example—and rewrite them, deforming their meaning in an asymmetrical way. It was not a question of simply negating, or contradicting, the meaning of the original text. The rewritings bend the original out of shape. By calling the procedure "plagiarism," however, Lautréamont-Ducasse emphasized the importance of citation. Citation introduces an interdiscursive structure, a shift in discursive level. In Lautréamont-Ducasse's "corrections" it was just this irrecuperable difference—a difference of repetition *of enunciation*—which neutralizes the possibility of any plane of reference for the interdiscursive collisions, or juxtapositions, he performs.[21] Lautréamont-Ducasse himself points out in the text of *Poésies* that the "plagiarism" erases, or neutralizes, any truth value that might have attached to the utterance.[22] To this extent, it also negates any stable plane of reference for meaning, since the initial framework of enunciation is not carried over into the lifting of the citation.

Already a devoted enthusiast of the *Chants de Maldoror*, Breton discovered the manuscript of *Poésies* in the Bibliothèque Nationale about a year before he first saw the collages of Ernst. In a letter to his fiancée Simone, composed after his discovery of this manuscript, Breton expressed his profound interest in the technique of "plagiarism." What specifically struck Breton was that the rewritings or " corrections" did not involve the systematic negation of the original. They neither refute nor respect the identity of the given text; they make the given one different without negating it. "It is by this means," Breton writes, speaking of the nondialectical contradiction at work in the plagiarisms, "that Ducasse achieves this kind of *angelic truth*—*Les Poésies* of Isidore Ducasse or earthly paradise [*le paradis terrestre*]" (original emphasis). Whereupon he adds, in a more confidential tone, "I am speaking to you of myself, and only of myself; in this letter it is uniquely a question of my taste for innocence" (B 1226).

If we apply the lesson of Lautréamont's *Poésies* we see that what ensures the absence of any frame of reference that Breton remarks in the collages of Ernst is the operation of citation implied in the borrowing of anterior images.[23] Wrenched from their contexts in a neutral mode, deactivated with respect to truth or reference, they appear to offer themselves up to be rearranged at whim.[24] The freedom of juxtaposition is enhanced by this disengagement from representation. The entirely synthetic space

Ernst engenders through the photographic reproduction of his collages is a space of pure fiction—without any plane of reference.

What Breton learns from *Poésies*, in other words, and recognizes in the work of Ernst, is a mode of meaning (or figuration) that is free of the discursive burden of representation. The lesson of Lautréamont is the paradox of a nonrepresentational figuration, the kind we find in the work of Magritte, of whom Ernst wrote in *Beyond Painting* that "he painted collages entirely by hand." My argument is that Breton has discovered a new notion of the fictive in the collages of Ernst which he will subsequently elaborate in terms of the surrealist image. This is what surrealism will affirm as an alternative to the "failed" projects of symbolism and Cubism. The lesson of angelic truth, then, is that one has more freedom from the constraints of representation when one takes representation as a point of departure—through an anterior *parole* in text or image—than when one resists representation through abstraction, as both symbolism and Cubism can be said to attempt to do. The content to be restored to form, then, as Breton put it in the confession, involves a mode of meaning—signifieds—suspended through a gesture of citation. In this sense, one could say that this meaning is in a sense not only restored, but returned *to form.*

Whereas Cubism presents a response to the question of relativity in relation to the outside world, Breton argues in his essay "Max Ernst," surrealism does so in relation to the inner world.[25] Ernst, Breton writes, "projects before our eyes the most captivating film in the world . . . by illuminating, in the most profound way, with a most exceptional light [*d'un jour sans égal*] our inner life" (B 246, my emphasis). "Inner life" is to be understood in terms of memory and time—that estrangement in our own memory enabled by collage. In the opening sentence of the essay we were invited to take automatism as a "veritable photography of thought," presumably in relation to the thought of the writer. In the closing image, however, Breton suggests that Ernst provides a film of *our* inner life, that is, of the inner experience of the reader/viewer, or, perhaps, of writer and reader together. The subjective positions are interchangeable because of the "estrangement" that results from the absence of any system of reference and because of the demise of the principle of identity Breton announces toward the end of the essay.

Of this "marvelous faculty of collage" Breton asks, "can it not do better than a poet?" The rhetorical question is important because it marks the displacement of the notion of poetry to include a poetry of mental operations in and of themselves—something like what Valéry had already appreciated as the interior drama of *l'esprit à l'œuvre* and presented in that fiction of modern lyricism, *Monsieur Teste.* The operations of collage are quintessentially poetic, for poetry involves juxtaposition and displacement. The lesson of Max Ernst, however, is that a freedom of juxtaposition, of *ordonnance*, is not pertinent in and of itself, but in relation to a level of preexisting signifying material.

The Man and the Window—and the "Light of the Image"

In the Surrealist Manifesto (1924) Breton defines surrealism as pure psychic automatism. This involves a "mode of expression" that presents "the real operation of thought" unimpeded by constraints of logic, esthetics, or morality. Breton sometimes refers to this psychic automatism as an inner murmuring, or a magic dictation; in principle, automatic writing or drawing simply records the flow of mental activity. The surrealists did not invent automatism, which had been practiced in the Dada milieu in writing, drawing, and photography. But when Breton decides to make automatism the centerpiece of what he calls "surrealism," he gives it new value. In the Dada context, Breton had spoken of the power of automatic writing to "ruin literature." In the Manifesto, automatism involves an affirmation. It returns us to the sources of poetic inspiration, and, above all, it yields revelatory images. The mind is carried away by these images that delight it (*ravir*, which means both to delight and to carry away) into the most beautiful of nights, the night of lightning bolts (*la nuit des éclairs*). Automatism may ruin one conception of literature, but thanks to the sublime effect of the "light of the image" it affirms another notion of poetic force, one linked to "emotive force and poetic reality."

If, at the moment of the Ernst exhibition, Breton still had expectations for Dada, by the following year he rejects Dada as merely the "crude image of a state of mind that it in no way helped create." He accuses the Paris Dada group of the vulgarization of important ideas.[26] "For myself, I will try to make a more radical commitment" (B 261), Breton announces, and he adds: "for a long time the risk has been elsewhere" (B 263). The account of the hypnotic sessions presented in "L'Entrée des Médiums" indicates where, for Breton, the real risk lies. It is in this context that Breton appropriates the term "surrealism," introduced earlier by Apollinaire, and defines it as "a certain psychic automatism which corresponds quite well to the dream state" (B 274).

In the First Manifesto, Breton presents the constellation of values—the ethos, or *morale*—that surrounds the practices discussed in "L'Entrée des Médiums": imagination, *liberté d'esprit*, and a fascination with the realm of the possible in opposition to the constraints of logic and practical necessity. Here we recognize the *courroie de transmission* that attaches to symbolism, since all these themes can be found in Valéry's essay on Leonardo. What is specific to surrealism is that it designates a "new mode of pure expression" that yields the light of the image.

In the Manifesto Breton begins his explanation of the surrealist image by quoting the poet Pierre Reverdy, who had defined the lyrical poetic image in the following terms:

> The image is a pure creation of the spirit [*l'esprit*].
> It cannot emerge from a comparison, but from the coming
> together of two distant realities.
> The more the relations between these two realities are distant
> and right, the stronger the image will be—the more it will
> have emotive force and poetic reality.

Reverdy's definition emphasizes that the image is not merely a comparison or analogy between two terms but a direct bringing together of things that appear to have little in common. In the Manifesto, Breton adjusts Reverdy's definition from the perspective of automatism. Not only is it a question of replacing mere comparison with a strong notion of metaphor that fuses the two disparate terms, it is a question of going beyond rhetoric, in the traditional sense, altogether. In contrast to the symbolist notion of poetic effort (in the tradition of Poe, Baudelaire, and Valéry), Breton affirms that the two terms that collide in the image emerge spontaneously from psychic automatism. The image occurs almost like a chemical reaction or a nuclear fusion. Two terms, which ordinarily belong to two different worlds, are thrown together by the speed and dynamic mobility of thought. Surrealist images are precipitates. This was Breton's initial title for the work published as *Les Champs magnétiques*, and it is the term Breton will use in 1928 to characterize the paintings of Masson.

Breton's first example of automatic writing in the Manifesto of 1924 also serves as an example of the surrealist image, and may be considered both a form of citation and a mode of collage. Breton writes that one evening, before going to sleep, a strange phrase came into his head, "or dare I say," he adds, "knocked at the window." He says he perceived this strange phrase "clearly articulated but independent of any voice," in a mode, therefore, of something like citation. The words, he reports, were accompanied by "a feeble visual representation." He claims to have been struck by the "organic" aspect of the sentence, the way it all fit together as one phrase.[27] By the time Breton writes the Manifesto, however, he has forgotten the exact sentence that flew into his head. It was, he writes, "something like: 'there is a man cut in two by the window'." Had he been a painter, he acknowledges, he would have focused on the visual image; as a poet, he claims to be most struck by the verbal sequence. And yet it is the visual image that enables him to puzzle out what the words say. The visual image provides a kind of signified (or mental idea) of the verbal signifiers that hover without a voice. Breton sees a man in an upright position divided in two sections by a window that cuts through him at right angles. "Without any doubt," he concludes, "it was merely a question of a vertical realignment [*redressement*] of a man who was leaning out a window."[28]

The "peculiar phrase," as he calls it, is a kind of verbal equivalent of the freedom of *ordonnance* with respect to given signifieds that Breton admired in the work of Ernst. We have two terms, a man and a window, which have simply been rearranged in relation to one another; the rearrangement confounds our habitual manner of seeing them, and, in this way, conveys poetic reality. Breton is struck by the force of this image: "I immediately wanted to incorporate it into the building material of my poetic construction," he tells us. He does so, as we shall see momentarily, in *Les Champs magnétiques*.

The image carried by the peculiar phrase given to exemplify the surrealist image is not as arbitrary as it might appear. A man who leans out a window is involved in an act of unmediated perception of the outer world. The image, in other words, dramatizes the figure for linguistic transparency we analyzed in our discussion of Sartre. Instead of looking through a window to the outside world, however, we have an exaggeration of that figure: a man leaning out an open window. This figures the operation of photography Breton discussed in the essay on Ernst, suggesting the immediacy of its trace, and, by association, the literary realism the critic attacks in the Manifesto. The ninety-degree rotation displaces this figure. The transparent glass of the pane is now implicitly reinscribed and instead of giving out onto an external scene the window opens into the man, suggesting an act of looking into the self (estrangement within memory, perhaps) and the "inner photography" of automatism. By virtue of the statement that the strange phrase "knocked at the windowpane"—presumably of Breton's awareness—the window as figure of consciousness is already in play. But the phrase that knocked on one window, the window of Breton's consciousness, carries another, one that cuts through the body instead of figuring the mind.

The image returns in *Les Champs magnétiques*, where the window of the image opens onto the heart. "The window cut into our flesh opens onto our heart. One sees an immense lake. . . . One laughs also, but you must not look for long without a telescope. Everyone can pass through this bloody corridor [*couloir*]" (B 57).[29] It is a question of cutting a path, or a corridor, into "inner life." In the Manifesto Breton writes: "I would like to give the key to this corridor," alluding to the corridor (*couloir*) that would provide access to the psychic processes of dream and lead into the lyrical register of feeling and imagination. "Everyone can enter into this bloody corridor," we read in *Les Champs magnétiques*; if the corridor is bloody, it is because the heart is evoked in the register of the body.[30] The French word *couloir* relates to the verb *couler* (to flow) and suggests the flow (*coulée*) of psychic automatism, the magic dictation Breton refers to as "the flow that concerns us" (B 332). For Breton, the surrealist image is a *couloir*, and what flows through this corridor are more images. The window that cuts the man in two figures the operation of the surrealist image itself and its effect—"the light of the image." Images are windows that cut into the heart of the automatic text.

Presumably on the basis of his own experience with the peculiar phrase, Breton adjusts Reverdy's definition of the image from the perspective of automatism. "Nothing is grasped consciously," he insists. The writer does not intentionally select the two terms that interact in the image:

> It is not within man's power, in my opinion, to perform the contact between such distant realities. . . . We must therefore admit that the two terms of the image are not deduced one from the other in order to produce a spark, but that they are the simultaneous products of the activity I call surrealist, the role of reason being limited to acknowledging and appreciating the luminous phenomenon. (B 338)

The image is the product of what Breton calls "surrealist activity." The spark marks the shock, the esthetic effect, of the image; its light stands for the revelation it yields. Surrealist activity engenders both elements of the image and provokes their coming together. Defined here as "psychic automatism," surrealism is thus presented as a process of image production; automatically—spontaneously—it engenders images that carry emotive force. "The esthetic of Reverdy," Breton writes, "had me taking effects for causes." The image is not the cause of surreality, it is the effect of surrealist activity—its precipitate.[31]

Breton proceeds to elaborate his own version of the surrealist image through an electrochemical figure:

> And just as the size of the spark increases when the spark is produced through rarefied gases, the surrealist atmosphere created by mechanical writing [*écriture mécanique*] . . . lends itself particularly well to the production of the most beautiful images. One could even say that in this dizzying race [*course vertigineuse*] the images are like the only handlebars of the spirit [*les seuls guidons de l'esprit*]. The mind [*l'esprit*] convinces itself gradually of the supreme reality of these images. Undergoing these images at first, one soon notices that they flatter one's reason, expanding its knowledge. . . . It proceeds, carried by these images that ravish it . . . it is the night of lightning bolts [*la nuit des éclairs*]: in comparison to this, day is night. (B 338)

It is the torrential flow of the automatic process—the *débit* (which also means declamation) of the *course vertigineuse*—that yields the two terms that fuse together in the image. They are posed as "simultaneous products" of this activity on the model of the chemical precipitate. Sequence does not function to imply logical priority of one term over another. We might extrapolate that the rarefied atmosphere of surrealist activity is a function of that absence of any frame of reference that Breton referred to in the essay on Ernst. The atmosphere created by this absence enhances the difference of charge or current (*différence de potentiel*) between the two elements of the image; it refuses any context that might tame the wildness of the relation. The mind (*l'esprit*), Breton writes, "becomes conscious of the unlimited expanses where its desires manifest themselves, where the for and the against always neutralize themselves [*se réduisent*]" (B 338). The difference of logical opposition is reduced by the light of the image, or the image as light. It is reduced in the specific sense of being consumed, as fire consumes into ash, or heat is said to "reduce" a liquid, returning liquid to gas.

"I believe in the future resolution of these two states, dream and reality, which are so contradictory in appearance, into a sort of surreality . . . this is the object of my conquest," Breton affirms. In *Les Vases communicants* he speaks of a "sublime point" where contradictions cease to be contradictory. As we have seen in previous chapters, these affirmations have gotten Breton into enormous trouble with French commentators, from Bataille in the early 1930's to Sartre in the 1940's all the way up to Foucault in the 1960's and beyond to Philippe Sollers and other *Tel Quel* critics in the 1970's and 1980's. Breton's affirmations have always been taken to mean that surreality implies some transcendent realm over and above the real, a domain of dialectical synthesis in a fundamentally idealist—that is, Hegelian—sense. Bataille is consistently counterposed to Breton on this point in theoretical discussions.

Breton's electrochemical figure for the surrealist image, however, suggests another way to read this "sublime point." Surreality, which, as we have seen, is an effect of the image, not its cause, should be interpreted in terms of the "supreme reality" of the image. The "future resolution" of logically contrary terms should be read in terms of the chemistry of the image itself, that is, in relation to the burning "reduction" of the "for and against" (Pascal's disparaging formula for rational disputation) associated with the "night of lightning bolts." In the phrase "future resolution of these two states, dream and reality, which are so contradictory in appearance," the word "resolution" is usually read in relation to the verb *résoudre*, understood as "to resolve," in the sense of resolving a problem or a contradiction. But in this case it is a question of a *se résoudre* (as we saw in the passage just cited) which also signifies "to reduce": to transform something into its smallest elements, or to make it disappear (we speak of reducing a broth in cooking, for example). The exact form Breton uses is *se résoudre en*, which we find in the following example given by the Robert: "Hail clouds resolve [*se réduisent en*] into water."[32] Instead of considering Breton's declaration in terms of a philosophical (or logical) problem in need of dialectical solution, we should read it as a description of a dynamic (al)chemical process.

In the context of Breton's critical development, the discursive resolution of the states of dream and reality occurs ten years after the First Manifesto. A theoretical resolution occurs in "Le Message automatique," Breton's "complete return to basic principles" concerning the question of automatism. "What is unique about surrealism," Breton writes here, "is to have proclaimed all normal human beings equal before the subliminal message. . . . All men, I say, all women, deserve to convince themselves of the absolute possibility of having recourse . . . to this language which is not surnatural and which is the very vehicle of revelation for one and all" (B 182).[33] Automatic writing or drawing is a vehicle for revelation because "it leads straight to hallucination."—"All the experimentation that is underway," he writes, "is meant to demonstrate that perception and representation—which, in the adult, seem to be so radically opposed to one another—should be taken merely as by-products of the dissociation of a single original faculty, which the eidetic image confirms. . . . I maintain that automatism alone can lead to this." How? Through the power of hallucination. Breton's presentation of this phenomenon recalls the terms of his declaration concerning the future resolution of the difference between dream and reality, for it is precisely in hallucination that the difference between reality and dream (or, in the language of "Le Message automatique," perception and representation) cannot be distinguished. With hallucination, Breton writes, it is a question of "the valid line of demarcation that would make it possible to isolate the imaginary object from the real one."[34] He cites a recent study to the effect that "one can affirm the presence or the perception of an object when it is present and perceived, when it is absent and perceived, or when it is neither present nor perceived."

In *Beyond Painting*, where collage and frottage are presented as "plastic equivalents of the surrealist image," Ernst also stresses the hallucinatory quality of the image. He emphasizes that this sort of image does not involve metamorphosis (as in *Les Chants de Maldoror*, for example) but involves a kind of fusion. The terms of the image are "fused without any intermediary." What Ernst suggests is that the surrealist image is not to be thought in rhetorical terms, that is, as comparison or metaphor. The

hallucinatory image produces an ambiguity between identity and difference, an equivocation between perception and representation, between
subjectivity and objectivity, or dream and reality. As Breton makes clear
in "Le Message automatique," what is important is a confusion between
the real and the fictive. It is a question of a contamination of that difference such that something new is indeed given to sense.

Surrealist automatism, then, could be said to yield the "resolution" of
surreality to the extent that it "leads directly to hallucination," for hallucination obliterates the distinction between dream and reality. Instead of
elaborating this "resolution" in dialectical terms, as a forward movement
beyond antinomy toward synthesis, Breton goes back (through a *re-
soudre*, a linking together again) to an anterior unity—the unique faculty
of eidetic images. The solution is not dialectical but psychological, even
electrochemical. Surreality is not a question of dialectical movement but
of a "chemistry of intelligence."

The expression "chemistry of intelligence" comes from *Le Surréalisme
et la peinture*, an essay written in 1928 in response to a claim by Pierre
Naville that there could be no such things as surrealist painting because
the facture of painting precludes the spontaneity of automatism. "For us
today," Breton writes toward the beginning of that essay, "what is at stake
is reality itself."[35] What is at stake, once again, is the line between perception and representation as the question of hallucination returns. "For
a long time, I think, people will experience the need to go back up the
magic stream that flows from the eyes to its real source, *bathing in the
same light, things that are and things that are not*" (SP 7, my emphasis).
The metaphor of the flow that characterizes the "magic dictation" of automatic writing returns in relation to the eyes. Surrealism implies two
movements of flow, two registers of the magical, and two modes of the
automatic.

Poe also had used the expression "chemistry of intelligence." Breton cites
this striking passage from the *Marginalia* in *Le Surréalisme et la peinture*:

The pure Imagination . . . chooses, either from the Beautiful or the Ugly, the only
elements which, having not yet ever been associated together, are best suited for
its combinations . . . there is a singular analogy between natural chemical phenomena and those of the chemistry of intelligence; it often happens that the bringing together [*la réunion*] of the two elements gives birth to a new product that in
no way recalls the qualities of any particular one of its components, or even any of
them. (SP 35)

We recognize in Poe a version of the definition of the poetic image Reverdy
contributed to the First Manifesto. But Breton makes this figure his own.
"The words: 'chemistry of intelligence,'" he writes, speaking of Masson,

" . . . would always lead us to these paintings as before so many inevitable dazzling precipitates" (SP 36). Masson's paintings are compared to surrealist images as they emerge in texts thanks to the specific atmosphere of surrealist activity and the "chemistry" of automatic writing.

"It should be the painter's turn to speak," Breton wrote in "Le Message automatique," echoing Valéry's admiration for what he called Leonardo's "philosophy of painting." And we soon see why this is. The painter, according to Breton, enjoys a faculty of eidetic images; painting introduces us to the "domain of pure forms," to the "boundaries [*limites*] where the mind refuses to borrow anything from the outside world." Breton summarizes his line of argument with the following formula, one that we recognize from our interpretation of Valéry in relation to Bergson: "To See, to understand [*entendre*] is nothing . . . to Recognize (or not recognize) is everything. Between what I recognize and what I do not recognize there is me. . . . It is to the conception of this most fervent relation that surrealism has raised its thoughts and that it holds onto" (SP 44). It is in this context that Breton declares the immanence of surreality:

Everything I love, everything that I think and feel, inclines me to a particular philosophy of immanence according to which surreality would be contained *in reality itself*, and would be neither superior nor exterior to it. . . . I reject with all my might efforts which, in painting as in writing . . . end up subtracting thought from life (materialism) or placing life under the aegis of thought (idealism). (SP 46, my emphasis)

We are reminded of the essay on Ernst where it was a question of not leaving the field of our experience, and of an "estrangement [*dépaysement*] . . . *in our own memory*" (my emphasis). The "resolution" of the states of dream and reality has less to do with a spirit of contradiction—with a Hegelian synthesis or an idealist transcendence—than with what Breton calls here a "spirit of evasion"—that is, evasion in the quite specific sense he attributes to Picasso. Breton champions Picasso not as the inventor of a Cubist discourse, but as the painter who dared to make a radical break from imitation, and who thus opened the way for a painting of what Breton calls the "interior model." This kind of painting, exemplified by the early work of de Chirico as well as by Magritte, displays what Breton understood by the surrealist image. Ironically, it is the quintessentially Cubist painter, Picasso, who suggests to Breton the modernist path he went on to propose as an alternative to the "failed projects" of symbolism and Cubism.

"To See, to hear/understand [*entendre*], is nothing. To Recognize (or not recognize) is everything. Between what I recognize and what I do not recognize there stands myself. . . . It is, I believe, the concept of this most fervent relationship that has always inspired surrealism and to which it has remained faithful" (SP 43–44). Here we have a conception of recognition that has nothing to do with the Hegelian master/slave dialectic that informed the elaborations of both transgression and engagement. What Breton alludes to here is recognition in Bergson's sense. "The truth is that basic vision and audition do nothing but . . . furnish us with reference points, or better yet, trace out a frame that we fill with our memories," Bergson writes in *L'Energie Spirituelle*, published in 1919:

One would be strangely mistaken concerning the mechanism of recognition if one thought that one began by seeing and hearing/understanding [*entendre*] and then, once the perception was constituted, matched it with a similar memory in order to recognize it. The truth is that *it is memory that makes us see and hear/understand* [*entendre*] and that perception would be unable, by itself, to evoke the memory that resembles it . . . it only becomes complete perception and acquires a distinct form thanks to the memory, which insinuates itself into it and provides it with most of its matter. (HB 944, my emphasis)

Perception provides the frame for the memory tableau.

As we have seen in the preceding chapter, Bergson's theory of recognition (*reconnaissance*) is central to his psycho-philosophical reflections, his philosophy of life. Recognition is a temporal function that links past and present; it is "the act by which we recapture the past in the present" (HB 235, *Matière et mémoire*). For Bergson, it is an essential mental operation, one that is performed not only during perception but in other activities as well, such as remembering, dreaming, and even reading. Recognition is required in perception because perception is not static, or punctual, as we tend to conceive of it; it occupies a certain duration (HB 184). Perception occurs through the interplay of past, present, and future, which makes up the flow of dynamic time. To receive information from the external world through the senses it is necessary to recruit the memory of a past perception—a "representation of an absent object." It is necessary to connect this with the physical experience of new perceptual data in order to make it meaningful to consciousness as one prepares to act. But the role of memory is not simply cognitive or pragmatic. Memory marks the "having been lived" or "having been felt" of perceptions. It testifies to the subjectivity of past experience—that is, to *le vécu*. It is thus the locus both of freedom (freedom from determination) and of subjective experience and feeling. Memory is "what communicates to perception above all its subjective character" (HB 220). In this sense, memory is an important feature of modern lyricism.

Recognition matches a memory image spontaneously generated through "reflection" ("the external projection of an image actively created" by *l'es-*

prit) to incoming sense data. Without recognition, we would have no distance on the material of sense experience; we would be, as it were, glued up against the physical world, unable to act. To this extent recognition plays a role for Bergson analogous to the one the negativity of consciousness plays for Hegel. It opens up a distance from the external world that allows for subjective agency. On Bergson's account, however, the relation between subject and object is not one of objectivity, as it is when we speak in cognitive terms (that is, in relation to a framework of representation) or in Hegelian terms, where it is a question of the negativity of consciousness and the master/slave dialectic. "Questions pertaining to the subject and the object," Bergson insists, " . . . should be posed in relation to time rather than space" (HB 218). Thus the entire issue of the relation of subject to object—a question that is of capital importance for Breton, and which he claims the discovery of Ernst's procedures of frottage and photo-collage has resolved—is radically displaced by the thinking of Bergson, which challenges the ideology of truth as objective representation, and the neo-Kantian mentality of empirical science.

In the preceding chapter we saw that the death of Teste was marked by "the agonizing human gaze which loses recognition." The fact that this alludes to Bergsonian recognition was supported by an entry in Valéry's notebooks that reads: "the return, the repetition [*reprise*], is the essential fact. Property of the Present. Coincidence of a memory-perception [*perception-mémoire*] and a sensory perception [*perception-sensation*] which, by their coming together and complex composition, yields the system Me-Present [*Moi-Présent*]."[36] I have also indicated that Bergson's theory of recognition played an important role in his analysis of reading, one echoed in Valéry's course on poetics, as well as in Sartre. In Breton, the Bergsonian operation of recognition is pertinent to the "resolution" of the states of dream and reality, or, as he sometimes puts it, the acts of representation and perception. It informs the status of hallucination. For on Bergson's theory, perception blends the dimensions of subjectivity and objectivity together in a temporal dynamic. Recognition links representation and perception together in such a way that "one can no longer discern what is perception and what is memory." In *Matière et mémoire*, Bergson asks: "What is the use of these memory images? By preserving themselves in the memory, by reproducing themselves in consciousness, are they not going to distort [*dénaturer*] the practical nature [*caractère*] of life, *mixing dream with reality*?" (my emphasis). Bergson's rhetorical question is extremely pertinent to the issues that preoccupy Breton, both in *Le Surréalisme et la peinture* and in "Le Message automatique." It is just such a possibility, the possibility of mixing dream and reality, that appeals to Breton. It is in these terms, I would argue, that one should interpret Breton's remark to the effect that recognition ("what I recognize and what I don't recognize") is central to surrealist activity. "It is the conception of this most fervent relation that has always inspired surrealism and to which it has always remained faithful." It plays a crucial role in the "chemistry of intelligence."

"To evoke the past in the form of images," Bergson writes in *Matière et mémoire*, "one must be able to cut oneself off from [*s'abstraire de*] present action, one must know how to attach value to what is useless, one must want to dream" (HB 228). Here, dream is identified with the positive value of pure duration, and with what Bergson calls the "deep inner life" of "the feeling and passionate self." Listening to Bergson, however, we seem to hear Breton, the Breton of the First Manifesto, who rails against the alienation of the subject in the culture of rationalism and of empirical science, and calls for a retrieval of lost psychic energies and for a reunification of the self with the subliminal forces latent within it. Breton appeals to dream for the liberation of an alienated self just as Bergson does. The relation between memory and image in Bergson helps us understand what Breton might mean by a capacity to "estrange oneself / take a holiday [*se dépayser*] in one's own memory" and how what he calls an "interior model" might be the visual correlate to the textual surrealist image.

Nadja, the Angel of Evasion: False Recognition

If Breton credits Picasso with a "spirit of evasion," for his courageous refusal of the mimetic function in his early painting, the surrealist personification of the spirit of evasion is, of course, Nadja. "Close your eyes and say something. Anything, a number, a name," Nadja declares,

> like this (she closes her eyes): Two, two what? Two women. What are these women like? Dressed in black. Where are they? In a park. . . . And what are they doing? Come on, it's so easy, why don't you want to play? Well, this is how I talk to myself when I am alone . . . this is how I live. (B 690)

The author marks this passage with an asterisk, and, in a note at the bottom of the page, poses this rhetorical question: "Do we not touch upon the extreme term of the surrealist aspiration here, its most powerful, most radical idea?" Breton as much as declares that Nadja is an allegory of psychic automatism. If poetry is a state of mind for Breton (as it was for the Dada poets) Nadja is its personification. In the course of the narrative, she becomes thoroughly identified with a process of automatic production in both visual and verbal registers. "I no longer want to remember," Breton writes toward the end of *Nadja*, "anything but a few phrases, pronounced before me or written by her all at once before my eyes, the phrases through which I can best retrieve the tone of her voice, and whose resonance is so strong in me" (B 719). By the end, the character Nadja is all but replaced by her automatic drawings and her "strange phrases [*phrases bizarres*]" which Breton dutifully records. Her fragments even begin to thematize this resonance; her "avec la fin de mon souffle qui est le commencement du votre" (which can either be translated "with my last breath which is your first" or "with the end of my inspiration which is the beginning of yours") is followed by: "If you like, for you I would be nothing, or merely a trace" (B 719). And of course there is the symbolic portrait of the two of them: "the siren, in which form she always saw herself from the back, and from this angle, holding a roll of paper in her hand; the monster with the blazing eyes rises up from a sort of vase with the head of an eagle, covered with feathers that figure ideas" (B 721). Nadja has not only become the substance of her automatic productions, but these productions portray her as the mediator of Breton's own creative energies.

As the text opens, Breton emerges from a bookstore where he has been perusing a work by Trotsky.[37] The revolution won't be made by them, he muses as he surveys the bourgeois Parisians that fill the streets—and then he beholds the apparition of The Unknown Woman (*L'Inconnue*). Her eyes attract his attention, eyes that remind Breton of Blanche Duval playing the part of Solange in "Les Détraquées." With their dark makeup that belongs on the stage (but that Breton appreciates on the street), Nadja's eyes blur the line between real and imaginary realms. The Unknown Woman is already in a mode of trangression; she has already begun a subversion of real public space, contaminating it with the codes of the theater as scene of representation.

Nadja is an angel of evasion. She recognizes no boundaries, either between theater and life, or between past and present. Like Teste, though in quite a different way, she incarnates a principle of instability. Whereas Teste is a figure of intelligence "detached from any application," that is, a figure of genius as "man of attention [*l'homme d'attention*]," Nadja is a "free genius [*génie libre*]," the very incarnation of Bergsonian sympathy. Whereas Teste displays vigilant attention, Nadja, the "errant soul," lives with the kind of "inattention to life" that Bergson identifies with one extreme end of mental activity: dream. As we shall see in more detail in Chapter 6, for the philosopher dream and action are considered two extreme limits of mental activity. They do not differ radically in kind (as on a Freudian model, where the unconscious is separated from consciousness by forces of repression); they are distinguished by differences in degree of tension, or attention. "Whether asleep or awake," Bergson writes in *L'Energie spirituelle*, "*l'esprit* combines sensation with memory" (HB 890).

Whereas for Bergson dream is characterized by a state of mental relaxation (and a predominance of memory images), waking consciousness involves tension because it is focused directly on the present or approaching moment and its requirements for useful action. This preparedness for action—almost entirely lacking in Nadja—is what Bergson calls "attention to life."[38]

Readers of *Nadja* face a disturbing ambivalence that threatens any coherent interpretation of the text. For if Nadja is a figure of the highest aspirations of surrealism, she also appears to demystify the myth of these aspirations because of the culminating diagnosis of her madness. It is interesting to note in this context that for Bergson there is nothing aberrant in cases of "pathological" depersonalization. From his point of view, such phenomena simply reveal features of the customary operations of the psyche usually hidden from us because the "attention to life" of consciousness concentrates energies on incipient action. Truths about relations between the processes of recognition and perception, for example, come to light through experiences of second sight, or what Bergson calls "false recognition." What interests the philosopher in such cases is that present and past experiences overlap:

The distinction that we make between our present and our past is therefore, if not arbitrary, at least relative to the extent of the field that our attention to life can embrace. The "present" occupies just as much place as this effort. As soon as this particular attention lets go of something it held under its gaze, what it abandons of the present becomes *ipso facto* past. In a word, our present falls into the past when we cease to endow it with ongoing interest. (HB 1386, *La Pensée et le mouvant*)

Bergson goes on to describe exceptional cases in which "suddenly attention renounces the interest it took in life," and "immediately, as if by magic, the past becomes present again" (HB 1387). This disinterestedness is not the Kantian disinterestedness of esthetic contemplation, but the disinterest in pragmatic action that, on Bergson's theory, characterizes not only dream but also the activities of the artist. The senses and consciousness of the artist, Bergson writes, "adhere less to life" than those of most people. When it comes to artists, "nature forgot to attach their faculty of perception to their faculty of action." Artists, he states,

no longer perceive just for the sake of action; *they perceive for the sake of perception*—for no reason, for the pleasure of it. In a certain sense . . . they are born detached, they are painters or sculptors, musicians or poets. It is thus really a *more direct evasion of reality* that we find in the different arts; and it is because artists think [*songe*] less about using their perceptions that they perceive a greater number of things. (HB 1373, my emphasis)[39]

Nadja is an "angel of evasion" in just this sense, and it is for this reason that she can stand for the possibilities of automatism and the "highest aspirations" of surrealism. As if she were a walking example of that form of depersonalization specific to the artist—false recognition—Nadja seems to live her encounter with Breton as if there were no fundamental distinction between her perceptions and her memories or imaginative sympathies. "It seems to her," Breton writes of Nadja, "that she had never had a secret from me, even before knowing me." Nadja feels as if she has lived what she reads in Breton's *Le Poisson soluble*; it is as if she herself dissolves into this automatic text. When she reads the Jarry poem cited in the Manifesto she has a vision of the poet passing through the forest mentioned in the poem. Not only does she see him, as in the frozen moment of a photograph, but she follows him in action in a cinematic mode:

She sees the poet passing near this forest, it is as if she could follow him from afar: "No, he is turning around the forest. He cannot enter it, he doesn't enter it." Then she loses him and comes back to the poem, a little further on than the point where she left him, pausing over the words that most surprise her, giving each one an indication of complicity, the exact sign of assent it solicits. (B 689)

Walking through the garden of the Tuileries one night, Nadja and Breton come upon a fountain. "These are your and my thoughts," Nadja says to Breton, "See where they start from, how far they rise up and how it is even more beautiful when they fall back down. And then they melt together right away, they are taken up again by the same force, once again there is this broken soaring, this fall . . . and it goes on and on, indefinitely" (B 698). Coincidentally, Breton has just been struck by the very same image while reading Berkeley's *Dialogues between Hylas and Philonous*. In his edition of the text, a picture of a fountain appears on the frontispiece, one whose very movements Nadja appears to be describing, inspired by the fountain in the Tuileries. Breton provides a photo of this page for the reader's benefit.

A further coincidence, however, is that Bergson uses this same image to characterize the relation between perception and memory in the psyche.[40] A fountain in its double movement, he proposes, conveys the true functioning of mental operations. These are usually obscured by the attention to life of consciousness, but are revealed in cases of depersonalization, such as those we associate with false recognition or second sight. On Bergson's analysis, memory is generated alongside perception. The present, he writes, "splits in two at every moment, even in its shooting up, in two symmetrical streams, of which one falls back towards the past and the other soars off towards the future. The latter, which we call perception, is the only one that interests us." (HB 914, *L'Energie spirituelle*).[41]

"It is even more beautiful when they fall back down." Not surprisingly, when Nadja contemplates the waters of the fountain, she prefers the moment Bergson associates with the past. What Nadja sees in the fountain corresponds to Bergson's use of the same figure to explicate precisely the terms of Nadja's "pathology," her "spirit of evasion"—memory and perception as they operate in the phenomenon of second sight. Her state of derealization is what Bergson would call a "lowering of vital resiliency [*abaissement de ton vital*]," a reduction of psychic tension that enhances the dynamics of memory and dream at the expense of perception in its relation to consciousness and readiness for action. Nadja is in a state of what Breton elsewhere calls "wakeful dreaming [*rêve éveillé*]."[42] To the extent that memory and perception also correspond to Breton's terms "dream" and "reality," as they function in the celebrated declaration from the First Manifesto (subsequently rephrased in terms of representation and perception in relation to the question of hallucination in "Le Message automatique"), we can appreciate to what extent the coincidence of the fountain in *Nadja* is overdetermined for Breton. The fountain could be said to figure surreality itself and the "immanent transcendence" it designates.

In his account of such unusual mental states, Bergson makes the distinction between those that involve a fundamental deficiency and those that, on the contrary, "appear to add something extra to normal life and to enrich it instead of diminishing it." He cites hallucination as an example of the latter (HB 909). It is in this context that Bergson presents one of his most positive assessments of the psychic state of dream. "In one sense," he writes, "the perception and memory which are at work in the dream are more natural than those in waking life: *consciousness amuses itself by perceiving for the sake of perceiving, remembering for the sake of remembering, without any concern for life, I mean for an action to be performed*" (HB 911, my emphasis). "To perceive for the sake of perceiving" is the same expression Bergson used to characterize the artist in the passage cited earlier. There is a link between what Bergson calls "memory of the present" and the sympathy of intuition for which the model is the detached spirit of the artist. The mechanism of "memory of the present" also extends to a kind of future seeing: "this recognition in advance [*cette reconnaissance à venir*], that I feel is inevitable by virtue of the momentum [*élan*] gathered all along by my faculty of recognition, exerts in advance a retroactive effect upon my present state, placing me in the strange situation of someone who feels that they know what they know they don't know" (HB 919). This is precisely the position of Nadja. It is in the mode of something like a "memory of the present" that Nadja wanders through life, and through the streets of Paris. For Bergson, as for Breton, dream and hallucination enrich the consciousness of the artist.[43]

Nadja is all intuition, all sympathy, in Bergson's sense. This is what accounts for the exceptional force of her encounter with Breton; it is also what inspires Breton's sense of *hantise*. "I am the trace of your thought," Nadja affirms to Breton. To the extent that she is a figure for automatism, her wandering spirit haunts not only Breton but the movement of the text as well. *Nadja* opens with the question of identity: "Who am I? if exceptionally I refer back to an adage: why would not everything depend upon knowing who I 'haunt'?" (B 647). From the very beginning this question of identity is displaced toward an operation of recognition in Bergson's sense, that is, toward a play of perception and memory. The theme of being haunted (*hantise*) treats this very question. The limits between self and other become inextricably bound up with the question of the limits between past and present. The two come together here. Breton not only frequents Nadja, he haunts or obsesses her and is haunted by her in turn. "One day," she had pronounced, "you will write a book about me." Breton fulfills her identity only by writing her life in a way that problematizes his own identity. Nadja is haunted by Breton—this is the story told—and reciprocally, Breton is haunted by Nadja—this determines the mode of telling the story.

With *Nadja*, Breton's task is to attempt to "know what I should very well *recognize*" and to "learn a small part of what I have forgotten" (B 647, my emphasis). Breton's self-portrait dramatizes the formula Breton proposed in *Le Surréalisme et la peinture*: "To See, to hear/understand [*entendre*], is nothing. To Recognize (or not recognize) is everything. Between what I recognize and what I don't recognize, there stands myself" (44).

Nadja is a figure of psychic automatism. With the novel *Nadja*, it is a question of transposing the automatism *vécu* of Nadja into a narrative (or autobiographical) mode that is also "automatic." The writing of Nadja's story involves the juxtaposition of intense experiences in the life of Breton, episodes that arrive by chance. "Sudden rapprochements . . . petrifying coincidences": these are lived equivalents of the surrealist image, which Breton explicitly compares to the texture of automatic writing:

From these facts, of which I can only be the haggard witness, to others, which I flatter myself to think I get the drift of [*dont je me flatte de discerner les tenants*] and, to a certain extent, can presume to know the outcome of, there is perhaps as much distance, for the same observer, as between one of these affirmations . . . that make up the "automatic" sentence or text, and a sentence or a text . . . whose elements have been well thought out and weighed in advance. (B 652)

Nadja, the "errant soul," lives the processes of psychic automatism whereas Breton reconstructs them through the errancy of "*hantise*," that is, through chance encounters with haunting memory images. "I will limit

myself here to remembering, effortlessly, what . . . sometimes happened
to me. . . . I will speak of this without any preestablished order and according to the whim of the moment which just lets things float [*surnager*]
to the surface" (B 652).[44] Breton *scripteur* is an entirely passive medium,
just like the "writer" of an automatic text. Writing *Nadja*, then, involves
a form of chemistry between present (as time of writing) and past. The
random memories swim to consciousness capriciously. Here *surnager* also
implies "to subsist" (*se maintenir dans ce qui disparaît*) or to linger on as
memories do. Memories are phantoms; the self is a haunted house.

Before the narrative of *Nadja* properly begins, Breton relates a series
of coincidences, such as his first encounter with Paul Eluard. These initial
pages, which help frame the story of Breton's encounter with Nadja, perform something like a spiritual exercise in preparation for her entrance
on the scene. This preparation links Nadja's appearance (and her story)
to Breton as writer of this "automatic" text. The thickness of the frame
detracts from the centrality of the story of Nadja and attracts poetic attention back to Breton and to the process of writing. In the last pages of
the book, which close the frame of the narrative, Breton's discussion of
the photographs that accompany his text perform the same function. "I
began to look again at several of the places that this story happens to lead
to," he writes:

I wanted, in fact, just as with some people or some objects, to give a photographic
image that was taken from the particular angle from which I had myself considered them. . . . I discovered that they defended themselves, more or less, against
my undertaking, with the result that the illustrated part of *Nadja* was, in my opinion, insufficient. (B 746)

He gives several examples of photos he was unable to obtain: "Becque
surrounded by sinister-looking fences . . . the Théatre Moderne on its
guard," and laments the "total disappearance of almost everything that
relates to the Etreinte de la Pieuvre . . . " These details contribute a sense
of the passage of time, which separates the time of the events narrated
from the time of writing the text. They emphasize the problematic nature
of the relationship between representation (the photograph, but also the
text) and the "real."

Breton states in his preface to the 1962 edition that the role of the photographs in his text is to eliminate all description. In her notes to the Pléiade edition, M. Bonnet suggests that their role is to unify the text. Both
these views consider the photos to be illustrations of the text, in the usual
sense of illustrating the real to which the text refers. But there is another
possibility. Perhaps the photos attach not to the story told but to the process of telling the story, that is, to the dynamics of the "magic dictation"

itself or to automatism as "photography of thought [*de la pensée*]." Perhaps the photographs pertain to the story of Nadja not on the level of a realist reading, but on an allegorical one, a reading of Nadja as figure for the process of automatism. In this case the photographs would present memories as mental images. "Inwardly," Valéry wrote in his essay on Leonardo, "there is a drama . . . the actors here are mental images . . . the *esprit* . . . is their scene [*lieu*]" (V 1158–59). I am proposing that we consider the photographs we find in *Nadja* as mental images in something like this sense. The photos present the mental images that swim to the surface in the author's mind in the process of writing; they are like precipitates of involuntary memory, the memory work associated with the desire to "know what I should very well recognize," and the task of learning "a small part of what I have forgotten" (B 647).

Not unlike the famous sentence from Lautréamont concerning Maldoror: "I will say how he was good . . . it is done," the point of departure and the point of arrival of Breton's narrative are held together in the same sentence: "I will take the Hôtel des Grands Hommes, place du Panthéon, where I lived around 1918, as my point of departure and for my point of arrival [*et pour étape*] the Manoir d'Ango à Varengeville-sur-Mer, where I find myself in August, 1927." The sentence short-circuits the narrative and closes it back upon the time of writing.[45] The juxtaposition of the first two photographs—the Hôtel des Grands Hommes and the Manoir d'Ango—reinforces this effect of short circuit, for it puts both moments on an equal footing. It disrupts the chronological framework of the story told, interrupting it with a frame of retrospection that inscribes the time of writing. Once this interference has occurred on the visual level, the photographs can no longer be taken for granted as simple illustrations of the novel's story. Instead, they serve as "guidons de l'esprit [handlebars/ guidons of the mind]," navigating the writing of the "faits glissades [sliding events]" and the "faits précipices [events of the abyss]."[46]

But before the Hôtel des Grands Hommes and the Manoir d'Ango (or perhaps in the interval between them) comes the glass house. "For myself," writes Breton, "I will continue to live in my glass house, where one can see who comes to visit me at any hour . . . where I sleep at night on a glass bed with glass sheets, where who I am will appear to me sooner or later etched by diamond" (B 651). This image returns as the title of a photograph in *L'Amour fou*. What that photograph depicts, however, is not a house but a crystal, and beneath it Breton has written "my house, my life, what I write." In *Nadja*, the house, the life, and the writing also coincide. They are all a function of "petrifying coincidences" and of "sudden juxtapositions" (B 651), themselves figured by the diamond in Breton's text and by the crystal in the photo from *L'Amour fou*. One could

say that the photos in Breton's novel are part of the poet's building materials, as Breton put it in the First Manifesto. They are like the windows
that cut into the heart in *Les Champs magnétiques*. As such, they let the
reader "see . . . who comes to visit me . . . at any hour," or, in this particular context, which memory images haunt Breton at which point. They
are the markers of coincidence—petrified coincidences—which link *errance* (errancy) to *hantise*.

Considered as mental images, phantoms of signal events, the photographs play a role in generating the text, which could be said to flow
from their appearance. They give what the mind's eye sees. "Now I see
[*revois*] Robert Desnos again," Breton writes, and we see in the photograph what Breton sees in the interior vision of memory. Rather than the
photo illustrating a text, it seems in such cases that the text narrates a sequence of visions, the memory images the photos give us to see. To this
extent the photos do not take us into the world beyond the text; they bring
us inside Breton's mind, and, in overlapping fashion, inside the mind of
Nadja who functions as a "trace of [his] thought." Breton insists that the
photo of each monument or artifact was "taken from the particular angle from which I myself had considered [it]" (B 746). Instead of objectifying documents that reinforce the relation to the real—the relation of reference—they introduce the angle of the *vécu*, of subjective seeing. As
"photography of thought" they are to be read not as referents but as signifieds.[47]

By calling our attention to the disjunction between the apparently timeless sites or monuments represented in the photographs and the reality of
the devastations of time—the demise, for example, of the Théatre Moderne—Breton underscores the difference between the persistence of memory and the fragility of the real.[48] Thus paradoxically, while appearing to
play a role of documentation of the real, the photos (and Breton's discussion of them) serve to remark the difference from the real that is always
at play in memory and, to this extent, always part of the experience of the
real itself. We could say that the photographs play a double role. Appearing as referential indicators, they are representatives of a signified in
the mind or memory of the writer; they mark the difference between the
two.

Breton regrets not having been able to obtain the photo of a certain figure from the Musée Grévin, "even though there is no other mention of it
in this book." He regrets

the impossibility of obtaining authorization to photograph the adorable lure
[*leurre*] . . . in the Grévin museum, this woman pretending to hide in the shadows
to attach her garter, and who, in her immutable pose, is the only statue I know
that has eyes: eyes of provocation. (B 747–48)

An editor's note in the Pléiade attaches this image to Solange (the character from *Les Détraquées*) and to Breton's description of her "uncovering a marvelous thigh, there, a little above the dark garter." The editor sees in this another "way to secretly link one point of the story to another, one of those threads that the intentional discontinuity [of the text] hides," (B 1558). A thematic link between Solange and Nadja is undeniable, but the question of the photo is another matter. In the first place, there is Breton's explicit statement concerning the wax figure to the effect that "there is no other mention of it in this book." There is also the question of the placement of the photo. Once obtained, Breton did not put it near the account of *Les Détraquées*, but rather at the end of the text, as part of the meta-narrative frame.

There is also the question of the title. Breton does not give the photographs the name of the scene or object represented in them. Instead, a citation from the text serves as title, together with the page reference where this citation is to be found. This textual reference is always located within a page or two of the photograph in question. The picture of the woman adjusting her stocking is entitled "au musée Grévin," and the page reference attached to this title corresponds to the meta-narrative discussion of the impossibility of obtaining the photo for the text. This image remains singular. Not only does it pertain to something mentioned in the text as not being mentioned—"even though there is no other mention of it in this book"—but the absence of the photo is marked in the text and the placement of the photo in the later edition (and its title) refers the reader to this discussion of its absence.[49] For all these reasons, it invites interpretation in a different register from the other images.[50]

Breton describes the wax statue from the Musée Grévin as a lure. As such it might be taken as a figure for all the photos in *Nadja*, for they all function as lures for the reader. The first photos in the book appear to present public and stable points of reference, "documents" of the real, which attach us to perception. But as the novel progresses, we find various substitutes for this "real" world: a theatrical scene, the photograph of a printed text, strange objects and works of art, and finally Nadja's automatic drawings. We slip from the horizon of perception to that of representation by text and by image, or, in other words, from the plane of action in the real to the plane of dream.[51] There is no longer any "plane of reference" as these instances of virtual, imaginary, and real existence are all placed on the same "documentary" (or pseudo-documentary) level for us. They solicit us with a reassurance of the real only to problematize the real, enhancing the fringes of consciousness. They solicit complicities between the outer world of perception and action and the inner world of memory, dream, and imagination.[52] The photos in *Nadja* lure us into the elsewhere—the alibi—of the errant soul, Nadja, and into that concatenation of automatism and the real for which she stands—"this is how I live."

"One will therefore be surprised," Breton writes in the Second Manifesto, "that, clinging as close to *the truth* as we have done, we have been careful, overall, to arrange a literary, or other, alibi for ourselves rather than to throw ourselves into the water, not knowing how to swim, to enter into the fire, without believing in the phoenix, to attain this truth" (B 810–11, original emphasis). *Nadja* is such a literary alibi for the risk of that "extreme limit" of surrealist activity that Nadja ostensibly lived. Likewise, the empirical Nadja is the alibi of Nadja as figure for automatism. For in order to portray automatism in life (as opposed to art)—that is, to portray the passage to act of automatism—Breton needed the alibi of a certain realism. This is reinforced by the lure of the photographs. The realist story of an empirical Nadja is but a lure, a lure to the siren's song of a "detachment from the real" of the "star in finitude [*l'étoile dans le fini*]." The photographs reinforce the alibi of realism while at the same time they lure the reader into the perpetual elsewhere of the "angel of evasion" with a reassuring illusion of the real.

Surrealist Invention and Engagement

As Breton writes in *Les Vases communicants*, there is a surrealist desire to transform the world, as well as to interpret it; there is a "practical will which is the revolutionary will" (*VC* 135). This desire was announced in the Second Manifesto. Breton's support for the revolutionary politics of the Communist Party in the late 1920's prompted an exodus of dissident surrealists (Bataille among them) from Breton's milieu. Some years later, however, when Breton had been replaced by Sartre as principal cultural rival, Bataille credited Breton with the invention of engagement. "Not that I am opposed in any way to the principle of engaged literature," he wrote more than a bit disingenuously in the 1940's, adding, "How can we not rejoice today (even insidiously) to see it taken up again by Jean Paul Sartre? It nevertheless seems to me necessary to remember here that twenty years ago Breton staked the whole activity of surrealism on this principle."[53] Bataille strategically champions Breton as father of engaged literature in a gesture calculated to derail cultural stereotypes. But the stereotypes hold fast.

Thanks in part to Sartre's scathing attack against the surrealists in *Qu'est-ce que la littérature?*, Breton's engagement has never been taken seriously. The shift in Breton's discourse that accompanied his engagement, however—his appeal to the discourses of Hegel, Marx, and Freud—has been taken very seriously. It has been taken to account for the activity of surrealism from beginning to end. The question is not whether Breton's theoretical discourse is dialectical or Hegelian. There is no question that it becomes so once the commitment to Marxist revolution is made.[54] In the Second Manifesto, the whole project of surrealism is presented as a development of dialectical thinking.[55] In *Positions politiques du surréalisme*, Breton characterizes surrealism as a "mode of knowledge . . . developing within the framework of dialectical materialism, in application of Marx's password "more consciousness [*plus de conscience*]."[56] The appeal to "plus de conscience" becomes a theoretical focal point where the discourses of Marx and Freud meet and join forces. Freud's discourse corresponds, on the level of superstructure, to that of Marx's materialist dialectic on the level of infrastructure. The question is not, then, whether Breton's discourse is Hegelian or dialectical, but rather, what is the status of this Hegelianism in the context of the evolution of Breton's thinking concerning surrealism? Were the "new discursivities" of Marx and Freud essential to the emergence of the surrealist enterprise, or did surrealism just accommodate them, applying them for the sake of their rhetorical power?[57] Did Breton merely elaborate the fundamental aspirations of surrealism in terms compatible with his political ideology and invoke Freud as the superstructural equivalent of the Marxist discourse of emancipation? Or does a Hegelian notion of dialectic in fact account for the energies and aspirations of surrealism at the deepest level?

In the case of Bataille and transgression the answer would be yes. As we have seen, Bataille's notion of transgression in eroticism is elaborated through an intimate dialogue with, and subversion of, the Hegelian notion of absolute knowledge. The Hegelian dialectic of recognition is central both to Bataille's thinking of the transgression of eroticism and to Sartre's elaboration of engagement. In Breton, however, it is entirely absent. Our reading of Breton has substituted Bergson's notion of recognition for that of Hegel, shifting away from the discursive field usually associated with surrealism: Hegel, Marx, and Freud. I have argued against the conventional idealist interpretation of surrealism as a quest for a transcendent solution to a dialectical problem: the opposition between dream and reality. I have chosen instead to read surreality in terms of Breton's figures for the operation of the surreal image and what Breton calls the "chemistry of intelligence." In so doing I have also substituted a Bergsonian "unconsciousness" for either a Freudian or a Lacanian unconscious in our interpretation of what Breton understands by the dynamics of dream.[58]

Bergson did not consider unconsciousness (*inconscience*) to be radically distinct from consciousness. His analysis of dream as one extreme end of mental activity, one that privileges a free play of memory images, informs

Breton's characterization of surreality in terms of an "estrangement in our own memory." Bergson elaborates his theory of recognition in the very terms Breton explicitly invokes in "Le Message automatique" as well as in *Le Surréalisme et la peinture*: that is, as an interaction between representation and perception. These are the terms brought together in Breton's theory of surreality, which poses it as a question of "reality itself."

The appeal to Bergson encourages us to reject an interpretation of automatism in terms of a theory of the unconscious structured like a language. The Lacanian perspective invites a reading of automatic texts in rhetorical terms. This approach leads to a characterization of surrealism in terms of a negative formalism—that is, in terms of the violation or transgression of formal conventions. The Bergsonian perspective, on the other hand, proposes that we replace the Freudian or Lacanian unconscious with a more supple notion of unconsciousness, or *inconscience*, and that we consider this unconsciousness dynamically, in relation to an energetic continuum leading in and out of states of conscious "attention to life." In this way, we replace a topographic principle with an economic one that is also dynamic: the shifting degrees of tension or relaxation involved in various mental attitudes.[59] This point of view invites us to think a "travail de l'esprit," as both Bergson and Valéry put it, which includes a play of visual images. This visual register opens up a virtual field of memory. What the thinking of Bergson brings to our understanding of surrealism, then, is a heightened appreciation of the desire to fuse visual and verbal arts that Breton announces in *Le Surréalisme et la peinture*, including the kind of "fusion" of photograph and text that we find in *Nadja* and *L'Amour fou*. It helps us appreciate what Breton did not fully recognize at first in *Le Surréalisme et la peinture*, namely, that Magritte, whom Max Ernst described as an artist "who painted collages entirely by hand," had understood the surrealist image better than anyone.

In the years between 1910 and 1914, Bergson was at the height of his popularity, which went well beyond narrow professional circles.[60] Breton finished his lycée studies in 1912–13. He had reputedly demonstrated a particular interest in philosophy "in spite of the positivism of his professor André Cresson which he rejected."[61] If Cresson was a neo-Kantian empiricist, the philosopher who represented the antithetical point of view was of course Bergson—"the philosopher we listen to," as François Mauriac put it in 1912.

It has been suggested that in 1913 Bergson's *Essai sur les données immédiates de la conscience* and *Matière et Mémoire* "played at the beginning of the twentieth century an analogous role to the one played by *L'Allemagne* of Mme de Staël for the early French romantics."[62] Only in this case it is a question of the symbolist milieu. By 1904, Bergson had been publicly declared the philosopher of symbolism by Tancrède de Visan, a poet-philosopher who was a student and follower of Bergson. If de Visan's name is largely unknown to us today it is perhaps in part because he was the theorist of another symbolism, what he called "a contemplative lyricism," which was something quite distinct from the modernist symbolism of Mallarmé.

It is well known that Breton's reflections on modernity turned on the issue of a modern lyricism. These reflections are most intense around the time he begins to abandon the Mallarméan symbolist poetics of his early poems, that is, around 1919. We remember that long discussions between Breton and Pierre Reverdy reportedly took place on this subject and it is in this context that Breton receives from Reverdy the definition of the poetic image that he will subsequently borrow (with the slight adaptation we have traced) to characterize the surrealist image. Reverdy defined lyricism as "the result of the shock of two elements, if two notes produce a third sound, there is lyricism. If two notes produce two notes without harmony [*sans accord*] there is no lyricism." In another formulation Reverdy writes: "Lyricism is neither attitude nor beatitude: it is the modulation that springs from the shock of two thoughts and it is their exchange [*troc*]."[63] We have already suggested the shift that took place from this starting point in a meditation on lyricism as Breton elaborates his own notion of the surrealist image in relation to the dynamics of "photocollage" and automatic writing.

As de Visan's essay on lyricism reveals, something quite similar to Reverdy's discussion of lyricism (and to what is subsequently elaborated as the surrealist image) is to be found in Bergson's *Essai*. Appealing to the distinction he makes between the "deep self," in touch with pure duration, and the "superficial self," the subject of action, of social life, and of language, Bergson writes:

Digging beneath the surface contact between the self and external things, [if] we penetrate into the depths of organized and living intelligence we will witness the superimposition or rather the intimate fusion of many ideas which, once dissociated, seem to exclude one another as logically contradictory terms. The strangest dreams, where two images overlap with one another and present to us at the very same time two different people, who are nevertheless only one, will give us a feeble idea of the interpenetration of our concepts in the waking state. The imagination of the dreamer, isolated from the external world, reproduces through simple images and in its own way parodies the work that is constantly ongoing, on ideas, in the deepest regions of intellectual life. (HB 90)

When Breton defines automatism as a "veritable photography of thought," I would suggest that he has in mind Bergson's notion of thought as unconscious psychic operation of the "deep self."

My argument has been that we need to read Breton not from a retrospective vantage point (Hegel, Marx, Freud, Lacan as they pertain to the enterprise of theory) but, as Valéry put it in relation to Leonardo, from the point of view of its emergence, that is, in relation to a certain symbolism. This is not the symbolism of Mallarmé, however, which has been recuperated for the thinking of poststructuralism, but the lyrical symbolism of poets such as Maeterlinck, theorized by de Visan. It is this *courroie de transmission* that helps us appreciate the specificity, and the force, of Breton's critique of modernism as he saw it emerging in relation to the symbolism of Mallarmé and the Cubism of Picasso. It is for this reason that I have emphasized lyrical and fictive moments in surrealist automatism, and stressed not only the importance of the visual register for Breton, but the fact that the visual register is crucial to the activities of automatism even in the verbal mode. For Breton, the energies of lyrical meaning operate in the visual register, even when it is a question of texts. We must read automatic writing with our eyes—"les yeux de notre esprit [the eyes of our mind]."

In the Second Manifesto Breton expresses the desire to "clarify the relations between thought and matter" (B 794), a formulation that rephrases the question of relations between superstructure and infrastructure, which is also to say the question of engagement. This, for the surrealist, is both an esthetic and a political question that works itself out not only in relation to what Breton calls "la querelle sociale [the social struggle]," but also in relation to the surrealist object. It is in this context that Breton writes that surrealism has "succeeded in dialectically reconciling these two terms so violently contradictory for the adult man: perception, representation." Here we have an eclectic overlap of the discourses of Hegel and of Bergson. For along with the claim of a dialectical reconciliation, we find the terms of the operation of recognition, specifically the terms elaborated through Bergson's notion of recognition in the *Le Surréalisme et la peinture*. Here Breton claims that surrealism has "bridged the abyss" that separated perception and representation. "From now on painting and surrealist constructions," he adds, "have enabled the organization of perceptions with a tendency towards objectivity around subjective elements. By their tendency to impose themselves as objective, these perceptions appear overwhelming, revolutionary, in that they imperiously call to something in external reality that responds to them. One can foresee, to a large extent, that something *will be [quelquechose sera]*."[64]

In addition to Hegel and Bergson, then, we hear echoes of Valéry, the Valéry of the early Leonardo essay. We remember reading there that for the philosopher, "the limit one seeks to get back to [*rejoindre*] is simply what is," whereas the artist "spills out into the possible and makes himself *the agent of what will be*" (V 1243, original emphasis). This, as we have seen, is what Valéry understood by power and action, that is, the "pouvoir créer" of invention. The essay "La Position surréaliste de l'objet" picks up where Breton's discussion of Ernst left off and, to a certain extent, continues along the lines of the *courroie de transmission* of symbolism—the symbolist ethos, that is, if not its poetics. It marks the development from collage to construction as a literalization of a fiction in three-dimensional space. The important point here is the continuity of reflection between the two essays. The question of the surrealist object is one of the concretization of the phenomenon of hallucination already linked to automatism in "Le Message automatique" and, by Ernst, in relation to collage—"ne fait-il pas mieux qu'un poète?" Breton had asked rhetorically of Ernst. The practical meditations on the surrealist object represent the highest aspirations for what Breton calls poetry, hardly a uniquely verbal or linguistic phenomenon for him. The surrealist object fulfills the revolutionary program of surrealism, the dual operation of interpreting the world and transforming it. It materializes the alibi and concretizes the surrealist image.

Of course Breton's theoretical solution to the opposition between poetry and action, as it is advanced in relation to the surrealist object, is unacceptable to Sartre. For the philosopher of engagement, surrealism renders action impossible, to the extent that it deconstructs or invalidates the oppositions between the domains of the real and of the imaginary, as we have seen in our reading of Kristeva. Sartre comments, concerning Breton, "the proletariat engaged in struggle needs to distinguish between the past and the future, the real and the imaginary, life and death at every minute in order to succeed." And he adds: "just as it radicalized the negation of the useful in order to transform it into a refusal of project and of conscious life, surrealism radicalizes the old literary claim to gratuitousness."[65]

Sartre's attack is double-edged. On the one hand, negation is the very essence of surrealism; on the other hand, this negation is impotent, nothing but a variant of art for art's sake. In the context of this debate, Sartre is implicitly appealing to a Hegelian notion of action as negativity of consciousness operating in a dialectical movement. For him surrealism negates the categories of action because it negates both subjectivity and objectivity. It dissolves subjectivity because it involves an escape from self-consciousness. For Sartre, then, surrealism is radical negation (what Hegel alluded to as "the night in which all cows are black") to the extent that it does not presuppose a subject-object opposition. For Sartre, as we have seen, subjectivity requires recognition in Hegel's sense.

As our reading of Breton has indicated, however, the structure of the master/slave dialectic, so central to the thinking of transgression and of engagement, does not operate in relation to automatism. Indeed, the absence of this relation is precisely what Breton admired in the *Poésies* of Lautréamont-Ducasse and, perhaps, in the photo-collages of Max Ernst. Instead of a recognition scene, we have found recognition in Bergson's sense, that is, a dynamic interaction between perception and memory.[66] To this extent we can see that from Sartre's point of view, which presupposes a set of Hegelian categories, surrealism implies a destruction of subjectivity. From another point of view, however, one associated with Bergson (and perhaps with Valéry) the subject is to be thought in terms of dynamic (that is, temporal) interiority, the interiority of *le vécu*, which was figured by the two moments of the fountain in Bergson as in *Nadja*.

Although in his polemical moments Sartre relies upon Hegelan formulations and an instrumental concept of action, we have also seen that in his analysis of engagement—the analysis that enables a reconciliation of the contradictory positions of speech and action—action is considered as invention. This is what is introduced by the paradoxical dialectic of reading. Here, then, is the deeper proximity between Breton and Sartre, one buried beneath layers of polemical riposte.

Part III

Abstract

Part II has uncovered proximities between Sartre, Valéry, and Breton that problematize the conventional oppositions, or incompatibilities, between transgression, engagement, pure art, and automatism. In each case, the illumination of a Bergsonian subtext enables a different reading to emerge. Engagement does not subordinate literature to political action, nor does it depend upon a representational language. Pure art does not imply a formalist poetics of intentional effort. Surrealist automatism does not imply a Lacanian unconscious and is not a dialectical operation. Valéry's conception of pure poetry and Breton's conception of psychic automatism refer us to a Bergsonian operation of recognition [*reconnaissance*]. The opposition between Valéry and Breton can be described, as we have seen, in terms of an opposition between the voluntary and the automatic. This same opposition plays an important role in the thinking of Bergson. Although the meaning and value of the term "automatic" will reverse itself in the passage from Bergson to Breton, the discourse of Bergson organizes the issues that open onto the "incompatibilities" of the generation that follows him.

In Chapter 6 I present a close analysis of the Bergsonian terms I have introduced into my readings of Sartre, Valéry, and Breton. This analysis will show that the reversal that occurs with respect to the term "automatism" was prefigured by the texts of Bergson themselves, which display a strategic ambivalence with respect to the opposition between dream and action. It is just this ambivalence within Bergson's discourse that enables it to inform, in quite different ways, the three myths of the powers of literature: engagement, pure art, and automatism. To the extent that Bergson also provides us with a notion of action quite different from the one presupposed by Bataille when he declared the incompatibility between poetry and action, Bergson provides an intertext that enables us to appreciate the proximities, and to map the differences, between engagement, automatism, and pure art. To do this, I interpret Adorno's reevaluation of the stereotypical opposition between engaged art and pure art in relation to what is learned from my rereadings informed by the analysis of Bergson. This reevaluation underscores the traditional exclusion of surrealism from the modernist canon, and to this extent puts in perspective Breton's early critique of the modernist trajectory. In the last chapter I address the question of the effacement of Bergson's discourse from the history of modern thought, as well as the politics of this effacement, and return to Bataille to contextualize his thinking of action and of the sacred in relation to Bergson. Finally, in the Conclusion, I return to the question of transgression and the status of theory.

CHAPTER 6

The Voluntary and the Automatic

Sartre, Valéry, Breton, and Bergson

In our readings of Sartre, Valéry, and Breton, we have introduced Bergson's ideas concerning duration, invention, recognition, the vital, and the automatic. In this chapter, a closer analysis of the issues Bergson is concerned with will enable us to map proximities between engagement, pure art, and automatism. We will see that the displacement of the term "automatism" performed by Breton is prefigured in Bergson's own writings. Specifically, it is anticipated by a tension in Bergson's argument concerning relations between freedom and action. Freedom is identified with action in opposition to the passivity or reactivity of inert matter. At the same time, however, the experience of freedom is a function of time or duration, and action in the world—useful action—alienates us from the experience of duration as well as from the freedom of invention.

As we have already mentioned, Bergson proposes a philosophy of life in opposition to a Kantian (or Neo-Kantian) critical philosophy. A philosophy of life is not concerned with questions of knowledge or truth, but with action. Action, for Bergson, implies an inner knowledge. To this extent, a philosophy of life emphasizes not space (representation and quantification) but time—the dynamic time of lived experience that Bergson calls duration. It was a kind of existential point of view that prompted the shift from a perspective of knowledge to one of action: "Besides consciousness and knowledge [*science*] there is life."

"Any summary of my views would misrepresent them," Bergson wrote toward the end of his career,

if it did not place at the outset, and constantly return to, what I consider the very center of my doctrine: the intuition of duration . . . the representation of a multiplicity of quite different mutual penetrations, the representation of a heterogeneous, qualitative, creative duration, is my point of departure and the point to which I continually return. It will demand a very great mental effort, the bursting of many frames.[1]

Bergson's first published book, *Essai sur les données immédiates de la conscience*, is devoted to "the analysis of the ideas of duration and of voluntary determination" (HB 148). This work introduces a psychological perspective onto philosophical questions. Bergson presents the notion of duration (which challenges the spatial model of nature as representation received through Kant) in the context of a discussion of states of consciousness. He addresses qualities and intensities instead of objective entities such as quantities and extensions. The thrust of this study is that the intuition of duration requires the suspension of the framework of useful action. Bergson's point of departure is the Cartesian distinction between external change (movement) and internal change (spontaneity or freedom). Duration is associated with inner change (the unextended) in opposition to extension as the horizon of the quantifiable. Bergson examines this idea of inner change in relation to emotion, qualities, and intensities of feeling. He opposes affective states of the psyche (*l'âme*), known immediately through lived experience, to material things as objects of knowledge. Experience of intensities unfolds in the temporal milieu of pure duration and consists of various states of consciousness which are multiple and heterogeneous. They are not yet stretched out in the presumed sequences of chronological, homogeneous, or spatialized time. The *Essai* elaborates inner freedom or spontaneity dynamically, in the register of time. This is opposed to the static outside world, which is construed on a spatial model and symbolized through language. In pure duration, no separation is made between "the present state and anterior states." We recognize an anticipation of what Bataille will call "sacred continuity and fusion" in opposition to the profane world of useful action that considers things in their separation.[2]

Freedom, then, as inner change or dynamism is a function of *l'esprit*—the unextended—as opposed to the body. But how can one defend the hypothesis of freedom when one cannot point to the operations of something without extension? The answer Bergson gives in *Matière et mémoire* is memory: "If, then, spirit is a reality, it is here, in the phenomenon of memory, that we may come into touch with it experimentally."[3] Memory is the locus of freedom or spontaneity—the locus of *l'esprit*. It means, for Bergson, "independence, the inner force which permits one to separate oneself from the rhythm of the ongoing flow of things, to retain the past better and better in order to influence the future" (HB 355). In this sense memory plays a role for Bergson analogous to that which the negativity of consciousness plays for Hegel. It introduces the gap, the distance from the real of nature (what Hegel calls identity), which enables independence from the determinations of the givens of nature.

We remember that what distinguishes a philosophy of life is its emphasis on lived experience and on action. For Bergson, perception serves action, not knowledge. Indeed, he considers perception a kind of virtual action. Space and time are not transcendental forms of apperception, as in Kant: they are "the schemas of our action on matter" (HB 345). Action occurs as a function of biological need, which Bergson construes in terms of a category of "useful action." It is our needs, then, that prompt us to divide up what we would otherwise experience as the continuity of the real into separate entities that can be denoted by words. This is the role of perception, which in turn is served by language. Perception (what Bergson calls "pure perception") "consists in detaching, from the totality of objects, the possible action of my body on them" (HB 360). Bergson defines living (*vivre*) in terms of this activity of cutting up the real into serviceable categories that enable useful action—"to establish these very special relations between segments thus cut out from sensible reality is precisely what we call living" (HB 334).

But there are two modes of action. And this is where the category of the automatic comes into play, in opposition to the voluntary. There is automatic action, which involves a reaction dictated by necessity, or the reflex movement of the body; and there is voluntary action, which is spontaneous and linked to consciousness. For Bergson, free action involves a relation to time and memory, a relation made possible by the operation of recognition (*reconnaissance*): "the progressive movement through which the past and the present come into contact with one another" (HB 367). Bergson makes a distinction between pure perception—"a perception which exists in principle [*en droit*] rather than in fact [*en fait*]"—and concrete perception, which occurs in time. Because, as Bergson puts it, the latter "occupies a certain duration," it requires "an effort of memory which extends a plurality of moments into one another" (HB 184).[4] Recognition, then, means "the utilization of past experiences for present action" (HB 225). Indeed, the present is defined only through action and requires a reference to the body, "moving limit between the future and the past" (HB 224). The body is defined as being "always situated at the precise point where my past expires in an action" (HB 224). Action is "the point of contact with the real"—or with the present. An image becomes memory precisely when its attachment to the real is severed by the flow of time and action.[5]

The dynamics of free, voluntary action, with the intervention of memory, open up a range of states of consciousness, from the free imaginative productivity of dream to the focus of consciousness on incipient action as contact with the real. Considered as one extreme of mental activity on this scale—a state of tension or sharp focus—action is what contracts *la durée* and introduces separateness into the continuous experience of immediate intuition—"the living unity that was born of inner continuity" (HB 320). It slices up the real so that it can be acted upon effectively, a gesture corresponding to the operations of language, or of any form of symbolic representation.

Bergson represents the mind (or psyche) as an inverted cone whose broad top would correspond to the relaxed state of dream, and whose bottom point would mark the other mental extreme—action as it makes contact with the real through an inscription of the present (HB 302). Mental activity is considered to be dynamically at play at all of the levels, or virtual planes, that cut though this cone. It requires effort to shift levels of mental activity toward the plane of action by increasing focus. As the various (or "successive") levels of memory (HB 250) contract and come closer to the external perception, they approach the mode of action, the limit point of pure perception. Action thus involves the attempt to "get the memory to contract itself or rather to sharpen itself [*s'affiler*] more and more, until it presents only the cutting edge of its blade to the experience into which it penetrates" (HB 251). This is what would correspond to Valéry's notion of "travail de l'esprit," or intellectual effort.

After the exposition of duration and the experience of intensities in his *Essai*, Bergson changes register with *Matière et mémoire* and defends the hypothesis of freedom in the register of psychology as an experimental science. In relation to phenomena such as aphasia, memory can be studied clinically. Indeed, Bergson verifies his theory of recognition and reflection (this theory of the articulation of past and present necessary to the possibility of free voluntary action) on the basis of clinical data concerning operations of reading. Studies have shown, he argues, that reading does not occur through a process of accumulation, letter by letter (that is, in what Sartre would call series). "Ordinary reading," he writes, "is a veritable work of divination, our mind picking here and there some characteristic and filling in the gaps with memory images which, projected onto the paper, are substituted for the characters actually printed there and give us the illusion of them. Thus we create, or recreate, continually" (HB 249). Reading, as clinically observable activity, provides the theoretical model for Bergson's analysis of perception itself. It provides a model of perception as a circuit—"la perception réflechie [reflected/reflexive perception]."

Indeed, for Bergson reading marks a kind of middle ground with respect to the excessive tension of the mental plane of action on the one hand and the radical dispersion of the plane of dream on the other. It is reading, not action per se, which provides the basic paradigm for perception as well as for the philosophical activity of intuition. We can recognize Bergson's thinking in Sartre's theory of the "dialectical paradox of reading." On Sartre's account, the instances of perception and memory are distributed across the divide of writer and reader. The writer performs the function of fixing an image of the external world (albeit "spiritualized" by his or her own subjectivity) and the reader performs the work of recognition and reflection, that is, the work of memory or dream. Thus when Sartre corrects the Hegelian scene of recognition in *Qu'est-ce que la littérature?*, he does so through an appeal to Bergson's theory of recognition that was clinically supported by studies of aphasia and of reading. What is more, we have seen echoes of Bergson's theory of reading in Valéry as well as Sartre. It plays an analogous and crucially important role in the discourse of the pure poet and of the engaged writer.

For Bergson, then, freedom is *vie* which occurs as spontaneity and becomes actualized through action. Action means that the energies of the subject are brought to bear on the external world. We start out from an opposition—spirit/body—which lines up with an opposition between inside and outside. The body is what faces an outside real and acts upon it. Unlike lower species of the animal world, it does so freely, thanks to the activity of consciousness that chooses the particular action to be performed. Consciousness is identified with choice. But it can choose the nature of the contact to be made between the body and the real only thanks to memory, that is, thanks to the fact that *l'esprit* exists as temporal dynamism. Experience occurs in duration. Hence Bergson claims that "questions concerning subject and object . . . should be posed in terms of time rather than space" (HB 218).

The indetermination of will (*volonté*), then, is a function of this temporal dynamism of consciousness or interiority. In proto-Existentialist language, Bergson writes that "the mind exceeds . . . the body and . . . creates acts by creating itself again." Voluntary action is defined in *L'Essai sur les données immédiates de la conscience*, in terms of the temporal dynamics of consciousness itself: "consciousness . . . retains some of the past, coils it up upon itself, and with it prepares a future which it helps to create." Action is a point of contact with the real (HB 224) that actualizes the present instant. It determines the precise and effective conjunction between past and present with an appeal to the future. Thus, on the one hand, it marks an outside with respect to the interiority of *l'esprit*. At the same time, however, as we have seen, it names one mode of interiority, one mental plane. At the other extreme, there is what Bergson calls dream, a level of mental operation in which images coexist or interpenetrate in a dispersed manner. We see that the terms of the polemical opposition between Valéry and Breton, the voluntary and the automatic, are doubled in Bergson's discourse by another formulation of their difference, the opposition between action and dream. Mental activity, for Bergson, is thus a *travail de l'esprit* "[which] continually travels between the two extreme limits, the plane of action and the plane of dream" (HB 311).[6]

The voluntary vs. the automatic, on the one hand, and action vs. dream, on the other, are two formulas that appear to account for the incompatibility between Valéry and Breton. And yet these two fundamental sets of oppositions are not parallel in Bergson. They overlap or intersect, a fact that eventually produces tensions within Bergson's argument. In the first place, as we have seen, the opposition between the voluntary and the automatic implies a limit between inside and outside, or between subject and object. But both extreme ends of mental activity, action and dream, are included within the single term of the voluntary as it pertains to operation(s) of interiority. Next, both action and dream involve memory, for perception requires recognition or reflection. The complication is that there are two types of memory. There is what Bergson calls a memory of imagination, but there is also a memory of the body, which repeats automatically through habit or reflex. The memory of the body thus inscribes a feature of the "automatic" within the very principle of the voluntary: memory. The two sets of oppositions intersect with one another.

So instead of two parallel oppositions that would sustain a dualism, we have something like one opposition—dream/action—which cuts through one term of the other opposition. It cuts through the voluntary, giving it temporal depth and dynamic efficacy in opposition to the automatism of inert matter. The voluntary (the inner) versus the automatic (the outer) is cut through by the temporal opposition: dream (which composes the past as representation or memory images) and action (which inscribes the present, informed by memory, as it cuts towards the future). At the same time, through the memory of the body as it relates to the memory of imagination, the "automatic," or reactive, moment participates in the voluntary one. Metaphysical dualism, Bergson wrote in the *Essai*, is a function of wrongly posing metaphysical questions, that is, of posing them in Kantian or neo-Kantian terms. The way in which Bergson sets up his interrogation, specifically the lack of symmetry between the two oppositions dream/action and voluntary/automatic (or the mechanical) essentially blocks, or preventively deconstructs, any such dualism.

The opposition between the voluntary and the automatic thus includes a difference between a temporal horizon and a spatial one. To the extent that the voluntary term is implicitly privileged in relation to the categories of action and freedom, however, the opposition is not a neutral one. The complication is that in order to live the temporal dimension as a dimension of freedom, one must desist from action. Duration, in its radical heterogeneity, is characterized in its difference from the conventional consciousness that acts in the real, or in the social world. In the course of the development of Bergson's thinking, freedom becomes more and more identified with the temporal dynamic itself and with the spontaneity of invention. It becomes less and less identified with action, although it was initially introduced in terms of useful action in the real, according to a paradigm of biological need. The world of action as a spatialized and symbolized field covers over the freedom and spontaneity of temporal duration. The term "action" comes to be contaminated, as it were, by the spatialized horizon that contains it.

Freedom, then, is identified with action when it is a question of distinguishing the voluntary (or the vital) from the automatic, or of distinguishing the human from the animal realm. On the other hand, it is also identified with spontaneity itself—that is, with the vital activity of "pure" duration, with time lived as duration by what Bergson calls the deep self. Of the two extremes of mental activity, action and dream, it becomes clear that dream is closer to the experience of pure duration than action, for action involves engaging a concentrated subject on the superficial and conventional level of contact with outside things. This requires considering the self and the real through modes of symbolic representation (quantification, language) which map experience onto homogeneous space and quantifiable (that is, spatialized) units of time. To experience the deep self as freedom (or to engage in philosophical intuition), the subject must become disinterested in action. But this is precisely what characterizes the states of dream and intoxication. In dream, Bergson writes, "we no longer measure duration, we feel it" (HB 84, *Essai*).

There is thus a fundamental ambivalence in Bergson's writings concerning the status of dream. With respect to the opposition between the voluntary (or the vital) and the automatic, a distinction that depends on a certain privilege of action, dream representations are disparaged as useless phantoms. Dream is but a shadow play of gratuitous representations, usually suppressed into a subconscious register during waking hours when the demands of action are paramount. On the other hand, the horizon of free action is time, qualitative time as opposed to the quantitative time of repetition and reaction. In the *Essai*, where Bergson repeatedly affirms that the lived experience (*vécu*) of duration is ineffable, he invokes the dream state to suggest what an experience of pure duration would be like. "The inner self," he writes, "the one that feels and becomes passionate, the one that deliberates and decides, is a force whose states and modifications penetrate one another intimately, and undergo a profound alteration as soon as one separates these states out, detaching the ones from the others, in order to unroll them in space" (HB 83). This is the effect of our tendency to quantify or spatialize time. To resist this tendency, Bergson writes,

> it is enough to detach this more superficial layer of psychic facts or events [*faits*] . . . *dream places us in exactly this condition,* for sleep, by slowing down the play of organic functions, modifies the whole surface of communication between the self and things outside it. We no longer measure duration, we feel it; from quantity it returns to the state of qualities; mathematical calculation of past time no longer occurs . . . this yields to a confused instinct. (HB 84, my emphasis)

Here dream is identified with the positive value of pure duration and of the passionate self. We seem to hear Breton—the Breton of the First Manifesto—who rails against the alienation of the subject in the culture of rationalism and empirical science, and asserts the need to retrieve subliminal forces of the self that wait to be tapped beneath the limits of rational consciousness and within the constraints of social convention. Breton appeals to dream for the liberation of an alienated self; Bergson made the same appeal in the *Essai.*

We find a negative valence attaching to action by association in Bergson's uncompromising attack on language. The problem of language is part of the larger issue of symbolic representation as tool of the concrete self of social life (*le moi réel*). Pure duration is inexpressible because of its dynamic mobility and heterogeneity. Language, in contrast, consists of conventional signs, signs constituted through repetition. Words operate mechanically; because they homogenize, they are unable to say anything new. Whereas "feeling . . . lives," Bergson remarks, "the letter kills the spirit" (HB 719, *L'Evolution créatrice*). Words are inert. They belong to the realm of the automatic. For this reason language "crushes immediate consciousness," that is, the consciousness of pure heterogeneous duration. To the extent that language is part of social action, the term "action" becomes contaminated by the negative valence initially reserved for the automatic in the sense of the mechanical or inert.[7]

An exchange of values takes place. Whereas initially the vital was identified with the voluntary vs. the automatic, gradually Bergson shifts to an opposition between the vital and the voluntary. When it becomes too closely identified with useful action, the voluntary takes on the pejorative value of the automatic. When the vital is identified with duration, it implies a suspension of action. In *L'Evolution créatrice* the vital is positively valued in relation to instinct. Here the voluntary becomes linked with intelligence as opposed to instinct, while instinct becomes the register of the vital as involuntary, now invoked in the sense of disinterest with respect to useful action. We detect this exchange of values, for example, when we read that memory images "conserve themselves automatically," and recognize that here "automatic" is not being used in its usual pejorative sense. It is already on its way to being transvalued. At the same time, we also hear about a "conscience automate [automatic consciousness]," where the term "automatic" retains its negative value, but is displaced from the material to the spiritual, or voluntary, realm. Ultimately, then, a gap opens up between the voluntary, which presides over choice of action, and concrete freedom—*la liberté en acte*, epitomized by the spontaneous production of memory images that occurs through the process Bergson calls reflection.[8]

Two uses of the term "freedom" by Bergson are thus to be distinguished in this context. There is freedom as action on the real, in opposition to the automatic which is merely passive or reactive. There is also a notion of freedom as spontaneous "travail de l'esprit" which is entirely disinterested in action and is attuned to duration through its own dynamics of variation and its rhythms of heterogeneous multiplicity. It is from this second level (via Valéry's elaborations of the "travail de l'esprit") that we arrive at Breton's appeal to a psychic automatism that, by virtue of its separation from useful action and its difference from the pejorative automatism of the mechanical, transvalues automatism as it displaces it not only from body to mind, but also from the mental plane of action to that of dream.

When we let Bataille guide our reading of Bergson, we become more sensitive to the economic issues. This focus has helped us recognize the ambivalence in Bergson concerning action and dream. In Bergson, these two extreme states of mental operation are on a continuum. The difference between them is one of degree of tension or concentration. Dream is a modality of dispersion; action involves the concentration and focus of memory images under the demands of action brought to bear on the present moment. As Bergson makes clear, the operations of the two are not fundamentally distinct. In dream and in waking consciousness, Bergson writes "the same faculties are at work, in a state of tension, in the one case, and relaxation in the other. The dream is mental life in its entirety minus the effort of concentration" (HB 893, *L'Energie spirituelle*). Here the formulation in terms of a difference in tension (the "economic" difference as the term is used in discussions of Freud's *Beyond the Pleasure Principle*) actually serves to reinforce the continuity between consciousness and unconsciousness. For in Bergson these two interrelate dynamically, whereas in Freud they refer us to entirely separate topographies which are radically isolated from one another through the effects of repression. In Bergson, the difference between consciousness and unconsciousness is a function of different degrees and qualities of pyschic tension and attention.

But the economic issues (in Bataille's sense now) are pertinent on a larger scale as well. Bergson poses the question of freedom in opposition to a determinist or mechanist discourse that holds the law of the conservation of matter to be universal. He poses time as force or energy. To the extent that subjective interiority occurs temporally, and to the extent that memory can store up (*emmagasiner*) time, Bergson proposes free subjectivity in terms of something like what Bataille will call a general or excessive economy. Freedom requires this economy of excess. In Bergson (as in Valéry) *l'esprit* "gives more than it has" in a gesture of radical expenditure.

Along the same lines, the discourse of Bataille attunes us to the importance of the distinction between utility and uselessness that cuts through the concept of action in Bergson, dividing it into a kind of automatic action (in the mechanistic sense) on the one hand, and the free, radically voluntary action of invention on the other. In Bergson, the value given to dream occurs in the name of a privileged "fringe of uselessness [*frange de l'inutile*]" which empowers subjectivity. In relation to Bergson's thinking of duration, the opposition between heterogeneity and homogeneity (which will become so central to the thinking of Bataille) parallels the distinction between the useless and the useful. And, as in Bataille, the register of expenditure (*dépense*) (or of heterogeneity) attaches specifically to intensities and to affect. We could say that Bataille's use of the distinction between the sacred and the profane recapitulates the difference Bergson addresses between the vital and the automatic, that is, between pure duration and homogeneous time. The experience of duration is in many respects parallel, on the individual level, to the experience of the sacred, which, lived as heterogeneous fusion and continuity, breaks up the apparent coherence of a "superficial self" to arrive at the collective equivalent of a "fundamental self."

Virtual Readers

We have seen that the various incompatible positions we have investigated in this study—engagement, automatism, and pure art—all intersect with the discourse of Bergson in significant ways. The continuity Bergson affirms between the mental planes of dream and of action, and the way in which this opposition intersects with that between the voluntary and the automatic, renders this discourse a particularly helpful screen upon which to project and map the disparate positions of the next generation. As a heuristic device, then, one might imagine our incompatible figures—Sartre,

Valéry, and Breton—as virtual readers of Bergson. If we recall the dynamics of the two extreme states of mental activity on Bergson's account—the concentrated tension of the plane of action and the dispersed level of dream—we might attempt to determine the setting or "tonus" of each reading to determine, with respect to our "virtual readers," at what setting in the continuum from dream to action (or with respect to the opposition between the voluntary and the automatic) their own discourse would intersect with that of Bergson.

How would Sartre read Bergson? He would read him at the level of major distinctions, such as that between the voluntary and the automatic, without attending to the complications introduced by the cross cutting opposition between dream and action. He would read him for the big issues: the great divide between the animate and the inert, the question of freedom, and the struggle against all forms of determinism. He would read him for the notion of the organic, and for the process of totalization. This is the Bergson that returns in the *Critique of Dialectical Reason*. To the extent that duration interests him, it would be on the level of "duration and free choice" (HB 729, *L'Evolution créatrice*), that is, of duration as precondition for freedom. We could say that Sartre "reads" Bergson at the most superficial level—in Bergson's sense. He reads him at the level of "the superficial self." Sartre approaches duration from the surface edge, where it is a question of the imperative of action in the face of danger. He reads him at the level of "automatic consciousness [*la conscience automate*]." In Bergson's terms, this would involve a tight, or concentrated, setting. We think of Sartre, for example, when we read in Bergson: "originally we only think to act [*nous ne pensons que pour agir*]. Our intelligence has been poured into the mould of action" (HB 532, *L'Evolution créatrice*). For Bergson and for Sartre, to live is to act; it is a question of responding to biological need. "In reality," Bergson writes, "a human being is a center of action. S/he represents a certain amount of contingency which introduces itself into the world, that is, a certain quantity of possible action" (HB 717, *L'Evolution créatrice*). Nothing could be closer to Sartre's position. Furthermore, in Bergson, the difference between man and animal comes down to the question of choice of action—and this is precisely what is opened up by the advent of human consciousness. "Consciousness," Bergson writes, "is the light immanent to the zone of possible actions or of virtual actions which surround the action actually accomplished by the living being. It signifies hesitation or choice."[9]

As we have seen in Chapter 3, Bergson's philosophy of life opens the existential question. "What is . . . the exact meaning of the word 'to exist'?" Bergson asks in the opening line of *L'Evolution créatrice* (written in 1907, republished in 1941) which proposes the idea of the continual self-creation of the subject through action. What Bergson calls "invention" becomes on this level of "creation of self by self" a central tenet of Sartre's *L'Existentialisme est un humanisme*. Even the wording of Sartre's text reminds us of Bergson—"A man engages in his life, sketches out his figure, and beyond this figure, is nothing."[10] In *L'Existentialisme est un humanisme*, Sartre, like Bergson, compares the free constitution of the self to the work of the artist, specifically the artist of genius who does not follow any rule but the energies of his or her inner spirit. "Has one ever reproached an artist making a painting with not being inspired by rules established a priori?" Sartre asks rhetorically, "has one ever said what painting he should make? It is clear that there is no definitive painting to be accomplished, that the artist engages with the construction of his painting, and that the painting to be done is precisely the one he will have done." What art and ethics have in common, Sartre summarizes, is that in both cases it is a question of creation and invention. Invention, for Sartre as for Bergson, is the antithesis of an instrumental relation. In the figure of the portrait, action and invention are one.

The point I would like to stress here is that although Sartre will frequently inflect the term "action" in the direction of instrumentality (through an adaptation of Husserl's theory of intentional consciousness and Hegel's conception of the negativity of consciousness), there is another inscription of "action" that refers us to Bergson's understanding of freedom as invention. This, of course, is noninstrumental. "You are free," Sartre writes in *L'Existentialisme est un humanisme*, "choose, that is, invent" (47). This sense of the word "action" remains constant in Sartre. We find it in the discussion of history in *Qu'est-ce que la littérature?*, where the possibility of revolution is attached to a capacity for invention, and we find it again in the *Critique of Dialectical Reason*, where it is a question of the logic of praxis. To appreciate this tendency in Sartre's thinking we must remember that action, for Bergson, is on a continuum with dream. We must remember Bergson's dictum that "wherever something lives, somewhere a register is opened where time inscribes itself" (HB 508, *L'Evolution créatrice*) and his fundamental identification of time with invention: "time is invention, or it is nothing at all" (HB 784). For Bergson, the faculty of knowledge is "secondary to the faculty of action" (HB 489); "The universe endures [*dure*] . . . duration signifies invention" (HB 503). To a certain extent, for both Sartre and Bergson, action is simply a corollary of the dynamism of time—of the giving of "es gibt" as Heidegger would say.

We remember Bergson's injunction: "We must try . . . to see in order to see [*voir pour voir*] and not in order to act. Then the Absolute will reveal itself to be very near to us" (HB 747). Roquentin's nausea was a figure for, or anticipation of, his revelation of the absurd, or of contingency as absolute. It seems that Sartre's one literary encounter with this "voir pour voir" was enough. The revelation was at once liberating and repellent— a "marmalade." It is as if Sartre made the decision to apply the lesson of contingency to action in the domain of the relative, not the absolute. He will henceforth concern himself with the level of "voir pour agir." If the revelation of the absolute was accompanied by the breakdown of the signifying function in *La Nausée*, the importance of the bond between language and action was perhaps only reinforced for Sartre by this consideration. After a glimpse of the absolute, Sartre determines to remain emphatically at the surface. Literary engagement subsequently reabsorbs the artist/intellectual (back) into the existential paradigm of action as invention.

With respect to the ambivalence within Bergson's discourse concerning dream and action, we could say that Sartre reads Bergson at the level of action. We could rephrase the ambivalence we have analyzed in Bergson's thinking in the following terms. Freedom, in principle (*en droit*), is freedom from the grid of representation that accommodates determinisms and puts freedom at risk. This was essentially the lesson of the *Essai*: the need to retrieve the immediate knowledge given through pure duration. But concrete freedom (free action in the real) involves precisely the reinscription of that grid of representation—space and time as schemata (*schèmes*) of action—which coincides with the operation of discursive language. This tension within Bergson's discourse illuminates the apparently radical break between Sartre's account of prose in the first chapter of *Qu'est-ce que la littérature?* and his treatment of language in the second chapter. The myth of prose, which we read in terms of a Hegelian negativity of consciousness and a Husserlian notion of intentionality, can also be read in relation to one level of Bergson's thinking, that is, his analysis of what he calls "pure perception" as virtual action.

On this analysis, perception is identified with the body as point of contact with the real (and hence with the present). This, we remember, was Bergson's fundamental definition of action. At the same time, speech is presented (ambivalently) as an extension of perception. In Bergson, too, it becomes the kind of extension of the body Sartre proposes in his myth of prose. On Bergson's analysis, speech is fundamentally an extension of perception as action because it is the burden of action to cut up the heterogeneity of the real into things and words. Because of the link in Bergson between perception and action, and between action and the body, language itself can be considered a function of the body, just as we find it in Sartre's myth of prose. The notion of generality necessary to the iteration of language is analyzed by Bergson in terms of habit. This refers us to the memory of the body, and hence to mechanism and to automatism in the pejorative sense.[11] This is Bergson's analysis of the origin of language: "The understanding, also, has set up motor apparatuses, this time artificial ones, in order to respond, in terms of a limited number, to an unlimited multitude of individual objects: the totality [*ensemble*] of these mechanisms is articulated speech" (HB 301, *Matière et mémoire*). Action and language are structurally parallel.[12] The plane of action coincides with the act of uttering speech just as in Sartre's myth of prose. The plane of action and of language are one when it is a question of the distinction between levels of consciousness spanning the psychic distance (or temporal difference) between action and memory or dream. Considered in this light, we can identify Sartre's myth of prose in the first chapter of *Qu'est-ce que la littérature?* with Bergson's account of pure perception, and the account in the second chapter, where it is a question of the paradoxical dialectic of reading, with what Bergson called "concrete perception," which requires the operations of recognition and reflection. For unlike pure perception—"which exists in principle rather than in fact"—concrete perception occurs in time and occupies a certain duration.

To pursue the figure of "virtual readers," we could say that Valéry "reads" Bergson at the limit of his ambiguities (or ambivalence) concerning the two extremes of mental activity: dream and action. In Valéry we find a rhetoric of effort with no clear indication of how this effort functions. It does not act in an instrumental or objectifying manner, for it is said to occur in a mode of passive waiting.[13] Valéry's use of the term "effort" calls us back to the tradition from which the thinking of Bergson is said to emerge, that is, the thinking of Maine de Biran and his followers, for whom a feeling of effort was the phenomenal indication of free action (or of *volonté*) as cause of movements in the world of matter or extension. Bergson retains this sense of the word "effort" even as he shifts focus from the extended world of matter to the universe of time: the dynamic register of duration, memory and invention.

It is in this sense that we are to understand Bergson's analysis of intellectual effort or of the effort of invention. In Bergson, we could say that there are two modes of effort, just as there are two extremes of mental activity: dream and action. The dream mode of effort is portrayed in terms of waiting or anticipation (*attente*). Bergson writes concerning invention, for example, that "one can settle oneself into the schema and wait indefinitely for the image" (HB 949, *L'Energie spirituelle*). The schema (a purely formal principle Bergson invokes in his accounts of reading) consists in an "anticipation of images" (HB 957). This is the moment that returns in Valéry's lecture on poetics, where poetic effort involves waiting for "the missing word or image [*l'image, le mot qui manque*]." But in

Bergson, effort also occurs in a mode of tension or concentration, most notably in the act of philosophical intuition. "Our intuition is reflection," Bergson affirms (HB 1328, *La Pensée et le mouvant*), and he continues, in resonance with Valéry, "thus we repudiate facility. We recommend a certain difficult manner of thinking. Above all we value effort. . . . We will say nothing of those who would have our 'intuition' be instinct or feeling. Not a word that we have written lends itself to such an interpretation. And in what we have written there is an affirmation of the contrary: our intuition is reflection" (HB 1328).[14] To philosophize, he concludes, is to invert the usual direction of mental energies [*la direction habituelle du travail de la pensée*] (HB 1422, *La Pensée et le mouvant*). This is the kind of reversal, and the kind of effort, we find in *Monsieur Teste*.

In a variation on the charge of bad faith Sartre leveled against Baudelaire, we could say that Valéry aspires to essence and existence at the same time. He wants to seize and master the subject of invention itself. Hence his fascination with what Bergson calls "the inner world [and] the spectacle of its own operations" (HB 630, *L'Evolution créatrice*). Valéry is concerned with the poetic equivalent of the work that Bergson attributes to the philosopher of intuition who retrieves contact with a deeper reality. Bergson describes this as the effort required to pass from the level of the superficial self to that of the deep self. Valéry elaborates this in terms of the impersonal energies of the *soi*—"What had he done with his personality?" he asks of Teste.[15]

Valéry takes seriously the idea of esthetic invention as action. It is as if he borrowed Bergson's model of action and turned it away from the real toward the act of invention itself. This implies the artist's detachment from useful action; Bergson associates this detachment with dream or derealization. In other words, instead of choosing between the positions of dream (inward) and action (outward) Valéry directs the energies of action inward. This was the thrust of our reading of *Monsieur Teste*.[16]

If Valéry "reads" at this more sober, or tense, level of Bergson's thinking, Breton, as we have already indicated, reads him in the very loose setting of dream and artistic detachment.[17] In our earlier discussion of Breton we brought out a number of affinities between Breton's psychic automatism and the early Bergson of the *Essai* and of *Matière et mémoire*. We suggested that Breton shares Bergson's objections to language when it comes to the language of discursive prose and that surrealist automatism is, among other things, a way to evade the alienations associated with such language. And yet an important question remains. Can Breton fully accept Bergson's critique of language if he puts so much faith in automatic writing? In the *Essai*, Bergson wrote that thinking is incommensurable with language (HB 109). Yet automatic writing seems to presuppose just the opposite: namely, that language can keep pace with the movements of inner thought; indeed, that it can give us a kind of "photography of thought."

One explanation for this is that Bergson changes his attitude toward language. Whereas he criticized its immobilizing effect in the *Essai*, language becomes mobile in *L'Evolution créatrice*: "The intelligent sign," Bergson writes, "is a mobile sign . . . anything can designate anything," (HB 629), unlike the instinctual signs of animal behavior. Bergson discovers the arbitrariness of the sign.[18] Breton might almost be speaking of this shift in Bergson's thinking when he writes in "Les Mots sans rides" (in *Les Pas perdus*): "One began by being wary of words, all of a sudden one came to notice that they were asking to be treated differently from the little auxiliaries that one has always taken them for . . . in short, it was time to set them free . . . a true chemistry had succeeded the 'alchemy of the word'" (B 284). Language can now participate in the "chemistry of intelligence" that Breton alluded to, citing Poe, in *Le Surréalisme et la peinture*.

In *L'Evolution créatrice* language does not crush immediate consciousness. Thanks to its mobility, it plays an important role in the process of recognition. "The word," Bergson writes,

> made for going from one thing to another . . . can thus extend itself not only from one object of perception to another object of perception, but also from the perception of a thing to the memory of this thing, from the precise memory to the more elusive image, from the elusive image, but still represented, to the representation of the act through which one represents it to oneself, that is, the idea. Thus a whole inner world, the spectacle of its own operations, opens itself up to the eyes of intelligence that used to look outside. (HB 630, *L'Evolution créatrice*)

Such, indeed, was Valéry's dream. And this is where we find Breton, via Bergson, in proximity to Valéry. As if anticipating Breton, Bergson writes: "The mind profits from the fact that the word is itself a thing in order to be carried by it and to penetrate into the interior of its own work." He adds that "to evoke concrete duration . . . without immobilizing it, the writer must put words into movement." This is perhaps one point of departure both for Breton and for the modern conception of poetry in general, which extends to include the whole of literature in its difference from conventional language—*et tout le reste ne sera que littérature*.

What is also important here, however, is that unlike the immobilizing words that cut up the real into homogeneous elements of iteration, mobile words attach to images instead of things or referents. Mobile words, Bergson says, can get beyond their conventionalism (their conventional role of signification) when they "signify simple, mobile, almost fluid representations, always ready to mould themselves onto the elusive forms of intuition, that is to say, images."[19]

The question of lyricism, which I raised in the discussion of Breton, can be construed in relation to this association between language and interior images. It is here that we recognize the possibility of that "impure content" in art that Caillois opposed to the formalism of the mainstream tradition of modernism.[20] From this vantage point, it is possible to think about language (poetic language) in a way that includes the visual register without necessarily implying the existence of a transcendental signified (which would give us the visual idea of a referent of signification). Nor, however, does this mobile (poetic) conception of language commit us to a regime of significance, that is, to an indefinite deferral of meaning, because, in Bergson, signification is not modeled on Hegelian negativity.[21] Likewise, the question of meaning poses itself differently for Breton.

We remember that it was intense reflection on the question of lyricism (shared with Verlaine, among others) that led Breton to his conception of the surrealist image. We also remember that the issue of lyricism was central to Breton's criticism of the modernist paths of symbolism and Cubism in his essay on Max Ernst. It is helpful to remember, however, that lyricism was not a neutral issue during this period. As we indicated in the preceding chapter, Bergson was invoked by theorists of symbolism in the early 1900's precisely in relation to the question of a modern lyricism. In his *L'Attitude du lyrisme contemporain* (1911) Tancrède de Visan identifies symbolism with a modern lyricism, which he also calls a "pure" lyricism, to distinguish it from that of romanticism. Although Breton criticizes symbolism in his essay on Ernst (and, implicitly, in the "Confession dédaigneuse"), the object of his attack is not symbolism in general, but specifically the poetics of Mallarmé and Valéry which had influenced him so strongly in his early years. The Symbolism of which de Visan speaks is quite different from that of Mallarmé. It is this more lyrical symbolism which could be said to provide what Breton called the "courroie de transmission" from symbolism to surrealism.[22]

De Visan defines symbolism in terms of a notion of lyricism he derives from Bergson, and specifically from the *Essai sur les données immédiates de la conscience*, as we see when he characterizes modern lyricism as "a return to the immediate givens of consciousness and to our most vital self [*notre moi le plus vivant*]."[23] This is "a lyricism that draws its flight [*essor*] from the very life of the soul, from inner or cosmic dreams, from landscapes viewed from within and brought back to emotional surges [*élans*]" (LC 9). Lyric poetry of the modern spirit is a poetry of the *vécu*, where an idea is made manifest by lyrical images. "In the beginning there was action, said Faust," de Visan writes. "The essence of the world, the substance of beings is not intelligence but activity or will [*volonté*]" (LC 22–23).

De Visan goes on to discuss how the symbolist poets he admires have achieved lyrical effects, analyzing specific rhetorical operations. To explain Maeterlinck's use of what he calls accumulated images, de Visan cites this passage from Bergson's *Introduction à la métaphysique* (1903), one that would surely have held a special interest for Reverdy and Breton: "No image will replace the intuition of duration, but many diverse images, borrowed from very different orders of things, will be able, by the convergence of their action, to direct consciousness to the precise point where there is an intuition to be seized." Consulting the text, we find that Bergson continues as follows:

By choosing images as disparate as possible, one will prevent one or another among them from usurping the place of the intuition that it is supposed to call up, because it would be chased off right away by one of its rivals. By requiring that they each demand from our mind [*esprit*] the same kind of attention and the same degree of tension, in spite of their differences, one can gradually let consciousness become accustomed to a very particular disposition . . . *precisely the one it will need to adopt in order to appear to itself without a veil.* (HB 1399–1400, my emphasis)

Bergson is speaking here about philosophical intuition, and about images that the philosopher calls to mind when wanting to convey his experience to others. But this description of the image, or of a fusion or composition of multiple images, echoes Bergson's earlier discussion of the dream state in its proximity to the experience of duration. "If, digging beneath the surface of contact between the self and external things," Bergson writes, "we penetrate into the depths of organized and living intelligence, we will witness a superimposition or rather an intimate fusion of many ideas which, once dissociated, seem to mutually exclude one another as logically contradictory terms." This is the context for the passage we cited from the *Essai* in the previous chapter concerning dream: "The strangest dreams, where two images overlap and present to us at the same time two different people who are nevertheless one, will give a feeble idea of the interpenetration of our concepts during the waking state" (HB 90). Here we find something very much like the effect Ernst achieves in the collages that so impressed Breton. If Breton uses the term "chemistry of intelligence" to characterize this sort of operation in *Le Surréalisme et la peinture*, the same term appears in his essay "Les Mots sans rides," which distinguishes the ground of surrealism from the early experiments of Rimbaud in the following terms: "a true chemistry had succeeded the 'alchemy of the word [*alchimie du Verbe*].'"

Whereas de Visan applies the above cited passage from Bergson to poetic activity in the strict sense of a literary poetics, Bergson is talking about images which one sees in the mind's eye. For him it is a question of the "inner gaze of my consciousness . . . [that I] direct to my person." It is from this vantage point in Bergson that we are able to think the surrealist image in its richness, as that which does not exclude the visual register on the basis of a linguistic model but, on the contrary, aims at a fusion of the verbal and the visual to the greatest extent possible.

On one level of Bergson's thinking—the level of the positive value given to dream in its disinterestedness with respect to action, and its proximity to the "real" of duration (the absolute real)—Breton would have found the fundamental ethos of his surrealist affirmation. He would have found in Bergson the operation of recognition as mixture of the spontaneous representation of memory and perception. He would have found an account of language that plays an important role in this chemistry of recognition and a positive evaluation of the activities of unconscious mental states in view of their relation to subjective meanings or lyricism. All of this, which we find again in Breton, helps us to recognize the affirmative energies of surrealism. It helps us appreciate the "intimate mechanics" (to borrow a phrase from Valéry) between the linguistic register and that of the visual which is essential for an appreciation of surrealism on every level. Automatic writing, which produces hallucinatory images, needs to be read with the eyes—not rhetorically or stylistically. A surrealist text invites the reader to see with the mind's eye, with "les yeux de l'intelligence," as Bergson puts it, or, in Valéry's words, with "[les] yeux de l'esprit."

Stereotypes—Displacements

In *Notes to Literature*, Adorno attacks what he calls the simplistic and narrow-minded antithesis between engaged art and pure art: "It's a symptom of the disastrous tendency to stereotyping, to thinking in rigid and schematic formulas like the ones the culture industry produces in every domain."[24] When it comes to stereotypes, however, the attempt to correct or complicate one formula often involves reliance upon another as foil. Lamenting the stereotypical opposition of engaged art to pure art, Adorno goes on to develop a very complex analysis of Valéry: Valéry is the modernist hero who transcends the principle of art for art's sake through the identification of art and scientific knowledge, united through the double gesture of poetry and theory. But he does not nuance the position of Sartre to the same degree. He invokes the most conventional conception of literary engagement as discourse of realism. "The current theory of committed art . . . simply ignores . . . the fact that human beings are alienated from one another . . . this theory wants art to speak to human beings directly, as though the immediate could be realized directly in a world of universal mediation. But it thereby degrades word and form to a mere means, to an element in the context of the work as effect, to psychological manipulation; and it erodes the work's coherence and logic." Adorno goes on to oppose Valéry to Sartre: "Valéry has relevance for us today, and is the opposite of the aesthete which vulgar prejudice has stereotyped him as being, because he opposes the claim of a nonhuman cause to an overly hasty pragmatic spirit" (A 103).

For Adorno, modernist theorist of self-reflexive art, literary engagement stands for formal regression and blind adherence to a doctrine of content. As we have tried to show, this view is as caricatural as the reactionary portrait of Valéry. To relax the stereotyped opposition between engaged art and autonomous art it is not enough to revitalize one half of the equation. The interest in displacing stereotypes is to shift the question itself, not to vindicate one figure at the expense of another.

Adorno does point out, however, the ideological confusion created by the stereotypical view of literary engagement. The stereotype creates strange bedfellows. An intraliterary struggle—the debate about art—overtakes the ideological conflict in the political arena as the esthetically reactionary enter into alliance with the politically radical in opposition to the formally adventurous of any stripe.[25] As a corollary to this confused situation, the assumed continuity between literary engagement and militant or activist engagement is put in question. The appeal of engagement, Adorno writes, does not bear a consistent relation to the thesis of engagement in literature—"one would have to denounce all engagement that serves the world to satisfy the idea of the engaged work of art." This diagnosis of the internal (or circumstantial) contradiction within the framework of engagement brings us quite close to Blanchot's formulation of the problem in the late 1940's. "Today action, which as concrete intervention in the world is opposed to written speech [*la parole écrite*] which would be a passive manifestation at the surface of the world," Blanchot wrote, "and those who are on the side of action reject literature which does not act and those who seek passion become writers in order not to act."[26] Blanchot announces definitively that Sartre's attempt to reconcile the antinomy between speech and action has failed, but he nuances this affirmation in characteristic fashion. If writing is opposed to action, it is because it ruins action by placing us fictively in relation to totality.[27] In this precise sense Blanchot declares writing to be analogous to revolutionary action: "revolutionary action is in every respect analogous to action as it is embodied in literature: passage from nothing to everything [*du rien au tout*], affirmation of the absolute as event and of each event as absolute."

Here we are close to Bataille and his response to Sartre's *Baudelaire*—his call to take on the position of imposture, namely, that of desiring the impossible.[28] For Sartre, as he charged in his essay on Baudelaire, the imposture is the desire for essence and existence at the same time. Paradoxically, however, we are also close to Sartre, for whom, as we have seen, the essence of literature is "the subjectivity of a society in permanent revolution." When we pursue the logic of the opposition between speech and action as far as we can go, we come back around to something like the reconciliation of that antinomy as Sartre presented it in *Qu'est-ce que la littérature?*—literary engagement. As soon as we begin to nuance the stereotypical polemical positions, the lines of demarcation become less clear.

Objecting to the formulaic opposition of engaged art to pure art, Adorno reformulates the problem of engagement as a variation of the question of the possibility of poetry after Auschwitz. "The driving energy [*pulsion*] that animates engaged literature today," Adorno writes, "is the question: is art still possible?" But Adorno defines this question in terms of another incompatibility, one between "chance and the free act of creation." What is important here is how Adorno collapses various distinct incompatibilities into one when he rephrases the question of engagement in this way. Most specifically, he collapses the opposition between engaged and pure art into the incompatibility between surrealist automatism (Breton) and the modernist poetics of Valéry.

This rephrasing requires closer examination, for the incompatibilities in question are not parallel. We can distinguish three different formulations of the cultural confrontation over the issue of modern art. First there is the stereotype challenged by Adorno: the opposition between engaged art and pure, or autonomous, art. This involves the opposition Sartre/Valéry, on the one hand, and Sartre/Breton on the other, for Sartre's attack on poetry in *Qu'est-ce que la littérature?* participates in a broader debate concerning the intelligibility of modern art.[29] Second, there is the opposition between action and poetry formulated as two different "economies," or as a difference between existential and ontological registers. This is the thrust of Blanchot's formulation of the problem of engagement and these are the terms of Bataille's assertion of the incompatibility between poetry and action in general. In the third place, pure poetry (Valéry) is opposed by surrealist automatism (Breton, and, in a different way, Bataille). If we use Blanchot's formulation to organize the other two, we have something like the following schema:

action / passion (writing)
engaged art / pure art
pure art / automatism

The first thing that we notice when we organize the alternatives in this way is that the position of pure art shifts to the side of action when it is opposed to surrealist automatism. Furthermore, since Adorno equates engaged art with content and pure art with form, the associated positions of the content/form opposition also shift, as we see when we superimpose the two schemas:

action / passion
engaged art (content) / pure art (form)
pure art (form) / automatism (content)

This distribution of terms presents some surprises. In the first place we tend not to associate form with action. Second, we do not usually consider surrealist automatism in relation to a notion of content. Last, it is important to recognize that it is not the same notion of content that is at stake in each instance, a fact that further complicates any notion of form that would be derived through an opposition to content. In the case of engagement (as it is usually read), content implies message or intentional representation, as in discourses of realism. In the case of surrealism, however, content is, as Caillois puts it (borrowing from the discourse of the sacred), impure.[30]

The schema that analyzes Adorno's rephrasing of the question of engagement displaces the conventional view in ways that confirm the thrust of our readings of Valéry and Breton (Chapters 3 and 4). When Adorno poses the terms of the "urgent debate" concerning engaged literature as he does, he neglects the heterogeneity between the opposition engagement / pure art and that between pure art and automatism. He neglects the lack of parallelism between the different registers of incompatibility. It is precisely in this heterogeneity, however, that we find an anticipation of proximities between positions that have been locked in place by myths of incompatibility, and of the displacements or reconfigurations enabled by these proximities.

Adorno may have rephrased the question of engaged art as he did, however, because of a philosophical problem he diagnoses in the stereotyped opposition between engaged art and pure art, one pertaining to the question of the absolute. "Each of the terms of this alternative," Adorno writes,

negates itself and the other at the same time: engaged art, because it does away with the difference between art and reality, although it necessarily distinguishes itself from this term, because it is art; and art for art's sake because by virtue of wanting to be absolute it also negates this necessary relation [*relation obligée*] to reality that is implicitly contained in its emancipation with respect to the concrete, which is its polemical a priori. (*Notes sur la littérature* 286)

Now it is just this formulation of the problem, this opposition of the relative to the absolute, that is displaced by both Sartre and Valéry, on our reading. Sartre's analysis displaces the question of the absolute in relation to art in that it shifts the question of the absolute toward the intersubjective relation performed in the event of reading, an intersubjective relation mediated by text. As we have seen, it is precisely as paradoxical dialectic of reading that art, on Sartre's account, is distinguished from ordinary, determined empirical reality, and from the economy and operation of the instrumental relation. It is distinguished from empirical reality in, and as, a reciprocal dialectic of freedoms—or, as Sartre puts it, as the occasion of a bringing to consciousness (*se saisir*) of freedom. As we have seen, Valéry also emphasizes the dynamics of reading. If the event of reading distinguishes art from ordinary reality for Sartre, the act of reception as Valéry analyzes it in his course on poetics—reading as reinvention—grounds the absolute of art in the reality of experience. For Valéry, it is reading aloud that gives an otherwise inert text "the force and form of action." The relation of form does not operate in an intentional mode—that is, in a relation between subject and object, or between writer and work. It intervenes in the activation of reading. A poem, Valéry writes, "is a discourse that requires and entails a continual relation [*liaison*] between the voice that is, the voice that comes and the voice that ought to come . . . remove the voice and the requisite voice [*la voix qu'il faut*] and everything becomes arbitrary." [31] Valéry's notion of form cannot be read exclusively on the quantitative model of formal analysis (as Caillois might put it) latent in Adorno's concern with form as objectification.[32] And it is this adjustment of the notion of form that can account for the fact, as indicated in the schema above, that pure art can move across to the column of action when it is opposed by surrealist automatism. In this displacement of form toward an energetics of force and a certain concept of action, we find the term that helps us to reconfigure the sets of incompatibilities.[33] When Valéry's conception of form is read as a force of coming into form (poïein as formation of form)—that is to say, when it is read in relation to a notion of action in this sense of invention—things shift.[34]

As we have seen, Adorno's rephrasing of the question of engagement posed the issue in relationship to an incompatibility between free choice and chance, or in other words, between the voluntary and the automatic. Let us follow that formulation and see where it leads. From the 1920's to the 1940's major esthetic and cultural debates do turn on this opposition, though not always in accordance with our expectations. The opposition between the voluntary and the automatic unites both Valéry's high modernist poetics and Sartre's existentialism in opposition to the automatism of Breton and, in a different way, to the transgression of Bataille. Now, as we have seen, the opposition between the voluntary and the automatic plays a major role in the thinking of Bergson, along with that between dream and action as two extreme planes of mental activity. Although the value of the term "automatic" will shift, even reverse itself, from Bergson to Breton, the discourse of Bergson does organize the issues that will be formulated polemically, that is, as incompatible oppositions, in the next generation. For this reason it can orient a rereading of them. To the extent that Bergson also provides us with a notion of action quite different from the one presupposed by Bataille, his intertext enables us better to appreciate the proximities, and more precisely map the differences, between engagement, automatism, and pure art.

If the voluntary and the automatic on the one hand, and dream and action on the other characterize the incompatibility between pure art and surrealist automatism (Adorno's rephrasing of the problem of engagement), these terms all function in proximity to one another within the discourse of Bergson. Most significantly for our purposes, the opposition between action and dream as two planes of mental action cuts through the voluntary term, which for Bergson implied action as opposed to reaction. What this means is that "action" in Bergson (which, as we have seen, signifies *vivre*) includes a range of modalities of inner life. We could say (with reference to the schema shown in Fig. 2) that action and dream stand for the difference between Valéry and Breton, both of which involve modalities of the voluntary, in Sartre's and Bergson's sense, that is, in opposition to the material determination of the automatic, as understood by Bergson.

This schema characterizes Adorno's rephrasing of engagement, in relation to the question of the possibility of art. He poses his question assuming an incompatibility between free choice and chance. But when the problem is no longer posed instrumentally (that is, in relation to an opposition between subject and object) there is no longer any question of parallelism or lack of parallelism in the arrangement of these terms. Instead we have the intersection of the opposition between the voluntary (the indeterminate) and the automatic (the determinate) at the site of the existential question of Sartre. This opposition will become explicit in Sartre's *Critique of Dialectical Reason*, where it is precisely a question of correcting the determinism of materialist history with an appeal to the voluntary. In that work, Bergson's pejorative category of the automatic is elaborated in relation to the configuration of serialized totality and its associated reification, which precludes subjective freedom and hence the invention necessary for praxis.

At the same time, the voluntary includes the Bergsonian opposition be-

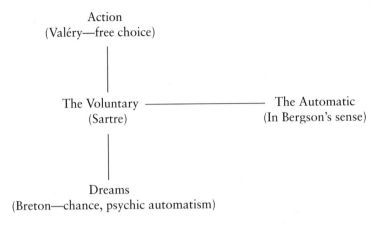

Action
(Valéry—free choice)

The Voluntary ———————————— The Automatic
(Sartre)   (In Bergson's sense)

Dreams
(Breton—chance, psychic automatism)

FIGURE 2

tween two planes of mental activity: action and dream. Here is where a *travail de l'esprit* occurs precisely as a shifting of levels or intermediate planes of mental operation.[35] We could say that the position for which Valéry stands—pure art—would be schematically situated in the "superficial" position of the plane of action. But the *travail de l'esprit* is directed first down to the level of dream, where it is a question of the spontaneous activity of reflection that images memory, and then back up to the level of tension required for poïein as a *faire de l'esprit*—what Valéry calls, in his "Première leçon," the passage from indeterminacy to act. Dream is the plane of Breton's transvaluation of automatism into psychic automatism, the pure spontaneity of *pensée* as it approximates the experience of duration. Hence surrealism involves the spontaneous production of the kind of image Bergson located in the dream register, which operates in closest proximity to the heterogeneous multiplicity of duration.

The proximities between the positions of Sartre, Breton, and Valéry are dynamic. In Bergson, as we remember, dream and action involve the same operations and the same faculties; they differ only in relation to their respective states of tension or relaxation. Dream, Bergson tells us, involves all the usual mental activity minus the tension of effort. Indeed, the difference in tension (perceived by some critics as itself too quantitative a formulation for the place it occupies in Bergson's argument) merely serves as a metaphor for two different dynamics of time: sharp time (time concentrated through tension as preparation for action) and slack time (the time of heterogeneous multiplicity, and in which different images and different temporal dimensions overlap). Sharp time is concentrated toward the present (even as anticipation or *attente*), whereas the slack time of dream accumulates energies of the past. Thus Breton writes that the surrealist image can "estrange us in our own memory." But for Breton too (especially in the later period, that is, in relation to the surrealist object) there is a moment of action as passage from the indeterminacy of interior image to act. If we consider the *travail de l'esprit* in Bergson's terms, that is, as a question of ranging back and forth across different levels of mental operation, then we can interpret Valéry's allusion to the concentration and dispersal of the *esprit* as a figure for these psychic energies. The image, of course, is Baudelairean, but the operation is Bergsonian.

When we look more closely, then, we realize that the different esthetic positions associated with the names of Valéry, Breton, and Sartre are put dynamically into play with one another in the thinking of Bergson, who elaborated the terms "dream" and "action" as the two extreme limits of mental activity. We also see that these differences are dynamically at play within each position—pure art, engagement, and automatism. In Valéry the *travail de l'esprit* involves the two states of tension and relaxation that would correspond to the planes of dream and action. Likewise, in Sartre the interaction between writer and reader (what Sartre calls the paradoxical dialectic of reading) also puts the plane of action together with the plane of dream. Here, however, these are distributed across the positions of enunciation—those of writer and reader. Sartre calls the reader's experience a "free dream [*rêve libre*]." The reader's task is one of reinvention. As we have seen, this involves retrieving meaning through memory, a process that, for Sartre, depends upon emotional response. We could say that in literary engagement, Sartre envisages a dynamic interaction between the levels of action and the level of dream. And it is just as *rêve libre*—that is, as an autonomous reinvention—that freedom occurs as the reciprocal recognition of the freedom of the other. This, for Sartre, is the essence of literature, which returns in the logic of praxis.

In Sartre, the dialectical paradox of reading involves something like a transposition of the formal circularity of the Kantian moral law, distributed across the positions of writer and reader. Just as the autonomous subject of the moral law both gives the law to herself and subjects herself to the law, so in the operations of reading the writer gives the text and the reader subjects herself to it only to reinvent it or to give it in turn. It is in this sense that literary engagement, far from separating the absolute of art from the real (as Adorno's formulation suggested), concerns the performance of the absolute—*la liberté en acte*, freedom in action or concrete freedom—through art or text. And it is only as absolute that the essence of literature can provide a paradigm for the dynamics of social revolution as perpetual revolution. Far from subordinating art to the real—to the world of instrumental relations, the world of the automatic in Bergson's sense, which corresponds to what Lukàcs will call reification—Sartre identifies art, freedom, and fiction. It is in this sense that it is a distortion of engagement to consider it in terms of literary realism. As a representational discourse, realism is considered to have a relation to meaning that is comparable to nonfictive discursive language—a language of truth. Yet here in *Qu'est-ce que la littérature?* it is precisely the status of fiction in its detachment from truth that guarantees the freedom of the reader, and hence the reciprocal recognition of freedom in the paradoxical dialectic of reading.

As we can see, there is a significant degree of common ground between Sartre, the philosopher of engagement, and Valéry, the pure poet. For Sartre, to write is "a certain form of desiring freedom"; for Valéry, literature is "freedom in action." For Sartre, the co-creating of writing and reading is a reciprocal act of generosity, in which each gives more than (s)he takes—and, in a certain sense, even more than each has. For Valéry, likewise, the economy of *charme* is one of continuing to give even as one imagines one is receiving. For all his rhetorical emphasis on action in *Qu'est-ce que la littérature?* Sartre defines the literary event as one of spiritualization. Valéry's poetics analyzes a "faire de l'esprit [action of the mind]." It is Bergson's definition of *l'esprit*—"the faculty of . . . drawing from itself . . . more than it contains . . . of giving back more than it receives, of giving more than it has" (HB 838, *L'Energie spirituelle*)—which introduces this excessive economy in the name of a rejection of determinism, or in the name of freedom.

The proximity of Valéry to Sartre, which is illuminated by this detour through Bergson, displaces the question of form in Valéry toward the energies of force and of action. To this extent it calls into question his conventional portrait as a (reactionary) formalist. At the same time, the proximity of Sartre to Valéry—precisely in relation to the "free dream" of reading—calls into question the conventional reading of Sartre as esthetically regressive, and of literary engagement as a matter of realism or of messages. The passage through Bergson helps us appreciate that it is not inconsistent for Sartre to privilege the genre of the novel (so disparaged by both Valéry and Breton), to refuse formalism, and, at the same time, to reject the conventions of realism and the fetishism of the message. In Bergson, the novel is a metaphor for the invention of duration and for organic unity. As we have seen, the genre of the novel is important to Sartre's analysis of literature precisely because of the process of totalization, one that returns to play a crucial role (in fundamentally Bergsonian terms) in the *Dialectic of Practical Reason*.

In other words, the intertext of Bergson enables us to adjust both sides of the stereotype of incompatibility that governs the opposition of liter-

ary engagement to pure art, instead of using one cliché as a foil for nu-
ancing or problematizing another position. It is precisely the ambivalence
in Bergson that illuminates Bataille's and Breton's proximity in opposition
to the ostensible position of Valéry. This ambivalence also organizes the
proximity between Sartre and Valéry in opposition to Breton. In effect,
then, it includes the shift I diagnosed in Adorno's recasting of engagement
as a question of modernism (is art still possible?); the central issue here is
the incompatibility between chance and "the free act of creation," or, in
other words, between automatism and a voluntarist (or formalist) poetics. It renders more coherent Valéry's association of form with a notion of
action as coming into form or coming into act. It also clarifies the association between content and surrealism: we see that we are no longer caught
in an opposition between form and content that considers content in relation to discursive meaning. Since surrealism is clearly not interested in
this kind of meaning it has often been read in terms of form, as a radical
transgression of formal conventions. But, as Roger Caillois reminds us,
there is another notion of content that does pertain to Breton—impure
content: an "imaginative content, this 'subject' that . . . has been so deliberately forgotten." Caillois wrote this in the 1940's.[36]

In relation to engagement (as it is traditionally read), content implies
message as intentional representation, which we usually understand in
terms of realist conventions. In the case of "impure art," however, there
is a content Caillois links to what he calls the empirical imagination and
to "the capacity to use the concrete to ends which are usually passionate"
(*AI* 47). He links this empirical imagination to "impure and delirious fabulation," which he discusses in terms of lyricism.

For Caillois, pure and impure art correspond to the axes of form and
content, respectively. Pure art, in other words, is that which refuses meaning both pure and impure. The elements of pure art, Caillois writes,

appear to be the booty of the interested pursuit of the mathematical structure of
the universe, made perceptible by the use of sensory mechanisms themselves constructed by number. . . . On the other hand, we will call impure the other elements
constitutive of art. Unlike the former which are formal . . . the latter draw their
origin from the actual or virtual content of consciousness: direct or symbolic sen-
timentality, desire and conscious or unconscious memories, etc. They make up the
"lived" [*vécu*], and therefore relatively individual, part of the work. It is in this
sense that they can be called subjective. (*AI* 46–47)

We see from this analysis that the emphasis on (impure) content attaches to the question of the lyrical and to the discourse of the *vécu*. It
pertains to interiority in the sense pertinent to Breton's elaborations of
psychic automatism. Indeed, Caillois goes on to charge pure art—pure

painting and pure poetry—with a "negation of the subject" (*AI* 42), and, in Bergsonian fashion, with the quantifiable as opposed to the qualitative. Concerning form, Caillois writes "harmonies of color, form and line, etc., boil down to number—it is always an invariable numerical relation which is perceived" (*AI* 43). Thus the content opposed to the formal horizon of pure art is, as Breton would put it, a "content of images" as opposed to the discursive content of messages. And yet the horizon of pure art, as I have tried to show in readings of Valéry, is not one of formalism as this is usually understood—as objectifying form imprinted through an intentional gesture. It is rather a formation *en acte*, a passage from indeterminacy to act.

Myths of incompatibility—such as the one Bataille announced concerning poetry and action—have given way to more complex relations between the figures under consideration. When we construe action not only negatively, through Hegel, but also positively, through vitalism, a different configuration emerges. When we read Sartre through Bergson's notion of invention, the concept of action—a central term in the polemic between Sartre and Bataille—is displaced. This vitalist understanding of action must be read along with the Hegelian one in order to grasp Sartre's theory of engagement—and of praxis—as a myth of the power of literature. When we retrieve the Bergsonian code we not only find a Bergsonian analysis of reading in Valéry that becomes central to Sartre's theory of engagement, we find a new *Monsieur Teste* (perhaps something closer to the one that was admired across ideological lines, that is, by Sartre as well as Breton) and a more supple notion of form—form as force of action understood as invention. This brings us closer to Breton and enables a reading of surrealism that emphasizes the importance of lyricism, a dynamic lyricism conceived in terms of the "impure" content of images, and Breton's incipient critique of the project of modernism. But how to demonstrate the impact of Bergson, taken for granted by contemporaries but generally suppressed since that time?[37] The next chapter will contextualize the reception of Bergson, in order to examine his erasure.

CHAPTER 7

The Politics of Erasure

The Modern and the Postmodern

"There is something unassimilable about him," Deleuze has written of Bergson, "object of so many hatreds."[1] Because of the range and intensity of ideological appropriations of his thought, and because of the violence of the attacks leveled against him, a virtual erasure of the discourse of Bergson occurred. In his *Tradition de l'existentialisme ou la philosophie de la vie*, which charged that existentialism was nothing but warmed-over Bergson, Julien Benda confronted the problem of erasure in 1947. Citing a passage from Simone de Beauvoir, Benda observed that one could swear one was reading *L'Evolution créatrice*. "Were we not right," he comments of existentialism, "to say that this metaphysic is nothing new? . . . Judging from the fact that it never cites Bergson, it seems to have the pretension of being new."[2] Benda's remark could be taken as merely anxiety of influence, but the fact that Benda himself devoted much of his career to attacking Bergson, often in vitriolic fashion, introduces an ideological factor into the equation. And Benda has not been alone in his crusade against the philosopher. He is joined by members of the far right (Maurras and Lasserre), the revolutionary left (George Politzer and Lukàcs), and even the Catholic Church. Is there any wonder, then, that the figures we have studied here rarely invoke Bergson by name? Or that, when Thibaudet mentioned to Valéry that he perceived an affinity between the poet's writing and that of the philosopher Valéry reportedly responded: "I have read Bergson as badly as possible [*j'ai lu Bergson aussi mal que j'ai pu*]"?[3] Is it any wonder that Valéry's denial has been taken at face value by most critics?[4]

Bergson's obliteration from the cultural scene is stunning. Between 1907 and the First World War, Bergson is said to have been "the most celebrated philosopher in the world."[5] Friend and foe agree on the range and intensity of the philosopher's impact upon his contemporaries. Benda, who tracks Bergson with the acuity of an enemy's eye, argues in 1926 that Bergsonism is no mere intellectual fashion; it is "a movement . . . that embraces the whole realm of the spirit . . . religion, literature, morality, painting, music."[6] The prestige of Bergson has been described as almost supernaturally intense by a friendly critic writing in 1942, soon after Bergson's death: "For almost fifty years now, the battle has been raging in France around a philosophy, his philosophy, various Bergsonisms composed the very atmosphere in which almost all French realities were steeped since 1900."[7] Today, as the editors of Deleuze's *Bergsonism* write, his work is almost forgotten; it is "reduced to the status of a footnote in histories of philosophy, making a brief appearance in studies of 'vitalism' or 'irrationalism.'"[8] His work "has now been almost entirely discredited."[9]

The disappearance of Bergson's philosophy was a function of the diversity of appropriations it underwent, and the intensity of the ideological stakes involved in them. We are reminded of Baudelaire's prose poem "Le Gâteau," in which hungry children fight over a piece of bread they insist upon calling cake, until it is reduced to nothing but crumbs mixed with sand. Before 1914 (during Breton's school years) Bergson's influence upon French youth, including lycée students, was said to have been "remarkable." The Binet report, a survey made in 1908 that inquired into the state of philosophy teaching in the schools (lycées and colleges), showed that "Bergson's ideas prevailed over all others among both faculty and students."[10] Binet reportedly interpreted these results to be a dangerous sign, an indication that the philosopher's thinking was encouraging a virulent antiintellectualism among French youth. His conclusions reflect the ideological pressures associated with an institutional conflict, the Sorbonne dispute, which erupted in response to education reforms put in place in 1902.[11]

This dispute symbolically pitted the two most popular academics of the day, Bergson and Durkheim, against one another. In institutional terms, the debate concerned issues of curriculum and reflected tensions that go back to the reforms that secularized education in the early years of the Third Republic. It was a question of the role of the humanities in an educational system that more and more emphasized scientific methods and values. The Sorbonne (and Durkheim in particular) represented the values of scientific rationalism, as well as republicanism (because of the role Durkheim and other members of this faculty had played during the Dreyfus affair). What is known as the "crisis of the New Sorbonne" was ignited when Charles Péguy, an ardent Catholic and a disciple of Bergson, attacked the Sorbonne in 1906 for suppressing classical education and Christian learning in favor of an official secular rationalism. The Sorbonne is accused of being antiphilosophical. Péguy charges that Durkheim and his colleagues had become "the secular priesthood of a new state cult."[12] Bergson, who was teaching at the Ecole Normale, and who had come out in favor of classical education and against Durkheim's science of sociology as early as 1895, was held up as the antithesis of this scientific rationalism. The teaching of the Sorbonne faculty is portrayed as the "official doctrine of the university"; Bergson is posed as the innovative thinker who challenges the old dogma of rationalism inherited from the previous century. Politically, however, the situation is more complicated. "The real complaint against the Sorbonne," wrote Alphonse Aulard, a historian at that institution,

is . . . neither literary nor pedagogical. It is political. It is religious. The Sorbonne has against it conservatives and clericals of every shade. . . . It is a rallying point for those who want to subject youth to the old political and religious dogmas.[13]

The Sorbonne dispute was exploited by right-wing groups such as L'Action Française—anti-Dreyfusards, anti-Semites, and anti-republicans— and by the most conservative elements of the French Academy. Thus if the "old," institutionalized position of the Sorbonne was opposed by those who favored something "new," this group included elements that represented cultural and political values that antedated the establishment of the Republic—monarchists and clericalists.

It is too simple, however, to say that the eclipse of Bergson was due to an association with the right-wing politics of a number of his most vociferous followers. Others—Valéry, Proust, and Baudelaire, to name but a few—have been labeled politically reactionary without disappearing from the cultural horizon. With Bergson the story is more complicated: not only is he identified with the political right, he is also violently attacked by them. In addition to the vitalism of the right that rallied its forces in the Sorbonne dispute, Bergson's philosophy is appropriated by a vitalism of the left. Georges Sorel, who specifically acknowledged his debt to Bergson, published *Réflections sur la violence* in 1908. In this work Sorel appeals to Bergson's conception of action and argues that the philosopher's thinking should be applied to the social realm.[14] He presents a revision of Marx from the point of view of Bergson.[15] Faced with an extreme-left appropriation of Bergson, the right turned against him. When he became a candidate for the French Academy, leaders of L'Action Française fought his election with vicious attacks and the kind of anti-Semitic innuendo that had been perfected during the years of the Dreyfus struggle. (Bergson was a Jew, although he was so strongly influenced by Catholicism that he was on the point of converting toward the end of his life.) Bergson's thinking was portrayed by Maurras as a feminine romanticism, and his patriotism was called into question. Is his philosophy truly French, Maurras asks?

In spite of the violent campaign against him, Bergson was elected to the French Academy in 1914. He reached the height of his glory—and of his infamy. The force of his impact can be measured by the resistance he inspired. By this date he had the educational and political establishment against him (liberal republicans of the Sorbonne), as well as a segment of the political right and the official voice of the Catholic Church, which put his works on the Index that year.[16] By the late 1920's, however, the left also launched a violent attack against him. In 1929, Georges Politzer viciously criticized him from a Marxist perspective in a book entitled *La Fin d'une parade philosophique*. He finds the philosopher's thinking to be bourgeois and reactionary, "an offensive return of idealism in the face of the definitive perfecting of materialism."[17] For admirers of Bergson such as Sartre, who was also a friend of Politzer, it became impossible to openly acknowledge Bergson. "His philosophy," Politzer concluded, "was nothing but a ten-year episode in bourgeois tactics. No longer corresponding to a central tactical necessity, Bergsonism is more and more on the decline. Soon it will hold no more important place in the arsenal of the bourgeoisie than the game of . . . bridge."[18] But it became necessary to toll the death knell for Bergsonism a second time. Politzer's book was republished in 1947 (under a new title, *Le Bergsonisme, une mystification philosophique*, because, as the 1946 preface to this edition announces, Bergsonism "once again . . . exerts a certain seduction on the minds of philosophers and intellectuals."[19] We can only infer that the influence of Bergson survived the thirties—the decade of Marxism—to renew its appeal in the forties. This is the period of Sartre's Existentialism, which Benda characterized as a reincarnation of Bergsonism.

Romanticism

Bergson's philosophy was a popular one, as Sartre's would be. In part for this reason, the appropriations and ideological deformations of his thinking were rich and ambivalent. "Bergsonism," Benda wrote, "was perhaps the only philosophy to have been really understood by the vulgar." If the populist appeal of "nonconformist" vitalism was directed against the institutions of parliamentary democracy, the same collectivist lyricism had been diagnosed as distinctly democratic in the years before the First World War. Benda identifies Bergsonism with democracy in strictly pejorative terms. He opposes an aristocratic society, "a society truly . . . reverential of states of reason," to democratic society, "a society in search of sensation alone," and he adds, "just as Cartesianism will have been the philosophy of an aristocracy, Bergsonism is strictly the philosophy of democracy."[20] Benda's remark is derisive, but it points to an important issue: the political dimension of esthetic discussions concerning romanticism and classicism. In this context, democracy is associated with romanticism in opposition to aristocratic classicism.

In a thinly disguised 1907 attack, Pierre Lasserre, the literary critic of the far-right review *L'Action Française*, accuses Bergson's thinking of being nothing but warmed-over romanticism. This was not merely an esthetic judgment; it was also both political and moral. In this milieu, the charge of romanticism amounted to an accusation of irrationalism, effeminacy, and unfaithfulness to the French national spirit. Romanticism, Lasserre writes in his book devoted to that subject, is "a disorder which, affecting feelings and ideas, disturbs [*bouleverse*] the whole economy of civilized human nature."[21] It involves "the decomposition of art because it is the decomposition of man" (L 320); in short, it is "originally pathological [*primitivement maladie*]" (L 18). Bergson is read via Rousseau. The proper economy of human nature is a virile rationalism; the decomposition of man, the malady, is effeminization: "Romantic idiosyncrasy is in essence feminine" (L 155), Lasserre writes, and Maurras also identifies Bergsonism with a "feminine romanticism." Benda will repeat this theme in 1926, when he identifies Bergsonism with a hatred of intelligence and notes "the preponderance of women in modern leadership concerning spiritual matters [*dans la direction moderne des choses de l'esprit*]."[22] He embellishes upon Lasserre's misogyny when he specifies that it is a question of "women *as women* [*femmes en tant que femmes*]" (my emphasis). Lasserre also makes a link between French romanticism and the German influence, which, he writes, "pushed the romantic spirit in its own direction." Although Bergson is not named here, Lasserre links this German influence to "the sophism of evolution" (L 461); in case anyone should miss the point, he concludes with the observation: "This book would illuminate today's history through the history of yesterday" (L 543).

Nationalistic sentiment was intense in France after the defeat in the Franco-Prussian War, and it continued up to the First World War (where it found vindication) and beyond.[23] It covered the whole political spectrum. We find it in the speeches of Gambetta in the 1870's. Invoked by the republicans in the context of the anticlerical movement for school reform, the theme is subsequently appropriated by the right with Barrès and Maurras, where it takes on a virulent intensity. To the extent that anti-German sentiment is entrenched in France, first in relation to the spirit of *revanche*, and subsequently in connection with the sacred union (*union sacrée*) of the war effort, we are not surprised to see Benda make the same set of identifications as Lasserre and Maurras: Bergson is associated with romanticism and with Germany. Benda insists pointedly on a specifically anti-French aspect of German romanticism, referring to its "anathematization of the intellectual nature of French literature."[24] Thus to label Bergson a romantic amounted to accusing him of siding with the enemy—Germany—through the affinities between Bergsonism and German pantheistic evolutionism, one strain of German romantic thinking. At the time of Lasserre's book (1907), of course, Germany represented the victorious enemy of the war of 1870, the war that had cost France Alsace and Lorraine and ushered in the democratic institutions of the Third Republic, under attack from so many quarters.

Whereas romanticism was viewed by many to be foreign to the French spirit, Cartesianism, the "aristocratic" philosophy, was considered to be the natural mentality of the self-respecting Frenchman. From the point of view of the far right (whose ideology was generally strong in the years after the First World War), to refuse Cartesianism was tantamount to national betrayal.[25] These accusations (or innuendoes) would endure for decades, since the Treaty of Versailles would hold Germany responsible for the massacre of so many French during the First World War (a war actively supported by Bergson), and Germany would become the enemy once again during the next war.[26] This layer of ideological pressure remained constant for more than five decades, even as the specific nature of the attacks on Bergson shifted, coming first from the middle (the milieu of the Sorbonne), then from the right (it was said to be Barrès who led the campaign against Bergson in the Academy), and then from the left. Politzer opens the reaction against Bergson in the thirties with his vituperative attack against Bergsonism from a Marxist perspective, first published in 1929 and subsequently republished in the forties. Here Bergson's romanticism is attacked as philosophical idealism from the perspective of dialectical materialism.[27] And yet the extreme leftist Georges Sorel acknowledges the indelible influence of Bergson.

Bergson is attacked as a romantic; romanticism is attacked in the name of national identity on the one hand (Lasserre, Benda), and of Marxist revolution on the other (Politzer). The voices we hear in the controversies concerning Bergson reveal the political underpinnings of the cultural stereotypes we have been dealing with in our exploration of incompatible positions concerning modern art. The politization of romanticism, and the delegitimation and subsequent erasure of the discourse of Bergson, have had a significant effect on the development of modernist discourse. Here again the position of Valéry is pivotal.

Valéry's assertions concerning Mallarmé's defenses against automatism—the virtues of his "resistance to the facile," and the characterization of this resistance in terms of effort and work—can be glossed through Lasserre's attack on romanticism. Lasserre criticized the subjectivism of romanticism as a "reign of facility" (L 489) and argued that this subjectivism involved an "abdication of [the] organizing and constructive energies" (L 158–59) of the artist. These are the virile energies Lasserre felt were pathologically effeminized through romanticism. Lasserre characterized genius as a "mania for perfection [*folie de la perfection*]" (L 314), and invoked action in the ostensibly masculine mode of the imposition of form. The pure artist, Lasserre affirmed, is the classic artist.

Here we have precisely the code of the reactionary classicism with which Valéry's name has been associated—Descartes yes, Bergson no. It is in this context that a comment Adorno makes in passing takes on specific interest. He remarks that Valéry establishes "a bridge between the two extremes of French philosophy, Bergson and Descartes."[28] We can now appreciate, however, that this "bridge" does not just concern a philosophical opposition. It amounts to a tightrope act over the ideological gulf that separates a political right from a political left. But even this formulation is inadequate to the complexity of the situation. If Bergson stands accused first by the right (romanticism is revolutionary and anarchic) and then by the left (romanticism is a philosophic idealism instead of being a dialectical materialism), a version of this ideological ambivalence attaches to the other side of the equation as well. Descartes, the French rational classicist, represents the aristocratic position for Lasserre and Benda, and yet this rationalism is also associated with the ideology of the Terror. Considered in this light, the gulf that separates Descartes and Bergson becomes more menacing.

More important, however, we recognize that the ambivalence we identified in our reading of Valéry might involve a strategy of ideological neutralization. Valéry applies a language of Cartesian classicism to Mallarmé. But he also composes an essay on Descartes depicting the rationalist philosopher as a romantic hero. The essays on Leonardo rhetorically insist upon the formula "obstinate rigor," which suggests Cartesian method, but Valéry approaches his subject according to the Bergsonian maxim of imaginative sympathy. What is more, his analysis explores a number of Bergsonian themes (the importance of memory, the drama of interiority, the spontaneous production of mental images) and presents a critique of language that corresponds to the one Bergson advanced in his *Essai*. Valéry even emphasizes the "lesson of Leonardo" that Max Ernst and Breton consider a primer in the virtues of automatism.[29] Finally, an amalgamation of the rhetoric of Descartes and of Bergson accounts for the complexity, and the mystery, of Teste. Teste is a "Monstrous Idea [*Ideé Monstre*]," in Valéry's words, precisely as the figure of a "virile" Bergsonism.

We have lost track of the Bergsonian code in Valéry and exaggerated the importance of the Cartesian one. The effacement of the discourse of Bergson, almost unrecognizable to today's readers, has reinforced the stereotype of Valéry as a reactionary classicist. According to conventional wisdom, Valéry's modernism is associated with a return to the Cartesian spirit after the excesses of romanticism. This return is read as an intensification of the modernist move of Baudelaire who revolted against certain aspects of the romantic tradition he inherited. Baudelaire not only appealed to the formal economy advocated by Poe, he couched this appeal in a rhetoric of the virtues of work and perfection. To this extent, the figure of Baudelaire legitimizes an identification of modernism with a certain neoclassicism, and Valéry, "the modernist," stands for a return to virile intelligence.[30]

If Valéry is considered neoclassicist, this modernist classicism is repudiated by Breton in the name of avant-gardism. Whereas the rhetoric of Breton's avant-gardism was taken up by the discourse of modernism, surrealist art was never admitted within the modernist canon. A suppression of surrealism has occurred that parallels the disparagement of romanticism we have traced back to the ideology of Lasserre. Sartre's explicit attack on surrealism as gratuitous negativity, his sarcastic portrayal of it as a mere amusement of sullen children in *Qu'est-ce que la littérature?*, appears to have stuck.[31] Surrealism is conventionally portrayed in negative terms. High-modernist inheritors of the symbolism of Mallarmé and Valéry often consider it mere antiart and antitradition. On the other hand, self-described avant-gardists, loyal to the spirit of Dada, charge Breton with having compromised the radical negativity of Dada in his determination to secure a place for surrealism within the cultural legacy of modernism. In literary criticism, studies of automatic writing frequently focus on the formally "transgressive" texture of automatic writing, attending principally to the rules of narrative or style that it breaks. This emphasis tends to reduce surrealism to the convention of the negation of convention, that is, to a negative formalism. *Tel Quel* critics nourished a myth of the reactionary character of surrealism in order to assert their own independence. From this perspective, surrealism is a failed preliminary attempt to achieve the agenda of *Tel Quel*: the reconciliation of Marx and Freud.[32] Automatism is reduced to a version of Freud's dream theory on the one hand and of the Lacanian unconscious on the other. The "dictée magique" of automatism is reductively identified with this unconscious while Breton the theorist is accused of naiveté. Aspects of surrealist activity that cannot be accounted for in contemporary theoretical terms tend to be ignored or repudiated.[33]

The depreciation of surrealism in recent decades receives support from

discourses of modernist art criticism and art history. Surrealism was violently rejected in these circles because it was not compatible with the high
modernist project as codified by its preeminent critic and theorist, Clement
Greenberg.[34] Greenberg invokes the language of difficulty and of form we
traced back to Lasserre, transposing it into discussions of plastic values
and a formalism associated with the materiality of the picture plane.[35]
Nonfigurative surrealist painters such as Masson or Miro, whose work
can be analyzed in formal terms, were admitted (marginally) into the modernist canon, a modernism Greenberg conceives of in relation to the
Anglo-American literary high modernism of Joyce, James, Eliot, and
Pound. But the surrealism of Magritte, the surrealism of the image that
affirms the desire to "restore content to form [*restituer le fond à la
forme*]," as Breton put it in his "Confession," cannot be so easily reconciled with the principles of modernism expounded by Greenberg or the
critics who followed him. In the same way, automatic writing that yields
to a stylistic approach is acceptable as long as it can be judged in terms of
the norms of transgression of representation. The art-critical discourse of
modernism echoes Valéry's discourse of perfection in its refusal of facility. Indeed, it is on just these grounds that Clement Greenberg (the critic
who forged the language of American modernism in the visual arts) rejects both surrealism and postmodernism.

Modernism, for Greenberg, begins with Baudelaire. It asserts the autonomy of esthetic value, which is directly linked to an experience of difficulty. Greenberg laments what he calls the "urge to relax," which in his
view threatens standards of quality in art. From his point of view "the
postmodern business is just one more expression of that urge." He traces
this "urge to relax" back to the avant-garde circles of Dada and surrealism, and even further back to "a certain confusion of standards brought
on by Romanticism." To him, both surrealism and postmodernism represent a retreat from quality and its attendant difficulty. Greenberg defines
modernism in opposition to this tendency; modernism is "the continuing
endeavor to stem the decline of aesthetic standards, threatened by the relative democratization of culture under industrialism."[36] We hear echoes
of Benda's characterization of Bergson's thinking as "democratic" because
it represented a quest for mere sensation, and of Lasserre's critique of romanticism.

Greenberg is not alone among modernist thinkers to disparage surrealism and postmodernism as responses to the crisis romanticism represented for art. Habermas, who defends modernity in philosophical terms
(and also designates Baudelaire as the origin of modernism), accuses surrealism of being an "extravagant program which . . . tried to negate modernity." The revolt did not succeed, Habermas argues, and he affirms that

this very failure "gave a new legitimacy . . . to the concentrated and planned character of artistic production."[37] We hear echoes of Adorno's rephrasing of the question of engagement (discussed in Chapter 6) to read, "Is art still possible?," given tensions between chance (automatism) and an esthetics of effort. Adorno himself does not hesitate to take sides on this issue. He rejects surrealism on the grounds of the importance of critical negativity in modern art. Adorno transposes the question of difficulty, which, as we have seen, goes back not only to Valéry but also to the literary criticism of Lasserre, into dialectical terms; he formulates it in Hegelian terms as a question of negativity. He links this negativity to the modernist project of purification of meaning—the inheritance of Valéry's myth of Mallarmé—which operates through formal dynamics. To the extent that this purification operates formally, Adorno argues, it dialectically articulates meaning as the negation of meaning.[38] This is the "negative capability" of modern art, one that has been associated with a Marxist politics by critics such as Adorno. And yet we recognize that it also involves a Hegelian rephrasing of the discourse of difficulty invoked by Lasserre in relation to the philosophical opposition between Descartes and Bergson— Descartes yes, Bergson no—and the political agenda associated with neoclassicism.

For Paul de Man, writing in 1965, modernism means self-consciousness.[39] In this respect, de Man's view is close to that of Adorno, for de Man understands self-consciousness in terms of negative capability.[40] Reacting against the high-modernist formalism of New Criticism, de Man charges that the New Critics have misunderstood romanticism. He argues that they have associated it with a facile reconciliation between man and nature. This is to say that they have neglected its antithetical force—and, by implication, its difficulty. De Man calls for a return to romanticism precisely to retrieve the kind of negative capability that Adorno, Habermas, and, in his way, Greenberg, all advanced in the name of modern art. He calls for a return to romanticism reread in discordant terms, that is, in terms of the sublime rather than the beautiful.[41] Whereas for Greenberg modernism arises in opposition to romanticism, for de Man, it radicalizes the negative energies of romanticism, energies lost sight of in the symbolist milieu which posed poetry as an operation of reconciliation.[42] Whereas Greenberg faults romanticism as a decline from major to minor in the realm of taste, de Man faults symbolism for metaphysical illusion. De Man's view of the modern, one that attaches it to a negativity associated with romanticism (and to this extent attributes a positive value to romanticism as energy of negativity), enables him to enlarge his conception of modernism beyond the restricted canon of high modernism, and, by implication, to include figures from the avant-garde.[43] Perhaps because of his identification of modernism with self-consciousness, however, de Man remains silent on the question of surrealism in these early essays; the Hegelian approach to surrealism yields little of interest.

Our analysis in the preceding chapters has associated surrealism—the term excluded from the discourse of modernism—with Bergson, not Hegel. In this way, I have brought surrealism into filiation with romanticism, via symbolism. But it is not a question of the same symbolism de Man rejects. It is a matter of the lyrical symbolism that posed itself as a further extension of romanticism. The question is, however, which one? The romanticism of Lasserre, that lingers on in Greenberg and the New Critics? Or the problematized romanticism of de Man? The answer depends on your reading of Bergson. From de Man's point of view, Bergson is implicated in the symbolist esthetic from which he would like to liberate modernism.[44] He invokes Bergson in relation to the metaphysical illusion of unmediated vision. Adorno suggests the same thing in his essay on Valéry, when, after suggesting the importance of Bergson for Valéry in a passing remark, he takes pains to distinguish Valéry's critical vision from Bergson, whom he associates with immediacy (as does de Man). Both Adorno and de Man distort Bergson on this point. For although Bergson's philosophy is a philosophy of intuition, what is at stake is an intuition *of duration*, which bears no relation to a phenomenological immediacy of experience, that is, to a subject's immediate perception of an object. We remember that for Bergson the subject-object relation must be thought in relation to the dimension of time, not space. According to Bergson, one does not encounter objects as such in the experience of duration, but rather mobile intensities in heterogeneous fusion.[45] As we have seen, Sartre's *La Nausée* gives us a novelistic approximation of Bergsonian immediacy with Roquentin's revelation of the absurd in the garden scene, an experience of qualities to which no words attach.

It would not be correct, however, to suggest that this reading of Bergson implies de Man's reading of romanticism. For precisely the interest of reintroducing Bergson into the discussion of modernism (and its other, surrealism) is that Bergson's thinking, as Deleuze has emphasized, is radically affirmative in nature. It rejects the thinking of contradiction, and hence does not engage with the question of negativity. It therefore cannot be assimilated to a notion of negative capability. It is this affirmative nature of Bergson's thinking that informs the fundamentally affirmative character of surrealism—affirmative, that is, in the sense of Nietzsche. Breton refuses negation in a manner reminiscent of Lautréamont-Ducasse's *Poésies*, and it is just this refusal that renders surrealism incapable of being assimilated within the discourse of modernism, which, in its filiation with neoclassicism reelaborated in Hegelian terms, depends upon a notion of negativity. It is this refusal of negation that is the strongest affinity between the surrealist affirmation and the thinking of Bergson.

"The philosophy of history admits to being nothing more than a gigantic mythology in which newcomers hide their predecessors, when they do not sterilize them. Suddenly, because he discovers Marx, the historian of ideas declares that he can no longer see Rousseau," François Châtelet wrote.[46] If we substitute Bergson for Rousseau (according to a code well in place, as we have seen, since Lasserre's book on romanticism) we have a precise description of what occurred in the case of Bergson. By the 1930's Bergsonism has for the most part been "sterilized" out of philosophical exchange; the dominant discourses of the decade were those of Hegel and Marx.[47]

Evacuated from the discourse of philosophy, the influence of Bergson is felt in the political arena during the late twenties and early thirties. If, before the First World War, vitalism had been intellectually appropriated by both the far right and the far left, in the 1930's, what Loubet calls the "spirit of the thirties" reveals a proximity of far left and far right ideologies of revolution.[48] The eclipse of Bergson's philosophical influence, then, coincided with a displacement of vitalist energies into the field of action, specifically in the "nonconformist" milieux of revolutionary activism in the early 1930's. I would like to return briefly to the question of Bataille's relation to this milieu.

In the early 1930's, a second wave of reaction against positivism and rationalism occurred, reminiscent of (and probably a continuation of) the Sorbonne dispute in the early years of the century, which pitted Bergson against Durkheim. This time the revolt was explicitly aimed at the bourgeoisie as a class. It was articulated as a rejection of parliamentary democracy, but it was not just a right-wing phenomenon. The young generation in the early 1930's refused the institutional channels for political organization—political parties—and sought to cross the traditional boundaries separating left from right. Benda, the critic of Bergson and author of *La Trahison des clercs*, became a target for this group of predominantly young writers and thinkers. He is attacked in the name of engagement, an engagement with a distinctly vitalist orientation.[49] In certain milieux, the influence of Bergson was combined with an interest in Freud and Nietzsche, and an enthusiasm for surrealism.[50] But the "spiritual" revolt in question was not only a marginal phenomenon. It is reflected in Valéry's essays, composed during the 1920's and 1930's, which announce a generalized "crisis of the spirit."[51]

For the young in 1930–31, it is the social aspect of this general crisis that is most compelling. In this climate of pre-Existentialist engagement, action means revolutionary action, although it is not always clear if the revolution in question is a materialist or a spiritual one. "Revolutionary means anything that works towards the overthrow of the established order"; the revolutions of communism, fascism, and national socialism all had a certain appeal as concrete realizations of this formula.[52]

Loubet argues that what began as a sense of spiritual malaise became increasingly politicized and that a tendency toward political activism increased after 1933. This period also sees the emergence of "revolutionary" critiques of Marxist communism that view orthodox Marxism as deterministic, and to this extent, as yet another version of intellectual mechanism. We remember that it was during these years that Bataille, the dissident surrealist, became involved with Le Cercle Démocratique, the dissident communist group organized by Boris Souvarine, who had launched one of the first leftist critiques of communism. It was in the review associated with this group, *La Critique Sociale*, that Bataille published both "La Notion de dépense" and "Structure psychologique du fascisme" in the same year—1933.

But he was a marginal member of this marginal group. Simone Weil, fellow member of Le Cercle Démocratique, expressed her dismay at finding Bataille to be a comrade whose view of revolution was so different from her own. "How to coexist in the same revolutionary organization," she asks, "when people have conflicting ideas of revolution? . . . for him [Bataille] the revolution means the triumph of the irrational, for me of the rational, for him it means catastrophe, for me a methodical action where it is necessary to try to limit damage, for him the liberation of the instincts and above all those considered pathological, for me a higher morality. . . . What do we have in common?"[53] It is in this context that Bataille's association with another ex-surrealist and fellow librarian at the Bibliothèque Nationale takes on a particular interest. Armand Dandieu was one of the leaders of a group called L'Ordre Nouveau which published a review by the same name. He was also the author (with Robert Aron) of an influential book, *La Révolution nécessaire*. Dandieu's thinking was strongly influenced by Bergson, Péguy (who, we remember, had launched the Sorbonne dispute), Sorel, Nietzsche, and Mauss.[54] Dandieu's conception of revolution, a contemporary reviewer wrote, was distinctly Bergsonian— "the Revolution is conceived of in terms of the Bergsonian notion of freedom: it is a leap, a creative rupture . . . the spirit [*esprit*] is above all the power to perform original acts [*poser les actes premiers*], the faculty of going beyond oneself. The revolution is thus in a way spiritual by definition since revolution and *esprit* are one and the same."[55] Michel Surya tells us that although Bataille was not known to have belonged to L'Ordre Nouveau, he was close friends with Dandieu and saw a great deal of him over the course of several years. He also tells us that Bataille helped write a chapter of *La Révolution nécessaire*, contributing his analysis of expenditure, which was central to his evolving theory of transgression.[56] The discourse of L'Ordre Nouveau sheds light on Bataille's notion of revolution during the 1930's, and on his political writings in the context of the group Contre-Attaque (L'Union de Lutte des Intellectuels Révolutionnaires), which was founded in 1935 by Bataille together with Breton. The two temporarily join forces again in this effort to fight fascism—and advance revolution—more aggressively than was being done by the Popular Front.

The explicitly Bergsonian language of Dandieu and of L'Ordre Nouveau exposes the vitalist intertext at play in Bataille's language of revolution. In "Vers la révolution réelle," published in the first issue of the *Cahiers de Contre-Attaque*, Bataille describes what he calls an "organic" revolutionary movement in terms that suggest the extreme-left Bergsonism of Sorel, and the milieu of L'Ordre Nouveau. In this short essay, Bataille gives a neat formulation of what Loubet called the "spirit of '30." Organic movements, he writes, differ from political parties of both the left and the right which are based on class interest: "[They] are not situated within permanent frames analogous to spatial divisions: they only manifest themselves in time"—we recognize the fundamental Bergsonian opposition here between space and time—"[they] constitute an *act of offense* [*un acte d'offensive*] unleashed against the established regime" (original emphasis). The main interest was to provoke "the passionate bringing together of *populist crowds from all over* [*des foules populaires de tous les pays*]."[57] Bataille goes on to stress the importance of aggressivity in these movements and the role of violent emotion in galvanizing the masses. Insurrection would result not from a certain political program, he argues, but rather from "collective exaltation" which erupts in revolutionary violence.[58] It is thus from this far-left version of vitalism that there emerged an association of mysticism and revolutionary thinking that we find in both Sorel and Bataille.[59] The group Contre-Attaque was disbanded in the spring of 1936. Bataille's next project was the review *Acéphale*, and the experiment of the secret society. Bataille embraced the sacred, which he would pursue, in a different register, in the enterprise of the Collège de Sociologie. Is it a question of the sociology of Durkheim, of an attempt to synthesize Mauss and Marx?[60]

In an essay from 1946, "Le Sens moral de la sociologie," Bataille discusses the turn toward sociology he and other founding participants in the Collège de Sociologie (Michel Leiris, Caillois, and Jules Monnerot) experienced. The attraction of sociology, he reveals, was initially political. "The desire for revolutionary social action had first of all attracted attention to Marxist sociology . . . privilege [*précellence*] of collective over individual creation by sociology and ethnography, especially . . . the Durkheimian theory defining religious activities and myths as manifestations of a collective being that is society."[61] The turn toward sociology, then, emerges in the context of the extreme-left activities of the milieu of the Cercle Démocratique and of the fascination with action that found expression in the projected activities of Contre-Attaque.

Although Bataille invokes the celebrated name of Durkheim, the orientation of the College of Sociology was not at all Durkheimian. Monnerot, Hollier tells us, was "violently anti-Durkheimian."[62] His "deep opposition to the Durkheimianism of the French School of Sociology," Hollier adds, "is an opposition whose themes are closely akin to the epistemological transgressions called for by Bataille and Caillois."[63] In addition to the work of Marcel Mauss, the sociology that was meaningful to the milieu of Bataille was probably closer to that of Simmel (which, as Aron writes, "attached too-human action to the social") than to the rationalist rigors of the French School.[64] The members of the Collège are not interested in rational analyses of the sacred; they are interested in the event of the sacred, and in its performance. It is not surprising, then, that the founders of the Collège mark their distance from Durkheim by distinguishing "sacred sociology" from general or religious sociology (*sociologie religieuse*).[65] Caillois declares that sociology means "knowledge of the vital elements of society."[66] Bataille also appeals to a certain vitalism in connection with the Collège: "This research might be held to be vital" (42), he writes in "Le Sens moral de la sociologie," as opposed to "the effeminate enchantments and tricks of art" (42) that Bataille and Caillois associate with surrealism during these years. With Acéphale and the Collège, then, we find a tragic (that is, Nietzschean) version of the energetics of action Bataille promoted in the days of Contre-Attaque. A certain form of vitalism returns in the thinking of the sacred that nourished Bataille's theory of transgression.

During this period, Bataille and Caillois criticize Breton's overinvestment in poetry. The surrealists, as Denis Hollier has put it, had become artists.[67] Against what they considered to be the powerless evasion of the surrealists—their retreat into literature—Bataille, Caillois, and Leiris appeal to the sacred as a discourse of action and power.[68] They oppose a discourse of action to Breton, a vitalist one entirely compatible with his theory of transgression.

In the period after the Second World War, however, the rhetoric will reverse itself. As we have seen, Bataille would oppose poetry to action, against Sartre. Bataille's view of revolution changed after the war. He now saw it as yet another scene of mechanistic calculation of means and ends and identified revolution with the utilitarian economy. During this period of Bataille's disengagement, he would oppose a vitalist conception of poetry—"the poetry of the event"—to Sartre's imperative of action, which he understood in instrumental terms. Bataille now considered freedom to be the very essence of poetry—"literature is the essential, or is nothing." The act of writing "[is] directed by the absolute of freedom," and transgression has become, among other things, a myth of the powers of literature.[69] Against Breton, he opposed a vitalist notion of action to literary estheticism. Against Sartre, he opposed a vitalist conception of poetry to an instrumental notion of action. Bataille's theory of transgression (anticipated in his 1933 essay "La Notion de dépense") serves both moments of Bataille's involvement in a polemical opposition of poetry and action. Perhaps this is why the theory of transgression can serve the theorists of *Tel Quel* so well in their reconciliation of the antinomies between art and revolution, or literature and action. It is just this link, however, that has been severed by the theoretical rereading of Bataille, and the appropriation of transgression as a theoretical term.

My attempt to contextualize the philosophy of Bergson led us back to Bataille and confirmed the hypothesis that Bataille shared a Bergsonian subtext with the other figures examined in this study—Sartre, Valéry, and Breton. We can now see more clearly what is at stake in the difference between Bataille the theorist and the multifaceted Bataille, who was the problematic interlocutor of both Breton and Sartre. We can appreciate what was lost when the sacred (in its vitalist filiation) was suppressed in the process of *Tel Quel*'s appropriation of Bataille. What was obscured (in part for political reasons) was not only the question of the social, but also the complex notion of action involved in the thinking of Bataille.[70] We see that Bataille's ideological opposition of literature to action in the 1940's and 1950's—his declaration of their radical incompatibility—must be read in relation to his earlier advocacy of action against literature. Both moments of this tension are necessary to understand Bataille's thinking of transgression, and to understand transgression as a myth of the powers of literature.

Conclusion

With the advent of theory, Bataille's notion of transgression becomes an indispensable operator, a "philosophy." Engagement, to all appearances, becomes a dead issue. With the new close relations between philosophy and psychoanalysis, the status of the subject is put so radically into question that the imperative of engagement loses all urgency in the face of the more comprehensive debate concerning a crisis of humanism in general. Engagement becomes little more than a convenient presupposition to be turned against the work of philosophers or critics whose political lives shock us, as if for some unexamined reason there should be a consistent correspondence between philosophical thinking and the unfolding of a particular biography.

If Sartre is considered outdated, does this mean that Breton, so fiercely attacked by Sartre, becomes once again more readable? Not at all. Paradoxically, while conventional wisdom considered Sartre an enemy of the avant-garde, it continued to credit his charges against Breton. And what about Valéry? Since it was the surrealists who discredited Valéry, and the surrealists were themselves discredited by Sartre, does that make Valéry more readable?[1] Not at all; Valéry "vanished without a trace."[2] Once again, the attack outlasts the credibility of the voice that utters it. Breton's critique of Valéry persists even after interest in surrealism has subsided. Whereas Mallarmé lives on in the poststructuralist canon, Valéry does not. As I argued in Chapter 3, it was the very way Valéry wrote the modernist myth of Mallarmé that enabled his subsequent transposition into an emblem of postmodernity. Although the poststructuralist profile of Mallarmé-text effaced the poetics of effort or intention, the dense, crystalline writing of the pure poet was nevertheless posed as an inaugural model of textual productivity in its quasi-automatic operation. Valéry, on the other hand, became frozen into the past thanks to the myth of his reactionary classicism, a myth reinforced by the apparent incompatibility with Breton. Of all the figures we have been considering here, Bataille alone lives on—in theory.

We can see that the myths of incompatibility that we have been exploring function negatively; they act as criteria of exclusion. This neutralization of one voice by another, however, supports the framework of theory, enhancing the illusion of its absolute novelty. The myths of radical incompatibility reinforce the theoretical depreciation of history, which was introduced in the early days of structuralism with the opposition of structure to history. Our rereadings, however, suggest that the authority enjoyed by theory during the last few decades owes a great deal to a displacement of powers previously ascribed to literature (or poetry).

Sollers all but declares as much in his preface to the 1980 reedition of *Théorie d'ensemble*. "What is essential in this book concerns a dream [*l'essentiel de ce livre porte sur un rêve*]," he writes, "to unify reflection and on this basis to unleash a generalized subversion." This dream of unification, he continues, "came from a sharp awareness of the possible powers of literature that a customary repression likes to minimize, hold back, subordinate." This allusion to the habitual repression of the powers of literature echoes the opening "Déclaration" of *Tel Quel* (1960) which invoked Valéry and the powers of poetry implicitly against the pressures of engagement. "What needs to be said today," Sollers continues, "is that writing is no longer conceivable without a clear anticipation [*prévision*] of its powers, a calm commensurate with the chaos from whence it awakens, a determination to give poetry the very highest value [*plus haute place de l'esprit*]. Then the work can truly become, in the words of Valéry, an 'enchanted edifice.' . . . All the rest will not be literature." The echo of the early high-modernist spirit of *Tel Quel* is then reinforced in the 1980 preface by the puzzling remark concerning what Sollers called "the dream of theory":

Not literature in the service of theory (as everyone seems to have thought of *Tel Quel*) but just the opposite. The sciences of language, philosophy, psychoanalysis helping to bring into relief an infinite web of fictions [*un tissu de fictions à proprement parler infini*]. Then there was Marxism: the dream seized upon it, following the formalists and the futurists, and thought that the revolution was in the process of coming back into its own [*rentrer dans son vrai lit*]. (original emphasis)

Here we can begin to read something like what Kristeva called the "dilemma of engagement" or its displacement by *Tel Quel*.

The first part of Sollers's sentence, "not literature in the service of theory," is straightforward. We recognize the familiar complaint leveled against theory in American universities throughout the last few decades, that literary readings were "theory-driven," or that literature was being used for the advancement of theory.[3] The second part, however, is puzzling: "not literature in the service of theory . . . but *just the opposite*." Is theory in the service of literature? Is it really a simple reversal of the formula of engagement as this is conventionally understood? This would imply not just an echo, but a wholesale return to the 1960 declaration and its profession of faith in poetry that was upheld against the "habitual repression" of engagement.

This would be surprising after nearly two decades of progressive commitment both to theory and to politics on the part of *Tel Quel*, developments punctuated by the essays gathered in the collection that this statement prefaces. The italics for "très exactement le contraire" register as ironic with a reader who has followed *Tel Quel* throughout the 1970's. This irony may distract us, but it does not dismiss the question of the echo. The powers of literature are clearly invoked in this 1980 preface. Sollers explicitly states that theory derives from a consciousness of the possible powers of literature, and not the other way around. Presumably it was from these same powers of literature that the subversive effect of theory might be said to derive. Such, at least, was the dream. But is this literature in the service of theory—or "très exactement le contraire"? Whatever its precise status, the intimate relation between theory and literature (or fiction) goes to the heart of the avant-garde program of *Tel Quel*. "Put theory and fiction into communication with one another" announced the 1968 manifesto, "La révolution ici maintenant," as a fundamental point on its revolutionary agenda. To read the preface of 1980, one must keep in mind the displacements that have already occurred with respect to the terms "theory" and "literature" (or fiction), not only since the "Déclaration" of 1960, but also since 1968. These are due precisely to the success of attempts to "put theory and fiction into communication with one another." The irony carried by the italics of "mais très exactement le contraire" in the passage just cited is perhaps meant to direct our attention to this fact.

The American reader must first attend to another potential misunderstanding, one that concerns different values and connotations associated with the term "theory" on opposite sides of the Atlantic. In "Mémoires," Kristeva recounts having been warmly received by an American university during the 1970's. She describes the atmosphere she encountered there as "generous, free and encouraging by its curiosity and intellectual naïveté"—"I find there is nothing more stimulating for my work than these visits across the Atlantic," she adds. To begin to understand the phenomenon of theory in the United States it is important to take seriously Kristeva's comment concerning the intellectual naïveté she encountered in the United States.[4] On this side of the Atlantic, "theory" came to represent an attempt to remedy precisely the kind of institutionalized naïveté Kristeva diagnosed, a function of the relative absence from the curriculum of what is popularly called "continental" philosophy. Theory provided the opportunity to introduce into the American university a whole corpus of material previously excluded from it. These exclusions were not incidental, since they amounted to precisely those works that dominated thinking in France during the 1930's, 1940's, and 1950's: Hegel, Marx, Heidegger, and (to a lesser degree) Nietzsche and Freud. To this list we could add names from the human sciences—psychoanalysts, anthropologists, and linguists—some of whom were studied in the American universities, but usually in relation to narrow fields of specialization. They were studied, when at all, in isolation from any broader literary or philosophical tradition.[5] Thus the naive enthusiasm with which Americans embraced French theory—giving it the warm reception enjoyed by Kristeva and so many other French visitors to the American academy during these decades—implied an intense desire to be cured of an entrenched "naïveté."

But there was also a question of prestige. In the American context, theory represented an intellectual coming of age. Here, structuralism leveraged the status of theory (and hence of the comparative literature departments that introduced theory into American universities) and of the humanities in general. It did so because of its association with the social sciences. In France, disciplines such as anthropology, sociology, and psychology are grouped together with history as "human sciences." They presuppose a general intellectual background in philosophy that is shared by scholars of letters. Here, on the other hand, the social sciences exist both institutionally and intellectually in closer proximity to the hard sciences than to the humanities, because of a common reliance upon methods of quantification. In its passage across the Atlantic, structuralism passed some of the epistemological prestige of the hard sciences onto the "soft" disciplines of the humanities. Theory, in the more culturally advanced American institutions, became the hard core of the humanities during the 1970's and 1980's.

In the French context, on the other hand, structuralism was a first step in a radical transvaluation of the very notion of theory. Althusser, for example, displaced theory from the domain of philosophy, which carried an unquestionable epistemological authority, to the political arenas of Marxism and the Communist Party. From its beginnings with Lévi-Strauss, structuralism posed an "epistemological critique of bourgeois thought."[6] It placed itself in an adversarial relationship both to scientific empiricism and to philosophical idealism, our two most legitimate points of reference for a stable distinction between fact (or truth) and fiction. The intimate relation between theory and literature, advocated by *Tel Quel*, should be considered in this light. Indeed, through structural analysis, theory is said to reach "realities" such as the unconscious or language, which are not available to experience. It gives us, in other words, something like what Foucault presents as a definition of the fictive: "the verbal vein of what is not, just as it is [*la nervure verbale de ce qui n'est pas, tel qu'il est*]."[7]

In this sense, structuralism simultaneously fulfilled a Kantian epistemology of truth as system and at the same time enabled Althusser to label Kantian epistemology (and, by association, the enterprise of empiricism it legitimized) "ideological." It is this dual status that renders structuralism so compatible with the modernist esthetic as Adorno had defined it: as a self-overcoming of reason. Since the same Kantian epistemology can be read as the foundation for esthetic realism (through the issue of representation, which is the principal question of the *Critique of Pure Reason*), the delegitimation of Kantian epistemology invalidates the esthetics of realism. This too can be construed as merely ideological—that is to say, bourgeois. We are perhaps already part way to a resolution of the "dilemma of engagement" as Breton had conceived it. For realism is no longer considered politically correct, as Lukàcs and other Marxist humanists had maintained. With structuralism, theory has become something like what Sollers calls a "web of fictions." After Althusser, it also becomes critique, the intellectual operation that separates ideology from "science." On two sides of the Atlantic, then, two quite different values attached to the word "science."[8]

But *Tel Quel* also inherited a positive notion of ideology from Althusser, one that became crucial to its program of intellectual avant-gardism. As is well known, Althusser replaces the dualist model of base and superstructure upon which the Marxist analysis of ideology depends with a triad of social instances: the economic, the political, and the ideological. The ideological includes cultural institutions (or, more generally, representations in the symbolic) which establish relations between the state (or state apparatus) and individuals. In this sense the ideological—now in a more positive sense—is itself construed as a "web of fictions." Only in this context the fabric in question is said to have material existence (and real impact) to the extent that these representations are considered to be embodied in social practices and hence open to forces of transformation. In this broad and fundamentally positive sense the ideological includes theory as a domain of the production of knowledge through critique. Critique is precisely meant to separate out the "ideological" (in the classical, or negative, sense) from the true, which is revolutionary. To the extent that the "dream" of *Tel Quel* seized upon Marxism (as Sollers put it in his preface), what it seized upon, and perhaps mastered, was a slippage between these two quite different registers of the ideological. One can be dismissed as the "mere fiction" of bourgeois ideology ("literature," as it will come to be written in *Tel Quel* within quotation marks). The other carries the positive value of cultural production. Poetry or text is no longer to be trivialized as a mere reflection of empirically verifiable substructural realities. It has become revolutionary.

If, as Kristeva writes in "Mémoires," *Tel Quel* marks the "turning point where the forefront of structuralism shifted into an analysis of subjectivity," this is because here is where the two registers of the ideological come together. *Tel Quel* can designate as ideological in the negative sense the traditional literary canon, especially the nineteenth-century realist novel— "and all the rest will be nothing but literature," as Verlaine had put it— and simultaneously propose as revolutionary the writing of the avant-garde, as Kristeva does in *La Révolution du langage poétique*. It is in this theoretical context that certain possible powers of literature would engender a unification (a tissue) of reflection with generalized subversive impact. If the ideological (in the limited sense) produces subjects for the state, then on the basis of the Althusserian notion of ideology, avant-garde art is posed as constitutive of the revolutionary subject, which overlaps with the subject of critique, and to this extent with the operations of text. If avant-garde art becomes paradigmatic for the revolutionary process, then theory, as a unification of reflection coming from the powers of literature (or art), does not operate as a mechanism of epistemological certainty at all, but "très exactement le contraire . . . "

"You know what profoundly reactionary ideology . . . 'literature' is the active symptom of in our society," Sollers wrote in his 1968 essay "Ecriture et révolution." He continues: "this symptom refers us to the whole of bourgeois ideology. . . . For this kind of economy (work, author, expression, etc.) *Tel Quel* signifies a devaluation . . . what we propose would like to be as subversive, with respect to 'literature,' as Marx's critique was to the classical economy."[9] Sollers then affirms that Derrida's general theory of writing proposes an "envers de la littérature." The difficulty of reading "not literature in the service of theory [as everyone seems to have believed of *Tel Quel*] but just the opposite" is that the quotation marks that distinguished the "wrong side of literature" (*l'envers de la littérature*— which can also mean "literature inside out") from its wrong side (*envers*)—or, if you will, a science of literature from ideology—have been removed. The work of the 1960's has already been accomplished; the term "literature" has been displaced. In the 1980 preface, therefore, the irony of the apparent reversal that resounds through the italicization of "*très exactement le contraire*" is that a dialecticization of the terms "theory" and "literature" has already occurred, and has displaced both terms simultaneously. The words themselves have been rendered radically ambivalent, thanks to the successful practice of putting theory and fiction into communication with one another. The question of "just the opposite" or of reading inside out requires us to read this *envers*. Is it a question of literature or of literature inside out? The question becomes more difficult when "literature inside out" has itself become institutionalized. This is what accounts for the symptomatic ambivalence of the 1980 preface—*Tel Quel* is old, as Sollers wrote in the declaration of *Infini*.

We must return to "Ecriture et révolution" with this sense of irony. "What we propose would like to be as subversive, with respect to 'literature,' as Marx's critique was to the classical economy," Sollers wrote. We recognize a link between the apparent devaluation of literature (or of a certain literature) and the insistent appeal to the "possible powers of literature" (literature without quotation marks) invoked by Sollers both in the 1960 "Déclaration" and again in the 1980 preface. The same sentence has been uttered before in relation to the powers of literature. In a note to the essay "Où va la littérature?" Blanchot wrote: "The important point is that it is a question of pursuing with respect to literature the same effort Marx made with respect to society."[10] In the same paragraph to which this note is appended, we read a meditation on the language of fiction that prefigures a number of the key theoretical moves of *Tel Quel* in the 1960's and 1970's. "It is enough to write the word 'bread' or 'angel,'" Blanchot writes, "in order to have available to our fantasy the beauty of the angel or the taste of bread—yes, but on what conditions? On condition that the world where we use those things has collapsed . . . and also that I no longer be myself and can no longer say 'me' [*je ne puisse plus dire moi*]"—"A formidable transformation [*transformation redoubtable*]," adds Blanchot, in a tone reminiscent of Hugo. I cite this passage from Blanchot as a reminder of the "false appearance of the present . . . advancing here . . . remembering there [*ici devançant, là remémorant*]," as Mallarmé put it in *Mimique*. This is not to claim a priority or privilege for Blanchot, but rather to emphasize the extent to which the questions of *Tel Quel* receive an important ingredient of their force from the thinking and writing of what Blanchot called the "question of literature," as it emerged in relation to the discourses of Breton and Sartre. They are thus embedded in a broader intertextual network that the immediate demands of *Tel Quel* (including simply a demand to be heard) forced into the shadows.

Sometimes rhetoric has an afterlife that exceeds the reach of conscious belief. We realize that theory did not come into being full-blown, and yet it is easy to be lulled by the language of radical beginning and not to attend to the ways in which theory emerged as a response to literary polemics of previous generations. The 1940's saw Sartre pit himself against

Breton and Bataille, saw imperatives of revolution in conflict with the esthetic necessity of formal innovation, a necessity easily appreciated in the
aftermath of the experience of the Russian avant-garde during the 1920's
and under the pressures of the ideology of socialist realism. We could say
that in the next generation "theory" displaced the prestige and authority
previously enjoyed by literature and yet managed to pose poetry itself as
the vehicle of engagement. The concerns of the previous generation were
worked through in theory in the context of *Tel Quel.*

The Modernism of Theory

This brings us to a final question. Where does theory (or poststructuralism) stand with respect to canonical modernism, or for that matter, with
respect to postmodernism? However accurately or inaccurately, poststructuralism is popularly identified with postmodernism. When cultural
studies is criticized in the press, for example, it is associated with the
names of Foucault and Derrida and identified as being both poststructuralist and postmodern. It is often attacked in the very same terms that
were used against poststructuralism before cultural studies (or political
correctness) became a subject of debate. On another level, Habermas has
identified poststructuralism as postmodernist. He charges both with political conservatism in a variation on the theme of "relaxation" of tension
expressed by Greenberg. He accuses both of relaxing the negative, or critical, relationship to culture he identifies with modernism. The debates that
took place between Habermas and Lyotard have reinforced the tendency
to identify poststructuralism and postmodernism, as Habermas opposed
both of these in the name of a rationalist modernism in the tradition of
the Enlightenment.

Critics such as Fredric Jameson and Ihab Hassan also confirm the identification of poststructuralism and postmodernism, although more ambiguously, for "postmodern" is also taken to be primarily a chronological marker. The art historian Rosalind Krauss declares flatly that "the historical period the avant-garde shared with modernism is over. That seems
an obvious fact."[11] Linda Hutcheons affirms that "the term 'post-modern'
has slowly come to be accepted as a general post-1960's period label."[12]
By implication, then, poststructuralism and postmodernism are identified
to the extent that both are said to emerge in the 1960's. All these voices
encourage us to accept an identification between theory (or poststructuralism) and postmodernism. And yet an ambiguity remains. Along with
blunt statements concerning the passing of modernism today, we hear dec-
larations of the demise of deconstruction.[13] If modernism is over, and deconstruction threatens to be over too, how can deconstruction be postmodern? Or is the postmodern also over?

Significant tensions between modernism and other forms of modern avant-gardism (Dada and surrealism) are glossed over too quickly if we simply identify poststructuralism with postmodernism. Indeed, one interpretation of postmodernism is that it emerges precisely because of such tensions. This view considers postmodernism a neo–avant-gardism that arose in reaction to the constraints of canonical modernism, which had lost its negative force as counterdiscourse and become a new academicism. We can situate the activities of *Tel Quel* in these terms. As we have seen, *Tel Quel* initially appealed to Valéry against the imperative of engagement. It echoed this appeal when it privileged the "possible powers of literature" over theory in the 1980 preface to *Théorie d'ensemble*. But *Tel Quel* also included figures such as Antonin Artaud and James Joyce. It kept modernism open by reintroducing energies of avant-gardism through an appeal to the figures already privileged by the surrealist avant-garde: Sade, Lautréamont, Rimbaud, and others. The French modernist tradition is much closer to the avant-garde than is American modernism, and perhaps for this reason the notion of postmodernism has not been energetically taken up in France.

Tel Quel's embrace of the avant-garde, however, respected two fundamental principles of modernism: esthetic autonomy (sometimes transvalued into a fetishization of text) and the purification of meaning associated with abstraction or formal innovation. For this reason, poststructuralism ought not to be identified with postmodernism. It represents a continuation of the high modernist line of development that comes down to us through the conventional reading of Valéry.[14] The poststructuralism of text and signifiance extends the purification of meaning that Caillois diagnosed as the program of modern art, or, at least, of the Mallarmé/Valéry current that identified modern art with pure art. Indeed, signifiance marks the culmination of this modernist trajectory, which is theorized in terms of a radical critique of representation. It involves the ultimate purification of meaning as indefinite deferral.[15] Modernism and poststructuralism each present us with versions of the same alternative Breton had already diagnosed as the dilemma of the modern artist: realism or formal innovation. In the American context, it is a question of figuration vs. abstraction. In the French context, the opposition has been presented in more philosophical (Hegelian) terms: sense (discourse) vs. nonsense (the radical negativity Artaud has come to represent) as transgression of meaning.[16] Variations on this opposition, of course, include the alternatives between the *lisible* and the *scriptible*, and between *plaisir* and *jouissance* (Barthes), as well as the distinction between work and text, and between the symbolic and the semiotic (Kristeva).[17]

A symptom of the modernist commitment of *Tel Quel* is the delegitimation of surrealism discussed in Chapter 7. As I have argued, surrealism emerged as a counterdiscourse both to Dada and to what became canonical modernism. Breton rejected the general trajectory of modernism early on when he announced the failure (*échec*) of symbolism and Cubism.[18] Against the purification of meaning in the tradition of Mallarmé and (by association) Valéry, Breton chose to "restore content to form." He opted for the "impure" meaning of the surrealist image, rejecting Cubism in favor of the path taken by De Chirico, Ernst, and Magritte. He committed himself to a modern lyricism, the "*courroie de transmission*," the drive belt, from a certain symbolism to surrealism. It is not a question of the modernist symbolism of Mallarmé, however, but of the explicitly romantic symbolism championed by Tancrède de Visan, who identified the lyricism of symbolism with the vitalism of Bergson—Bergson yes, Descartes no. "The symbolists," de Visan wrote, "continue romanticism, and broaden it."[19] For him, symbolism is "a lyrical consciousness," one he identifies with action. But he explicitly distinguishes his conception of action from the virile, instrumental action Lasserre prized and associated with artistic form-giving. It is not a question of a "will that presupposes a determined goal," de Visan writes, but of action in the sense of Nietzsche's affirmation and Bergson's invention.[20] It is action, then, in the sense Benda impugns when he complains that Bergsonism "exalts pure action," and that Bergsonian duration amounts to a "pure will and pure action."[21] In other words, it is action in the sense that appealed to both Sorel and Bataille in the 1930's.

The main point of my reading of Breton has been to oppose the modernist exclusion of surrealism and to give weight to Breton's prescient diagnosis of the limits of the modernist project. For this reason, I have emphasized the importance of lyrical and fictive moments in surrealist automatism. When Breton is read from the vantage point of poststructuralist theory—that is, via Lacan and a linguistic or semiotic paradigm—he is read in modernist terms. He ends up a poor modernist, devoid of special interest, because the modernist focus is incompatible with the affirmation of surrealism. The theoretical reading of Breton, which is fundamentally a modernist reading, neutralizes him.

I have argued that if we read Breton through Bergson we can begin to recover the thrust of Breton's early critique of an impasse of modernism, that is, his appreciation of the need to open another channel. Those channels are being opened today in a number of areas of art production. Criticism has lagged behind to the extent that it has no viable category of the fictive, or of the lyrical. In the French theoretical context, critical reflection on the fictive was cut short during the 1960's by the reaction against phenomenology that ushered in, or was ushered in by, poststructuralism. Derrida's critique of Husserl was followed by Lacan's category of the imaginary. This specular category was presented as a mere prelude to accession to the symbolic, privileged domain of the play of the signifier. In his study of Foucault, Deleuze refers to "a reaction against phenomenology" that resulted in "a privilege of the word over the visible."[22] In this context, the fictive was considered on the realist model, that is, as a simulacrum of the real, and, to this extent, of the discourse of truth or reference.[23] It is perhaps time to retrieve the question of the fictive, the question of virtual images or impure meaning, meaning that does not operate in relation to realist representation modeled after referential signification. In the same way, the poststructuralist critique of the subject blocked discussion of the lyrical, which was associated with the voice of a unified subject. My readings have attempted to open up another way of thinking lyricism and another dynamic of the fictive, one displayed, for example, in the nonrepresentational figuration of the paintings of Magritte. Surrealism is of theoretical interest for us today because it confronts us with these questions. With surrealism we have a lyricism of the exploded subject and fiction without representation.

Before we can begin to think coherently about postmodernity, we must dig back into layers of the modern, and seek out old fault lines. To rethink the possibilities of diverse modernisms, we must reexamine romanticism, specifically French romanticism and challenge a resistance to romanticism within the French context, one that is not unrelated to the issues and ideological pressures of the early decades of the century, which played themselves out in relation to the discourse of Bergson. If we include Bergson within French romanticism (taking our cue from the terms of Lasserre's argument and from the criticism of Tancrède de Visan) we retrieve a current of French romanticism that emerges in response not only to Descartes but also to eighteenth-century ideologues and mechanists, as well as to the early sociology of Auguste Comte. It is as an alternative to these specific ideological forces that a French theoretical romanticism would emerge as a channel capable of engendering a different path from the prevailing modernism, one which might provide a basis for elaborating a more meaningful thinking of the postmodern. In any case, we cannot even begin to account for the range of developments of the modern—not to mention elaborate a coherent category of the postmodern—until the inheritance of romanticism is reconsidered. We will then be in a position to appreciate the multiple stakes of modernism—or of virtual modernisms, such as surrealism.

But Breton cannot be read in isolation. To appreciate the possibility of rereading Breton in a direction opened up by Bergson, we had to follow what Breton called the "courroie de transmission" that leads from surrealism back to symbolism. The affirmation of a certain proximity to symbolism prompted a reconsideration of Valéry, at once the stereotypical representative of symbolism and the close interlocutor of Breton for many years. The rereading of Valéry challenged the notion of him as reactionary classicist and emphasized those moments in his writing that reveal him to be in sympathy both with the lyrical symbolism of de Visan and the psychic automatism of Breton. To the extent that both Breton and Valéry have traditionally been designated in terms of the formulaic opposition between engagement and pure art, it became necessary to reinvestigate the thinking of engagement. Read as a discourse of realism, engagement has been a foil for modernism as a perpetuation of the "classical" rejection of romanticism, the "intelligent" purification of meaning. When we read it in proximity to Valéry, or the discourse of pure art, however, it can no longer function in this capacity; instead it reinforces the need for thinking the fictive. The effect of myths of incompatibility is to link each figure to the others like pieces of an interlocking puzzle. In adjusting one piece, one also reconfigures the board. This is the remapping I have undertaken in this study.

"*Tel Quel* est vieux," *Infini* announced in 1983. Theory is no longer "what is happening [ce qui arrive]" as Sollers put it in the 1960's. But what does it mean for theory to grow old? What does it mean to inherit theory? "To inherit," Derrida has written, "is not essentially to receive anything, a given one can have. It is an active affirmation . . . it presupposes the initiative . . . of critical selection. . . . I love those gestures," he adds, " . . . that link together the hypercontemporary [*hyperactuel*] and the anachronistic."[24] Inheriting theory today might require such a gesture—the reinvention of Bergson on the way to thinking visuality in the twenty-first century.[25]

Reference Matter

Notes

Introduction

1. See Guerlac, *The Impersonal Sublime.*
2. For the concept of "après coup"—or "nachträglichkeit"—see Laplanche and Pontalis, *Vocabulaire de la psychanalyse.*
3. Althusser, *Pour Marx.*
4. Reprinted in *YFS* 78, 1990, p. 34 (my translation).
5. An example of these dynamics: the discourse of engagement is characterized as a "model of teleological-transcendental mystification, humanist and psychologistic, complicitous with the absolute obscurantism of the bourgeois state"—quite a put-down, especially in 1968 (*Tel Quel* 34, 1968).
6. As Philippe Soulez has written: "There is no ideology that does not have to combat a symmetrically opposed ideology. This means that thinking [*le penser*] is difference, ideology is opposition" (*Bergson politique*, p. 346, my translation).
7. As we shall see further on, this is even the case in the opening "Déclaration" of *Tel Quel*, which appeals to Valéry implicitly against the pressures of Sartrean engagement.
8. "Travail de l'esprit" could be translated as "mental activity." *L'esprit* is usually rendered as "mind"; in Valéry, however, it means something broader and less exclusively intellectual, something like "psyche." Valéry also thematizes the notion of *travail* (work) in a number of his critical essays. Given all of these resonances, I prefer to leave the expression "travail de l'esprit" untranslated.
9. See Deleuze, *Bergsonism*, and the discussion in Chapter 6.
10. For a comprehensive history of *Tel Quel* see Forest, *Histoire de "Tel Quel."*

Chapter One

1. Fourny, *Introduction à la lecture de Georges Bataille*, p. 19.
2. Philippe Sollers, "La Science de Lautréamont," reprinted in *Logiques*, p. 270.
3. I am simplifying here. More precisely, it is a question of developing the dialectic between Nietzsche and Hegel within Bataille's thinking in the direction of late Heidegger via Nietzsche. See Hollier's introduction to *Le Collège de Sociologie* concerning Bataille and Nietzsche.

4. See Derrida, *Writing and Difference*, trans. Alan Bass, for an English translation of this text.

5. *Tel Quel* 34, 1968.

6. Quite different conceptions of revolution are at stake here. Bataille, in the 1930's, identified revolution with transgression. But (as I shall discuss further in the Conclusion) his was hardly an orthodox understanding of revolution. Subsequently, he identified revolution with rationalism and the utilitarian economy. As we shall see, Kristeva tries to have it both ways in *La Révolution du langage poétique*. She relies upon Bataille's rhetoric of transgression but tries to realign grammatology with a specifically Marxist notion of revolution. See Chapter 2.

7. Philippe Sollers, preface to *Théorie d'ensemble*.

8. Bataille founded the review in the 1940's. *Critique* was the principal rival to Sartre's *Les Temps modernes*. See *Critique* 195–96, 1963. Subsequent references to this essay by Foucault will be given in the text within parentheses, marked PT (my translation).

9. This is consistent with his use of the term "se dessiner" in the passage quoted above.

10. We are moving closer to late Heidegger. Kant, Foucault writes, opened up the question of the limit but closed it again by turning his attention away from critical philosophy toward philosophical anthropology. Here, already, the "return to Kant" that began more than a decade later is prefigured as a return to the ontological questions subsequently addressed by Heidegger. The burden of dialectical thinking is thus laid at the feet of Kant, who stepped back from a "thinking of the limit."

11. "D'un tel langage, il est possible, sans doute, de retrouver chez Bataille les souches calcinées, la cendre prometteuse."

12. Philippe Sollers, "Le Toit," *Tel Quel* 29, 1967. Subsequent references will be given in the text within parentheses, marked T (my translation).

13. Whereas for Derrida "writing" is not to be taken literally, for Sollers "writing" carries less of the philosophical force of Derrida's analysis and usually implies something like "literature" (or "l'envers de la littérature") and to this extent does signify more or less literally.

14. Bataille seems not to be particularly interested in this polemic per se, that is, the literary concern that will connect up with the philosophical issue of the critique of representation. Obviously Bataille's economic distinction, and his opposition of the heterogeneous world of the sacred to the homogeneous one of the profane implies a disinterest in realism. And yet in the contemporary theoretical context, once the critique of literary realism is reinforced by the philosophical critique of representation, all forms of esthetic figuration become suspect. Bataille is never so restrictive. He will appeal to figuration, fictions, images, and operations of "dramatization" in the service of transgression and the experience of the sacred. Bataille will become friends with Magritte late in his life. Modernist purists, on the other hand, reject Magritte as "realist."

15. "L'érotisme—le fait que la théorie en soit faite seulement aujourd'hui dans le sillage de Sade—prend alors toute sa signification: non seulement il est ce qui, dans l'histoire, se présente comme fin de l'ère théologique, philosophique et pré-

scientifique—comme ce qui *met fin*, visiblement, à leurs présupposés logiques—, mais encore comme *le viol* de l'individu constitué par cette période, de l'unité organique et économique qui en a été le support: 'Toute la mise en œuvre érotique a pour principe une destruction de l'être fermé qu'est à l'état moral un partenaire de jeu . . . ' . . . En somme l'érotisme entendu comme la richesse dévoilée et l'aveu du langage—comme son pouvoir de dépense et de gratuité—occupe en un point une fonction de pénétration et de destruction du discours."

16. This phrase is particularly difficult to translate. It means both that theory and literature would speak to one another and that they would be open to one another in the sense of one room communicating with another. It implies that the limit between the two is to be made porous. From "La révolution ici maintenant," p. 68.

17. We shall return to this point in our discussion of Breton in Chapter 5, where I argue that Sollers and others have misinterpreted this passage from Breton. Denis Hollier also addresss this passage in his essay "Le dualisme matérialiste de Georges Bataille." He writes that, whereas for Breton "the point of the fusion of the opposites [*fusion des contraires*] defines the sacred . . . and distinguishes it from the profane," in Bataille, the sacred is understood in relation to a play of difference, specifically that between the "two worlds" of the sacred and the profane, of interdiction and transgression, etc. The sacred for Bataille is pertinent in and through the difference between the sacred and the profane, in and through the limit between them, and it is in this sense that the thinking of Bataille is a thinking of the limit." Although I do not agree with Hollier concerning the "idealism" of surrealism (especially if this implies a dialectical opposition between idealism and materialism), his analyses of the relations between Bataille and Breton (and Bataille and Sartre) are nuanced and detailed and extremely helpful to anyone interested in attempting to contextualize the issues taken up by *Tel Quel*.

18. Derrida, "De l'économie restreinte à l'économie générale." I have used the English text, in *Writing and Difference*, trans. Alan Bass.

19. Derrida, ibid.

20. See my "Sublime in Theory."

21. Philippe Sollers, preface to the second edition of *Théorie d'ensemble* (1980).

22. Denis Hollier, "Le Dualisme matérialiste de Georges Bataille."

23. Bergson, *L'Evolution créatrice*, p. 39. Subsequent references will be given in the text, marked *EC* (my translations).

24. Bataille, *L'Erotisme*, p. 129. Subsequent references will be given in the text, marked *E*.

25. Bataille writes this in a note to his essay "Histoire de l'érotisme," in *Œuvres complètes*, vol. 8, p. 549. Subsequent references to this work will be given in the text within parentheses marked H, and will refer to this edition (my translation).

26. Kojève's Hegel, Besnier writes, is anthropologized. For Kojève, "the central lesson would be delivered in the famous dialectic of master and slave" (*La Politique de l'impossible*, p. 139, my translation).

27. I say "his or her" for ideological reasons. But it should be remembered that it was the question of the very possibility of this reciprocity that launched Simone de Beauvoir's *The Second Sex*. To mark the point that feminine mastery was never

to be taken for granted, I will henceforth use the masculine gender in connection with the Hegelian scenario of the master/slave dialectic.

28. This note is cited in Derrida's essay. I have used the English version of this text in *Writing and Difference*, p. 275. The note appears on p. 36 of Bataille's *Erotism*.

29. This is discussed further in the Conclusion.

30. Cited in Kojève, *Lectures de Hegel*, p. 477.

31. See Bataille, "Lascaux ou la naissance de l'art" in *Œuvres complètes*, vol. 9, pp. 32–36.

32. See Bataille, "Le Dernier Instant," *Critique* 5, 1946.

33. See Bataille, "De l'âge de pierre à Jacques Prévert," *Critique* 3–4, 1946. Here Bataille elaborates a notion of "the poetry of the event [*la poésie de l'évène-ment*]" (p. 197) which he opposes specifically to Sartrean engagement. Sounding a lot like Valéry, he enjoins the poet to "cry out what is [*crier alors ce qui est*]" (p. 198). Although the language is different, what Bataille describes in terms of the event and the instant is not unlike what Bergson had earlier elaborated in relation to duration. We hear echoes of Bergson when Bataille writes that "la misère de la poésie [misery or destitution of poetry] is the desire for its permanence. Between the man who cries out and the event that is, language usually intervenes, whose generality and immaterial nature lead straight to duration, the timeless, and the Academy" (p. 207). Bataille echoes the critique of language presented in Bergson's *Essai* although he uses the term "duration [*durée*]" to express just the opposite of Bergsonian duration.

34. Ibid., p. 209.

35. Ibid., p. 210.

Chapter Two

1. In his essay "Position politique de l'art aujourd'hui," Breton wrote in the 1930's: "the situation . . . of writers and innovative artists is dramatic. . . . In fact, they find themselves faced with a dilemma. Either they must give up interpreting the world according to their inner life—here this is their own possibility of en-during that is at stake—or they must give up their participation in the transfor-mation of this world on the level of action" (*Positions politiques du surréalisme*, p. 190, my translation).

2. Foucault, "Distance, aspect, origine," p. 20.

3. Julia Kristeva, *La Révolution du langage poétique*. References to this work will be given in the text in parentheses, marked K. English translations are taken, with some adaptation, from *Revolution in Poetic Language*, trans. Margaret Waller; page references to this edition will be given in parentheses after the En-glish text.

4. The expression "procès de la signifiance" carries two meanings in French: the process of signification (or signifying) and also the putting on trial, or calling into question, of signification. I will leave the French word untranslated, in most instances, in order to keep both meanings in play.

5. In Waller's English translation *rejet* is translated as "rejection." Because of

the connotations of this word in English, I prefer to leave the French word untranslated here. The term "denial" alludes to the Freudian concept of *verneinung*; see Laplanche and Pontalis, *Vocabulaire de la psychanalyse*.

6. Allusions to transgression in *La Révolution du langage poétique* are too numerous to inventory here. The fact that one finds the word itself at least eight times, for example, between pages 58 and 68 is indicative of its pervasiveness. The word "franchissement" also refers to the operation of transgression, as do the metaphors of "le toit," or of the "deux versants" of signifiance. These metaphors allude to the analysis of Bataille and transgression presented by Sollers in his essay entitled "Le Toit" (see Chapter 1).

7. "We might as well admit the obvious [*Autant reconnaître l'évidence*]," Bataille comments concerning Breton during the 1940's, "although surrealism seems dead . . . when it comes to the wrenching of man from himself [*en matière d'arrachement de l'homme à lui-même*], there is no competition for surrealism [*il y a le surréalisme et rien*]" (p. 101, in *Change 7*).

8. The *rejet* "produces new cultural and social formations which are innovative and . . . subversive" (p. 162) and to this extent acts as a revolutionary subject.

9. I am borrowing the term from Todorov, *Qu'est-ce que le structuralisme?*

10. Sartre, *Qu'est-ce que la littérature?*, pp. 298–301 (my translation).

11. Here what Kristeva calls the thetic phase corresponds to a moment in the emergence of the subject when the subject accedes to what Lacan calls the symbolic, entering into the realm of language and into subject-object relations. The thetic subject is the subject that poses the phenomenal world before him- or herself.

12. Kristeva writes that "modern poetic language . . . attacks not only denotation (the positions of the object) but also meaning [*sens*] (the position of the speaking subject)" (p. 58).

13. The full quote reads as follows: "This means that the question of the second stage of heterogeneous contradiction, namely that of the *interpretant* or *meaning* in which this contradiction must irrupt, is of crucial importance. What is at stake is not just the survival of the social function of 'art' but also, beyond this . . . modern society's preservation of signifying practices that have a sizeable audience" (p. 190, original emphasis).

14. "In narrative, instinctual dyads [*la dyade pulsionnelle*] (. . . affirmation/ negation, life drive / death drive) are articulated as a non-disjunction. In other words, the two 'terms' are distinct, differentiated and opposed; but the opposition is later disavowed [*après-coup déniée*] and there is an identification of the two" (p. 90). Is Breton's "highest point of the spirit" to be achieved, then, through narrative? Kristeva continues: "One could say that the matrix/womb [*matrice*] of enunciation structures is a subjectal space . . . where the signifying process is ordered, that is, endowed with meaning" (p. 90). Kristeva also says in this chapter that text can absorb, or subsume, various moments or modes of signifying activity: narrative, metalinguistic, etc.

15. See Chapter 1.

16. Lévi-Strauss, *Introduction à la lecture de Marcel Mauss*, p. 63.

17. Breton, "Second Manifeste du surréalisme" in *Manifestes du Surréalisme*, pp. 126–27 (my translation).

18. References to this work will be given in the text, in parentheses (my translation).

19. Kristeva, "Mémoires," p. 48.

Chapter Three

1. Bataille, "Incompatibilities," letter to René Char, republished in *YFS* 78 (1990), p. 34. "Although the debate concerning literature and 'engagement' appears to have subsided," Bataille continues (writing in the 1950's) "its decisive nature has not yet been clearly perceived."

2. Simone de Beauvoir, *La Force des choses*.

3. "Literature in action [*la littérature en acte*] can only coincide with its full essence in a classless society. . . . In such a society it would overcome [*dépasserait*] the antinomy between speech and action" (pp. 162–63).

4. The *Robert* gives "la différence entre deux personnes" where "différence" is to be understood in the sense of "différend"—struggle or conflict.

5. If we take this scene seriously as an inscription of the Hegelian master/slave dialectic, then we can read the emphasis on the signifying force of prose in the opening pages of the essay in terms of negativity of consciousness. This is precisely what is at stake in the difference between the signifying force of prose, which, according to Sartre, establishes this negativity as separation from the immediacy of nature, and the "unreadable" character of poetry and painting, portrayed as being glued fast to material being. The superiority of prose over poetry, as portrayed in the opening pages of the text, is a function of its structural resemblance to the negativity of consciousness.

6. Derrida, *Speech and Phenomena*, p. 22.

7. My translation, in adaptation of a translation by James Kirkup, published in Valéry, *Selected Poems*. Here is the translation of Mr. Kirkup: "A slave with slant eyes weighed down by subtle fetters / Changes the water in the vases, in mirrors / Swims, lavishes on the mysterious bed her pure / Caress; brings a woman into this enclosure / Who, moving unobtrusively across my dream / Passes before my eyes yet does not break their calm / Withdrawal, as a glass will move across the sun / Simply, without the mechanicals of reason."

8. "L'œuvre d'art est valeur parce qu'elle est appel."

9. Anna Boschetti makes this point in *Sartre et "Les Temps Modernes."*

10. Human consciousness is defined in this context as "the means by which things manifest themselves" (p. 45). As Descartes and Kant affirm, only divine reason could be said to do so.

11. This anticipation (*attente*) confirms the objectivity of the work: "when we read we anticipate [*on prévoit*], we await [*on attend*]. . . . Without the waiting . . . there is no objectivity" (p. 48).

12. As we shall see further on, both Valéry and Bergson elaborate a very similar account of reading, one that also corresponds to what Heidegger presents as the dual activites of creating and preserving, which together bring the work of art into being in "The Origin of the Work of Art."

13. "Thus," Sartre writes, "from the beginning, the meaning is no longer con-

tained in the words since that is what, on the contrary, permits one to understand the meaning of each one of them." ("dès le départ, le sens n'est plus contenu dans les mots puisque c'est lui [le sens], au contraire, qui permet de comprendre la signification de chacun d'eux") (p. 50).

14. "the literary object has no other substance than the subjectivity of the reader," Sartre writes, p. 52.

15. It replaces the woman in Bataille's dialectic of eroticism, just as the word replaced the woman in Sartre's adaptation of Valéry's poem "Intérieur" to characterize the mental state (*état d'esprit*) of prose.

16. The French text reads: "Seulement cette personne se donnera avec générosité, la liberté la traverse de part en part et vient transformer les masses les plus obscures de sa sensibilité" (p. 57).

17. The term "generosity" is also a part of the discourse of Catholic modernism. See Grogin, *Bergsonian Controversy*, chapter 6.

18. The French text reads: "quand je lis, j'exige; ce que je lis ainsi, si mes exigences sont remplies, m'incite à exiger d'avantage de l'auteur, ce qui signifie: à exiger de l'auteur qu'il exige d'avantage de moi. Et réciproquement l'exigence de l'auteur c'est que je porte au plus haut degré mes exigences, ainsi ma liberté en se manifestant dévoile la liberté de l'autre."

19. Sartre echoes Valéry, here, who echoes Bergson. For further discussion of this point see Chapter 3 and Chapter 5, as well as further on in this chapter.

20. Lévi-Strauss, *Elementary Structures of Kinship*, pp. 52–53. The gift exchange, as analyzed by Mauss and recapitulated by Lévi-Strauss, involves "a passion for the gift, accompanied by the ritual obligation on the recipient to accept and to give" (p. 54). Gifts are "either exchanged immediately for equivalent gifts or are received by the beneficiaries on condition that at a later date they will give counter-gifts often exceeding the original goods in value, but which in their turn bring about a subsequent right to receive new gifts surpassing the original ones in sumptuousness." Subsequent references will refer to this edition and will be given within parentheses in the text, marked LS.

21. It is in relation to the activity of reading that the anthropological structures come into play with the greatest pertinence. Reading, according to Sartre's analysis, involves a "pact of generosity between the author and the reader." Sartre portrays reading as a passion "in the Christian sense of the word, that is, a freedom that puts itself resolutely in a state of passivity in order to obtain, through sacrifice, a certain transcendent effect. The reader makes him or herself credulous [*se fait crédule*], descends into this credulity, and thus . . . at every instant is accompanied by the consciousness of being free" (p. 56, my translation). It is through this gesture of sacrifice, or self-sacrifice, that the reader's freedom receives a form of recognition. The metaphor of the Passion is used more systematically than we might at first notice. It returns in "Situation of the Writer in 1947" when Sartre characterizes writers as "condemned to undergo something like a Passion," that is, the "double requirement [*double exigence*]" that exists because of the class division within the writer's public. The metaphor of the Passion introduces the notion of the sacred associated with what Sartre calls the "consecration" of reading, as well as with the pact of generosity—art as gift ceremony. Sartre links the figure of the

Passion and the theme of sacrifice to passivity and to *croyance*. The metaphor of the Passion suggests a submission to the passivity of the body, which is to say, following Sartre's analysis in *Esquisse d'une théorie des émotions*, a submission to the body's emotions. The "directed creation" of reading operates through these passions: "It is precisely with feelings that one recreates the esthetic object; if it is moving, it only appears through our tears; if it is comic, it will be recognized by our laughter" (p. 56). If reading is a "pact of generosity," what the reader gives (like Christ) is "the gift of his or her whole person [*le don de toute sa personne*]" (p. 56). And it is for this reason that the pact (and the anthropological structure of reciprocity) is cemented by an act of belief, *croyance*. The "belief by engagement" is an "imaginary belief." Thus, although the pathos of body and emotion is quite the opposite of the Kantian realm of freedom (which is separated from the domain of what Kant calls the "pathological"—passively determined by sensory reception, that is, by the forms of space and time, by an abyss)—here emotions are free specifically because they are freely and generously given—solicited by mere fictions.

22. Sartre, *Esquisse d'une théorie des émotions*, p. 60. Subsequent references will be to this edition (translations mine) and will be quoted in the text within parentheses, marked E.

23. Here is the continuation of the passage already quoted above: "[words] are there as traps to elicit our feelings and reflect them toward us . . . the literary object has no other substance than the subjectivity of the reader: the anticipation [*attente*] of Raskolnikoff is my anticipation that I lend to him . . . his hatred . . . is my hatred, solicited, captured by signs . . . that is what animates it, it is its flesh."

24. And he adds, "we might easily associate this with the 'rational intuition' that Kant reserves for Divine Reason."

25. Sartre, *Plaidoyer pour les intellectuels*, p. 434 (my translation). Sartre's discussion of the superiority of the artist over the intellectual supports our reading of *Qu'est-ce que la littérature?* We emphasized Sartre's allusion to the silence, the *non-savoir* of the written text, and the way in which Sartre ironized, and then evaded, the question of the author's message. In *Plaidoyer*, Sartre explicitly writes that literary writers have no message. They have nothing to communicate to the reader, he declares, "nothing that can be said, nothing meaningful [*rien du dicible . . . rien de signifiant*]" (P 437). They convey only a "non-savoir silencieux" (P 437) because their goal "n'est pas de communiquer un savoir." Repeating the theme introduced only tangentially in *Qu'est-ce que la littérature?*, he announces that "the true relation of the reading to the author remains unknowingness [*le non-savoir*]." Echoes of Bataille.

26. This becomes clear in Sartre's study of Mallarmé as well as in his study of Genet.

27. For an interesting discussion of the importance of the universal singular in Sartre, see Philip Wood, *From Existentialism to Poststructuralism*.

28. See Philip Knee, "Sartre et la praxis littéraire," on this point.

29. The French text reads: "Si l'œuvre d'art a tous les caractères d'un universel singulier, tout se passe comme si l'auteur avait pris le paradoxe de sa *condition humaine* comme moyen et l'objectification au milieu du monde de cette même con-

dition dans un objet comme fin. Ainsi la beauté, aujourd'hui, n'est autre que la *condition humaine présentée non comme une facticité* mais comme produit par une liberté créatrice (celle de l'auteur). Et, dans la mesure où cette liberté créatrice vise à la communication, elle s'adresse à la liberté créatrice du lecteur et l'incite à recomposer l'œuvre par la lecture (qui est, elle aussi, création), bref, à saisir librement son propre être-dans-le monde comme s'il était le produit de sa liberté; autrement dit, comme s'il était l'auteur responsable de son être-dans-le monde tout en le subissant ou, si l'on veut, comme s'il était le monde librement incarné."

30. The French text reads: "utilise les phrases comme agents d'ambiguité, comme presentification du tout structuré qu'est la langue, il joue sur la pluralité des sens, il se sert de l'histoire des vocables aberrantes; loin de vouloir combattre les limites de son langage, il en use . . . le style, en effet, ne communique aucun savoir; *il produit l'universel singulier* en montrant à la fois le langage comme généralité produisant l'écrivain et le conditionnant tout entier dans sa facticité et l'écrivain comme aventure, se retournant sur son langage, ou assumant les idiotismes et les ambiguïtés pour donner témoignage de sa singularité pratique et pour emprisonner son rapport au monde, en tant que vécu, dans la présence matérielle des mots."

31. Simone de Beauvoir, *La Force des choses*, p. 15. Subsequent references will be to this edition and will be given in the text, within parentheses, marked FC (my translation).

32. Boschetti, *Sartre et "Les Temps Modernes,"* pp. 143–44.

33. Ibid.

34. "Devoted to the very marrow of his bones to the adventure of writing," de Beauvoir writes, "suddenly, everything fell apart [*se détraqua*]; eternity broke into pieces . . . he understood that living not in the absolute but in the domain of the transitory, he had to renounce being for the sake of doing [*faire*] . . . practice won out over contemplation" (FC 15)

35. Ibid., p. 53 (my emphasis).

36. Ibid. In this context Simone de Beauvoir recalls a remark by Sartre to the effect that the refusal of posterity ought to give him posterity.

37. Ibid.

38. Boschetti writes of an "attempt to get out of an indirect and vague engagement—through literature—theorized during the preceding period, and, in particular, to take a position with respect to the Communist Party" (p. 258). This citation indicates that although Boschetti asserts that Sartre's theory of engagement was in fact a defense of literature, as I have already indicated, she abandons this insight and returns to the more conventional narrative of a gradual weaning from literature, where literary engagement marks a first step in a gradual progression toward the full-fledged engagement of Sartre the militant Marxist theorist.

39. The full quote reads as follows: "il fallait que l'homme . . . confondit [la littérature] avec son existence même. . . . Sartre respectait la littérature au point d'en confondre le destin avec celui de l'humanité" (FC 54).

40. De Beauvoir writes that during the 1940's Sartre "était loin encore d'avoir compris la fécondité de l'idée dialectique et du matérialisme marxiste" (FC 56). Ronald Aronson in *Jean-Paul Sartre* concurs.

41. FC 57. The French quote reads: "il analysait . . . le matérialisme en tant que mythe révolutionnaire. A ce moment sa pensée tournait court car sur la relation liberté-situation, il flottait, et davantage encore sur l'histoire."

42. Sartre, *The Critique of Dialectical Reason*, p. 28. Subsequent references will be to this edition and will be given in the text, within parentheses, marked CR.

43. In Sartre's historical argument, the writer's public marks the concrete or historical equivalent of the abstract "formal" position of the reader analyzed in the preceding chapter. It also provides a paradigm for society at large. For this reason the position of the reader in chapter 2—the reader recognized in his or her freedom and reciprocating this recognition—is the paradigm not only for the historically concrete literary public but for society as a whole.

44. At this point the problem of the message, already diagnosed, would vanish. For the writer's subject, humanity in the world, would coincide with the writer's interlocutor, the universal public in the mode of freedom. "The writer," Sartre writes, "has only one subject: freedom" (p. 70).

45. In *Qu'est-ce que la littérature?* the literary absolute remains merely a paradigm for the social or political end—"the city of ends." Literature is revolutionary in its essence—ontologically. But, as Sartre depicts it in his sketch of concrete relations between writer and public, the historical process itself unfolds in terms of the binary structure of self and other invoked in the first chapter of his essay, where prose was defined as a "secondary moment" of action—"action by unveiling"—and the master/slave dialectic was not structurally corrected but merely sublimated into the domain of language. In chapter 3 of *Qu'est-ce que la littérature?* the vicissitudes of writer and public play out relations of alienated recognition. Only the result, or effect, of the three-term relation introduced in chapter 2, where it is a question of the reciprocal recognition of freedom mediated by the text, makes itself felt in Sartre's argument. With respect to history, this effect plays the ideological, or mythic, role of regulative idea.

46. The formation of the group in fusion, he writes, involves a "ternary relation of free, individual action, or free reciprocity, and of a mediating third party" (p. 366).

47. If we follow the logic of the gift closely, we realize that in the literary event, as in the group in fusion, any of the three terms—writer, work, reader; or self, other, and third party—might be considered the third term, which is also to say the gift. Is it surprising, in light of these connections, that Sartre labels the position of the third term the "sovereign" position? If we read the group in fusion in relation to the excessive economy of the gift in *Qu'est-ce que la littérature?*, then perhaps "sovereignty" should be read in relation to Bataille. An allusion to Bataille's *La Part maudite* in a note to the *Critique* would support such an interpretation. In this light, we could say that in the *Critique of Dialectical Reason* Sartre has written together elements of the discourses of Bataille and Marx. He has done so through the ontological structure of the literary work in order to "revolutionize" art and defend its autonomy against pressures exerted by the Communist Party.

48. The third party, Sartre writes, "transcends me toward his projects insofar as I transcend him: this is simple reciprocity" (*CR* 376). Integrated into the group in fusion by totalization (a process of temporalization that recalls the temporality of Sartre's account of reading) the third party is "quasi-transcendent through the mediation of the group since I am in fact to integrate myself with him into the community and since . . . I remain in tension, at the limit of immanence and transcendence . . . and he is transcendent-immanent to me" (*CR* 377). And here, as I suggested in the reading given here of *Qu'est-ce que la littérature?*, it is this new structure itself, the paradoxical dialectic, that is the foundation of the notion of project. "This new structure," Sartre writes in the *Critique*, "(which lies at the origin of all so called 'projective' actions or actions 'of project') resides in the fundamental characteristics of mediation" (*CR* 377). In the *Critique* Sartre appears to explicitly criticize the simple version of the gift that we read in *Elementary Patterns of Kinship*, where Lévi-Strauss poses it explicitly as a kind of remedy for the master/slave dialectic. On the face of it this might call into question our reading of *Qu'est-ce que la littérature?*, except that what Sartre returns to in the *Critique* is precisely that which the rhetoric and structure of the gift enabled in the paradoxical dialectic of reading, namely, what Sartre calls in the *Critique* "mediated reciprocity."

49. Lévi-Strauss, *The Savage Mind*, p. 254. Subsequent references will be to this edition and will be given in the text within parentheses, marked *SM*.

50. Sartre repeatedly criticizes the conventions of the realist novel, specifically the function of the omniscient narrator, which denies us access to the character's inner life.

51. Of the fused group Sartre writes in the *Critique*, "The internal, synthetic constitution of me by the group is simply totalization" (p. 376). Of the third party he writes: "I am among third parties and have no privileged status. But this operation does not transform me into an object because totalization by the third party only reveals a free praxis" (p. 379). Again we hear echoes of the master/slave dialectic (or its objectification) which is corrected through totalization.

52. See Gérard Genette, *Figures III*, translated as *Narrative Discourse*.

53. A corollary to this is that poetry (and Sartre is concerned with modern poetry) does not propose or sustain a fiction. We have seen that it is this shared fiction ("fiction" here does not necessarily imply realism) that is essential to the reciprocal recognition of freedom in the practice of reading on Sartre's analysis. It is the grid of fiction that engages our belief or *croyance* such that our emotions follow and enter into the process of reading. As we have noted, language does not generate meaning through an accumulation of words. It does not generate meaning in series, as it were. The meaning of a word depends upon the meaning of a phrase or sequence of phrases. It is in this sense that the narrative model serves Sartre's philosophical interest: it facilitates totalization, which is a central feature of Sartre's theory of reading.

For further explanation of the distinction between totality and totalization the reader should refer to chapters of the *Critique of Dialectical Reason* that present the concept of the group in fusion. It may be helpful to consider the following set of oppositions which might be considered parallel to the one between totality and totalization: series / group in fusion, instrumental / noninstrumental, analytic / synthetic, perception / reading, inorganic / organic, causality / finality.

54. *L'esprit* is usually translated as "mind," but this is too intellectual to convey the richness of the term, as Valéry uses it to denote something like psychic force or energies. Since "psychic" has other connotations in English, I prefer to leave the term untranslated.

55. Valéry, *Œuvres complètes* I (Paris: Gallimard, 1957), p. 1350. Subsequent references will be to this edition and will be given within parentheses in the text (my translations).

56. Anna Boschetti writes that "in its intellectualism, the work of Valéry was an important reference for Sartre, contrary to what some superficial objections might lead one to believe." *Sartre et "Les Temps Modernes,"* p. 47. Ronald Aronson in *Jean-Paul Sartre* agrees.

57. Henri Bergson, *Matière et mémoire*, in *Œuvres complètes*, p. 262. Subsequent references will be to this edition and will be given in the text, in parentheses, marked HB.

58. Bergson also gives the musical melody as an image for pure duration in the *Essai sur les données immédiates de la conscience* (HB 70). I shall discuss Bergson's thinking of duration in more detail in Chapter 6. As we shall see, Bergson's analysis of reading serves as a model for his analysis of perception, which involves the dynamics of what Bergson calls "recognition [*reconnaissance*]." Bergson's recognition has nothing to do with Hegelian recognition. The difference between these two is particularly important in relation to our reading of Breton. See Chapter 5.

59. Although Sartre (along with almost everyone else) subsequently repudiated or ignored Bergson, Ronald Aronson tells us that Sartre's dissatisfaction with Bergson was that Bergson did not go far enough. Critics as diverse as Boschetti, Aronson, Benda, Cohen-Solal, and Paul de Man all acknowledge the impact Bergson had on Sartre.

60. Bergson, *L'Evolution créatrice*, in *Œuvres complètes*, p. 498 (my translation). Subsequent references to this edition will be given in the text in parentheses, marked HB.

61. It also became a central tenet in Sartre's *L'Existentialisme est un humanisme*, where we read: "A man engages with his life [*s'engage dans sa vie*], sketches its figure, and beyond this figure, is nothing" (p. 57). "You are free," Sartre writes here, "choose, that is, invent" (p. 47). In this essay Sartre presents the fundamental principal of existentialism in distinctly Bergsonian terms. He asserts that "one must take subjectivity as the point of departure," and glosses subjectivity as "le vécu," or lived experience. In *L'Existentialisme est un humanisme* Sartre, like Bergson, compares the free constitution of the self to the work of the artist of genius, that is, of the artist who does not follow any rule but the energies of his or her inner spirit. "Has one ever reproached an artist who is making a painting for not being inspired by a priori rules?" he asks rhetorically; "has one ever prescribed what painting he must paint? It is well understood that there is no definitive painting to be made, that the artist engages with the construction of his or her painting, and that the painting to be made is precisely the one he or she will have

made." What art and ethics have in common, Sartre summarizes, is that in both cases it is a question of creation and invention. Invention for Sartre, as for Bergson, is the antithesis of an instrumental relation. In the figure of the portrait, action and invention are one.

62. Henri Bergson, *Essai sur les données*, in *Œuvres complètes*, p. 88 (my translation). Subsequent references to this edition will be given in the text in parentheses, marked HB.

63. An earlier version of *La Nausée* explicitly concerned the problem of contingency, a central issue in Bergson's reflections. In a note to *L'évolution créatrice* Bergson makes explicit the relation between duration and contingency which he repeatedly alludes to when he uses the terms indeterminacy (*indétermination*), voluntary (*volontaire*), as well as *invention, création*, and *liberté*. He writes: "There is radical contingency in the incommensurable progress between what precedes and what follows, in other words, duration" (HB 518–19). And, in the body of his text, he adds, "To represent this irreducibility and this irreversibility to ourselves, we must break the scientific habits which correspond to the fundamental requirements of thought, we must do violence to the mind [*esprit*], climb back up the natural slope of intelligence. But that is precisely the role of philosophy" (HB 519). Such was also the role of M. Teste, of whom Sartre was an avid admirer. Indeed, in these comments by Valéry concerning his hero Teste, we seem to find an anticipation of Roquentin: "I once tried to describe a man, *camped out* in his life, a sort of intellectual animal, a Mongol, sparing with stupidities and errors, cavalier and ugly [*leste et laid*], without any attachments, a voyager without any regrets, solitary, remorseless—entirely given over to his inner practices, to his deep prey, lodged in his hotel with his suitcase, without books" (V OCII 1383, original emphasis).

64. Sartre, *La Nausée*, Gallimard, 1938, p. 42 (original emphasis). Subsequent references will be given in the text in parentheses, marked N (my translation).

65. For Bergson, in an experience of the qualitative time of duration the inner states of consciousness add together dynamically, "and organize themselves together the way the notes of a melody do, that we let ourselves be rocked by. In short, pure duration could well be nothing but a succession of qualitative changes that melt together [*se fondent*], that penetrate one another, without any precise outlines, without any tendency to exteriorize themselves with respect to one another, without any relation to number: this would be pure heterogeneity" (HB 70). Here is Sartre's rendering of this state of fusion and organization which Bergson had challenged a novelist to portray: "Balls of fire roll around in the mirrors; smoke rings circle round and turn, veiling and unveiling the hard smile of the light . . . the movement of my art unfolded like a brilliant musical theme [*s'est développé comme un thème majesteux*], it slid along the song of the Negress; it seemed to me I was dancing" (N 42). In *La Nausée* we find this other allusion to the problem of duration: "I no longer distinguish the present from the future and yet it endures [*ça dure*], it becomes realized little by little. . . . That's time, naked time, it comes into existence slowly, it makes you wait for it, and when it comes, one is *disgusted/nauseous* [*écoeuré*] because one notices that it had already been there for a long time" (pp. 53–54, my emphasis).

66. "Encouraged by him [the bad novelist]," Bergson wrote, "we have momentarily *removed the veil* that we interposed between our consciousness and ourselves" (HB 89, my emphasis).

67. "Contingency is not a false pretense [*un faux semblant*], an appearance one can dissipate, it is the absolute" (N 187).

68. Sasso, *Georges Bataille*, p. 110.

69. Bataille, "De l'âge de pierre," p. 212.

70. Ibid. We shall see in Chapter 4 how close this comes to certain features of Valéry's poetics.

71. Bataille, "Le Dernier instant," p. 456.

72. Bataille writes: "L'économie générale . . . n'aurait pu se constituer avant le développement d'une philosophie de l'intériorité mais dès l'abord il faut mettre en terre cette philosophie" (p. 141). Bergson writes: "Il faut voir pour voir, et non pas pour agir, et alors l'absolu se révèle à vous."

73. I return to this point in Chapter 7.

74. Bataille, "De l'âge de pierre," p. 197 (my translation).

75. Bataille, "De l'existentialisme," p. 131.

76. Bataille's involvement with Le Cercle Démocratique begins earlier, in 1931. Contre-Attaque exists between 1935 and 1936. The experiments of Acéphale and of the Collège de Sociologie have a dimension of engagement, as we shall see in more detail in the conclusion.

77. Cited in Surya, *Georges Bataille, La Mort à l'œuvre*. See pp. 196–99.

78. As we have already seen in relation to Bataille, Kojève's reading of Hegel calls attention to the paradox of Hegel's scene of recognition. The master, in the very moment that is meant to determine his subjective autonomy and essentiality in opposition to the dependent status of the slave, depends upon the servility of the slave for the recognition, or objective confirmation, of his mastery. Sartre capitalizes on this paradox in a way different from that of Bataille, whose theory of eroticism, as we have seen, involves recognition by a woman—the gift herself! Sartre places the paradox of the recognition scene at the center of his analysis of esthetic experience, at the core of his "dialectical paradox of reading." He renders it explicit. The essentiality desired by the writer is only possible through the intermediary of the reader. The paradox of the recognition scene thus becomes the enabling moment of the esthetic correction of the violent quest for mastery through the alliance of reciprocity. The "master" (the writer who seeks essentiality) needs the "slave" (the reader) for recognition, but he needs the reader precisely *not* to be a slave; he needs the freedom of the reader and the free gift of that freedom. The reciprocity involved in the paradoxical dialectic of reading—the bridge, in Sartre, between anthropology (Mauss) and ethics (Kant)—depends upon the fictive status of the literary work. By cutting us off from the determinations of space and time, the fictive or imaginary world engages us by soliciting our feelings in their freedom, unconditioned by reality or referential truth. For Sartre, contact between reason and the realm of nature as representation (in Kant's sense) occurs primarily through the reciprocity of writing and reading mediated by the literary object, and only secondarily as practical reason. The esthetic imperative may be modeled after the ethical one at some deeper level—"beneath the esthetic imper-

ative we discern the categorical imperative"—but it is the esthetic imperative that counts.

79. In his 1947 study *Tradition de l'existentialisme ou les philosophes de la vie*, Julien Benda made a similar observation. "For Sartre and for his school," he writes, "engagement is not a consequence of freedom, it is freedom itself" (p. 69, my translation). Benda, as we shall see, argues that existentialism is a rehash of Bergsonism.

Chapter Four

1. *Tel Quel* 1, 1960, pp. 3–4 (my translation). An implicit allusion to Sartre is discernable in context.

2. Adorno, *Notes to Literature*, p. 138. Subsequent references will refer to this edition and will be given in the text, in parentheses, marked A (all translations are my own).

3. Chronologically, of course, this incompatibility arises first with the opposition of Dada and surrealism to the modernist "pure" poetics of Valéry.

4. Paul Valéry, *Œuvres complètes* I, p. 707. Subsequent references will be given in text, marked V. All translations are my own.

5. I am using the opposition "modern/postmodern" lightly here to allude to the conventional identification of poststructuralism with postmodernism. I will challenge this view and discuss these notions in more detail in a later chapter.

6. *Tel Quel* took its distance from Sartre initially through Valéry and later through its adaptation of surrealist positions. But it then took its distance from surrealism not only through Bataille (the disaffected surrealist) but also through Mallarmé. Through the interposition of Mallarmé, signifiance (or text) became dissociated from surrealist automatism. Through the reinterpretation of the myth of Mallarmé, *Tel Quel* also distanced itself from Valéry.

7. Valéry writes: "There is no doubt that he reasoned about their figures, explored the inner space where the words appear to be now *causes*, now *effects*" (p. 655, "Je disais quelquefois," original emphasis).

8. "Mallarmé," Valéry writes in "Lettre sur Mallarmé, "considered literature as no one had done before him with a depth, a rigor, a sort of instinct of generalization that, without his being aware of it, brought our great poet closer to one of our modern geometers who have reestablished the foundation of science, giving it a new breadth and a new power by means of an ever more refined analysis of its fundamental notions and its essential conventions" (V 700, "Existence du symbolisme"). He also refers to Mallarmé's "enumeration, in the manner of Descartes, of the possibilities of language" (p. 709, "Mallarmé"), and to the "clear and distinct ideas" ("notions pures et distinctes") of Mallarmé in "Lettre sur Mallarmé," (p. 635). In "Dernière Visite à Mallarmé" Valéry writes: "Ordinary literature seemed to me to be comparable to an arithmetic . . . that which he conceived of seemed to me analogous to an algebra" (p. 631); and again, in "Sorte de Préface": "Syntax for this poet was an algebra that he cultivated for its own sake," (p. 685); in "Mallarmé" we read: "Mais notre Mallarmé . . . se voua sans répit . . . à l'entreprise inouïe de saisir en toute sa généralité la nature de son art, et par un

dénombrement à la Descartes des possibilités du langage, d'en distinguer tous les moyens. . . . J'ai comparé jadis cette recherche à celle qui, de l'arithmétique . . . a conduit à l'invention de l'algèbre" (p. 709).

9. Bergson, *L'Evolution créatrice*, in *Œuvres complètes*, p. 685 (all translations are mine).

10. "The automatic," as we shall see, means a number of different things for Valéry. It stands for the operation of a romantic notion of inspiration (see, for example, p. 707, "Mallarmé"), for chance effects or "natural" processes, and for what Mallarmé called "la parole brute," ordinary language that, for Valéry, in this context, includes the ordinary clichés of literary convention.

11. "It is here that literature touches the domain of ethics . . . that we find the conflict between the natural and effort . . . [and] that virtue manifests itself" (p. 641).

12. In a less elegant way Breton concurs with Valéry's opinion of the sorry state of letters when he calls for a "definitive cleansing of the whole literary stable [*nettoyage définitif de toute l'écurie littéraire*]" in "Le Message Automatique" (in *Point du Jour*, p. 171). We will discuss the relations between surrealist automatism and Valéry further in Chapter 5. Breton is perhaps rephrasing Valéry who had called for a "cleansing of language [*nettoyage de langage*]," a phrase that returns in Sartre's *Qu'est-ce que la littérature?*

13. Breton writes that automatic writing and *récits de rêves* are "as detached as possible from the will to signify" (*Œuvres*, p. 809). In the First Manifesto he also emphasizes that "the virtue of speech (and, all the more so, of writing) seemed to me to have to do with its ability to cut things short in a striking manner" (p. 323); he adds: "I came to especially cherish words for the space that they left around them, for their tangencies with innumerable other words that I did not pronounce. The poem FORÊT-NOIRE was written in precisely this spirit."

14. Derrida alludes to this aspect of *l'esprit* in Valéry (*l'esprit* as "power of transformation," as Valéry writes in "La Politique de l'esprit") both in *Spectres de Marx*, pp. 24–30 and in *L'Autre cap* (Minuit, 1992). However, the Derrida text that most closely anticipates the lines of my reading here (if one only substitutes Bergson for Nietzsche) is the early "Qual Quelle" (in *Marges*). When I first read this essay I had not yet read Valéry; I returned to it only after this chapter was completed.

15. Valéry redefines poetics in the narrow prescriptive sense as "poïetics" from the Greek word *poïein*, which he translates as "mental action [*le faire de l'esprit*]."

16. Baudelaire, *Œuvres*, p. 1271 (my translation).

17. It also refers us to Bergson, who writes in *Matière et mémoire* of "the double movement of contraction and expansion by which consciousness tightens [*resserre*] or loosens [*élargit*] the development of its contents." Bergson describes this double movement in terms of resemblance and contiguity (or metaphor and metonymy, in anticipation of Jakobson and Lacan) (HB 305).

18. Valéry uses the phrase "extrême perfection du travail." In the "Première leçon," it is the idea of work that precipitates the economic metaphors of production and consumption that Valéry invokes to refer to the activities (and in-

stances) of writing and reading. "Without insisting on my economic comparison," Valéry remarks, "it is clear that the idea of work, the ideas of creation and of accumulation of wealth, of supply and demand, present themselves quite naturally in the domain that interests us" (p. 1344).

19. The mysterious relations between desire and event (or accomplishment) are explicated in the following terms: "a voluntary action . . . that can require long hours of work . . . comes to adapt itself, in the operation of art, to a state of being that is completely irreducible in itself to finite expression, that refers to no localizable object that one can determine . . . and this ending up as this work [*et ceci aboutissant à cette œuvre*]" (p. 1357).

20. Adorno writes of Valéry: "the absurd moment of chance [is] a veritable value-limit in the space-time that he associates with Bergsonian duration, the involuntary memory as only form of survival [*survie*]. For in the anarchy of history this memory is itself contingent. For Valéry this defines the dignity of chance" (A 148–49).

21. Cited in Adorno (A 159).

22. In the lecture he declares his interest in "the creative act itself [*l'action qui fait*]" more than in "the thing created [*la chose faite*]." In the essay "Descartes" he writes that his curiosity "is more interested in the *esprit* itself than in the things represented there" and "gets excited by the vain desire to perceive the very workings of thought [*le travail propre de la pensée*]" (pp. 795–96).

23. We recognize an allusion to the theory of reading which we discussed in relation to Sartre and traced back to Bergson via Valéry: reading as directed creation [création dirigée] which involves anticipation or *attente*.

24. In Valéry's "nous faire entendre soi-même," the "soi-même" is ambiguous, suggesting both a "himself" and a "oneself." This is a variation on the theme introduced in the "Première leçon": that the effect of the work "should be to recreate in the other person a state analogous to the one initially experienced by the producer" (p. 1357). "Works of the mind [esprit], poems or other, only relate back to *what engenders whatever engendered themselves* and to absolutely nothing else" (p. 1350, original emphasis). This is the *mimique* of reading, where the work creates in the reader the analogous state of the conditions of its own production. The *Discourse* of Descartes is a "mute soliloquy" that invites the reader into the recreation of its own interior monologue.

25. For Valéry the content of Descarte's writings amounts to what Pascal would call mere "reversals of for and against [*renversements du pour au contre*]," a process that, in the end, exhausts the thinker's philosophical contribution and reduces it to "the sort of dead creature [*mort*] attested to by a mention in history and an inscription in school curricula"—"one no longer discusses with these mummies." (This resonates with Sartre's mockery of the library and of the messages contained in the books on those shelves in *Qu'est-ce que la littérature?*) "What do we do with these terms that one can not specify without recreating?" Valéry asks. "Thought [*Pensée*], the mind [*l'esprit*] itself, reason, intelligence, understanding, intuition, or inspiration? . . . Each of these names is by turn a means and an end, a problem and a resolution, a state of being and an idea" (p. 797). The word *in-*

spiration makes explicit the problem of genius, which is the central issue here and the poetic question par excellence. Valéry takes a Pascalian attitude to the question of the philosophical content itself.

26. "By itself . . . *l'esprit* possesses no means to have done with its essential activity" (p. 796).

27. Here we are at one extreme end of Valéry's poetic sensibility, one that comes quite close to Bataille, who also characterizes poetry as an act of "crying out what is," and who insists on the relation between poetry and the instant. This is what Bataille calls "the poetry of event." See "De l'âge de pierre à Jacques Prévert," *Critique* 3–4 (1946): 197–98.

28. We return to the question of Valéry's use of a vitalist notion of the will specifically in relation to Descartes, and discuss this as a strategic gesture, in Chapter 7.

29. In the case of Descartes, Valéry speaks of an "intellectual effort disengaged from all application" and adds "and what is more pure and more audacious than its development along this abstract path?" This disengaged intellectual effort marks Descartes as the pure philosopher, on analogy with the pure poet, just as Mallarmé, the pure poet, was the algebrist, etc.

30. "He gives himself a sort of reason of State [*raison d'Etat*] against which nothing can prevail, and which always ends up freeing the Self energetically of all difficulties or parasitical notions that have been engraved upon it *without having been discovered from within*" (p. 826, original emphasis).

31. His intellectual career is marked by the "struggle . . . between his will to clarity in the organization of knowledge, and uncertainty, the accidental, confusion and the inconsequential, which are the most likely attributes of most of our thoughts" (p. 824).

32. Both Adorno, in his essay in *Notes to Literature*, and Derrida, in his early essay "Qual Quelle" (in *Marges de la philosophie*) illuminate this aspect of Valéry's poetics. Derrida makes a connection between Valéry and Nietzsche (whereas I shall elaborate this aspect of Valéry's thinking in relation to Bergson). Adorno notes the ambivalence in Valéry concerning chance and the arbitrary, yet he insists upon the primacy of form, which he considers the central point of Valéry's esthetics. He does not problematize this notion of form, but considers it in Hegelian terms, that is, as concretization and objectivation—"The absolute mastery of the self [*du soi*] by the subject signifies that it sublates itself into something objective " (A 172, translation altered). For an interesting reading of Valéry that discusses the writing of the *Cahiers* in terms of impersonal production, see Daniel Oster, *Monsieur Valéry*.

33. As we shall see in connection with the essays on Leonardo, gestures of identification are systematic and strategic for Valéry as they are for Baudelaire. See my *Impersonal Sublime*.

34. *Monsieur Teste* in Valéry, *Œuvres complètes* t. II, p. 18. Subsequent references will be given in the text and will refer to this edition.

35. That is, automatic now in a sense close to what Breton means when he uses the term. I have been tracing within Valéry a shift from the Bergsonian pejorative sense of "automatic" to the positive sense we find in Breton as a reversal of Bergson's term; that is, a psychic automatism instead of a material repetition. Breton

elaborates the reversal, but it is prepared for by the slippages we have been tracing within the discourse of Valéry.

36. Bergson, *Matière et mémoire*, in *Œuvres complètes*, p. 221. Subsequent references to this work will be to this edition (PUF) and will be given in parentheses in the text, marked HB (translations mine).

37. In *L'Evolution créatrice* Bergson writes: "animal life consists of 1) obtaining a supply of energy, 2) expending it [*la dépenser*]" (HB 709).

38. Bergson, *Œuvres complètes*, p. 747 (my translation). The citation reads in French: "Alors l'Absolu se révèle très près de nous, et, dans une certaine mesure, en nous. . . . Il vit avec nous. Comme nous, mais, par certains côtés, infiniment plus concentré et il dure."

39. In French the quote reads: "[il] port[ait] les dissociations, les substitutions, les similitudes au point extrême, mais avec un retour assuré, une opération inverse infaillible." When Valéry uses the term *intellectuel* in such cases, it is as an adjective for the noun *esprit*. It is not limited to acts of intellection. If Valéry speaks of an "intellectual effort detached from any application," we should not take the word "intellectual" in too restrictive a sense. It is rather a question of psychic effort or energy. The "se saisir" involved here is not specular and does not involve knowledge. It is rather a question of a reappropriation of the energies of the self related to what Valéry called "egoism" in the case of Descartes.

40. Here we do, perhaps, have an equivalent to the dialectic of recognition which we do not find in Bergson but which we have traced in relation to Bataille and Sartre. But here the "se saisir" is to be understood, I think, in relation to Baudelaire and his discussion in the Wagner essay of the poet's need to "raisonner son art," that is, to be critic as well as poet.

41. The act of witnessing would be comparable to what Bergson calls "veiller," when he writes "veiller et vouloir sont une seule et même chose" (HB 893, *L'Energie spirituelle*). Teste is a figure of consciousness as witness.

42. I prefer to translate *voir* by "seeing" rather than "vision" to emphasize the active or verbal feature of it instead of the nominal one. The French text reads: "et ne pouvant être que par consommation de possible et recharge. . . . De ceci, supposer un individu qui en soit comme l'allégorie et le héros." Bergson defines intuition in terms of an act of "finding true duration again." He distinguishes his own philosophy of intuition from that of other philosophers in the following way. The others, he writes, consider intelligence to operate in time and conclude that to get beyond intelligence one must escape from time. Whereas for Bergson, as he writes, "to pass from intelligence to vision, from the relative to the absolute, it is not a question of getting out of time (we are already outside of it); on the contrary, we must place ourselves in duration again and once more seize reality in its mobility which is its essence" (HB 1271, *La Pensée et le mouvant*). Intuition, Bergson adds "pertains above all to inner duration . . . it is the direct vision of the *esprit* by itself . . . a form of knowledge as contact and even coincidence" (HB 1273).

43. Indeed, Teste is so "mentally rich [*riche d'esprit*]" that "the development of his attention is infinite and . . . the idea of finishing with it *would no longer have meaning*" (p. 43, my emphasis). Teste would correspond to the work of mental action depicted in the lecture on poetics" before the hand that intervenes.

44. Concerning intuition, Bergson also speaks of "the enlarged consciousness, pressing on the borders of an unconscious which yields and resists . . . which demonstrates to us that the unconscious is there; against strict logic, it affirms that even if the psychological is conscious [*le psychologique a beau être du conscient*] there is nevertheless a psychological unconscious . . . the intuition we have of ourselves" (HB 1273, *La Pensée et le mouvant*).

45. Cited in Judith Robinson, *L'Analyse de l'esprit dans les Cahiers de Valéry*, p. 146 (my translation). Subsequent references to this work will be given in the text in parentheses and marked R.

46. Consciousness, as vigilance, implies a relation to the future but also to the past. "Valéry often reminds us," Robinson writes, "that awakening is above all a return of memory . . . in awakening the memory is the first thing to come back, that is, the recognition of what one sees and of one's relation to what one knows"(R 136).

47. Valéry's undertaking reminds us of Bergson's recommendation to study internal phenomena, "phenomena in the process of occurring, as they constitute, by their mutual penetration, the continual development of a free person" (HB 149, *Essai*, my translation). For the free self (*le moi libre*), according to Bergson, is the agent of invention; it is the self of genius. It is in this context, also, that Valéry writes: "Il y a là toute une mécanique intime, très délicate, dans laquelle des durées particulières jouent le plus grand rôle, sont incluses les unes dans les autres" (V 1163, "Introduction à la méthode de Léonard de Vinci").

48. This, as we shall see in Chapter 5, is a formulation that both echoes Bergson (specifically passages from the *Essai* and from *L'Introduction à la métaphysique*) and anticipates Breton's interest in the collages of Max Ernst, and his definition of the surrealist image.

49. Here we have an echo of Bergson's affirmation in the *Essai* that duration is unrepresentable. Hence Bergson's critique of language as alienating and reifying (to borrow a term that Lukàcs will elaborate on the basis of ideas taken from Bergson). On the relation between Bergson and Lukàcs, see *The Crisis in Modernism*, ed. Burwick and Douglas.

50. Once again Valéry sounds much like Bergson in the *Essai*, who condemns language in terms of repetition and the inert (that is, the automatic in the negative sense). This is the basis for his claim that duration, in all its spontaneity and instability, is unrepresentable. It is interesting, in this context, to remember that Valéry writes: "mon moi-même s'est formé de 1890 jusqu'à sa maturité (1910)" (note to "Mauvaises pensées et autres," p. 1527), that is, precisely during the years of the publication of Bergson's early work.

Chapter Five

1. Cited in Brochier, *L'Aventure des surréalistes, 1914–1940*, p. 53. The French text reads: "La critique de notre temps est très injuste envers le symbolisme . . . vous me dites que le surréalisme ne s'est pas donné pour tâche de la mettre en valeur; historiquement, il était inévitable qu'il s'opposât à lui, mais la critique n'avait pas à lui emboîter le pas. C'était à lui de retrouver, de mettre en place la courroie de transmission." The expression *courroie de transmission* literally means

"drive belt," a term of automobile mechanics, but also suggests "current of trans-mission" (*courant* instead of *courroie*), in the sense of electrical current, a meta-phor Breton frequently uses, as we shall see. I will henceforth leave the term in French, in order to suggest both registers and retain the playfulness of Breton's language.

2. When I refer to the "voluntarist poetics" of Valéry in this chapter I am al-luding to the conventional view of Valéry as formalist modernist, for this is the Valéry that Breton attacked. Of course my reading in the previous chapter is in-tended to problematize this perspective.

3. Valéry, "Littérature," in *Œuvres complètes*, p. 546. The French text reads: "Il ne peut être autre chose. . . . Fête: c'est un jeu, mais solennel, mais réglé, mais significatif; image de ce qu'on n'est pas d'ordinaire, de l'état où les efforts sont ry-thmés, rachetés."

4. Breton, "Notes sur la poésie," in *Œuvres complètes*, p. 1014. This and sub-sequent translations are mine. Subsequent references will be given in the text, and will refer to this edition. The French text reads: "Un poème doit être un débacle de l'intellect. Il ne peut être autre chose. . . . Débâcle: c'est un sauve-qui-peut, mais solennel, mais probant: image de ce qu'on devrait être, de l'état où les efforts ne comptent plus." Subsequent references to this edition will be given in the text, in parentheses, marked B.

5. In *Poésies*, Lautréamont-Ducasse writes: "If one were to correct the sophisms via the truths associated with these sophisms, the correction alone would be true; while the work thus recast would have the right not to call itself false anymore. The rest would be outside the true [*hors de vrai*], with a trace of falsehood, and therefore of necessity considered null and void," *Œuvres complètes*, p. 51 (my translation). For a discussion of the *plagiat*, see my *Impersonal Sublime*, chap. 4.

6. "L'Existence du Symbolism," Valéry, *Œuvres complètes* I, pp. 690–93. This analysis is particularly interesting because elsewhere Valéry insists that these were the years "où je me suis fait." He also alludes to the importance of the "thèses psycho-physiologiques à la mode" in the years 1883–90. Bergson's *Essai* was pub-lished during this period and this statement is one of the few that can be taken to point to the influence of Bergson, which Valéry otherwise stubbornly denies.

7. Valéry writes of "intellectual nothingness and the powerlessness that results from it."

8. The word "dictature," which conveys absolute power, also suggests dicta-tion in the sense of Breton's definition of automatism as a "magic dictation [*dic-tée magique*]." If the lecture on poetics appears to be too late to have had a for-mative impact on Breton, the early essays on Mallarmé, Descartes, and Leonardo, as well as the early "Crise de l'esprit," were composed in the twenties, that is, dur-ing the most formative years in the career of the young Breton. The chronology of publication dates does not give us a full picture of the possible interactions be-tween Breton and the less notorious side of Valéry's reflections upon poetry—his mystical commitment to the forces of inner life and his understanding of the op-erations of "l'esprit en acte." Valéry's essays emerge as an unfolding set of varia-tions on abiding concerns: the question of genius and the drama of mental action. The essays on Mallarmé date from 1920 ("Le Coup de dés, lettre au directeur des

Marges") to 1933. The classes on poetics at the Collège de France began in 1937. But there is no reason to think that the material presented at the Collège de France had not been meditated over a longer period of time. The earliest essay on Descartes was published in 1925, and subsequent essays appear into the 1930's and 1940's. Likewise, the Teste cycle was generated between 1896 and the year of Valéry's death. The date given for the "Première leçon du cours de poétique" is 1937, much later than Breton's elaborations of automatism and the emergence of his thoughts concerning surrealism. Indeed, Breton had undertaken the experiment that led to the *Champs magnétiques* before the composition of the essays on Mallarmé. But, as Béhar points out in his biography, *André Breton*, the initial experiment with automatism that yielded the *Champs magnétiques* was not at first recognized by Breton as a major event. The technique of automatism, like those of collage and *réclame*, had already been advanced in the milieu of Dada and published in Dada revues. It is a question here not of the invention of automatism, but rather of the importance Breton came to give it as he subsequently elaborated it and held to it as a core phenomenon of surrealism.

9. It is helpful, in this context, to recall certain general features of Breton's own career. Breton did not just fall into an avant-garde milieu. To enter it he effectively sacrificed his entrée into the official literary world, where a place had been held open for him. When he had the backing of the literary establishment—Valéry, Gide, and Proust—to receive financial support to continue his work as a poet he submitted for the competition not one of his early poems in the manner of Valéry and Mallarmé (poems that had already met with success in this milieu) but an experiment in the spirit of Dada. Needless to say he did not win the fellowship. He made a choice concerning two different conceptions of poetry: the traditional view of poetry as expression and the Dada conception of poetry as, in the words of Tzara, a "dictatorship of *l'esprit*." In the same way he did not haphazardly fall away from the Dada group. He broke from that milieu deliberately to take a divergent path.

10. The title, Mme. Bonnet suggests, was in Breton's mind since at least 1920. A number of the articles were first published earlier still: "Guillaume Apollinaire," 1918; "Alfred Jarry," 1919; "Jacques Vaché," 1919; "Deux Manifestes Dada," 1920; "Pour dada," 1920; "Max Ernst," 1921. See Breton, *Œuvres complètes*, p. 1216 (notes to *Les Pas perdus*).

11. Valéry, OC I, 1036. The essay by Valéry in which this exact expression, "crise de confiance," is used appears after Breton's composition of "La Confession dédaigneuse." But Valéry refers here to earlier versions of these meditations that go back to 1919. Valéry emphasizes the continuity between them—"The pieces since 1919 have not changed a lot, and I think that the pages that I wrote then still represent quite precisely the uncertainty and anxiety of the present day" (V 1022, "La Politique de l'esprit"). Whatever the exact wording, given that Breton is in close contact with Valéry during this period, it would not be surprising that this otherwise unusual expression, "the terrible difficulties consciousness has with confidence" alludes to the dialogue with Valéry.

12. Cited in Werner Spies, *Max Erst, Collages*, p. 19. From Aragon, *La Pein-*

ture au Défi, 1930. Breton also writes, in *Entretiens* (1952), "It is no exaggeration to state that Max Ernst's first collages, of incredible suggestive force, struck us as a revelation," cited in Spies, n. 35, p. 250.

13. Spies, *Max Ernst.* Cited in n. 426, p. 258, from Breton "Genèse et perspective artistique du surréalisme" (translation mine). For another discussion of relations between Ernst and Breton, see Rosalind Krauss, *Optical Unconscious.*

14. Spies writes that "Ernst's method initially turned Cubist papier collé inside out: rather than inserting 'nonesthetic' borrowed elements into a picture, he began with a 'nonesthetic' image and, by means of drawn and painted additions or subtractions, gave it 'esthetic' character," p. 30. For a discussion of distinctions between collage, papier collé, and Duchamp's readymades, see Spies, especially pp. 42–44. Concerning the papier collé see also Yve-Alain Bois, *Painting as Model.* Concerning Cubist collage, see Rosalind Krauss, "In the Name of Picasso," in *The Originality of the Avant-Garde and Other Modernist Myths.*

15. Max Ernst, *Beyond Painting,* p. 14. This passage comes after a short discussion of the "Lesson of Leonardo," which for Ernst involved the practice of frottage—the projection of spontaneous conceptions of the imagination onto the "screen" of a natural material. Ernst calls the irrational the "conquest of collage," and reminds us that another conquest is surrealist painting. He names Magritte, "whose pictures are collages entirely painted by hand," as well as Dali (p. 17).

16. See Spies, *Max Ernst,* chapter 4 and especially pp. 66–67. Spies gives plates of a number of collages from 1920.

17. *Pensée* (idea or thought) is not to be understood in an epistemological or intellectual sense but rather in terms of Valéry's "symbolist" term "inner life [*vie intérieure*]" and his notion of *l'esprit,* conceived as force of transformation. In this sense, as we shall see more clearly further on, *pensée* for Breton is linked to the notion of spontaneity. *Pensée* here should be understood in relation to what Breton calls "spoken thought [*la pensée parlée*]," that which gives "the trace of the real operations of thought," or "the thinking of real spontaneity." Automatism, then, Breton suggests, would give us the trace of what Valéry calls "le travail de l'esprit."

18. The same argument is summarized in *Position politique du surréalisme.* It was a commonplace of the time; Léger and Magritte, among others, make the same point.

19. This Congress never takes place, in part due to the lack of participation of Tzara. The essay "Quelques caractéristiques," included in *Les Pas perdus,* takes up the questions Breton was thinking about in connection with the planned Congress.

20. For the distinction between langue and parole see Saussure, *Cours de linguistique générale.* When I use "speech" in the sense of Saussure's term *parole* I am referring not only to language, but to images as well.

21. For a discussion of this "repetition of enunciation" and shifts in discursive level in *Poésies* see my *Impersonal Sublime.*

22. In *Poésies* we read: "If one were to correct the sophisms via the truths associated with these sophisms, the correction alone would be true; while the work

thus recast would have the right not to call itself false anymore. The rest would be outside the true [*hors du vrai*], with a trace of falsehood, and therefore, of necessity considered null and void." Lautréamont-Ducasse, *Poésies*, p. 51.

23. Spies refers to an "esthetic of quotation" in relation to Ernst, "a technique by which to exploit the discovery that when real things are combined, their meanings shift" (p. 82); he does not discuss the *plagiat* of *Poésies* in this connection, or develop the notion of citation in the direction undertaken here. He does mention, however, that Lautréamont used material from the same sort of catalogues as Ernst, as source material for the *Chants de Maldoror*. In fact the writing practice of *Poésies* was to some extent already utilized, though less sytematically, in the *Chants*.

24. It is interesting to note in this context that, as Spies tells us, one of Ernst's works takes a copy of a Dürer etching and "artfully renders it unrecognizable"—this was precisely the practice of Lautréamont-Ducasse in the *plagiat*. Spies also tells us that Ernst was charged with plagiarism in the 1950's, when source material of one of his collages was uncovered and identified.

25. In Breton's essay on Ernst, the allusion is to cinematic pictures as objectifications of the fact of the subjective relativity of time— *temps locaux*.

26. In "Lâchez tout" (a response to Tzara's reponse to Breton's "Après Dada") he writes: "We are subjected to a kind of mental mimicry that prohibits us from going deeper into anything and makes us consider with hostility what used to be most dear to us" (B 263).

27. The "peculiar phrase" was therefore poetic according to the definition of Valéry: poetry is different from prose in that with poetry we feel compelled to repeat the words exactly; there is no possibility of paraphrase.

28. When we look more closely, however, we see that the verbal and visual registers are actually intertwined. The visual image is hardly a mere illustration of an autonomous text; it may be that it is just the other way around. For when we read "there is a man cut in two by the window," the direct article (*la* fenêtre) refers to the window given in the visual representation: "the faint visual representation of a man walking and cut in two, in the middle, by a window perpendicular to the axis of his body." The interpretation which follows—"certainly it was a question of the simple vertical displacement in space of a man looking out a window"—reintroduces the definite article because the expression "to lean out the window"—"se pencher de la fenêtre"—requires it. This being the case, it seems that the definite article present in the initial statement of the sentence was already not merely a description of the visual representation itself, but a description of the interpretation—the visual interpretation of the spatial translation of a ninety-degree angle.

29. The French text reads: "La fenêtre creusée dans notre chair s'ouvre sur notre coeur. On y voit un immense lac. . . . On rit aussi, mais il ne faut pas regarder longtemps sans longue-vue. Tout le monde peut y passer dans ce couloir sanglant." The *Champs magnétiques* is published before the Manifesto. However, we remember that the phrase had come to Breton earlier. Enough time had elapsed so that Breton had forgotten the exact sentence by the time he composed the Manifesto. Presumably it came to him in connection with experiments with automa-

tism undertaken within the Dada context that produced *Les Champs magnétiques*. In any case the metaphors of building material and construction are surprising, since the "building" into which Breton incorporates this image is an automatic text.

30. There is also implicitly an image of birthing. Here it is a question of the coming to light of a deeper self—what Bergson would call the *moi profonde* or the *esprit libre*. Rebirth is one of the major themes of the opening pages of the Manifesto.

31. *Précipités* was Breton's initial title for what became *Les Champs matgnétiques*.

32. Although *résoudre* (as a transitive verb) can signify the resolution of a problem or an enigma, in Breton's sentence it is a question of a "se résoudre en"—a "résolution . . . de deux états . . . en une sorte de surréalité"—which corresponds to the syntax of the dictionary example of resolution in the chemical sense: "les nuages de grêle se résoudent en eau." A constellation of chemical figures has already been introduced to account for the "supreme reality" of the surrealist image—"précipités," fusion, *étincelles*, *différences de potentiel*. The dynamics of a "se réduire" are presented as a function of a surrealist "atmosphere." In the notorious declaration, the resolution in question pertains to dream and reality as "deux états," which, in a chemical vocabulary, would refer to the states of solid, liquid, and gas. It is in very similar terms, as we shall see, that Bergson distinguished between what he called the two extreme states of "l'esprit": dream and action. Here, in Breton, it is a question of the resolution of these states into a third: surreality. But we have already seen surreality presented through the chemical figure of an atmosphere. The resolution in question, then, is not the dialectical resolution of a logical problem, but rather a change of state, a transformation through reduction. In this sense it would be closer to a dissolution, a kind of atomization into the "solution" of the surrealist atmosphere.

33. Breton, "Le Message automatique," in *Point du jour*, p. 182. Subsequent references will be to this edition and will be given in the text, in parentheses, marked MA. Language, here, is to be understood in both linguistic and visual terms.

34. The full quote reads: "la ligne de démarcation valable qui permette d'isoler l'objet imaginaire de l'objet réel . . . tant toutefois admis que, jusqu'à nouvelle ordre, le second ne peut aisément disparaître du champs de la conscience et le premier y apparaître, que subjectivement leurs propriétés se montrent interchangeables" (MA 187).

35. Breton, *Le Surréalisme et la peinture*, p. 3. Subsequent references will refer to this edition and will be given in the text, marked SP. This statement has been generally neglected by commentators on surrealism from the 1960's and 1970's who interpreted Breton's "sublime point" as an ideal dialectical transcendence. As we saw in the first chapter, Foucault, Hollier, and others have emphasized an idealist (Hegelian) reading of Breton's "sublime point" where contradictions cease. They situate surreality in a transcendent realm. Likewise, *Tel Quel* publishes Bataille's article "La Vieille taupe" (also republished, in translation, in Allan Stoekle's *Bataille Reader*) which accuses Breton of philosophical idealism. On the

contrary, surreality is immanent to the real, in filiation not from Hegel but, as we shall argue, from Bergson, and probably from the "surnaturalisme" of Baudelaire.

Nevertheless, as I indicated in Chapter 1, Sollers opposes Bataille's theory of eroticism, figured by "le toit," to Breton's "mental point where life and death . . . are no longer perceived as contradictory," commenting: "The difference between these two formulations is essential (it would no doubt enable us to understand how Bataille and Breton are in irreconcilable positions with respect to Hegel)" (my translation). See "Le Toit."

36. Cited in Judith Robinson, *L'Analyse*, p. 136. The French text reads, "le retour, la reprise, fait essentiel. Propriété du Présent. Coincidence d'une perception-mémoire avec une perception-sensation qui donnent par leur réunion et rapprochement et composition complexe le système Moi-Présent." The similarity to Breton's invocation of recognition in *Le Surréalisme et la peinture* is striking.

37. For an interesting reading of Breton's *Nadja*, and for an original analysis of Breton's engagement—his "surrealist Marxism"—see Margaret Cohen's *Profane Illumination*. Cohen's analysis supports the broad lines of the reading given here. She argues that "dismantling the dialectic as it has been rigidified by historical materialism is central to Breton's modern materialism," and suggests that "Breton's concerns are not as opposed to those of Bataille's during the same period as their heated exchanges might suggest" (p. 122).

38. Nadja's destitution reflects this as does, even more, her proud assumption of it—"seventeen, yes, eighteen, no!" she says in response to the offer of a higher wage than what she had anticipated, when she is looking for work.

39. It is interesting to note that Bergson models the role of the philosopher of intuition on this portrait of the artist. For the philosopher it is a question of a "conversion of attention" (see HB 1373–74)—anticipations of Bataille.

40. Yet another coincidence: Deleuze ends his *Bergsonism* with this question. A few lines from the end of his book in the afterword to the English translation, "Return to Bergson," we read: "In an outstanding article on 'paramnesia' (false recognition), Bergson invokes metaphysics to show how a memory is not constituted after present perception, but is strictly contemporaneous with it, since at each instant duration divides into two simultaneous tendencies, one of which goes towards the future, and the other falls back into the past" (p. 118).

41. The French text reads: "se dédouble à tout instant, dans son jaillissement même, en deux jets symétriques, dont l'un retombe vers le passé tandis que l'autre s'élance vers l'avenir. Ce dernier, que nous appelons perception, est le seul qui nous intéresse." The image of the fountain returns, implicitly, when Bergson characterizes perception and memory in the following terms: "Our actual existence, as it unfolds in time, doubles itself with a virtual existence, a mirror image. Every moment of our life thus presents two aspects: it is actual and virtual, perception on the one hand and memory on the other. It divides in two at the same time that it presents itself. Or rather it consists in this division itself, for, the present instant, always moving forward, the ever-escaping limit between the immediate past which no longer is and the immediate future which is not yet, would be reduced to a simple abstraction if it were not precisely the mobile mirror which continually reflects perception into memory" (HB 917–18, *L'Energie spirituelle*).

42. *Les Vases communicants*, p. 128. There are a number of interesting parallels between Breton's account of himself in these pages and his description of Nadja. We remember, too, that Sartre characterizes the act of reading in just these terms, that is, as *rêve libre*, in *Qu'est-ce que la littérature?*

43. Bergson expresses the paradoxical experience of second sight in terms that elucidate what Breton might have in mind when he speaks of the power of collage (or the surrealist image) to "estrange us in our own memory." "What doubles itself at every moment in perceptions and memories," Bergson writes, "is the totality of what we see, understand, experience, everything that we are together with everything that surrounds us. If we become aware of this doubling, it is the whole of our present [*l'intégralité de notre présent*] that will appear to us both as perception and as memory. . . . The situation is strange, paradoxical . . . it is a memory of a moment in the very moment of its actuality. It is *past with respect to its form and present with respect to its content*" (HB 917–18, *L'Energie spirituelle*, my emphasis). In *Matière et mémoire* he also writes that "the feeling of 'déja vu' comes from a juxtaposition or fusion of perception and memory" (HB 236).

44. The French text reads: "Je me bornerai ici à me souvenir sans effort de ce qui, ne répondant à aucune démarche de ma part, m'est quelquefois advenu . . . j'en parlerai sans ordre établi, et selon le caprice de l'heure qui laisse surnager ce qui surnage." (We hear echoes in this passage of Lautréamont-Ducasse's "correction" of Pascal in *Poésies*.)

45. In the Second Manifesto Breton writes: "In poetry, in painting, surrealism has done everything [*a fait l'impossible*] to multiply short circuits" (B 809).

46. "Guidons de l'esprit" is Breton's figure for the surrealist image in the First Manifesto.

47. Breton often uses the word *pensée* in the same way that Bergson does, that is, to designate memory images in the mind.

48. It is a question of the kind of difference Breton describes so well in the case of De Chirico: "Certes l'œuvre qui en résultait restait liée d'un lien étroit avec ce qui avait provoqué sa naissance mais ne lui ressemblait qu'à la façon étrange dont se ressemblent deux frères, ou plutôt l'image en rêve d'une personne déterminée et cette personne réelle. C'est, en même temps ce n'est pas, la même personne réelle" (B 649).

49. In other words, the text remains constant throughout various editions. But the photo is subsequently obtained and given in the text. Thus we read of a photo that is unobtainable and then we see the photo after all, whose title refers us to the mention of it as unobtainable.

50. This is the only explicitly erotic image in the book. This fact, together with its appearance on the frame of the story of Nadja, might suggest that it is meant to announce the passion that Breton reveals at the end of the text for the woman he addresses directly as "Toi." This would explain its proximity to the photograph of "Les Aubes," the name of the restaurant where Breton dined with his new lover, marking the beginning of their liaison. The erotic presence and the signal of the dawn both mark the promise of a new beginning. But this interpretation does not account for the note that Breton attaches to his description of the wax figure— "the only statue I know that has eyes: the eyes of provocation"—a note that con-

cerns Nadja and a mode of provocation that is not primarily erotic, though it is passionate. In the note, it is explicitly a question of the radical subversiveness of Nadja: "Until that day I had not been able to [*Il ne m'avait pas été donné de*] draw out [*dégager*] everything, in Nadja's attitude toward me, that involved the application of a total principle of subversion, more or less conscious." What is involved here is a reflection concerning the relations between automatism (or "l'esprit d'errance") and subversion in a political register. It is in this sense that the wax statue could be said to mediate between the figures of substitution, Nadja and "toi," just as Nadja, through the "eyes" of the wax statue, is revealed to be the mediation (Mélusine) between automatism (in its relation to desire) and action—or automatic engagement.

51. These are Bergson's categories in *Matière et mémoire* for "the two extreme planes of mental activity that we have called the plane of action and the plane of dream" (HB 372). The plane of action is the one where the body has "contracted its past in motor habits" and the other is "the plane of pure memory" (HB 371). Thus we have the "real" fountain and then the virtual one in the drawing from the frontispiece of the *Dialogues entre Hylas et Philonous*. Likewise we have a painting by an old master followed by the historical postcards being peddled by the poor beggar at the cafe, in the episode ending with the improvised drawings of Nadja.

52. For an interesting discussion of the status of the photos in *Nadja* see Michel Beaujour, "Qu'est-ce que 'Nadja'?" Beaujour also holds that the photos do not replace description in *Nadja* (p. 786). Although he does not mention Bergson by name, his analysis anticipates the broad lines of the argument made here for he emphasizes a return from discontinuity to continuity and "the duration of sacred time." "You have to let time distend, soften and flow like an undifferentiated liquid substance, where the before and the after melt into one another and end up coexisting in the instant. This way of living time is evidently the greatest scandal of the surrealist adventure: it is radically opposed to our usual conception of a linear duration . . . which our industrious and industrial society glorifies" (p. 789, my translation).

53. The French text reads: "Il me semble néanmoins nécessaire ici de rappeler qu'il y a vingt ans, Breton misa sur ce principe toute l'activité du surréalisme" (Bataille, "Le Surréalisme au jour le jour").

54. Mme Bonnet cites Léon Pierre Quint in the *Revue de France*, Oct. 1931, to the effect that "In the Second Manifesto, Breton goes back to the very sources of Marxism and of the absolute idealism of Hegel to attach surrealism to them." In *Positions politiques du surréalisme*, Breton speaks explicitly of the "dialectical resolution of old antinomies" (p. 63).

55. "How can we believe that the dialectical method can be applied with validity only to the resolution of social problems?" Breton asks, and declares: "the whole ambition of Surrealism is to furnish possibilities of application in no way in competition with one another in the most immediate conscious domain," possibilities, that is, in the realms of passionate love, madness, art, and religion (B 793).

56. Breton, *Positions politiques du surréalisme*, p. 63. *Conscience*, of course,

also means "conscience" in French, and *plus de conscience* can suggest "no more consciousness."

57. "New discursivities" is Foucault's term from *The Archeology of Knowledge*.

58. Starobinski's essay "Freud, Breton, Myers" supports this point of view to the extent that it calls attention to fundamental incompatibilities between surrealist automatism and the Freudian theory of the unconscious. Starobinski points out that when Freud explores the forces of the unconscious, he does not valorize them per se; he emphasizes the need to organize, channel, and interpret the energies of the unconscious and their meanings. Breton, on the contrary, finds a "subjective treasure" in the unconscious (which, during the years of engagement, he will redescribe as a "collective treasure"). Starobinski stresses the need to link Breton's thinking of psychic automatism to a diversity of nineteenth-century psychologies. Whereas he proposes Myers as the principal theoretical source for Breton's notion of automatism, other critics disagree. In *Le Surréalisme* Jacqueline Chénieux-Gendron considers Starobinski's extrapolation excessive (78) and insists that "Breton est loin de renvoyer à l'ensemble de la théorie de Myers." Yet Starobinski's analysis is revealing. It is symptomatic of a more general effacement of the discourse of Bergson. What Breton would have retained from Myers, Starobinski suggests, was the positive value Myers attributed to unconscious processes, and specifically the notion of what he called a subliminal self. "On a reconnu," Starobinski acknowledges, "une distinction analogue à celle qu'établit Bergson à peu près au même moment, entre le moi social and le moi profond; et ce n'est pas un hasard si Bergson s'est laissé tenter, lui aussi, par les promesses de la parapsychologie" (165). What Starobinksi does not mention is that Bergson was a significant influence on Meyers (see "The Perpetual Crises of Modernism and the Traditions of Enlightenment Vitalism: With a Note on Mikhail Bakhtin" in *The Crisis in Modernism: Bergson and the Vitalist Controversy*). Indeed, beyond this one parenthetical remark, Starobinski says not another word about Bergson.

59. "The degree of spontaneity that individuals, taken separately, are capable of, alone decides concerning the fall [*chute*] or ascension [*ascension*] of the pans of the balance," Breton writes. The *plateau de balance* refers to the degree of dream or reality (or of representation or perception) at play in the mental operations. Here, as in Bergson's thinking, the relation between dream and reality (or between representation and perception) is an economic one, that is, a question of relative degrees of tension. It is a function of the kind of Baudelairean movement of dispersal and concentration that we saw at play in Valéry's conception of "le travail de l'esprit."

60. Romeo Arbour, *Henri Bergson et les lettres françaises*, pp. 375–76.

61. Breton, *Œuvres complètes*, p. xxxii.

62. Arbour, *Bergson*, p. 180 cites Tancrède de Visan (my translation).

63. Bonnet, *André Breton*, p. 131. Bonnet writes of Reverdy: "It is around this problem of lyricism and its corollary, the nature of poetic emotion, that [Reverdy's] discussions with Breton largely turned, according to the latter, as confirmed by some unpublished letters of Reverdy."

64. Breton, *Positions politiques du surréalisme*, pp. 167–68.

65. Sartre, *Qu'est-ce que la littérature?*, p. 189.

66. Bergson's recognition is a displacement of the Kantian schematism in the register of memory instead of cognition.

Chapter Six

1. "Tout résumé de mes vues les déformera, s'il ne place pas de prime abord et s'il ne revient pas sans cesse à ce que je considère comme le centre même de la doctrine: l'intuition de la durée . . . la representation d'une multiplicité de pénétration réciproque toute différente de la multiplicité numérique, la représentation d'une durée héterogène, qualitative, créatrice, est le point d'où je suis parti et où je suis constamment revenu. Elle demandera à l'esprit un très grand effort, la rupture de beaucoup de cadres," cited in Papadopoulo, *Un Philosophe entre deux défaites*, p. 120.

2. See the opening lines of *L'Erotisme*. Bergson's notion of duration invites us to think "succession without distinction, something like a mutual penetration, a solidarity, an intimate organization, of which each part is representative of the whole, does not distinguish itself from it, and is not isolated from it except for a mode of thought capable of abstraction," (HB 68).

3. Bergson, *Matter and Memory*, trans. Nancy Margaret Paul and W. Scott Palmer, p. 81.

4. Action involves a change to be fulfilled in time, that is, in future time: "We have no grasp on the future without an equal and corresponding perspective on the past" (HB 213). Perception activates memory, which helps determine the choice of action to pursue in a given situation: "because the memory of analogous previous intuitions is more useful than intuition itself, being bound within our memory to the whole series of subsequent events and, therefore, being better able to clarify our decision, they displace real intuition, whose role becomes nothing more than to . . . appeal to memory, to embody it, to render it active, and to this extent actual . . . perception ends up being nothing more than an occasion for memory . . . these two acts, therefore, perception and memory, always interpenetrate" (HB 213–14).

5. Recognition articulates memory and perception, or past and present. But it has nothing to do with an actual linkage between past and present in the sense of repetition. It is rather a question of what Bergson calls "recognition in the instantaneous" (HB 238). This consists not of representation but of action. But there is also what Bergson calls an "attentive recognition" (HB 244). Here recognition becomes reflection. Memory "creates . . . again the present perception, or rather it doubles this perception by referring it either to its own image, or to some memory image of the same kind." Reflection works on a principle of analogy. It involves "the exterior projection of an actively created image, identicial or similar to the object and which moulds itself on its contours" (HB 248).

6. As I have mentioned earlier, "dream" does not necessarily mean "sleep" for Bergson. It refers to a plane of mental activity that occurs at a certain distance from action. When action is suspended by sleep, we can be attentive to dream ac-

tivity (dream images). When action demands our attention, dream activity is veiled by consciousness, which is directed to action and is in this sense intentional. For Bergson, then, dream activity continues during waking hours. We are simply not conscious of it; it occurs in a mode of "unconsciousness [*inconscience*]." "What needs to be explained," Bergson writes in *Matière et mémoire*, "is no longer the cohesion of inner states, but the double movement of contraction and expansion by means of which consciousness tightens or enlarges the development of its contents . . . it is also easy to see why the 'associations' that we seem to form all through this movement exhaust [*épuisent*] all the successive degrees of contiguity and resemblance" (HB 305).

7. Bergson writes: "This influence of language on sensation is more profound than one might think. . . . Not only does language make us believe in the invariability of our sensations, but it will sometimes trick us concerning the nature of the sensation experienced. . . . In short, the word with its sharp outlines, the blunt word [*le mot brutal*], that stores up what there is that is stable, common, and consequently impersonal in the impressions of humanity, crushes or at least covers over the delicate and fugitive impressions of our individual consciousness. . . . This crushing of immediate consciousness is nowhere more striking than in phenomena of feeling [*sentiment*], a violent love, a deep melancholy invading our soul: these involve a thousand deep elements that melt together [*se fondent*], that penetrate one another . . . their originality is at this price. . . . Earlier each one borrowed an indefinable coloration from its milieu: here it is colorless [*décoloré*], and ready to receive a name" (HB 87–88, *Essai*).

8. This might be the basis for a notion of action implied in the theoretical term "textual productivity."

9. Examples of this point are numerous. Here are a few: "The awakening of consciousness in a living being . . . is all the more complete when s/he has a greater lattitude of choice and a larger quantitity of action has been accorded to him or her . . . the brain and consciousness correspond with one another because they both measure . . . the quantity of choice available to the living being" (HB 718, *L'Evolution créatrice*); "the role of intelligence is to preside over actions" (HB 747).

10. Sartre, *L'Existentialisme est un humanisme*, p. 57. Other Sartrean formulas echo Bergson: "Man is nothing but his project . . . he is nothing but the totality of his acts, nothing other than his life" (55); The fundamental notion of existentialism, we read here, is that "it is necessary to start from subjectivity" (17), that is, *le vécu* (69). The first principle of existentialism, for Sartre, is that "Man is nothing other than what he does," for "there is no determinism, man is free, man is freedom" (36–37). Existentialism "defines man by action" (62).

11. The idea of generality necessary to the operations of language, Bergson writes, "was, originally, only our consciousness of an identity in a diversity of situations; it was habit itself, moving back up from the sphere of movements towards that of thought. But from genres thus mechanically sketched out by habit, we have passed from an achieved effort of reflection on this very operation to the general idea of genre; and once this idea is constituted, we have built, this time voluntarily, a limited number of general ideas" (HB 301).

12. In *Matière et mémoire*, Bergson returns to the figure of the inverted cone already mentioned in order to characterize mental operations. Here it is a question of a cone whose point he names "S" and identifies with "the actual perception of my body," and the base which he lables AB where "my dreams in their totality . . . will be laid out [*seront disposés*]." "In the cone determined in this manner, the general idea will continually oscillate between the summit S and the base AB. In S it will take on the well-defined form of a bodily attitude"—i.e., a physical action—"*or of a pronounced word*" (HB 301, my emphasis). Speech is a strict equivalent to action here, as it will be in Sartre.

13. In a thorough book-length study of Valéry it would be necessary to consider relations between Valéry and the philosopher Alain, commentator on *Charmes*. But the discourse of Bergson informs Valéry's puzzling discussion of effort (crucial feature of Valéry's modernism) and problematizes our usual assumptions concerning his formalism; these are the questions which concern us here.

14. He continues here in *La Pensée et le mouvant*: "In general, action requires a solid basis, and the living being essentially tends to effective action. This is why we have considered a certain stabilization of things to be the primary function of consciousness. Installed within universal mobility, we said, consciousness contracts in an almost instantaneous vision an immensely long history which unfolds outside it." Along these lines, see HB 1329 concerning intuition and language. Bergson continues in even stronger terms: "The higher the consciousness, the greater the tension of its duration in relation to that of things. . . . Tension, concentration, these are the words by which we characterize a method that requires on the part of the mind, an entirely new effort for each new problem."

15. Valéry's critique of philosophy is sometimes taken as evidence that Valéry could not have been influenced by Bergson (an influence Valéry in any case denies). However, it is equally plausible that Valéry received his critique of language through Bergson, the "anti-philosopher," and that Valéry's critique of philosophy is parallel to Bergson's. For Bergson as anti-philosopher see Deleuze, *Dialogues* (with Claire Parnet) and *Bergsonism*.

16. For organizational reasons, the readings of *Monsieur Teste*, *La Nausée*, and *Nadja* are dispersed through various chapters of this book. However, they were intended to be considered together. Sartre and Breton, in their different ways, were fascinated by the depersonalization of Teste. All three texts can profitably be read in relation to the discourse of Bergson.

17. Critics who consider the question of the influence of Bergson on Surrealism are divided. Arbour says no. On the other hand critics closer to the period in question take this influence for granted. See for example Paulhan in *Les Fleurs de Tarbes* and Benda in *Tradition de l'existentialisme*. Benda writes that the influences of Bergson (as well as of Nietzsche) "are distinctly expressed by the surrealist poets." His *Belphégor, essai sur l'esthétique de la présente société française* is published before the emergence of surrealism per se (1918), but the analysis of the pervasiveness of Bergsonism in French culture in the years leading up to World War I would support the claims of an influence upon the surrealist milieu. We return to the question of the importance of Bergson to the symbolist milieu futher on in this chapter. Concerning the detachment of the artist, we read in Bergson:

"The creative writer becomes disinterested in effective action in order to replace himself . . . in the life of dream" (HB 95); "the detachment that is necessary in order for him to turn again towards the past, makes him descend into dream, dispersion, the scattering of the personality" (cited in Arbour, *Henri Bergson et les lettres françaises*, p. 95).

18. Again, "The word, made to go from one thing to another, is in fact essentially capable of being displaced and free" (HB 629, *L'Evolution créatrice*).

19. Cited in Arbour, *Henri Bergson et les lettres françaises*, p. 120. Since for Bergson there are three levels of the image—the image sensation, which pertains to the material object as it emerges thanks to the operations of recognition in perception, interior objects, or memory images spontaneously produced by the memory of imagination, and the me-image (*moi-image*) which pertains to the body. This formulation of the semiotic activity of the word does not close off, or limit, the operations of words; that is, it does not predetermine their field of activity— or their temporal horizon.

20. See Caillois, *Approches à l'imaginaire*. He refers to "impurity in art" in relation to the question of lyricism and defines this in terms of "the empirical imagination," glossed as "the capacity to utilize the concrete toward ends which are usually passionate." He associates this with fabulation, which he calls a lyrical function.

21. Deleuze, among others, insists on Bergson's refusal of negation (or contradiction) in his exclusively affirmative thinking. Deleuze reads Bergson in terms similar to those I used in my reading of Lautréamont-Ducasse in *The Impersonal Sublime*; this coincidence is perhaps pertinent to Breton and to what I am calling the affirmation of Surrealism.

22. This expression, translated literally, means "drive belt." Breton is obviously playing on something like a "current of transmission." For further discussion, see Chapter 5.

23. Tancrède de Visan, *L'Attitude du lyrisme contemporain*, p. 10. Subsequent references will be to this edition and will be given in the text within parentheses, marked *LC*.

24. Adorno, *Notes to Literature*, p. 99. Subsequent references will refer to this edition and will be given within parentheses in the text, marked A (translations altered at times). When the quote cannot be found in the English edition, I will use the French version of the work: *Notes sur la littérature*.

25. "The social function of the discourse of engagement has become somewhat confused," Adorno writes, " . . . conservative minds who require the work of art to speak are in alliance with their political adversaries against the hermetic work, which lacks finality" (*Notes sur la littérature*, 287, my translation).

26. Blanchot, "Le Règne Animal de l'esprit," p. 398 (my translation).

27. Ibid., pp. 400–402.

28. For an important discussion of Blanchot, concerning resonances between political and esthetic contexts, see Steven Ungar.

29. Concerning this broader debate see, for example, Octavio Paz, *The Intelligibility of Modern Art*.

30. I return to this point further on in this chapter.

31. Valéry, "Première leçon du cours de poétique," *Œuvres complètes*, p. 1349.

32. Even though Adorno goes a long way to problematizing Valéry's formalism, it nevertheless remains the case that Valéry is of special interest to Adorno precisely because Adorno continues to construe him as a formalist—perhaps at the limit of the possibility of formalism.

33. This identification of form and force was elaborated by Focillon, among others. See *The Life of Forms in Art*, trans. Charles Beecher Hogan and George Kubler.

34. This notion of action, it should be clear by now, is quite different from the conception of action Bataille had in mind when he declared poetry and action to be incompatible.

35. Bergson defines a "travail de l'esprit" in just these terms, i.e., as the work of passing from one level of mental operation to another, a passage that occurs as an increase or decrease of attention or inattention.

36. Caillois, *Approches à l'imaginaire*, p. 53–54. Subsequent references to this work will be given in parentheses in the text, marked *AI* (my translation).

37. If the importance of Bergson's thinking is difficult to demonstrate from today's vantage point, it was taken for granted by contemporaries. See Paulhan, *Les Fleurs de Tarbes*, and Benda, *Belphégor*.

Chapter Seven

1. Deleuze, *Dialogues*, with Claire Parnet, p. 22 (my translation).

2. "Avions-nous raison à dire . . . que cette métaphysique [L'Existentialisme] n'a rien de nouveau?. . . . toutefois il semble qu'elle y prétende, si l'on juge par le fait qu'elle en cite jamais Bergson," Julien Benda, *Tradition de l'existentialisme*, pp. 53–54.

3. Cited in Arbour, *Bergson et les lettres françaises*, p. 31.

4. François Roustang declares the lesson of psychoanalysis to be that "historical truth does not exist" ("Elle ne lâche plus," p. 63). At the same time he defines psychoanalysis as "the movement through which the subject regains his or her own story/history [*histoire*]" (p. 66). This occurs through a process of construction: "The analyst proposes to the analysand a fragment of his or her prehistory that the analyst hypothetically supposes or guesses" (p. 47). Whereas historical truth implies objectivity and the truth of a totalizing representation, the movement of psychoanalysis involves a collaborative effort of construction (together with rememoration and conviction) that recalls the reciprocity of invention and reinvention at play in Bergson's account of reading, subsequently taken up by Valéry and Sartre.

My gesture of contextualization is undertaken in the spirit of the psychoanalytic encounter and not historical truth. This study does not attempt to demonstrate influence. I have been interested in texts that make other texts readable and in the circumstances of their force and their effacement. To this extent, my approach is intertextual. But reading is construed by theorists of intertextuality as a performance of productivity of text, considered as an infinite chain of signifiers. The limits of intertextuality as method are a function of this infinite reach of the signifying chain. As usually practiced, it does not respect circumstances beyond the text.

When denial is a function of collective pressures that are ideological, intertextuality alone is not adequate to deal with the problem. It can respond to denial of meaning or influence but only in terms of structures of individual desire (Kristeva) or of individual crises of anxiety of influence (Bloom) and their associated systems of rhetorical displacement. To detect the intertextual relation in cases of ideological erasure, one must be familiar with the codes at play. To diagnose erasure one must take into account extralinguistic factors bearing upon various publics and their reception of texts. As Hans Robert Jauss has written, the public is not simply "a passive element" (*Pour une esthétique de la réception*). Writing in the 1970's, Jauss relied upon the traditional categories of author and public. The shift from work to text, however, does not significantly alter the issues at stake here. For from *texte, écriture,* or *productivité* it is not easy to pass to phenomena of reception.

5. Grogin, *Bergsonian Controversy,* p. 185.

6. Benda, *Sur le succès du Bergsonisme,* p. 169 (my translation).

7. Alexandre Papadopoulo, *Un philosophe entre deux défaites,* p. 2 (my translation).

8. The citation is from the translators' introduction to Deleuze's *Bergsonism,* p. 7. The exception to this is Deleuze's study itself (1966) and the ways in which Deleuze has made use of Bergson in his analysis of film. In terms of the figures we have been studying here, neither Sartre (with the exception of *L'Imaginaire*), Breton, Valéry, nor Bataille mentions Bergson by name, even when they engage with his discourse. Benjamin does, in his essay on Baudelaire, but in a kind of formulaic way. Adorno mentions in passing that "the common denominator between Proust and Valéry is none other than Bergson" (*Notes to Literature,* p. 144) but he says no more. More interestingly, he affirms that "Valéry the theorist established a bridge [*passarelle*] between the two opposed extremes, Descartes and Bergson" (p. 140). But he does not elaborate. He does state that Valéry critiques immediacy (p. 141), as if to distance Valéry from Bergson. Yet the immediacy of Bergson is completely different from the one Adorno attributes to the position of Sartre. Adorno also mentions that Benjamin's esthetics owes more to Valéry than to anyone else. If one puts two and two together, a configuration emerges that relates Bergson, Valéry, and Benjamin. This would be interesting to explore, although it is not explicitly mentioned by Adorno and only emerges when one reads between the lines. To take another example of a dismissive mention of Bergson, Starobinksi, in his article on Breton affirming the influence of Myers, names Bergson parenthetically but does not discuss him at all. In another register, if one consults surveys of twentieth-century studies intended to prepare French students of letters at the level of *premier cycle,* again one finds no mention of Bergson. Finally, in still another context, a recent exposition at the Grand Palais in Paris, *L'Ame et le corps,* which examined relations between science and art since the eighteenth century and emphasized the importance of currents of vitalism for artistic developments in the symbolist and avant-garde milieux at the beginning of the century, made no mention of Bergson (although Diderot appears in the section of the exhibit devoted to the eighteenth century). At the very least we might say that serious dis-

cussion of Bergson is disproportionate to the impact of his thinking in the early decades of the century.

9. This is the phrase of Jacques Monod, cited in Tzavara, "Bergson and the Neuropsychiatric Tradition," p. 189. This volume attempts to correct the view expressed by Monod, but is exceptional in this respect.

10. Grogin, *Bergsonian Controversy*, p. 126.

11. These were a result of the Ribot Commission, established in 1899. See ibid., chap. 5.

12. Ibid., p. 118. The substance of Péguy's attack was repeated in 1911 in another pamphlet, "L'Esprit de la Nouvelle Sorbonne. La crise de la culture classique. La crise du français," which was written by two other Bergson followers, Henri Massi and Alfred de Tarde, and signed anonymously, Agathon. Alluding to Pascal, Agathon describes a struggle between a "spirit of geometry" represented by the Sorbonne and a "spirit of subtlety [*esprit de finesse*]"—"the true spirit of French culture"—represented by Bergson, who was by this time lecturing at the Collège de France.

13. Cited in Grogin, *Bergsonian Controversy*, p. 131.

14. Philip Soulez cites Bergson: "A man of action is someone who, at a given moment, knows more quickly how to silence the faculty of reason, closes his eyes to the difficulties that prolonged reflection would inevitably present and throws himself into action" (my translation). He comments: "It is on the basis of this kind of conception of the man of action that we can understand the paradoxical reversals of the Sorelians," *Bergson Politique*, p. 336 (my translation).

15. Antliff writes: "Sorel's theory of social myths was premised on what he termed a revision of Marx from a Bergsonian perspective." See *Inventing Bergson*, p. 157.

16. Although Jacques Maritain had been converted to Catholicism from a secular rationalism thanks to the influence of Bergson's critique of mechanism, he subsequently becomes a Thomist and rejects Bergson's critique of intellect. He considers Bergsonian intuitionism and rationalist scientism to represent two extreme versions of the same mistake, a misunderstanding of the nature of reason; and he believed that true understanding involved a synthesis between intellect and intuition. When Bergson's writings were put on the Index, however, it was due to the association of Bergsonism and Catholic modernism, which, in doctrinal divergence from Thomism, was considered a serious threat to the institution of the Church. See Grogin.

17. Georges Politzer, *La Fin d'une parade philosophique* (published under the pseudonym François Arouet in 1929), p. 99 (my translation).

18. Politzer, *Le Bergsonisme*, p. 110.

19. The quote continues to say that the new edition of this text is meant to be of service to those "who no longer want to be duped by an anti-intellectualism whose reigning ideology (during the last five years) . . . has taught us to understand its real intentions deliberately turned toward the past, if not toward fascism, which confuses lyricism and delirium, life and the orgy."

20. Benda, *Sur le succès du bergsonisme*, p. 218 (my translation). Benda ex-

tends the compliment to existentialism, another popular philosophy, and to Nietz-scheanism (*Tradition de l'existentialisme*, p. 25).

21. Pierre Lasserre, *Le Romantisme français*, p. 309. Subsequent references to this work will be given in the text within parentheses, marked L, and will refer to this edition (translations mine).

22. Benda, *Sur le succès du bergsonisme*, p. 140 (my translations). T. E. Hulme also called Bergsonism "the last disguise of romanticism," see Grogin, *Bergsonian Controversy*, p. 185.

23. For an interesting account of the influence of ideologies of nationalism on French cultural developments in the visual arts during the First World War and in the aftermath of the war, see Kenneth E. Silver, *Esprit de Corps*. For a discussion of Bergsonism and its ideological appropriations as these affected the art world, see Mark Antliff, *Inventing Bergson*.

24. Benda, *Tradition de l'existentialisme*, p. 23.

25. On the influence of far-right ideology upon cultural life in France during and after the First World War, see Kenneth Silver, *Esprit de Corps*.

26. Concerning the role of Bergson in the war effort, see the excellent study of Philippe Soulez, *Bergson Politique*.

27. Soulez reminds us that "there are ideological Bergsonisms, there is no Bergsonian politics," in *Bergson Politique*, p. 242 (my translation). Politzer and Benda, he comments, were "destinataires intrus [intruding interlocutors]" for Bergson, p. 244.

28. Adorno, *Notes to Literature*, p. 140.

29. In his notebooks Leonardo mentions an exercise he gave to his students. He asked them to stare at a blank wall, in order to stimulate their powers of imagination. Students were then asked to draw what they "saw," a seeing that was prompted by an inner vision. Valéry mentions this exercise in his essay. Max Ernst calls it the "lesson of Leonardo" and discusses it in *Beyond Painting*.

30. This interpretation of Baudelaire neglects the complexity of Baudelaire's amalgamation of romantic (or transgressive) themes with an appeal to formal economy. It also neglects the decidedly romantic Baudelaire we find, for example, in the essays on Delacroix and Wagner.

31. The opening pages of *Qu'est-ce que la littérature?*, which disparage poetry in favor of the signifying force of prose as action, are directed not so much against Valéry and his version of pure poetry as against the transvaluation of literature into "poetry" performed by Breton and his associates since the early days of the review *Littérature*. The opacity of poetry disparaged by Sartre in the first chapter of his essay ("What is called writing?") coincides precisely with the discovery of the liberation of language from its subordinate utilitarian function set forth in Breton's essay "Les Mots sans rides," subsequently published in *Les Pas perdus*. If the specific target of the criticism of poetry has been lost on subsequent readers, it is in part because of Sartre's attack on Breton and surrealism that engagement itself has been misread. To the extent that it was considered a rejection of the formal innovation in literature championed by the surrealist avant-gardism, it has been identified with the position of literary realism. From here it is but a short step

to considering engagement to mark the subordination of literature to social or political agendas—the subjection of art to politics. This view, which I have attempted to problematize in my reading of Sartre in Chapter 3, has contributed to a depreciation of Sartre during the last few decades, decades marked by a fascination with the possibilities of avant-gardism in all its forms. At the same time, however, Sartre's critique of Breton contributed to the depreciation of Breton, and hence facilitated the effacement of all filiation on the part of the *Tel Quel* generation to the preceding two generations, enabling the *Tel Quel* group to pose itself as a pure origin, one that would inscribe itself in history only rhetorically and in relation to figures at the safe distance of the previous century.

32. *Tel Quel* repeats the charge Sartre makes concerning a conservative or reformist surrealism in the 1930's and 1940's. See also Denis Hollier (*Le Collège de Sociologie*) on this point. However, this shift has served as pretext for minimizing the impact of the early years of surrealism and for neglecting further exploration of what I am calling the surrealist affirmation.

33. An example of the modernist rejection of surrealism would be Romeo Arbour's *Henri Bergson et les lettres françaises*, which denies any influence of Bergson upon the surrealists, who are portrayed as too marginal and too radical to be worthy of mention along with the eminent French philosopher. The argument to the effect that the real avant-garde was Dada, which made all the important formal innovations long before surrealism, is a familiar one. For a formal reading of automatic writing see Laurent Jenny, "Le Surréalisme et les signes narratifs." Concerning *Tel Quel* see the numerous articles in the 1960's devoted to a critique of surrealism, including the article by Houdebine. For what I am calling a "retrospective reading" of surrealism (readings that inject contemporary theory retroactively), see Jacqueline Chénieux-Gendron's *Le Surréalisme*. The author analyzes automatism as a "coulée" of signifiers and approves the view of Robert Brechon (*Le Surréalisme*), whom she cites to the effect that the surrealist "magic dictation" involves a language from the unconscious, which is itself structured like a language. The implication is that the unconscious is a text and automatism provides us with the tracing of this text (p. 72). Chénieux-Gendron also privileges the linguistic over the visual in her analysis of Breton's theoretical writings (reading Breton's reference to "perceptions" in "Le Message automatique" as "signifiers") and treating the question of the visual arts separately from the broader discussion of surrealism and the thinking of automatism. Lastly, Chénieux-Gendron exemplifies the attitude to Breton that, after reading him retrospectively in terms of theory, finds him theoretically naive. She writes of his "dated psychology" and his "theoretical laxity." Thus she finds Lacanian theory to be the truth of automatism but relegates Breton to the role of inept precursor of the radical beginning of theory.

34. With respect to the visual arts and the exclusion of surrealist art from the modernist canon (with the exception of certain figures who worked along the margins of surrealist and modernist tendencies—figures such as Masson, Miro, and Arp) see Clement Greenberg, "The Notion of the Postmodern" in *Zeitgeist in Babel*, ed. Ingeborg Hoesterey. I will return to this question.

35. I am using the term "modernist" in Greenberg's sense here.

36. Clement Greenberg, "The Notion of 'Postmodern'" in *Zeitgeist in Babel*,

ed. Hoesterey, pp. 46–47. He adds that "the making of superior art is arduous, usually. But under Modernism the appreciation, even more than the making, of it has become more taxing, the satisfaction and exhilaration to be gotten from the best new art more hardwon." He then laments what he calls "the urge to relax" which "threatens and keeps on threatening standards of quality" and adds that "the postmodern business is one more expression of that urge." For an interesting discussion of Greenberg see *Modernism in Dispute*, Wood et al.

37. Habermas, *The Philosophical Discourse of Modernity*, pp. 100–101.

38. On this point see Albrecht Wellmer, *The Persistence of Modernity*, p. 10. For Adorno, Wellmer writes, both art and philosophy have an "antithetical relationship to the world of the instrumental spirit; that is the origin of their inherent negativity" (p. 5). He cites Adorno to the effect that "art is true to the extent to which it is discordant and antagonistic in its language and in its whole essence. . . . Its paradoxical task is to attest to the lack of concord while at the same time working to abolish discordance" (p. 9).

39. He writes that self-consciousness is "the truly central insight of modernity." See "What Is Modern?" in *Paul de Man: Critical Writings 1953–78*, ed. Waters, p. 143.

40. In his introduction to *Paul de Man: Critical Writings*, Waters cites a passage from de Man's dissertation on Mallarmé that sounds much like Adorno: "The poet knows that he cannot live within the plenitude of a natural unity of being; he also knows that his language is powerless to recapture this unity, since it is the main cause of the separation. But he surmounts despair at this discovery by objectifying his negative knowledge, and making it into a form which has this knowledge for its content. In so doing the poet hopes to safeguard the future possibility of his work by substituting the contemplation of his failure to a useless quest for unity," quoted in "Paul de Man his life and works," p. il, Introduction to *Paul de Man: Critical Writings*.

41. De Man elaborates this, for the most part, in relation to English romanticism. This view influenced my *Impersonal Sublime*, which attempted to make a similar gesture in relation to French romanticism.

42. For de Man, this symbolist mentality is exemplified by the traditional reading of Baudelaire's "Correspondances" as the blueprint for a symbolist esthetic. To this de Man opposes his own reading of the poem, as well as of what he considers to be its counterpart poem, "Obsession." See *Rhetoric of Romanticism*.

43. In his early essay "What Is Modern?" de Man alludes to a "fallacious prewar illusion of modernism" and identifies this with the high modernist canon of Yeats, Joyce, Eliot, Lawrence, Proust, Valéry, Gide, Mann, Rilke, and Kafka (p. 138). He writes that modernism should be considered from a wider perspective, starting "not with the aestheticism of 1880 but earlier, with romanticism, and ending, not with Yeats-Valéry-Rilke or Proust-Joyce-Mann, but with writing that does not belong to the heritage of symbolism" (p. 39). He names Robbe-Grillet, Dubuffet, and—Sartre.

44. "Modern Poetics in France and Germany" (1965), p. 154 in *Critical Writings*. De Man writes: "It has been shown . . . that Bergson's conception is a close equivalent, in philosophical language, of the kind of imagery used by symbolist

writers, from Baudelaire to Proust." Here de Man does not lend support to the argument I have been making concerning symbolism and Bergson. He has in mind a particular reading of symbolism (and of Bergson) which does not coincide with the one I have presented.

45. See the *Essai sur les données immédiates de la conscience* and the discussion in Chapter 5 of the present work. For a corrective to the view suggested by de Man and Adorno see Deleuze, *Bergsonism*. Bergson begins to be identified with idealism thanks to the critique of Politzer, the dialectical materialist. Derrida has also criticized Bergson in the same terms in which he has criticized Heidegger, that is, for "still being metaphysical." Of course, he also acknowledges that there is no escape from metaphysics. For a discussion of this point see Joseph N. Riddel, "Modern Times: Stein, Bergson and the Ellipses of American Writing," in *The Crisis of Modernism: Bergson and the Vitalist Controversy*, ed. Burwick and Douglass.

46. Châtelet, *Politique de la philosophie*, p. 50.

47. There was also, increasingly, an interest in Freud in philosophical circles. Raymond Aron writes that the 1920's were the years of a return to Kant and the 1930's a return to Hegel. Bergson, he writes, "did not belong to the French posterity of the German philosophers. Bergson defined himself neither with respect to Kant nor to Hegel." *On Sartre. History and Dialectic of Violence*, p. xii. Anna Boschetti writes in *Sartre et "Les Temps Modernes"* that Bergsonism was superseded by the discourses of Hegel, Marx, and Freud, but that the current of spiritualism remained active beneath the discursive change. Critics disagree concerning the impact of Bergson in the twenties. Some claim that the decline of his influence occurred immediately after the First World War. Others affirm the growing influence of Bergsonism in the 1920's. It seems that Bergsonism was less influential among philosophers after the war, but continues to have a broad cultural influence through the twenties, as Benda's remark, cited earlier, suggests, and even in the thirties in the political field.

48. See J.-L. Loubet, *Les Nonconformistes des années trente*.

49. "The image of the classical 'homo rationalis' . . . which had already been violently shaken by the war," Loubet argues in *Les Nonconformistes*, was further challenged by the emergence of Freudianism. This work analyses "Reviews and political movements of the young during the years 1930–1940" and presents a synthetic view of what the author calls "the spirit of 1930." Benda is attacked as "symbol of idealism and of academic rationalism towards which young writers and philosophers of the thirties were extremely critical." Cited in Loubet, p. 238 (my translation). See also p. 262.

50. Loubet, *Les Nonconformistes*, p. 263–64.

51. Valéry, *Œuvres complètes*; see "Essais quasi politiques." These essays were published between 1897 and 1936. The best known are "La Crise de l'Esprit" (1919) and "La Politique de l'esprit" (1936).

52. According to Thierry Maulnier, cited in Loubet, *Les Nonconformistes*, p. 272. See this discussion of the confusion and ambivalence concerning the respective merits of communist, fascist, and national socialist revolutions.

53. Cited in Michel Surya, *Georges Bataille, La Mort à l'œuvre*, pp. 175–76 (my translation). Surya comments, "Obviously, Bataille again put himself in the

position of getting into dialogue with, and acting with, members of an organization with whom he neither shares an analysis, nor a set of goals. Simone Weil expresses more or less the same thing, in the Circle, that Breton had reproached him for earlier." (p. 176).

54. A contemporary reports that Dandieu, who was considered both extremely sharp and charismatic, "would have been our Bergson" but for a very early death. Cited in Loubet, *Les Nonconformistes*.

55. Loubet, ibid., pp. 351–52, cites Jean Lacroix, who reviewed *La Révolution Nécessaire* for the review *L'Esprit* (my translation).

56. Jean Piel reports that Bataille and Dandieu "saw each other regularly for several years." See note to p. 183 in Surya, *Georges Bataille, la mort à l'œuvre* (my translation). This note should be read carefully; its language is extremely slippery concerning this association between Bataille and Dandieu. Bataille, Surya writes, as if to dismiss the whole matter, "in any case never mentioned any of this." He denies that Bataille wrote the chapter of *La Révolution Nécessaire*, but affirms that he "supposedly furnished certain elements of the elaboration of the chapter 'Exchange and Credits.'"

57. Bataille, *OC* I, p. 428). In relation to Contre-Attaque, Bataille was engaged in a "decisive struggle whose sole possible aim is to take power" (*OC* I, p. 384, my translation).

58. Bataille, *OC* I, p. 423. He speaks of collective exaltation in "Front Populaire dans la rue" where he writes: "We must contribute to the sense of power of the popular masses; we are certain that force results less from strategy than from collective exultation, and exultation can only come from words that touch the passion of the masses, not reason" (p. 411, my translation). See also the inaugural manifesto of Contre-Attaque, p. 379–80, especially numbers five and thirteen. Bataille also writes: "As always in insurrection, an organic movement carries those it attracts to violence and organizes them with a rigorous discipline. . . . The program of an organic movement cannot be an abstract and schematic program. . . . It cannot be directly subordinated to rational concepts. It is necessarily tied to immediate needs . . . to the aspirations that actually animate the given masses of a particular place and time," (*OC* I, p. 423, my translation). Breton is said to have left Contre-Attaque because he (as well as many other of Bataille's associates) was made uneasy by what was considered Bataille's "surfascisme." See Fourny, *Georges Bataille*, p. 69. Besnier also discusses Bataille's mixture of the influence of Nietzsche with a certain vitalism. For Bataille, he writes, "engagement should be the effect of a passion" ("Georges Bataille," p. 32, my translation). Besnier emphasizes the importance of Nietzsche in the 1930's and writes that for Bataille "the tragic calls for a form of activism" which he associates with what Aron called "the lyricism of the uncontrollable." Marmande also notes the complicated relationship to Marxism exhibited in the context of Contre-Attaque which involves the "elaboration of a doctrine founded upon immediate experiences" (*Georges Bataille politique*, p. 54). I am not interested in judging Bataille's political investments here, but rather in demonstrating the importance of a certain vitalism in his thinking.

59. Soulez, *Bergson politique*, 340. See also Antliff's discussion of Sorel in *Inventing Bergson*. Antliff writes that "since Sorel wished to incite the emotional,

revolutionary spirit of the proletarian, he appealed to their intuitive sensibilities, by describing his myth of revolution as composed of a body of images capable of invoking instinctively . . . the sentiments" (p. 156). Antliff points out that in his *Réflexions sur la violence*, "Sorel based this definition on the very section from Bergson's *Introduction to Metaphysics* that served as the basis of Visan's idea of accumulated images . . . and Severini's conception of simultaneity" (p. 158). Meanwhile, Bergson could be said to be moving in the direction of Bataille. He publishes his last major book, *Les Deux sources de la morale*, in 1932. This takes up issues of spirituality and social relations, addressing questions of ethnology and sociology. The harsh critic of Durkheim from the 1890's now acknowledges the validity of certain aspects of the French School of Sociology, although he affirms that Durkheim's science of ethnology "sees only the more superficial aspect of the human mind and therefore fails to comprehend the more profound significance of religious inspiration" (Sanford Schwartz, "Bergson and the Politics of Vitalism," p. 300). As Philippe Soulez points out, Bergson's analyses of war in *Les Deux sources* anticipated the analyses of Bataille and Caillois concerning war as "celebration and irruption of the sacred into the monotony of daily life" (Soulez, p. 269, my translation). Soulez also points out that Bergson included an analysis of totemism in *Les Deux sources* that was subsequently acknowledged by Lévi-Strauss in his *Le Totémisme aujourd'hui* (Paris: PUF, 1962). Soulez writes that in this book, Lévi-Strauss "acknowledges that Bergson put his finger on the essential point of totemism." On this subject see also Guy La France, *La Philosophie sociale de Bergson: sources et interprétations* (Ottawa, Canada: Ed. de l'Université d'Ottowa, 1974). Bergson ends his study on a note of warning concerning the survival of the human race. In anticipation, again, of Bataille's *La Part maudite*, "the question of the survival of humanity plays itself out on the level of energetics," writes Soulez (p. 284, my translation). Bergson proposes, he continues, that "the drama of humanity derives from the fact that the rationality of technicians [*la rationalité technicienne*] organizes its investments around things that are not the true reasons of desire. . . . Henceforth this rationality can very easily be moved, without knowing it, by the war instinct and lead all of humanity to a catastrophic end" (p. 291). Soulez comments: "the frenetic reversal of terms . . . gives a law that more or less resembles the 'paroxystic' evolution of Bataille" (n. 112, p. 294, my translation).

60. Fourny describes "La Notion de dépense" in these terms (p. 67). He explains that Bataille wants to correct Marx "by placing the study of social superstructures . . . at the basis of all revolutionary action" (citing André Thirion, p. 68, my translation). He then describes the sacred sociology of the Collège as existing "in the name of Durkheim and Mauss" (p. 77).

61. In this essay on the moral sense of sociology, Bataille explicitly appeals to Monnerot's use of the opposition sacred/profane, which he links to an opposition between the homogeneous and the heterogeneous that had been introduced earlier by Bergson. Here he identifies the sacred as one form of heterogeneous experience. The association with Bergsonian duration comes through more clearly in the following remark: the heterogeneous, Bataille writes in this essay, "is not, like the sacred, principally determined from the outside," as in ethnology, "but in a

general way from within and from without when it is a question of reactions we ourselves live," (p. 42, my translation). This suggests a relation to the *vécu* of real duration, and also that the sacred is a modality of this inner experience, one that is precipitated or determined by an external event.

62. Denis Hollier, *Le Collège de Sociologie*, p. xxiv.

63. Ibid., p. 48. Leiris, Caillois, and Monnerot took courses with Mauss and their relation to Durkheim was probably mediated by his influence; Mauss's work at times threatened the exclusively rationalist emphasis of his uncle, Durkheim. Lévi-Strauss's *Introduction to a Reading of Marcel Mauss* reveals these moments even as it attempts, for its own reasons, to bring Mauss back into the rationalist mainstream. See Raymond Aron, *La Sociologie allemande contemporaine*, p. 7, and in particular his discussion of the role of the "hau" in Mauss's theory of the gift.

64. Aron, *La Sociologie allemande contemporaine*, p. 3. Heimonet, in his article "Le Collège de Sociologie—un gigantesque malentendu" (p. 42), makes the point that Bataille is interested not in Durkheim and Marx, but in a new German sociology that "values direct recourse to lived experience." This points to Georges Simmel, a precursor of the sociology of religion who participated in movements of the vitalism of the left. Whereas Durkheim maintained that social facts are things, Monnerot published a book in 1946 entitled *Les Faits sociaux ne sont pas les choses* (Gallimard). Bataille's fascination with Nietzsche during this period is further evidence that he would be at odds with Durkheim's sociology. "We must call Nietzsche to the rescue," Bataille wrote, continuing: "Nietzsche against the state, whether it be Hitlerian or Stalinist. Nietzsche for man against the masses, whether they be fascist, American or Soviet. Nietzsche against rationalism, whether it be from Rome, from Moscow, or from the Sorbonne" (cited in Besnier, p. 89, my translation). The allusion to the Sorbonne, of course, refers to the Sorbonne dispute, discussed earlier, which pitted Durkheim (representing the Sorbonne) against Bergson. Concerning Simmel, see also Raymond Aron, *La Sociologie contemporaine allemande*, p. 7. The German sociologist had been a follower of Bergson and had lectured on the French philosopher in Germany in the 1890's. Durkheim translated Simmel, who, according to Aron, was well known in France. Atoji writes that Simmel's philosophy of life (in the mode of Dilthey and Bergson) "lies at the root" of his sociology (p. 25).

65. Hollier makes this point in the *Collège de Sociologie*, p. 48. R. Caillois and Jules Monnerot both also collaborate with the review *Acéphale*, which has a distinctly Nietzschean orientation, hardly compatible with the rationalism of Durkheim. For Bataille, *Acéphale* and the Collège were related enterprises.

66. Caillois, *Approches à l'imaginaire*, p. 71 (my translation).

67. Hollier, *Le Collège de Sociologie*, p. viii. Hollier continues: "This transformation of surrealists into artists is itself only the consequence of a more fundamental betrayal: their automatic adherence to organizational models borrowed from the political avant-garde . . . It is because they began by interiorizing the model of the Leninist groupuscule that when Stalinism at the end of the 30's made this legacy unbearable, they had no position to fall back on other than the art mar-

ket" (p. ix). In *Qu'est-ce que la littérature?* Sartre also attacks the conservatism of surrealism in this period, referring to a "surrealism free from scandal." *Tel Quel* will criticize surrealism in the same terms.

68. This is the period of Caillois's *Le Procès intellectuel de l'art.* Hollier writes that a rejection of literature was "the common denominator of the three texts 'For a College of Sociology,'" (*Le Collège de Sociologie,* xxiv).

69. Cited in Marmande, *Georges Bataille politique,* p. 140, 113, respectively (my translation).

70. We could say that along with Breton, Bataille was subjected to a modernist reading in the context of *Tel Quel.* The results, however, were quite different because Bataille, unlike Breton, was profoundly involved with the philosophy of Hegel (and Kojève).

Conclusion

1. "The Surrealists have given Valéry a bad name," Adorno writes in *Notes to Literature,* p. 139.

2. Fredric Jameson, *Postmodernism or the Logic of Late Capitalism* (Durham: Duke University Press, 1992), p. 303.

3. We can also read an allusion to a vulgar conception of engagement in which literature is subordinated to a political idea.

4. Kristeva was regularly invited to Cornell and Columbia during this period, probably two of the least naive of American universities at the time.

5. I am thinking of figures such as Piaget or Lévi-Strauss.

6. Miriam Glucksman, *Structural Analysis in Contemporary Social Thought.*

7. Michel Foucault, "Distance, aspect, origine," in *Théorie d'ensemble,* p. 21 (my translation).

8. This double register is repeatedly exploited by Lacan, who both attempts to found psychoanalysis as a science, as François Roustang has brilliantly analyzed in his *Lacan,* and also ironizes this gesture with a nod to the corrected meaning of science as it was at play in the context of Althusser's critique of ideology.

9. Sollers, in *Théorie d'ensemble* (my translation).

10. Blanchot, *Livre à venir,* pp. 282–83.

11. Rosalind Krauss, *The Origin of the Avant-Garde and Other Myths,* p. 6.

12. Linda Hutcheons in *A Postmodern Reader,* ed. Natoli and Hutcheons, p. vii.

13. When Derrida agrees to deny the death of deconstruction in a cover article for the *New York Times Magazine,* the situation has become serious.

14. While revising this chapter I came across "Mapping the Postmodern" by Andreas Huyssens, who agrees on this point: "Actually both in France and in the U.S. post-structuralism is much closer to modernism than is usually assumed by the advocates of post-modernism." He writes, " . . . I will argue that post-structuralism is primarily a discourse of and about modernism" (135)—"post-structuralism can be perceived, to a significant degree, as a theory of modernism" (136). In *A Postmodern Reader* I recommend this essay.

15. We have seen in our analysis of Kristeva that she wrestles with this prob-

lem in *La Révolution du langage poétique*. Her solution, to "revolutionize" différance through an appeal to meaning, is problematic, as we have tried to show,
and depends upon the ambivalence of Bataille's term, "transgression."

16. An interesting intersection between these two fields occurs in the essay by
Jean-François Lyotard, "Presenting the Unpresentable: The Sublime," *Artforum*,
April 1982. Eclectic postmodernism, he writes, "strips artists of their responsibility to the question of the nondemonstrable. That question is to me, the only one
worthy of life's high stakes. . . . Any denial of this question is a menace." p. 69.
He defends the avant-garde tradition that (in the tradition of negative dialectic)
"can only convey itself through the dialectic of refutation and questioning" (p. 68).
He opposes to this avant-garde activity "certain realisms . . . that have tried to offer the public accessible works of art which will allow it to identify with specific
ideas (race, socialism, nation, etc*). We know these attempts always call for the elim-
ination of the avant-garde*" (p. 67, my emphasis). This article, which dates from a
specific moment in Paris–New York exchange, is a symptom of the configuration I
am discussing here. In 1982 Lyotard essentially defended the avant-garde tradition
against the position of engagement (and an emerging multiculturalism). Ironically,
however, Sartre has defined engagement in precisely the same terms Lyotard up-
holds—"the engagement of the writer aims to communicate the incommunicable
and to maintain the tension between the whole and the part, the totality and the
totalization, the world and being in the world as the means of his work."

17. "Signifiance nous fait saisir la production du sens comme, par définition,
hétérogène à tout représentable," Ducrot and Todorov write, announcing the
"Copernican revolution" of the new thinking of text and *sémanalyse*: See Guerlac, "The Sublime in Theory," pp. 895–909. It is precisely in the name of the sublime and its refusal of representation that Lyotard defended modern avant-garde
and in this case minimal painting against the incursions of a postmodern figuration, historicism, and a different irony in his article in *Artforum*. This intervention suggests that the boundary line affirmed by Michael Fried in his early essay
"Art and Objecthood" was merely temporary, and that, in painting at least, min-
imalism in a sense radicalizes the purification of meaning that is intrinsic to the
modern.

18. See Breton, "Max Ernst," in *Les Pas perdus*, and Chapter Five of this study.
My discussion of modernism in the visual arts has been schematic to the extent
that I have taken Clement Greenberg as point of reference. Although I think that
many contemporary critics remain within the set of issues Greenberg set up, however much they displace and rephrase them, the reader should consult more nuanced views of esthetic modernism which take issue with Greenberg's positions.
See Yve-Alain Bois, *Painting as Model* and Rosalind Krauss, *The Originality of
the Avant-Garde and Other Modernist Myths* and *The Optical Unconscious*.

19. Tancrède de Visan, *Attitude du lyrisme contemporain*, p. 10 (my translation). For an interesting discussion of de Visan see Antliff, *Inventing Bergson*, chap.
1. I am aware that the thrust of my argument goes completely against the argument Antliff has put forth concerning the importance of Bergsonism for the early
development of Cubism. Given the range of Bergsonisms, however, our interpre-
tations are not necessarily mutually exclusive. An early cubism might have been

influenced by certain Bergsonisms in significant ways while the trajectory of the modernist tradition, which anchored itself in the cubist experiment, moved in another direction. In any case the divergence of our lines of argument supports my main point—the need to diversify modernisms.

20. De Visan, *Lyrisme contemporain*, p. 273 (my translation). Concerning Lasserre see Chapter 7 above. Concerning de Visan see Chapter 5 and Antliff, *Inventing Bergson*.

21. Benda, *Sur le succès du bergsonisme*, p. 199. This, of course, is the distinction emphasized in my reading of Valéry.

22. Deleuze, *Foucault*, p. 58 (my translations).

23. Even Baudrillard's notion of the simulacrum attaches very closely to a category of the real. The simulacrum involves a radical impoverishment (even the obliteration) of the real, but it is indiscernible from it. It does not help us think the kind of fiction we find, for example, in the collages of Ernst, or the paintings of Magritte, where it is a question of poetic fiction—fiction as invention.

24. Derrida, "La Déconstruction de l'actualité," p. 64 (my translation).

25. "One only knows, only understands, what one can reinvent," Bergson writes (HB 1327, my translation). I am thinking of a rereading of Bergson, beyond what I have attempted here, in light of poststructuralist critique. This would involve examining proximities between certain aspects of Bergson and of Heidegger. Rereading Bergson in the light of poststructuralism might enable us to retain one line of poststructuralist critique—the critique of phenomenology as suppression of the force of time (difference, multiplicity, heterogeneity)—without sacrificing the register of the visual and the play of (nontranscendental, or virtual) signifieds to a paradigm of writing or linguistic signifiers.

It would permit us to explore a certain lyricism without regressing to the naive notion of a unified subject. As an instance of heterogeneous intensities whose very being means being subject to time, the subject in Bergson is profoundly unstable. In his study of Foucault, Deleuze remarked that toward the end of his career, Foucault became interested in rethinking a notion of the subject in relation to time. "For a long time," he writes, "Foucault had considered the outside [*le dehors*] as an ultimate spatiality more profound than time; his last works suggest again the possibility of putting time outside [*de mettre le temps au dehors*] and of thinking the outside as time." See Deleuze, *Foucault*, p. 115. Deleuze concludes that "a certain vitalism culminates the thinking of Foucault" (p. 98). Although Deleuze does not explicitly mention Bergson by name, his analysis of Foucault insistently echoes his study of Bergson. Concerning visuality in the information age see William J. Mitchell, *The Reconfigured Eye*.

Bibliography

Adolphe, Lydie. *La Dialectique des images chez Bergson*. Paris: Presses Universitaires de France, 1951.

Adorno, Theodor. *Notes sur la littérature*, French trans. Sibylle Muller. Paris: Flammarion, 1984. English trans. Shierry Weber Nicholson as *Notes to Literature*, ed. Rolf Tiedemann. New York: Columbia University Press, 1991.

———. *Théorie esthétique*. Paris: Klincksieck, 1971.

Alexandrian, Sarane. *Surrealist Art*. Trans. Gordon Clough. London: Thames and Hudson, 1970.

Alquié, Fernand. *Philosophie du surréalisme*. Paris: Flammarion, 1977.

Althusser, Louis. *Positions*. Paris: Editions sociales, 1976.

Antliff, Mark. *Inventing Bergson: Cultural Politics and the Parisian Avant-Garde*. Princeton: Princeton University Press, 1993.

Apollinaire, Guillaume. *Les Peintres cubistes*. Paris: Berg International, 1986.

Arac, Jonathan, and Barbara Johnson, eds. *Consequences of Theory*. Baltimore: Johns Hopkins University Press, 1991.

Arbour, Romeo. *Bergson et les lettres françaises*. Paris: José Corti, 1955.

Aron, Raymond. *History and the Dialectic of Violence: An Analysis of Sartre's Critique de la raison dialectique*. Trans. Barry Cooper. New York: Harper Torchbooks, 1976.

———. *La Sociologie allemande contemporaine*. Paris: PUF, 1950.

Aronson, Ronald. *Jean-Paul Sartre: Philosophy in the World*. London: New Left Books, 1980.

———. *Sartre's Second Critique*. Chicago: University of Chicago Press, 1987.

Asari, Makoto. "Au delà de l'affirmation et de la négation; Les mythes en question: Bataille, Breton, Heidegger." *Pleine Marge* 8 (Dec. 1988): 717.

Assouline, Pierre. *L'Homme de l'art: D.-H. Kahnweiler 1884–1979*. Paris: Balland, 1988.

Atoji, Yoshio. *Sociology at the Turn of the Century: On G. Simmel in Comparison with F. Tönnies, M. Weber and E. Durkheim*. Tokyo: Dobunkan, 1981.

Audry, C. "Alain et le roman." *Revue de Métaphysique et de Morale* 57 (1952).

Balakian, Anna. *André Breton, Magus of Surrealism*. Oxford: Oxford University Press, 1971.

———. *Literary Origins of Surrealism: A New Mysticism in French Poetry*. New York: Kings Point Press, 1947.

———. *The Road to the Absolute*. New York: Dutton, 1970.

Barthes, Roland. *Essais critiques*. Paris: Seuil, 1981.

———. *Le Plaisir du texte*. Paris: Seuil, 1973.

Bataille, Georges. "Conférence sur le non-savoir." *Tel Quel* 10 (1962).

———. "De l'age de pierre à Jacques Prévert." *Critique* 3–4 (1946).

———. "De l'existentialisme au primat de l'économie." *Critique* 21 (1948).

———. "Le Dernier Instant." *Critique* 5 (1946).

———. *L'Erotisme*. Paris: Minuit, 1957.

———. "Expérience mystique et littérature." *Critique* 2 (1946).

———. "La Guerre et la philosophie du sacré." *Critique* 45 (1951).

———. "Letter to René Char." Repr. *YFS* 78 (1990).

———. *La Littérature et le mal*. Paris: Gallimard, 1957. Trans. Alastair Hamilton as *Literature and Evil*. London: M. Boyars, 1985.

———. *Œuvres complètes*, vol. 8. Paris: Gallimard, 1976.

———. *La Part maudite, précédé de la notion de dépense*. Paris: Minuit, 1967.

———. "Les Problèmes du surréalisme." *Change* 7 (1973).

———. "Le Surréalisme au jour le jour." *Change* 7 (1973).

———. "Le Surréalisme dans sa différence avec 'existentialisme.'" *Critique* 2 (1946).

Barthes, Roland, J.-P. Sartre, and Hyppolite. "Discussion sur le péché." In *Dieu Vivant*, 4 Cahier (Ed. du Seuil, 1915). Rprt. in *Œuvres complètes*, vol. 6.

Baudelaire, Charles. *Œuvres complètes*. Paris: Gallimard, 1961.

Beaujour, Michel. "A propos de l'écart dans la *Révolution du langage poétique* de Julia Kristeva." *Romanic Review* 3 (May 1975): 214–33.

———. "La Poétique de l'automatisme chez André Breton." *Poétique* 25 (1976).

———. "Qu'est-ce que *Nadja*?" *La Nouvelle Revue Française* 15, 172 (Apr. 1967): 780–99.

Béhar, Henri. *André Breton: le grand indésirable*. Paris: Calmann-Lévy, 1990.

Béhar, Henri, and Michel Carassou. *Dada, histoire d'une subversion*. Paris: Fayard, 1990.

Béhar, Henri, and Michel Carassou, eds. *Le Surréalisme, textes et débats*. Paris: Librairie Générale Française, 1981.

Benda, Julien. *Belphéghor, essai sur l'esthétique de la présente société française*. Paris: Emile Paul Frères, 1918.

———. *Sur le succès du Bergsonisme*. Paris: Mercure de France, 1936.

———. *La Tradition de l'existentialisme ou les philosophes de la vie*. Paris: Grasset, 1947.

———. *La Trahison des clercs*. Paris: Grasset, 1975; original ed. 1927.

Bergson, Henri. *L'Evolution créatrice*. Paris: Quadrige/PUF, 1941.

———. *Matière et mémoire*. Paris: Quadrige/PUF, 1939. Trans. Nancy Margaret Paul and W. Scott Palmer as *Matter and Memory*. London: George Allen, 1950.

———. *Œuvres complètes*. Paris: PUF, 1959. In the OC:

Les Deux sources de la morale et de la religion;
L'Energie spirituelle;

Essai sur les données immédiates de la conscience;
L'Evolution créatrice;
"Introduction à la métaphysique." In *La Pensée et la mouvant*;
Matière et mémoire;
La Pensée et le mouvant.

——. *The Two Sources of Morality and Religion*. Trans. R. Ashley Audra and Cloudesley Brereton, with the assistance of W. Horsfall Carter. New York: Henry Holt, 1935.

Besnier, Jean Michel. "Georges Bataille in the 1930's: A Politics of the Impossible." *YFS* 78. 1990.

——. *La Politique de l'impossible: l'intellectuel entre révolte et engagement*. Paris: La Découverte, 1988.

Blanchot, Maurice. *La Communauté inavouable*. Paris: Minuit, 1983.

——. "Le Jeu de la pensée." *Critique* 195–96 (1963).

——. *Le Livre à venir*. Paris: Gallimard, 1959.

——. *La Part du feu*. Paris: Gallimard, 1949.

——. *Le Pas au-delà*. Paris: Gallimard, 1973.

——. "Le Règne Animal de l'esprit." *Critique* 17 (1947).

——. "René Char." *Critique* 5 (1946).

Blood, Susan. *Baudelaire and the Esthetics of Bad Faith*. Stanford: Stanford University Press, forthcoming.

Bois, Yve-Alain. *Painting as Model*. Cambridge, Mass.: MIT Press, 1990.

Bonnet, Marguérite. *André Breton, naissance de l'aventure surréaliste*. Paris: José Corti, 1975.

Boschetti, Anna. *Sartre et "Les Temps Modernes," une entreprise intellectuelle*. Paris: Minuit, 1985.

Boyer, Philippe. "Grand Jeu." *Change* 7 (1963).

Brandt, Per Aage. "La Revue *Tel Quel*: une présentation" *Orbis Litterarum: International Review of Literary Studies* 27 (1972): 296–310.

Brechon, Robert. *Le Surréalisme*. Paris: Armand Collin, 1971.

——. "Le Jeu de la pensée." *Critique* 195–96 (1963).

Breton, André. *L'Amour fou*. Paris: Gallimard, 1937. Repr. 1970.

——. "Le Message automatique." In *Point du jour*. Paris: Gallimard, 1992.

——. *Œuvres complètes*. Paris: Gallimard, 1988.

——. *Point du jour*. Paris: Gallimard, 1992.

——. *Positions politiques du surréalisme*. Paris: Pauvert, 1971.

——. *Le Surréalisme et la peinture*. Paris: Gallimard, 1928. Repr. 1965.

——. *Les Vases communicants*. Paris: Gallimard, 1955.

Brochier, Jean-Jacques. *L'Aventure des surréalistes, 1914–1940*. Paris: Stock, 1977.

Bruno, Jean. "Les techniques de la dramatization chez Bataille." *Critique* 195–96 (1963).

Burwick, Frederick, and Paul Douglass, eds. *The Crisis of Modernism: Bergson and the Vitalist Controversy*. Cambridge, Eng.: Cambridge University Press, 1992.

Caillois, Roger. *Approches à l'imaginaire*. Paris: Gallimard, 1974.

——. "Divergences et Complicités." *NRF* (Apr. 1967).

———. *L'Homme et le sacré*. Paris: Gallimard, 1950.

———. *Le Procès intellectuel de l'art*. 1934.

Canguilhem, George. "Réflexions sur la création artistique chez Alain." *Revue de Métaphysique et de Morale* 57 (1952).

Caws, Mary Ann. *Surrealism and the Literary Imagination*. The Hague: Mouton, 1961.

Caws, Peter. *Sartre*. London: Routledge and Kegan Paul, 1984.

Celeyrette-Pietri, N., ed. *Problèmes du langage chez Valéry*. Paris: Les Lettres Modernes, 1987.

Châtelet, François. *La Politique de la philosophie*. Paris: Grasset, 1976.

Chénieux-Gendron, Jacqueline. "De la sauvagerie comme non savoir à la convulsion comme savoir absolu." *Pleine Marge* 13 (June 1991).

———. *Le Surréalisme*. Paris: PUF, 1984.

———, ed. *Lire le regard: André Breton et la peinture*. Lachenal et Rotter, 1993.

Chipp, Herschel B., "The Case of Breton." *MLN* 104, 4 (Sept. 1989): 819–44.

Chipp, Herschel B., ed. *Theories of Modern Art*. Berkeley: University of California Press, 1968.

Cohen, Margaret. *Profane Illumination: Walter Benjamin and the Paris of Surrealist Revolution*. Berkeley: University of California Press, 1993.

Cohen-Solal, Annie. *Sartre, A Life*. Trans. Anna Cancogni. New York: Pantheon, 1987.

Contat, Michel, and Michel Rybalka. *Les Ecrits de Sartre*. Paris: Gallimard, 1970.

de Beauvoir, Simone. *La Force des choses*. Paris: Gallimard, 1963.

de Man, Paul. "Against Theory." In *Critical Writings*, ed. Lindsay Waters. Minneapolis: University of Minnesota Press, 1989.

———. *The Rhetoric of Romanticism*. New York: Columbia University Press, 1984.

de Visan, Tancrède. *Attitude du Lyrisme Contemporain*. Paris: Mercure de France, 1911.

Deleuze, Gilles. *Bergsonism*. Trans. Hugh Tomlinson and Barbara Habberjam. New York: Zone Books, 1991.

———. *Foucault*. Paris: Minuit, 1986.

Deleuze, Gilles, with Claire Parnet. *Dialogues*. Paris: Flammarion, 1977.

Derrida, Jacques. *L'Autre cap*. Paris: Minuit, 1992.

———. "La déconstruction de l'actualité." *Passages* (Sept. 1993).

———. *L'Ecriture et la différence*. Paris: Seuil, 1967. Trans. Alan Bass as *Writing and Difference*. Chicago: Chicago University Press, 1978.

———. *Marges de la philosophie*. Paris: Minuit, 1972.

———. "Où commence et comment finit un corps enseignant." In Châtelet, *Politique de la philosophie*.

———. *Spectres de Marx*. Paris: Galilée, 1993.

———. *Speech and Phenomena and Other Essays on Husserl's Theory of Signs*. Evanston, Ill.: Northwestern University Press, 1972.

Descombes, Vincent. "L'Equivoque du symbolique." *Confrontation* 3 (1980).

———. *Le Même et l'autre*. Paris: Minuit, 1977. Trans. L. Scott-Fox and J. M.

Harding as *Modern French Philosophy*. Cambridge, Eng.: Cambridge University Press, 1980.

Ducasse, Isidore [Le, Comte de Lautréamont, pseud.]. *Œuvres complètes*. Paris: Garnier Flammarion, 1969.

———. *Poésies and Complete Miscellanea by Isidore Ducasse, Also known as Lautréamont*. Trans. Alexis Lykiard. London: Allison and Busby, 1978.

Ducrot, Oswald, and Tzvetan Todorov. *Dictionnaire encyclopédique des sciences du langage*. Paris: Seuil, 1972. Trans. as *Encyclopedic Dictionary of the Sciences of Language*. Baltimore: Johns Hopkins University Press, 1979.

Eigeldinger, Marc, ed. *André Breton, Essais et Témoignages*. Neuchâtel: à la Baconière, 1950.

Ernst, Max. *Beyond Painting*. Wittenburg: Schultz, 1948.

Flynn, Thomas R. "Another Sartrean Torso: Critique of Dialectical Reason." *Social Theory and Practice* 6, 1 (Spring 1980): 91–107.

———. "Mediated Reciprocity and the Genius of the Third in the Philosophy of Sartre." In *The Philosophy of Jean-Paul Sartre*, ed. Paul Arthur Schilpp. La Salle, Ill.: Open Court, 1981.

———. "The Role of the Image in Sartre's Esthetic." *Journal of Aesthetics and Art Criticism* 33, 4 (Summer 1975): 431–42.

Focillon, Henri. *La Vie de formes*. 7th ed. Paris: PUF, 1981. Trans. Charles Beecher-Hogan and George Kubler as *The Life of Forms in Art*. New York: Zone Books, 1992.

Forest, Philippe. *Histoire de "Tel Quel," 1960–1982*. Paris: Seuil, 1995.

Foucault, Michel. *L'Archéologie du savoir*. Paris: Gallimard, 1969. Trans. A. M. Sheridan Smith as *The Archeology of Knowledge*. New York: Pantheon, 1972.

———. "Distance, aspect, origine." In *Théorie d'ensemble*. Paris: Seuil, 1980.

———. "Préface à la Transgression." *Critique* 195–96 (1963).

Fourny, Jean-François. *Introduction à la lecture de Georges Bataille*. New York: Peter Lang, 1988.

Fried, Michael. "Art and Objecthood." In *Minimal Art: A Critical Anthology*, ed. Gregory Battcock. New York: Dutton, 1968.

Friedman, Susan Stanford. "Post-post-structuralist Feminist Critique." *NLH* 22, 2 (Spring 1991).

Freud, Sigmund. *Beyond the Pleasure Principle*. Trans. James Strachey. New York: Liveright, 1950.

Genette, Gérard. *Narrative Discourse: An Essay in Method*. Trans. Jane E. Lewin. Ithaca: Cornell University Press, 1980.

Gide, André. *La Littérature engagée*. Paris: Gallimard, 1950.

Glucksman, Miriam. *Structuralist Analysis in Contemporary Social Thought: A Comparison of the Theories of Claude Lévi-Strauss and Louis Althusser*. London: Routledge and Kegan Paul, 1974.

Goux, Jean-Joseph. "General Economics and Postmodern Capitalism." *YFS* 78 (1990).

Greenberg, Clement. *The Collected Essays and Criticism*. Ed. John O'Brien. Chicago: University of Chicago Press, 1986.

Grogin, R. C. *The Bergsonian Controversy in France.* Alberta: University of Calgary Press, 1988.

Guerlac, Suzanne. *The Impersonal Sublime: Hugo, Baudelaire, Lautréamont, and the Esthetics of the Sublime.* Stanford: Stanford University Press, 1990.

———. "Recognition by a Woman!" *YFS* 78 (1990).

———. "Sartre and the Powers of Literature: The Myth of Prose and the Practice of Reading." *MLN* 108 (1993): 805–24.

———. "The Sublime in Theory." *MLN* 106 (1991).

———. "Transgression in Theory: Genius and the Subject of *La Révolution du langage poétique.*" In *Ethics, Politics, and Difference in Julia Kristeva's Writing,* ed. Kelly Oliver. New York: Routledge, 1993.

Habermas, Jürgen. *The Philosophical Discourse of Modernity: Twelve Lectures.* Trans. Frederick G. Lawrence. Cambridge, Mass.: MIT Press, 1992.

Heidegger, Martin. "De 'la ligne.'" In *Questions I.* Paris: Gallimard, n.d.

———. "The Origin of the Work of Art." In *Poetry Language Thought,* trans. Albert Hofstadter. New York: Harper and Row, 1975.

Heimonet, Jean-Michel. "Le College de Sociologie—un gigantesque malentendu." *Esprit* 89 (May 1984).

———. *Négativité et communication.* Paris: Jean Michel Place, 1990.

Hoesterey, Ingeborg, ed. *Zeitgeist in Babel: The Post-Modernist Controversy.* Bloomington: Indiana University Press, 1991.

Hollier, Denis. "Le Dualisme matérialiste de Georges Bataille." *Tel Quel* 25 (1966).

———. *La Politique de la prose.* Paris: Gallimard, 1982.

———. *La Prise de la concorde: essais sur George Bataille.* Paris: Gallimard, 1974.

———. "Le Savoir formel." *Tel Quel* 34 (1968).

———. "Le Sujet de la transgression." *Sémiotexte* 1 (1974).

Hollier, Denis, ed. *Le Collège de Sociologie 1937–1939. Textes de Georges Bataille.* Paris: Gallimard, 1979. Trans. Betsy Wing as *The College of Sociology, 1937–39.* Minneapolis: University of Minnesota Press, 1988.

Houdebine, Jean-Louis. "L'Ennemi du dedans (Bataille et le surréalisme: éléments, prise de partis)." *Tel Quel* 52 (1972).

———. "Méconnaissance de la psychanalyse dans le discours surréaliste." *Tel Quel* 46 (1971).

———. "Position politique et ideologique du néo-surréalisme." *Tel Quel* 46 (1971).

Howells, Christina. *Sartre's Theory of Literature.* London: Modern Humanities Research Association, 1979.

Hutcheon, Linda, and Joseph Natoli, eds. *A Postmodern Reader.* Albany: State University of New York Press, 1991.

Ireland, John. *Sartre. Un art déloyal, théâtralité et engagement.* Paris: Jean Michel Place, 1995.

Isacharoff, M., ed. *Sartre et la mise en signe.* Paris: Klincksieck, 1982.

Jameson, Fredric. *Marxism and Form: Twentieth-Century Dialectical Theories of Literature.* Princeton: Princeton University Press, 1971.

———. *Postmodernism or the Cultural Logic of Late Capitalism.* Durham, N.C.: Duke University Press, 1992.

Janet, Pierre. *L'Automatisme psychologique: Essai de psychologie expérimentale sur les formes inférieures de l'activité humaine.* Paris: Félix Alcan, 1993 (1889).

Jarrety, Michel. *Valéry devant la littérature: Mesure de la limite.* Paris: PUF, 1991.

Jauss, H. R. *Pour une esthétique de la réception.* Trans. Claude Maillard. Paris: Gallimard, 1978.

Jay, Martin. "The Disenchantment of the Eye: Surrealism and the Crisis of Ocularcentrism." *Visual Anthropology Review* 7, 1 (Spring 1991): 15–38.

Jenny, Laurent. "Le Surréalisme et ses signes narratifs." *Poétique* 16 (1973).

Kant, Immanuel. *The Critique of Judgment.* Trans. J. H. Bernard. New York: Hafner Press, 1974.

Kavanagh, Thomas M., ed. *The Limits of Theory.* Stanford: Stanford University Press, 1989.

Klossowski, Pierre. "A propos du simulacre dans la communication de G. Bataille." *Critique* 195–96 (1963).

———. "De contre-attaque à Acéphale." *Change* 7 (1973).

Knee, Philip. "Sartre et la praxis littéraire." *Laval théologique et philosophique* 34, 1 (Feb. 1983).

Kojève, Alexander. *Introduction à la lecture de Hegel. Leçons sur la phénoménologie de l'esprit.* Paris: Gallimard, 1947.

Krauss, Rosalind. *L'Amour Fou: Photography and Surrealism.* Washington, D.C.: Corcoran Gallery of Art, 1985.

———. *The Optical Unconscious.* Cambridge, Mass.: MIT Press, 1993.

———. *The Originality of the Avant-Garde and Other Modernist Myths.* Cambridge, Mass.: MIT Press, 1985.

Kristeva, Julia. *Desire and Language: A Semiotic Approach to Literature and Art.* Ed. Léon S. Roudiez; trans. Tom Gora, Alice Jardine, and Léon Roudiez. New York: Columbia University Press, 1980.

———. *Langue, Discours, Société.* Paris: Seuil, 1973.

———. "Mémoires." *Infini* 1 (1983).

———. *La Révolution du langage poétique. L'Avant-garde à la fin du XIXe siècle: Lautréamont et Mallarmé.* Paris: Seuil, 1974. Trans. Margaret Waller as *Revolution in Poetic Language.* New York: Columbia University Press, 1984.

Kritzman, Lawrence. "The Changing Political Ideology of Tel Quel." *Contemporary French Civilization* 2 (1978): 405–21.

Lacapra, Dominik. *A Preface to Sartre.* Ithaca: Cornell University Press, 1978.

Lacoue-Labarthe, Philippe, and Jean-Luc Nancy, *L'Absolu littéraire: théorie de la littérature du romantisme allemand.* Paris: Seuil, 1978. Trans. Philip Barnard and Cheryl Lester as *The Literary Absolute: The Theory of Literature in German Romanticism.* Albany: SUNY Press, 1988.

La France, Guy. *La Philosophie sociale de Bergson, sources et interprètations.* Ottawa, Can.: Ed. de l'Université d'Ottawa, 1974.

Lala, Marie-Christine. "The Conversions of Writing in George Bataille's *L'Impossible.*" *YFS* 78 (1990).

Laplanche, Jean, and J.-B. Pontalis. *Vocabulaire de la pyschanalyse.* Paris: PUF, 1973.

Lasserre, Pierre. *Le Romantisme français.* Paris: Société de Mercure de France, 1907.

Legrand, Gérard. *André Breton et son temps.* Paris: Le Soleil Noir, 1976.

Leiris, Michel. "L'impossible 'Documents.'" *Critique,* nos. 195–96 (1963).

———. "Le Sacré dans la vie quotidienne." *Change* 7 (1973). Originally published in *NRF* (July 1938).

Lévi-Strauss, Claude. *The Elementary Structures of Kinship.* London: Eyre & Spottswoode, 1969.

———. *Introduction to the Work of Marcel Mauss.* Trans. Felicity Baker. London: Routledge and Kegan Paul, 1987.

———. *The Savage Mind.* London: Weidenfeld and Nicolson, 1966.

Lotringer, Sylvère. "Artaud Bataille" *Substance* 5–6 (Spring 1973).

Loubet, J.-L. *Les Nonconformistes des années trente.* Paris: Seuil, 1969.

Lyotard, Jean-François. *La Condition postmoderne: rapport sur le savoir.* Paris: Minuit, 1977. Trans. Geoff Bennington and Brian Massumi as *The Postmodern Condition: A Report on Knowledge.* Minneapolis: University of Minnesota Press, 1984.

———. "Painting and the Sublime." *Artforum* (April 1982).

———. *Le Postmoderne expliqué aux enfants, correspondance 1982–1985.* Paris: Galilée, 1986.

———. *Réécrire la Modernité.* Lille: Cahiers de la Philosophie, 1988.

Mackay, Agnes Ethel. *The Universal Self: A Study of Paul Valéry.* London: Routledge and Kegan Paul, 1961.

Magritte, René. *Ecrits complets.* Paris: Flammarion 1979.

Mallarmé, Stéphane. "Mimique." In *Œuvres complètes.* Paris: Gallimard, 1945.

Marmande, François. *Georges Bataille politique.* Lyon: Presses Universitaires de Lyon, 1985.

Mayeur, Jean-Marc. *La Vie politique sous la Troisième République.* Paris: Seuil, 1984.

Mitchell, William J. *The Reconfigured Eye: Visual Truth in the Post-Photographic Era.* Cambridge, Mass.: MIT Press, 1994.

Nadeau, Maurice. *The History of Surrealism.* New York: Macmillan, 1968.

Nancy, Jean-Luc. *La Communauté désœuvrée.* Paris: Bourgois, 1990.

Nash, Suzanne. *Paul Valéry, album et vers anciens.* Princeton: Princeton University Press, 1983.

Naville, Pierre. *Le Temps du surréel.* Paris: Galilée, 1977.

O'Neill, James C. "An Intellectual Affinity: Bergson and Valéry." *PMLA* 66 (March 1951).

Ortega y Gasset, José. *The Dehumanization of Art and Other Essays on Art, Culture, and Literature.* Princeton: Princeton University Press, 1968.

Oster, Daniel. *Monsieur Valéry, Essai.* Paris: Seuil, 1981.

Papadopoulo, Alexandre. *Un Philosophe entre deux défaites (Henri Bergson entre 1870 et 1940).* Paris: Ed. de la revue de Caire, 1942.

Papanicolau, Andrew C., and Pete A. Y. Gunter, eds. *Bergson and Modern Thought: Towards an Unified Science.* Chur, Switzerland: Harwood Academic Publishers, 1987.

Pasi, Carlo. "Nadja ou l'écriture erratique." *Pleine Marge* 10 (Dec. 1989), 83–99.

Paulhan, Jean. *Les Fleurs de Tarbes ou la terreur dans les lettres*. Paris: Gallimard, 1941.

Peytar, Jean. *Lautréamont et la cohérence de l'écriture*. Paris: Didier, 1977.

Piel, Jean. "Bataille et le monde, de la notion de dépense à la part maudite." *Critique* 195–96 (1963).

Pilkington, A. E. *Bergson and His Influence*. Cambridge, Eng.: Cambridge University Press, 1976.

Politzer, George. *Le Bergsonisme, une mystification philosophique*. Paris: Editions Sociales 1947. First published under the name François Arouet as *Fin d'une parade philosophique* in 1929.

Poster, Mark. *Sartre's Marxism*. Cambridge, Eng.: Cambridge University Press, 1982.

Prince, Gerald. *L'Œuvre Romanesque de Sartre: Métaphysique et technique dans l'œuvre romanesque de Sartre*. Geneva: Droz, 1973.

Richman, Michèle. "Bataille Moraliste?: *Critique* and the Postwar Writings." *YFS* 78 (1990).

———. *Reading Georges Bataille: Beyond the Gift*. Baltimore: Johns Hopkins University Press, 1982.

Robinson, Judith. *L'Analyse de l'esprit dans les Cahiers de Valéry*. Paris: José Corti, 1960.

Rodefelt, Jurgen Schmidt. *Paul Valéry, linguiste dans les Cahiers*. Paris: Klincksieck, 1970.

Rottenberg, Pierre. "Esquisse cartographique du nouveau surréalisme." *Tel Quel* 46 (1971).

Roustang, François. *Elle ne lâche plus*. Trans. as *Psychoanalysis Never Lets Go*. Baltimore: Johns Hopkins University Press, 1983.

———. *Lacan*. Trans. as *The Lacanian Delusion*. Oxford: Oxford University Press, 1990.

Rybalka, Michel, ed. *Sartre, un théatre de situations*. Paris: Gallimard, 1973.

Sanouillet, Michel. *Dada à Paris*. Paris: J. J. Pauvert, 1965.

Sartre, Jean-Paul. *Baudelaire*. Paris: Gallimard, 1963.

———. *Critique of Dialectical Reason*. London: Verso, 1976.

———. *Esquisse d'une théorie des émotions*. Paris: Hermann, 1965.

———. *L'Etre et le néant: essai d'ontologie phénoménologique*. Paris: Gallimard, 1980.

———. *L'Existentialisme est un humanisme*. Paris: Nagel, 1970.

———. *L'Imaginaire*. Trans. Bernard Frechtman as *The Psychology of the Imagination*. Secaucus, N.J.: The Citadel Press, 1966.

———. *Mallarmé*. Paris: Gallimard, 1986.

———. *Les Mots*. Paris: Gallimard, 1964.

———. *La Nausée*. Paris: Gallimard, 1938.

———. *Plaidoyer pour les intellectuels*. Paris: Gallimard, 1972. Trans. as "A Plea for Intellectuals." In *Between Marxism and Existentialism*, ed. John Matthews. New York: Pantheon, 1983.

———. *Qu'est-ce que la littérature?* Paris: Gallimard, 1948. Trans. Bernard Frechtman as *What Is Literature?* New York: Harper & Row, 1965.

———. *Situations*. Paris: Gallimard, 1947– . I–X.

Sasso, Robert. *Georges Bataille: Le Système du non-savoir, une ontologie du jeu.* Paris: Minuit, 1978.

Saussure, Ferdinand. *Course in General Linguistics.* Ed. Charles Bally and Albert Reidlinger; trans. Wade Baskin. New York: Philosophical Library, 1959.

Scarpetta, Guy. "Limite-frontière du surréalisme." *Tel Quel* 46 (1971): 59–66.

Schlipp, Paul Arthur, ed. *The Philosophy of Jean Paul Sartre.* La Salle, Ill.: Open Court, 1981.

Sheringham, Michael. "Genèse de la parole poétique: lecture de Carnet (1924) d'André Breton." *Pleine Marge* 11 (June 1990).

Silver, Kenneth. *Esprit de Corps: The Art of the Parisian Avant-Garde and the First World War, 1914–1925.* Princeton: Princeton University Press, 1989.

Sollers, Philippe. "Déclaration," *Tel Quel* 1 (1960).

———. "Déclaration," *Infini* 1 (1983).

———. "De grandes irrégularités du langage." *Critique* 195–96 (1963).

———. *L'Ecriture et l'expérience des limites.* Paris: Seuil, 1968.

———. *Logiques.* Paris: Seuil, 1968.

———. "La Pratique formelle de l'avant-garde." *Tel Quel* 46 (1971): 103–4.

———. "Le Toit," *Tel Quel* 29 (Spring 1967).

Sollers, Philippe, ed. *Théorie d'ensemble.* Paris: Seuil, 1968, 1980.

Soulez, Philippe. *Bergson politique.* Paris: PUF, 1989.

Spies, Werner. *Max Ernst Collages: The Invention of the Surrealist Universe.* London: Thames and Hudson, 1988.

Starobinski, Jean. "Freud, Breton, Myers." *L'Arc* 34 (1968).

Stoekle, Alan. *The Agony of the Intellectual: Commitment, Subjectivity, and the Performative in the Twentieth-Century French Tradition.* Lincoln: University of Nebraska Press, 1992.

———. *Visions of Excess: Selected Writings, 1927–1939, Georges Bataille.* Minneapolis: University of Minnesota Press, 1985.

Suckling, Norman. *Paul Valéry, The Civilized Mind.* London: Oxford University Press, 1954.

Surya, M. *Bataille, la mort à l'œuvre.* Paris: Séguier, 1987.

Suzuki, Masao. "En attendant la mort rose: une analyse de Carnet," *Pleine marge* 11 (June 1990).

Todorov, Tzvetan. *Qu'est-ce-que le structuralisme? 2. Poétique.* Paris: Seuil, 1968.

Turquet-Milnes, G. *Paul Valéry.* London: Jonathan Cape, 1934.

Tzavara, Athanaze. "Bergson and the Neuropsychiatric Tradition." In *Bergson and Modern Thought: Towards a Unified Science*, ed. Andrew C. Papanicolau and Pete A. Y. Gunter. Chur, Switzerland: Harwood Academic Publishers, 1987.

Ungar, Steven. *Scandal and Aftereffect: Blanchot and France Since 1930.* Minneapolis: University of Minnesota Press, 1995.

Valéry, Paul. *Lettres à quelques-uns.* Paris: Gallimard, 1965.

———. *Œuvres complètes*, vols. I, II. Paris: Gallimard, 1987. In vol. I:

"Le coup de dés, lettre au directeur de *Marges*," pp. 622–30;
"La crise de l'esprit," pp. 988–1014;

"Dernière visite à Mallarmé," pp. 630–33;
"Descartes," pp. 792–810;
"Discours sur Bergson," pp. 883–86;
"Fragment d'un Descartes," pp. 787–92;
INSTANTS, pp. 373–400;
"Introduction à la méthode de Léonard de Vinci," pp. 1153–99;
"Je disais quelquefois à Stéphane Mallarmé," pp. 644–60;
"Léonard et les philosophes," pp. 1234–69;
"Lettre sur Mallarmé," pp. 633–44;
"Mallarmé," pp. 706–10;
"La Politique de l'esprit," pp. 1014–40;
"Première leçon du cours de poétique," pp. 1340–59;
"Stéphane Mallarmé," pp. 619–22;
"Une vue de Descartes," pp. 810–42.

———. *Selected Poems*. New York: New Directions, 1950.

Waldberg, Patrick. *Chemins du surréalisme*. Bruxelles: Ed. de la Connaissance, 1965.

Wellmar, Albrecht. *The Persistence of Modernity: Essays on Aesthetics, Ethics and Postmodernism*. Cambridge, Mass.: MIT Press, 1993.

Wood, Paul, et al. *Modernism in Dispute: Art Since the Forties*. New Haven: Yale University Press, 1993.

Wood, Philip. *From Existentialism to Poststructuralism, and the Coming of the Postindustrial Age*. Stanford University Press, forthcoming.

———. *Understanding Jean-Paul Sartre*. Columbia: University of South Carolina Press, 1990.

Index

In this index an "f" after a number indicates a separate reference on the next page, and an "ff" indicates separate references on the next two pages. A continuous discussion over two or more pages is indicated by a span of page numbers, e.g., "57–59." *Passim* is used for a cluster of references in close but not consecutive sequence. Entries are alphabetized letter by letter, ignoring word breaks, hyphens, and accents.

Library of Congress Cataloging-in-Publication Data

Guerlac, Suzanne, 1950–
    Literary polemics : Bataille, Sartre, Valéry, Breton /
Suzanne Guerlac.
       p.   cm.
    Includes bibliographic references and index.
    ISBN 0-8047-2715-5 (cloth : alk. paper)
    1. French literature—20th century—History and crit-
icism. 2. Avant-garde (Aesthetics)—France.   3. Literature—philosophy. 4. Bataille, Georges, 1897–1962—
Philosophy.   5. Sartre, Jean Paul, 1905– .   6. Valéry,
Paul, 1871–1945—Philosophy. 7. Breton, André,
1896–1966—Philosophy.   I. Title.
PQ305.G78   1997
840.9'0091—dc20

                                    96-27399
                                       CIP

∞   This book is printed on acid-free paper

Original printing 1997
Last figure below indicates year of this printing
06 05 04 03 02 01 00 99 98 97

esprit 123